FROM THE ABODE OF ISLAM TO THE TURKISH VATAN

Map of the Republic of Turkey.

BEHLÜL ÖZKAN

From the Abode of Islam to the Turkish Vatan

THE MAKING OF A NATIONAL

HOMELAND IN TURKEY

Yale UNIVERSITY PRESS

NEW HAVEN AND LONDON

Copyright © 2012 by Behlül Özkan. All rights reserved. This book may not be reproduced, in whole or in part, including illustrations, in any form (beyond that copying permitted by Sections 107 and 108 of the U.S. Copyright Law and except by reviewers for the public press), without written permission from the publishers.

Yale University Press books may be purchased in quantity for educational, business, or promotional use. For information, please e-mail sales.press@yale.edu (U.S. office) or sales@yaleup.co.uk (U.K. office).

Set in Scala type by Westchester Book Group.

Library of Congress Cataloging-in-Publication Data

Özkan, Behlül, 1975–
   From the abode of Islam to the Turkish vatan : the making of a national homeland in Turkey / Behlül Özkan.
      p. cm.
   Includes bibliographical references and index.
   ISBN 978-0-300-17201-0 (pbk.)
   1. Nationalism—Turkey—History.   2. National characteristics, Turkish.
3. Turkey—History—Ottoman Empire, 1288–1918.   4. Turkey—History—20th century.
5. Turkey—Boundaries—History.   6. Turkey—Foreign relations.   I. Title.
   DR576.O95 2012
   320.5409561—dc23

                                                              2011042675

A catalogue record for this book is available from the British Library.

To My Parents, Nihat and Saime Özkan

p.3 (102) Remzi Oguz Arik
geography becomes Vatan
...man and land take
...ch other's name.
...re Borders in 1920

Figure 2.2 (84) Imperial Multi Ethnic
Kemal excluded Aleppo vs Ghana
losing his compact territorial
and ethnic national
...sion. - Reduce geography
    to concentrate
...gure 2.3 (99)
...o boundary between
Iraq and Turkey
Erases ethnic zones
like Lazistan, Kurdistan
regime's
erasure of ethnic markers
from public

- Ataturks ideals of national sovereignty
and modernism needed bounded, secular,
homogenous Turkish spaces.
 ↳ Maps in schools, atlases were changed
 ↳ They exclude non-Turkish groups like
  Kurds, Armenians, Greeks. Reinforcing
  ethnic homogenization.
- Ataturk rejected Pan-Turkism and Pan
 Islamism as the maps cut ties
 with imperial geography
 ↳ Different from imperial pluralism
 ↳ Maps excluded connections to
  Turkic lands in Central Asia
 - Figure 3.5 (119) Could have gone
          of racial-imperial
  Interesting because the book
  romanticized Pan-Turkic expansion
  what Ataturk's nationalism rejected
- Figure 3.12 (133)
 Shows it in Lausanne Treaty,
 which contrasts so heavily with
 3.11, which had partitioned among
 nations, showing the success of
 nationalism
 Established the outer limit of Turkishness
 where all else is foreign
- The map rejects Central Asian expansion
 ↳ Enshrines secular, Anatolian-Centered
  nationalism

CONTENTS

Acknowledgments ix

Introduction 1

1 Searching for a New Legitimacy: Ottoman Patriotism and Imperial Vatan 12

2 From Imperial to National Vatan 56

3 From Geography to Vatan 102

4 Vatan and Turkey's Foreign Policy 146

Conclusion 211

Notes 215

Illustration Credits 259

Index 261

ACKNOWLEDGMENTS

AT THE END OF MANY LONG YEARS OF STUDY, I am indebted to many people. I am first grateful to my parents, Nihat and Saime Özkan, who did everything possible to make my dreams reality. Without their support, this study would not have been possible. I dedicate this book to them.

Although I cannot adequately express the depth of my gratitude to my professors and advisors, I would like to acknowledge Andrew C. Hess at the Fletcher School of Law and Diplomacy. He introduced me to critical and interdisciplinary thinking. I also wish to convey my enormous debt to Feroz Ahmad, who guided me through my academic studies in both Boston and Istanbul, and to Georges Prevelakis, whose support, advice, and encouragement during his three years at the Fletcher School of Law and Diplomacy helped me gain a mastery of geopolitics. In addition, I would like to thank Soli Özel for his continuous support since my undergraduate studies. His course on political sociology was the most thought-provoking course that I attended at Boğaziçi University. Later in my life I had the privilege to be his friend.

While I would like to express my thanks to all of my friends, Emre Kayhan and Gürkan Zengin deserve special mention because of the many constructive hours we spent together discussing politics and history. Also, Michael Rodriguez, Ozan Özkan, and Mehmet Savan greatly assisted in the editing of the manuscript.

Introduction

MAX WEBER'S DEFINITION OF THE STATE as "a human community that (successfully) claims the *monopoly of the legitimate use of force within a given territory*" (emphasis in original) became a well-established dictum in the social sciences of the twentieth century.[1] In line with Weber, who accepted the territorial element as given and focused on examining the legitimate use of force, most political scientists have long been ensnared in the "territorial trap," because they have neglected problematizing and questioning the territoriality of the nation-state.[2] As James Anderson noted, "Nations, like states, are not simply located in geographic space—which is the case with all social organizations—rather they explicitly claim particular territories and derive distinctiveness for them."[3] The concept of homeland, the essential part of the nation-state paradigm establishing the link between the people and the territory, territorializes the national identity by creating the sense of belonging to the sacred soil and turning the imagined boundaries into physical ones. In Turkey, the nation-state accrued enormous power by convincing millions of its citizens of the need for unity, even if that meant sacrificing their lives for the national homeland's defense. While homeland provides physical space for the nation-state, it also reinforces the national identity by generating symbolic acts about the territory through geographical imagination.

This study is contextualized within the conflict of time and space and clashes over national territories that have arisen out of this fundamental conflict. It examines the development of national spatial consciousness within Turkey that makes it possible to view a particular space as embodying the vatan of the Turkish nation. Vatan signifies the territory of the Turkish nation-state and has been considered the most important factor in maintaining the cohesion of the society. Vatan—which, in Arabic, means the place of one's birth—can be translated as "homeland" in English. But this translation is problematic and does not fully reflect the implied meaning of the word in the Turkish language. In English, "homeland" refers to the territory of the nation-state, but in Turkish, vatan occupies a unique predominating status in political discourse. It refers not only to the national territory but also to major political and legal concepts derived from the word vatan, including citizen (*vatandaş*), patriotism (*vatanseverlik*), heimatlos (*vatansız*), high treason (*vatana ihanet*), and traitor to homeland (*vatan haini*). The first sentence of the constitution of Turkey underlines "the eternal presence of Turkish vatan and nation." According to Article 66, the only criterion to deprive someone of citizenship is "an act incompatible with the loyalty to vatan." Furthermore, according to Articles 81 and 103, both the president and the members of the Parliament should take an oath on assuming office that they will defend "the indivisible integrity of vatan and nation."

In the twentieth century, as Muslim societies began to be shaped by the newly founded nation-states, the modernizing ruling elites faced an arduous task of creating national societies and national vatans in place of Islamic community (*ummah*) and the Abode of Islam (*Dar al-Islam*). The national homeland differs from previous entities that occupied the space of today's Turkey not only in terms of geographical shape but also in the nature of conception of space and sovereignty. Nationalist perceptions of space and of the need to defend the homeland from the dangers of enemies confers hegemonic status to the holders of political power. Belonging to the same vatan invoked national affection by insisting upon the kinship of individuals who were not related; national homeland thus served as the linchpin in overcoming the differences among various ethnic groups. Rather than accepting national homeland as self-evident and innocent as perpetuated by the nationalist ideology, this study criticizes the established conventions about Turkish vatan and its intersections with politics and foreign policy. It seeks to displace the logic of nationalism by pointing to how national homeland is discursively constructed. As vatan has always been situated in a discourse, it should be analyzed in a contextual approach. Therefore, the rich details of Islamic and imperial territoriality are incorporated into this long-term case study of the making of the Turkish vatan. This study seeks to map out the role of vatan in Turkish politics, nationalism, and foreign policy and the critical socio-spatial background shaping it.

Before the establishment of the Turkish nation-state, sovereignty had not been associated with territorial boundary. The discourse of Western and modern geography displaced and vanquished pre-modern Islamic-Ottoman geographical understanding and replaced the historic romantic affection for vatan with strategic political allegiance. The newly established Republic of Turkey adopted the modern discourse of nationalism, presenting the nation's territorial conception as a naturalized and uncontested fact. Indeed, the circumstances that make possible the Turkish vatan constitute new conditions of knowledge production. Republican elites claimed that the roots of the Turkish nation-state were located in ancient Anatolian civilizations. At the same time, they rearticulated political concepts such as vatan and *millet* (nation) in a nationalist ideology that had been used by Ottoman elites in an imperial discourse since the beginning of the nineteenth century to sustain the empire's territorial integrity against the rising nationalist movements first in the Balkans, then in the Middle East and Anatolia.

Turkish nationalism reconfigured vatan's pre-modern Islamic-Ottoman meaning of one's birthplace to a "geo-body" of the Turkish nation, within which resided one's national brothers who were never known and would never be known.[4] One comes readily to know other members of the nation through the construction of new maps, histories, and memories about the vatan. The construction of the Turkish vatan in the first three decades of the twentieth century occurred simultaneously with the transformation of the meaning of millet from a religiously defined entity to a nationally defined imagined community. After 1923, the Republican regime encouraged the selective remembrance of pre-Ottoman roots of Turks in Central Asia and pre-Islamic Anatolian civilizations. In so doing, it transfigured vatan from a local birthplace and the Abode of Islam to a land of origins, namely, a national homeland. While modern geography and mapping of the space produced this geo-body, advocates of Turkish nationalism envisioned vatan as a sacred territorial body to love and be devoted to, to possess and be protected from enemy intrusions, and to kill and to die for, all of these elements playing a crucial role in representing a compact and solid national territory. The idea of defending the national homeland significantly answers part of the question raised by Benedict Anderson about nationalism: How can an idea so philosophically deficient and incoherent evoke such political power that men are willing to kill and die for it?[5]

Unlike the Islamic vatan, whose territorial borders were indistinctive, modern Turkey is, above all, a territorially well-defined geo-body. Its borders were demarcated as a result of the victory in the National Liberation War that terminated the Ottoman Empire and established the Republic of Turkey. The best exemplification of the transformation of imperial to national discourse occurred when the Ottoman territories were titled officially the Well Protected Domains of the Ottomans, signifying the unity of various provinces, while the name the Republic of Turkey emphasized a cohesive geographical unit, namely, Turkish vatan. However, as nationalist elites sought to initiate a radical break with Ottoman history and geography to legitimize the newly established nation-state, their policy of transforming an imperial space into a national vatan engendered an aporia in Turkey's geopolitical discourse. On the one hand, there was a huge loss of territories in the Middle East and the Balkans that were considered as vatan and had been ruled by Ottomans for centuries. In the last century of the Ottoman Empire, millions of people had migrated from these lost territories. On the other hand, the nationalist elites had to construct a national identity and solidarity to unite people from different ethnic backgrounds based on the glorification of the liberated territories in Anatolia, which is only a small section of the enormous Ottoman vatan.

The notion of a common Turkish vatan was deployed to override differences within the society. Republican reforms were unprecedented in terms of combining Turkish identity with territoriality. With the establishment of the Turkish nation-state, a sense of nationalism substituted servitude to the sultan and religion with loyalty to the homeland. This was revolutionary in that the nation was disassociated from Islam and God as the community of believers and from the Ottoman sultan as his loyal servants and now was anchored to the life-giving homeland. The rejuvenation of vatan became a central project of Turkish nationalism, and repositioning the people's loyalty from the sultan onto the vatan radically changed Turkish politics. The practice of politics, which had been dominated by the sultan, was recoded as embodied within the right of the nation. Children of vatan became the new source of sovereignty, and they sought to promote the welfare of the Turkish homeland and to participate in its progress. Similarly, nationalism, previously considered by Ottoman statesmen as acts of disorder undertaken by unruly subjects, was proclaimed as the people's endeavor to regenerate the long-gone glories of Anatolia. Turkish nationalists argued that they would rehabilitate the wretched Turkish vatan, which had deteriorated under the tyranny of the Ottoman sultans.

Since the establishment of the Republic, vatan has been the constitutive dimension of Turkish politics. However, far from a static territorial structure as suggested by nationalist ideology, vatan has been continuously deterritorialized and reterritorialized by the hegemonic political discourse according to changing internal and external political and social conditions. The Kemalists waged the National Liberation War to save the vatan from invasion by European powers as proclaimed in the National Pact (*Misak-ı Milli*), which identified the geographical borders of the vatan in 1920. Kemalists fought for vatan against imperialist powers and cooperated with the Soviet Union during National Liberation. However, after World War II, ruling elites argued that the same vatan was threatened by Soviet expansionism and, therefore, Turkey's entry into the Western bloc was the only way to protect the vatan from the "communist threat." While Turkey's participation in the Korean War was represented as a defense of vatan against communism on the far side of Asia, in the second half of the twentieth century Cyprus became the baby-vatan (*yavru-vatan*) in the foreign policy discourse, and unifying it with the mother-vatan (*ana-vatan*) constituted the popular national cause.

The ruling elites have dominated the "socio-spatial consciousness" to impose order and identity, thereby making the contemporary world comprehensible to the Turkish people.[6] In 2001, Prime Minister Bülent Ecevit, arguably one of the most democratic prime ministers in Turkey's modern republic, said, "in Turkey, the Turkish Armed Forces have a very special role defined by the nation's unique geographical circumstances.

In terms of security, Turkey is located in a critically vulnerable region compared to Western European countries. Therefore, its internal and external security is indivisible. From this vantage point, European countries cannot set the example because Turkey is a sui generis embedded in a very delicate geopolitical position."[7] Ecevit's statement was not an extraordinary one in Turkish politics. On the contrary, it reflected the well-established rationale that Turkey's "special" geography requires a customized type of democracy, a principle that has been repeatedly articulated by generals, politicians, and foreign ministry bureaucrats since the end of World War II.

The perception of Turkey in a continuous state of emergency due to its geographical location continued after the end of the Cold War. As late as 2008, General İlker Başbuğ, in his first speech as the commander of Turkish Armed Forces delivered during the handover ceremony, underlined the fact that Turkey is located in the middle of a turbulent region, and quoting Napoleon he said that Turkey's geography determines its fate: "If you look at the geography of Anatolia and the history of this geography, you realize that only strong states can survive and weak ones disappear soon from history's stage ... In its thorny geography, Turkey faces symmetrical and asymmetrical risks and threats. Therefore, it has to possess solid political, economic, technological, socio-cultural and military strengths that support each other ... Contrary to the conventional ideas, Turkey's conditions and difficulties due to its geography are not similar to some European countries. Such conventional ideas will cause tremendous delusions and irreparable results."[8]

This geographical rationale, which depicts Turkey as seeking to maintain its territorial integrity against internal and external "threats" within the context of a "dangerous" geography, gained an ontological, if not practically a metaphysical, status in Turkish politics. Any argument criticizing this rationale was easily dismissed as marginal and failing to account for Turkey's special geopolitical characteristics. As prime minister, Bülent Ecevit, who had strenuously criticized the military coups and interventions of the 1970s and 1980s, internalized this geopolitical rationale in due course and defended it in the 2000s, when Turkey's membership in the European Union (EU) necessitated limiting the military's role in Turkish politics. Ecevit criticized the demands for more political reforms in order to enhance Turkey's democracy by saying that "Turkey's special geopolitical conditions require a special type of democracy."⁹

The well-established nationalistic stance in Turkish politics and society argues that since people in Turkey's "dangerous" geography are surrounded by enemies, they have to prepare themselves to live in a continuous state of emergency. The only way to maintain Turkey's integrity in this state of emergency is to embrace the vatan as the most precious asset of the Turkish nation and to be ready to defend it for any sacrifice. Explicit references to the Turkish homeland's "dangerous" geographical location have been made not only by military officials but also in day-to-day politics, school textbooks, and newspaper columns by politicians, academics, and journalists. Democracy, foreign policy, and ethnic problems have all been depoliticized and interpreted from the perspective of geographical determinism, which considers the Turkish homeland in a permanent state of emergency. A textbook for national security classes, which is compulsory for every student in the tenth grade, warns students that "the Republic of Turkey, because of its geographical position, has had to face schemes devised by external powers. The Turkish youth needs to be prepared to deal with such schemes."[10] Since 1933, every morning millions of students gather in primary school courts to take an oath together. They shout in unison that their primary "principle" is "to love the homeland and the nation more than my being" and that they will be ready to "sacrifice my life for the Turkish being." State buildings including schools, police stations, and army headquarters put up billboards on their outside walls that display mottos such as "vatan first" and "who loves his vatan most is the one who fulfills his duty best." At the beginning of each football game, fans in the stadiums shout "the martyrs won't die and the vatan is indivisible" as a reaction against the armed Kurdish insurgency that has claimed more than forty thousand lives in the last thirty-five years. By doing so, they emphasize that they are ready to sacrifice themselves for the defense of Turkish vatan.

Contrary to this deterministic discourse, geography is not a product of nature. It is an outcome of a historical struggle over the control of territorial space. As Henri Lefebvre has argued, "space has been shaped and moulded from historical elements, but this has been a political process.

Space is political and ideological. It is a product literally filled with ideologies. There is an ideology of space. Why? Because space, which seems homogenous, which seems to be completely objective in its pure form . . . is a social product."[11] Parallel to this position, "when space is acknowledged as a physical fact, it is acknowledged by a subject; already here a man/space relation enters political knowledge as something indubitable, and space takes on political meaning as a clue to the sovereignty of a state; territory is naturalized right from the start."[12] This study aims to deconstruct the taken-for-granted assumption that "only strong states can survive in Turkey's geography" by identifying and analyzing its sources in politics.[13] The nation-state, national identity, and vatan in Turkey are not already existing and pre-political entities. On the contrary, competing political groups always contest them.

Once the vatan is deconstructed, the erected tower of conventional wisdom and political truisms collapses onto itself. This book is focused on the modes of representation of space as national homeland in both theoretical formulations and political practices. On the one hand, it analyzes the nationalist ways of seeing the world that have been sponsored by academic geography and how Turkish vatan is constructed to fit into schemas of security interests of ruling elites. On the other hand, it examines how vatan is embedded in popular culture. Turkish state continues to rely on the motto "everything is for vatan," proclaiming it on garrison walls and putting it on the mountains of Eastern Anatolia, which is mainly populated by Kurds. In the 2000s, people and groups who urged for the peaceful settlement of the Cyprus question in order to clear Turkey's way for full EU membership were labeled as "traitors to vatan" and were accused of "selling vatan to Greeks." Even the increasing volume of property purchases in Turkey by foreigners after 2003, as a result of liberal reforms, were depicted, by nationalists and Eurosceptics, as "selling vatan's soil to foreigners." Although defending territorial borders has become more difficult for the Turkish state as a result of increasing globalization, the state's practice of patrolling the cyber-borders of vatan by blocking access to more than a thousand websites—including YouTube—makes Turkey one of the world's strictest and most aggressive censors of cyberspace. Besides questioning the long-acknowledged fundamentals of national identity and territory, this study gives particular attention to how everyday political practices discursively produced and disseminated the concept of vatan.

As in social studies that ignore the relationship between space and nationalism, vatan remains peculiarly unexplored and conspicuously absent from the analytical radar in state-centric approaches despite its overwhelming role and influence in Turkish politics. As Jens Bartelson has emphasized, "in political discourse, centrality and ambiguity usually condition each other over time. A concept becomes central to the extent that other concepts are defined in terms of it, or depend on it for their coherent meaning and use within discourse."[14] Vatan has acquired an ahistorical and ontological status, considered, as it is, a timeless natural symbol of the reality of Turkish nation and state. However, far from being neutral and authentic, vatan has been a historically constructed spatial grid, upon which various political forces have battled for control of the national power structure and for hegemony in physically controlling and representing the vatan. The hegemonic political discourse carries an enormous authority in its capacity to define the physical and imagined boundaries of vatan and, therefore, the difference between the inside and the outside. Correspondingly, such an authority allows the hegemonic political discourse to dictate who can stay inside the vatan and to exclude alternative representations of vatan by using the process of othering. By refusing to acknowledge vatan as a preordained, static, and unchanging spatial platform, this study aims to overcome the problem of "spatial blindness" and to explore how vatan has been conceptualized, reinstated, and transformed as a constitutive territorial parameter for the Turkish nation-state.[15] It seeks to politicize the uncontested principle of a natural link between Turkish vatan and nation. Therefore, it focuses on the processes rather than the essences involved in vatan's imaginations and representations.[16] By problematizing the established geographical assumption of Turkey's foreign policy that the nation is engulfed and surrounded by internal and external threats, the study concludes that defending the vatan legitimizes and confers hegemonic status to the holders of political power.

The methodology used herein is based on a range of critical writings in political theory, geography, sociology, and history to help enrich the understanding of the reciprocal relations shaped and dictated by the construction of national territories, the question of the Other, and struggles over national identities. References are made to Michel Foucault and Ernesto Laclau on power-knowledge relationships and discourse theory, to Gearóid Ó Tuathail and David Campbell on geographical representation, and to Anssi Paasi on the role of education in inculcating national consciousness.[17] This interdisciplinary approach effectively reveals the way that territorial transformations in Turkey are themselves reflective of state power in shaping the nation's social and cultural life. Political struggles among different groups and classes to control aspects of spatial socialization consistently echo the significance of the Turkish vatan, through which Turkish people internalize collective territorial identity and socialize as members of the territorially bounded spatial entity. Supplementing theoretical analysis with deep qualitative and empirical research, this study seeks to lay out a compelling map of the vatan through a largely diversified body of resources, such as archives, memoirs, geography textbooks, maps, newspapers, novels, and governmental sources. In an informed, provocative way, it outlines the ways in which vatan was precisely standardized for each period represented in the book, which covers the late Ottoman and the Republican periods.

Chapter 1 examines the thorny transformation of the Abode of Islam to the Western nation-state paradigm, which required constructing physical and mental borders of the Ottoman identity and space formed by multiple religious and ethnic groups, segmented horizontally and separated by fluid frontier zones. Chapter 2 chronicles how the spatial consciousness of the Ottoman ruling elite and society was transformed from an imperial vatan to a national one between the years of 1908 and 1923. Analyzing the change from a heterogeneous imperial vatan to a homogenous national vatan reveals how national discourses and practices nationalized education, politics, and daily life in order to maintain social integration and order. In Chapter 3, I examine how a nationalist discourse prevailed in educational materials, particularly in how the state education system infused national ideals into geography textbooks, promoting Turkish national identity and the country's spatial and cultural features. The comparison of the pedagogy of space in Turkey before and after 1923 reveals how the newly established Turkish state effectively used geography education to construct spatial consciousness about the national homeland and to popularize collective national duties. Chapter 4 studies how Turkey's foreign policy discourse generated specific systems of meaning, common sense, and regimes of truth in order to legitimize the Turkish state as a political unit. By using representations of threats and dangers to vatan, ruling elites formed a historical bloc to discipline Turkish people and eliminate other antagonistic groups that challenged the ruling class's power and hegemony.

CHAPTER ONE

Searching for a New Legitimacy: Ottoman Patriotism and Imperial Vatan

IN THE LAST TWO CENTURIES, nation-states have become the prevailing form of political and social organization. The success of the nation-state largely depends on its construction of individual and group identities based on bounded territories, in which it legitimizes its monopoly of power. To put it briefly, territoriality emerged as a significant form of power. However, to attain uniformity within its territory, nation-states had to abolish the heterogenic organizational structure of the political system it succeeded. In the case of Turkey, the millet system bound people to their autonomous religious institutions, which were the backbone of the political and legal system that played an intermediary role between people and state. This system was later replaced with direct loyalty to and identification of citizens with the state. It was a very complicated process, as it required the constructing of borders of the national identity and territory in an imperial space formed by multiple religious groups segmented horizontally and separated by fluid frontier zones.

In Turkey and in other Middle Eastern societies, this process also necessitated the transformation of a value-based ontological self-perception (*Selbstverständnis*) as an Islamic civilization into a completely different mechanism-based self-perception as a Western civilization.[1] According to Ahmet Davutoğlu, whereas "the axiological foundations of Islamic political legitimacy are eternal values given by a supreme divine being which is sovereign over the human being and nature," political participation is fundamental for Western legitimation: "The political mechanism is the formation of a new base of sovereignty: national or popular sovereignty. The rising importance of this mechanism led to a shift in political theory toward finding the best way to fulfill this aspect of procedural legitimacy. Liberal democratic tradition and socialist/popularist democracies began to defend the supremacy of their systems due to their appropriateness for political participation rather than due to their attachment to a value system. Thus, political participation as a means of political legitimation became a value by itself and began to reproduce the norms of political life."[2] The difference between these self-perceptions can be most clearly seen in political concepts such as nation-state and *ummah*, which can be translated as "the worldwide Muslim community." It is difficult to find a corresponding term for "nation-state" in Turkish, Persian, and Arabic and similarly difficult to find an appropriate translation for "ummah" in Western languages.

According to the Koran, all Muslims comprise a single community, namely, ummah: "Verily, this ummah of yours is a single ummah, and I am your lord and cherisher: therefore serve me."[3] Islamic political understanding underlines the unity of ummah by disregarding ethnic and racial differences. As Davutoğlu emphasized, "the oneness of ummah depends on the common ontological approach of its members rather than on linguistic, geographic, cultural, or biological factors and is directly connected to the concept of Allah and to the specific imago mundi originating from this belief in tawhid."[4] Islamic jurists divided the world into two units: the Abode of Islam and the Abode of War. The Abode of Islam means "territories in which Islam and Islamic religious law prevail." The explanation of the Abode of War is more difficult and problematic. It indicates "territories where Islam does not prevail."[5] Contrary to Bernard Lewis and other Orientalist scholars, this does not mean that "there is a morally necessary, legally and religiously obligatory state of war" between these two.[6] Indeed, there is not a single reference to these concepts in the Koran and *hadiths*. These two concepts developed as a result of historical conditions and the expanding Muslim rule after the seventh century. After the tenth century, Islamic scholars started to use them more frequently as a reaction to the Crusades, the Mongol invasion of Islamic lands, and the end of Muslim rule in the Iberian Peninsula.

The Islamic identification of a non-Muslim country as the Abode of War resembles that of the Cold War's military blocs rather than a constant state of warfare between the two. Although these blocs maintain armies for a possible conflict, the standard relations are based on accommodation and coexistence since ongoing trade and political links serve the reciprocal interests of both sides.[7] It is striking that Prince Juan Manuel coined the term the "Cold War" in the early fourteenth century to define the political and military confrontation between Muslims and Christians in the Iberian Peninsula.[8]

The political legitimacy of the Ottoman state was based on its ability to defend the ummah and maintain its welfare within the Abode of Islam. However, far from accepting the relations between the Abode of Islam and the rest as an incessant warfare, Ottomans acknowledged the existence of an alternative political and religious order on the other side of the frontier. Their success rising from a small nomadic principality located in Bithynia—a frontier region between the Abode of Islam and the Abode of War—to a great empire cannot be solely explained by Holy War and *gaza* ideology based on religious zeal and commitment.[9] As the title of Cemal Kafadar's book *Between Two Worlds* so aptly reveals, Ottomans used the opportunities provided by the frontier. They benefited from the Byzantine administrative model and adapted it to Turco-Islamic realities.[10] Ottomans also changed the classical Islamic theory of legitimacy that stated that the caliph must be descended from the Quraish tribe to which the Prophet Muhammad belonged. According to Ottoman political understanding, the sultan was the sovereign by divine right.[11] The concept of Holy War was employed to legitimize the dynasty, and Ottoman sultans were depicted as the greatest Holy Warriors after the Prophet Muhammad. Ebu's-su'ud Efendi, who was the *sheikh ul-Islam*—the highest authority on the issues of Islam for three decades during the era of the Sultan Suleiman the Magnificent in the sixteenth century—presented the Ottoman sultans, not the Muslim community, as "the mighty annexer of the realm of war [Dar al-Harb] to the realm of Islam [Dar al-Islam]."[12]

In the fifteenth century, Ottoman sultans initiated successful military campaigns against other Turco-Muslim principalities to establish their political and military hegemony in Anatolia. This fighting against other Muslims was presented as a Holy War, as the Ottoman religious elite argued that these Muslim principalities in Anatolia hindered the Ottoman advance toward the West by making arrangements with infidels against the Ottomans.[13] In the sixteenth century, Ottoman sultans "granted the necessary guarantees for residence, travel and trade in the Ottoman territories . . . to those non-Muslims from the Abode of War who gave the pledge of 'friendship and sincere goodwill,'" namely, British and French merchants, whereas trade with the Habsburgs did not develop until the eighteenth century because of the adversarial relations between the two empires.[14] During the same era, Safavids in Iran threatened Ottoman political-religious legitimacy by supporting Shiism among the Eastern Anatolian population. To counter the increasing Safavid influence, Ottoman sheikh ul-Islam declared Holy War against them and wrote a religious opinion to justify fighting against another Muslim state: "If the schismatics of Persia (May God abandon them) who live in the land of Persia under the rule of the sons of Shah Ismail consider as disbelievers those who recognize Abu-Bakr, Umar and Uthman as rightful caliphs, and they themselves hold the rest after Ali as possessors of nobility (May God's approbation be upon them) . . . and if they consider them [the first three caliphs] as apostates and backbiters and openly curse and vilify them while considering themselves devout and believe that the killing of Muslims who are the people of the Sunnah is canonically lawful . . . the place where the cursers and believers of such things live, is it the Abode of War? Yes, it is the Abode of War and they can be considered as apostates."[15] Similarly Ebu's-su'ud Efendi declared Safavids and their followers as infidels and argued that the war against them was a Holy War.[16]

At the end of the seventeenth century, Ottoman territorial expansion was halted as a result of the military defeats against the Habsburg Empire. According to the well-established historical understanding, the Treaty of Karlowitz signed between the Habsburg and Ottoman empires in 1699 signified the decline of Ottoman power. The treaty also signified the end of the expansion of the Ottoman frontier, namely, the Abode of Islam, in Europe. For the first time, the Ottomans were forced to acknowledge the territorial integrity of their major adversary in Europe and formed a joint boundary demarcation commission with the Habsburg Empire. What was more striking about the Treaty of Karlowitz was that although it was a peace instead of a truce treaty, the Ottoman statesmen represented it as a temporary cessation of hostilities with infidels. In order to avoid criticisms about the unpopular treaty that marked the Ottoman territorial losses and to stabilize the border between two empires, the Ottoman Grandvizier Amcazade Hüseyin Pasha ordered the historian Naima to write a report to defend his policy. Naima compared the Treaty of Karlowitz with the Hudaybiyah Truce signed in 627 between forces of the Prophet Muhammad and the Meccans and argued that the cessation of hostilities with the infidels was preferable if the continuation of war was detrimental for Muslims.

Although the Ottoman statesmen sought to conceal the weakening of the empire against other European powers at the beginning of the eighteenth century, toward the end of the century the empire lost the first territory inhabited by Muslims, Crimea. Edward Weisband emphasized that the Treaty of Küçük Kaynarca signed between the Russian and Ottoman empires in 1774 "was the most humiliating the Sublime Porte had ever been forced to sign, for the Ottomans were forced, for the first time, to concede to the despised *gavurs* (infidels) a section of the Dar al-Islam."[17] The loss of Crimea and its Muslim population to Russia was so appalling to the Ottomans that Sultan Selim the Third wrote an emotional poem about the lost Muslim territories:

> "To the Divine Majesty I hath turned my face
> In my heart I hath enjoyed His Messenger's grace
> Let us go to war against the heathen's place
> Shall we let our country remain thus?
> Though upon Islam the heathen casts spells
> Here we still stand with our magnificence
> While every single Tatar is in chains
> Shall we let Crimea remain in heathen hands?"

After the Russian invasion of Crimea in 1774, thousands of Muslim Tatars left their ancestral lands, which turned into the Abode of War since *shariah*, the Islamic law, could not be implemented under the Russian rule. By following Prophet Muhammad and his followers' emigration from Mecca to Medina—the *hijra*, according to Islamic discourse—Crimean Muslims migrated to the Ottoman Empire, which was considered the Abode of Islam. As Brian Glyn Williams argues, the migration of thousands of Crimean Tatars from Russian-controlled Crimea to Ottoman territories reveals that territorial patriotism did not exist among them:

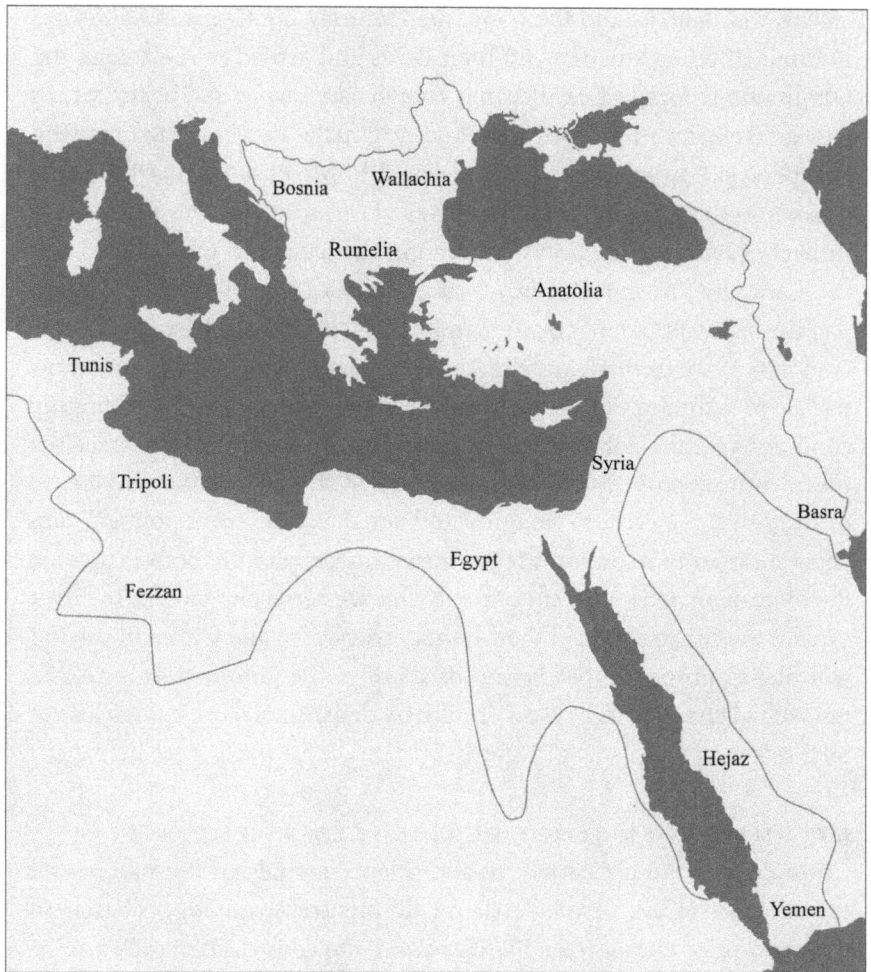

FIGURE 1.1 Map of the Ottoman Empire in the early nineteenth century.

"Far from articulating a unique ethnic right or claim to the Crimea as the eighteenth and nineteenth century Crimean Tatars' sacred *Vaterland* or *patrie*, the widely accepted tenants of Hanafi Islam therefore seems to have actually dictated that the Crimean peninsula (as a land where the laws of the unbeliever prevailed over the shariah) was to be abandoned by all pious Muslims."[18]

Contrary to Sultan Selim the Third's desire to regain Crimea from "infidels," the empire lost almost all of its territories in the Balkans and the Caucasus by 1918 (Figure 1.1). Because of the gradual retreat of Ottoman rule in the Balkans and the Caucasus, not only the Crimean Tatars but millions of other Muslims left their lands and settled in the remaining Ottoman territories. They became known as *muhajirs* in Turkey, which was derived from the word *hijra* and originally used for Muslims who fled persecution in Mecca and migrated to Medina. During the same era, while the Muslim population was starting to face the devastating impact of nationalism prevalent among Christians in the Balkans and the Caucasus, the modernizing ruling elites of the Ottoman Empire had the arduous task of creating an imperial patriotism based on homeland in place of ummah and the Abode of Islam. Although the Ottomans had been adapting the meaning of these two concepts to the changing conditions for the political and religious legitimacy of the state since the fourteenth century, ruling elites realized at the end of the eighteenth century that they had to imagine and construct different political concepts in order to maintain the territorial integrity of the empire against the increasing nationalist movements and Western colonialism. To better explain the construction of the Ottoman patriotism and Ottoman vatan, I will first examine the perception of space in the Ottoman Empire and how it had changed as a result of military defeats and continuous loss of territory.

OTTOMAN COSMOLOGY CHALLENGED BY THE WEST

Cosmology is the philosophical and scientific study of the nature and the structure of the universe. Islamic theocentric cosmology is based on the concept of *tawhid* (*La ilaha illa Allah*), the code declaring God to be one and not composed of parts. The most important consequence of tawhid is that it created an ontological hierarchy from God to human being and from human being to nature in which the "transcendence and unity of Allah are the prime and only cause of all that take place."[19] The difference between the God-centered Islamic political justification and the nature-centered Western political justification has significant political and social consequences. Western political philosophy put the state of nature at its center and developed mechanisms of sovereignty to legitimize state authority. In the case of Islamic political philosophy, the main objective is to establish a state to fulfill justice on behalf of Allah on earth. Whereas the former prioritized political institutionalization and contractual-consensual methods to rationalize obedience to the political authority and to law, the latter emphasized the dependence of political authority on the divinely based eternal value system. The values of social order and justice constituted the basic political philosophy of the Ottoman Empire summarized in the formula of the "Circle of Equity": "a ruler can have no power without soldiers, no soldiers without money, no money without the well-being of his subjects, and no popular well-being without justice."[20]

The Ottoman worldview (*Weltanschauung*) organized knowledge about the world in four dimensions.[21] Two dimensions were related to space. The first is the Islamic cosmography, which explains creation, the cosmos, and the physical realities in the world as a manifestation of the omnipotence of God. The second dimension is geography, which sought to explain physical conditions of regions and laws of nature. However, it was completely different from the modern understanding of geography, as political and military approaches were mostly disregarded by Ottoman authors. Aesthetic enjoyment played a more important role in maps and miniatures, and geographical books about other parts of the world were interested mainly in exotic creatures, supernatural forces, and mythical legends. According to pre-modern Ottoman cosmographers and geographers, every entity and creature, especially strange and exotic ones, confirmed the magnificence and omnipotence of God. The remarkable work of Piri Reis—a world map charting recent discoveries (in 1513) that included more information than Columbus knew after his last voyage—showed North and South America in detail. Piri Reis's map represented a radical break from previous Islamic and Ottoman geography that called the Atlantic Ocean "The Gloomy Sea" (*al-Bahr al-Muzlim*) or "Sea of Darkness" (*Bahr al-Zulumat*). However, it did not arouse major interest until it was rediscovered in 1929, since the Ottoman elites were more committed to pious speculations about the cosmos than to cartography and maps. In a similar way, *Tarih-i Hind-i Garbi* (A History of the *West India*), a book about the New World written around 1580, was more interested in illustrating animals and local inhabitants than in the activities of Europeans. In the sixteenth century, when the empire was expanding, the Ottomans did not need to incorporate their extensive knowledge of geographic discoveries into their political practices. For the Ottomans, conquering Egypt, with its prosperous resources, made much more sense than pondering the unknown New World.[22]

The third dimension of the Ottoman worldview is time in a historical conception. In traditional Ottoman history, the empire occupied the central position of the universe based on the Ptolemaic geocentric model. The empire was regarded as the inheritor of the Muslim dynasty, which started with the Prophet Muhammad and continued with four caliphs, the Umayyads, and Abbasids down to the Ottomans. The fourth dimension, theology, which explains the relation between man and God, is the dominant one in interpreting cosmology, geography, and history. Metaphorically, "looking around (geography) and looking back (history) are inextricably linked to looking up (theology)."[23]

In the seventeenth century, this Ottoman worldview was challenged on all four levels. In the dimension of theology, the emergence of unorthodox religious sects such as the Kadızadeli and Sabetai movements destabilized the political-religious structure of the empire. In history and cosmology, most Ottoman intellectuals recognized in an Ibn Khaldunian manner that the empire passed its zenith during the rule of Süleyman the Lawgiver (1520–1566) and that it was not the center of the universe anymore.[24] While the stability of the political-religious state structure was shaking and the conquest toward infidel lands was brought to a standstill, some Ottoman polymaths started to question the traditional spatial consciousness.

Katip Çelebi (1609–1657) is one of the most prominent geographers in the empire's long seven-centuries' history. Contrary to his precursors, Katip Çelebi considered geography an important tool for statesmen to be versed in political and military strategies. Geography provided them the opportunity both to journey to foreign countries and to acquire information from maps without traveling in these countries:

> For those who are in charge of affairs of the state, the science of geography is a matter of which knowledge is necessary. It may be not easy for them to be familiar with what the entire globe is like, but they ought at least to know the map of the Ottoman Empire and of those countries adjoining it. Then, when they have sent forces on campaign, they can proceed on the basis of the knowledge, and so the invasion of the enemy's land and also the protection and defense of the frontiers becomes an easier task. Taking counsel with individuals who

are ignorant of that science is no satisfactory substitute, not even when such men are local experts. Most such local experts are entirely unable to sketch the map of their regions. Sufficient and convincing proof of the necessity for learning this science is the fact that the infidels, by their application to and their esteem for those branches of learning, have discovered the New World and have over-run the markets of India. Even the despicable Venetians, coming to the straits of the Ottoman Empire, have opposed the power of our noble state, which rules from the east to the west.[25]

Katip Çelebi's views reflect a shift in the traditional Ottoman spatial consciousness. The reason for this shift was that the "infidels" were no longer limited to their part of the world but were conquering the New World and India. Although Europeans had not invaded the Ottoman Empire's territories yet, their supremacy in sailing—which resulted in control over the trade routes—was threatening the Ottomans' economic and political interests. For Katip Çelebi, to counter the European advance rulers could not continue to be ignorant about the affairs of "infidels" and instead needed to expand their cartographical and geographical knowledge.

Katip Çelebi wrote his most admired work, *Cihannüma*, between the years 1648 and 1654, and his intention was to compile a universal geography book. Even the name of the book—which means literally "roof terrace with a wide view" and can be interpreted as "the mirror of the world" (*Cosmorama* in Latin)—hints at this intention. Because of the importance of the information it included, *Cihannüma* became one of the seventeen books printed in the Ottoman's first printing office in 1732, eight decades after it was written.[26] The foremost characteristic of *Cihannüma*, which was unsurpassed by any Ottoman study until the nineteenth century, was its systematic methodology. In the science of geography, partitioning the world to describe the differences in the earth's surface is a major challenge. Islamic geographers before Katip Çelebi had divided the known world according to people's inhabitation into seven *iklims* (*klima* in Greek and "climate" in English), a mathematical and astronomical concept derived from Ptolemy's system.[27] Although Katip Çelebi did not completely reject this understanding, he partitioned the world into six continents: Europe, Asia, Africa, America, Magellenica (Australia), and the North and South Poles.[28] Then he divided the continents into territorial units called *memleket*, which means "country" in English. Çelebi believed that a geographer should inform his readers about the history and politics of the memleket. This represents a transition from "the additive structure of older Islamic geography to analytical regional geography which describes a region in its entirety."[29] According to Çelebi, if a geographer restricts himself to the physical characteristics of space, "he will turn [in]to a painter who portrays a naked dead body."[30] He criticized previous Islamic geographical works for trying to portray the world with only words and sentences, ignoring maps. On the first page of *Cihannüma*, he mentioned the importance of cartography for geographical studies. For him voyagers who traveled the world in their lifetime cannot match people who acquired geographical knowledge from maps. One of the most important features of *Cihannüma* is that it is the first Ottoman scientific study that extensively used and synthesized Western sources with Islamic ones. Indeed, Katip Çelebi started to write the first version of *Cihannüma* based only on Islamic sources. Nonetheless, he soon realized that the existent Islamic sources were not adequate to complete a universal geography book and so he stopped working on this first manuscript. In the second version of *Cihannüma*, he drew on Abraham Ortelius's *Theatrum orbis terrarum*, Cluverius's *Introductio geographica tam vetera quam nova*, and Gerardus Mercator's *Atlas Minor*. Heavily influenced by Mercator's views, Katip Çelebi underlined geography's instrumental value for the interests of the state:

> In some recent books, geography is divided into three
> branches, the third of which is termed politics. Basically
> referring to statesmanship, this branch divides the earth into
> sultanates and governments, i.e. into sultans, kings and other
> sovereigns, and consists of its representation and description
> in such manner . . . Geography is one of the sciences quite beneficial and useful in civil and social lives of men, and mastering
> this science is more important than all things else for ministers and senior officials. Philosophers have valued and preferred it to other rational sciences. For one ignorant of this
> science would be like a blind and deaf man when studying any

work, and in case of any dispute in the borders of states, this science would help resolve a difficulty, and it yields unquestionable benefits even in matters of more limited nature. Furthermore, it is such a science of wonder that it contains matters of curiosity obsessing the minds of men, thereby making them experienced and insightful about the world and realms ... Especially in the case of politics, this science is useful than all, and a man with knowledge of and insight into this science surely enjoys honor and praise.[31]

These original thoughts reflect a clear break from the Islamic understanding of the world. Geography is considered a science that depicts all characteristics of the earth.[32] The fourth dimension of the Ottoman worldview, theology, is degraded and used only in the preface of the book for legitimating the author's views. What is groundbreaking in *Cihannüma* is Katip Çelebi's scholarly attitude toward geographical knowledge and his factual style. In contrast to the Ottoman geographers, who took an overwhelming interest in personal narratives of travelers and tales about strange events about foreign countries to entertain the ruling elite of the empire, such as the well-known Ottoman traveler Evliya Çelebi, Katip Çelebi considered geography a practical science for statecraft and relied on European books, stories from merchants doing business with both West and East, and Ottoman officials' accounts. Although Katip Çelebi traveled Anatolia extensively, he did not even incorporate his impressions into his narrative when describing this region. Katip Çelebi is one of the first Ottoman intellectuals to question the reasons for the military successes of the Europeans, attributing them to their superiority of geographical knowledge.[33] From the window opened by Katip Çelebi, other scholars entered into Western geographical knowledge.

Another notable Ottoman geographer, Ebu Bekr ibn Behram el-Dimaşki, translated Joan Blaeu's *Atlas Maior* under orders of the Ottoman vizier Fazıl Ahmet Pasha. The translation took ten years and was completed in 1685. This monumental nine-volume book with 252 maps was called *Coğrafya-i Kebir* (Grand Geography). Similar to a state almanac, it took a utilitarian approach to inform the reader about the land, population, and cities of the Ottoman Empire. In fact, during the second siege of Vienna (1683), the information in the *Atlas Maior* about Hungary and Germany was used by the grand vizier Kara Mustafa Pasha. What is noteworthy about *Coğrafya-i Kebir* was that it was the first Ottoman book that mentioned Copernicus's heliocentric scientific theory 142 years after its development. However, since the maps of the Ottoman regions did not have any information that indicated that these territories were under the control of the Ottoman Empire, it can be said that "political geography as a means to represent statehood was not a concept emphasized by Abu Bakr [Ebu Bekr ibn Behram el-Dimaşki] or the painters who produced maps in the later copies."[34]

İbrahim Müteferrika, who used to call himself a geographer and added substantive information to the printed version of *Cihannüma*, made an important contribution to the development of geographical knowledge with his book *Usul el-Hikem fi Nizam el-Ümem* (Scientific Methods in the Structure of Nations). This book was written during the turbulent years of the Patrona Halil Revolt in 1730 that ended the Tulip Era and its reforms started in 1718. Müteferrika asked a crucial question in his book: "Why do Christians, who were so weak, degenerate, and inferior in the past compared with Muslims, begin to expand into the world and dominate so many lands and even defeat the once victorious Ottoman armies?"[35] His study attributed the Christian expansion to two factors. The first entailed new methods and techniques developed by European states in warfare and the organization of their armies. He discussed at length the significance of the army as a class for order and stability in states and societies.[36] Müteferrika attributed the recent Ottoman defeats against the well-organized and disciplined Habsburg and Russian armies to the ignorance of new military strategies and techniques. From this perspective he examined the success of reforms in Russia in the previous thirty years and how Peter the Great had invited experts from England and the Netherlands to modernize the state organization and military. Obviously, Russia was considered an example of Westernization for the Ottoman audience. Second, Müteferrika argued that in European countries, reason replaced the authority of religion in the state administration and implementation of laws. As it was too risky to advise replacing reason with religion in the Ottoman Empire, he instead discussed the indispensability of the science of geography for Ottoman statesmen to comprehend the physical and social conditions of their own state and those of their enemies. Indeed, one out of three chapters of the book discusses geography as a scientific guide for the statesmen. For Müteferrika, "geography is the mirror of the world. The world nations' capacities and conditions can be observed through geography. It is a kind of mirror of whether daily news and developments in the world are true or false and which can be verified with geography."[37] He advised the ruling elites to augment their geographical knowledge not only about their enemies but also about other Islamic peoples and countries all over the world. Sultans should utilize geography to unite all Muslims under the umbrella of the Ottoman Empire and defend them against the attacks of infidels.[38] These thoughts are the seeds of pan-Islamism, which became an influential ideology after the Tanzimat reforms in 1839.

Beginning in the second half of the seventeenth century, some Ottoman scholars realized the significance of scientific geography and the necessity to develop knowledge about their own and neighboring countries for use in military organization and state administration. These scholars argued that with the help of geographical knowledge, statesman can differentiate correct from inaccurate information and base their decisions on facts rather than superstitions and legends. However, their spatial consciousness diverges from the modern one and reflects the zeitgeist of the early modern period. The foundational stones of the Ottoman worldview before the nineteenth century were extraterritoriality, diasporas, and networks. Unlike a territorially defined, clearly bordered homogenous modern society, "the Ottoman world consisted of a tapestry of differing cultures."[39] This does not mean that Ottoman society was essentially open-minded and humanitarian, as some contemporary Turkish scholars have idealized it anachronistically as a precursor of liberal society.[40] The Ottomans tolerated different religions for pragmatic reasons. They utilized commercial and cultural diasporas, such as those that were Jewish, Greek, and Armenian, with their networks all over Europe, for the economic and political interests of the state. These communities were valuable not only in developing exports and imports but also in gathering economic, political, and military intelligence. Whereas in Europe the religious wars between Catholic and Protestant communities were engendering the condition of *cuius regio eius religio* (whose realm, his religion), in which people were forced to accept the religion of their king, the Ottomans provided extraterritoriality for Venetian and Genoese merchant communities. Ambassadors and consuls had legal jurisdiction over their communities, and they were allowed to have their own church in Ottoman territories.[41] Contrary to claims about the feeling of "timelessness," which is allegedly dominant among Muslim writers' perceptions of Europe "that nothing really changes," Ottomans were keen to update their information about their European rivals.[42] Abraham Ortelius's *Theatrum Orbis Terrarum*, which is the first true modern atlas with maps and supporting text bounded in book format, was brought to Istanbul in 1573, three years after it was published in Vienna.[43]

As the works of Piri Reis, Katip Çelebi, Ebu Bekr ibn Behram el-Dimaşki, and İbrahim Müteferrika reveal, these scholars followed Western advances in geography and other sciences. However, the question that İbrahim Müteferrika asked—why Europe had surpassed in power the Ottoman Empire and had started to dominate in other parts—has a point in terms of comparison between these two civilizations. Scholars and geographers often could not see the real difference between Europe and the Ottoman Empire. The answer might be found in the replies of these scholars. They argued that to compete against the West, the Ottoman ruling elites should change their attitude toward science and geography. By restricting themselves to diagnosing the troubles of their state and proposing practical solutions, they missed the crucial point that the Western advance in geography was not due to political motivation. Portuguese and English navigational achievements were economically and commercially motivated by the emerging merchant class in these two countries. Andrew Hess has argued this convincingly:

> While the Portuguese created a commercial and oceanic empire, the Ottomans pushed their frontiers into the water surrounding the eastern Mediterranean to create a seaborne state conditioned by the military and administrative requirements of a land-based Turko-Muslim state. In the course of their voyages rulers and merchants from Portugal and other Christian states participated in overseas commercial and military ventures that, in the East, rarely went beyond the establishment of a fortified trading post. While Portugal rejected the conquering tradition of her warrior aristocracy to lean almost entirely upon maritime commerce as the primary reason for imperial naval expansion in the East, the Ottomans,

in contrast sought to conquer territories in order to gain tax revenues from newly acquired agricultural and commercial economies.[44]

In the same way, in the second half of the sixteenth century, when the English Crown was not able to pay for cartographic projects due to the financial crises affecting all the monarchies in Europe, the merchant class became the patron of mapmakers to obtain scientifically produced charts for much-needed new markets.[45] None of the Ottoman scholars noticed the importance of the emerging various centers of power in the European societies that played an important role in the expansion of knowledge. Indeed, all their proposals were based on how to strengthen the social and political center of the Ottoman state to compete against the West. While decentralization of power led to the development of the economy and commerce in Europe, the extensive road and postal network of the Ottoman Empire enabled central authority to control and distribute imperial orders even to its remote provinces, such as Libya. In the Ottoman Empire, political power dominated the economic and commercial interests, not vice versa. The empire's patrimonial agrarian structure—aimed at maximizing its revenues from land tax—restrained the accumulation of wealth and development of innovative methods in the private sphere.[46]

The commercial and technological dominance of European states became more evident in the second half of the eighteenth century. With the defeat of the empire in the war against Russia in 1774, the military situation of the empire changed dramatically. The armies of "infidels" were no longer a distant threat for the Ottomans anymore. Russia's conquest of Crimea signaled the approaching "longest century" of the empire and its terminal decline. However, in the nineteenth century, the threat was not only the economic and military superiority of the West. If the world economy was reshaped as a result of the success of commercial Western European states, world politics in the nineteenth century was formed by the French Revolution and its vocabulary of liberty, equality, and fraternity. The powerful ideology of nationalism sealed the fate of the Ottoman Empire. The emergence of nationalism among Ottoman peoples resulted in the transformation of imperial spaces and multiethnic structures into nation-state territories and national identities. When the empire's borders were in constant flux, maps, territory, and geography would have completely different meanings for its people.

THE FRENCH REVOLUTION AND REMAKING THE VATAN

The French Revolution engendered a new political culture based on a thorough social and political change by means of mass mobilization and voluntary action. It not only influenced Western Europe but had, for example, repercussions on the liberation movements against the colonial powers in Asia, Africa, and the Middle East. The *Marseillaise*, the national anthem of the French Revolution, was sung during the 1908 Revolution in the Ottoman Empire and the Russian Revolution in 1917 and constantly played by Radio Baghdad in 1958 after the military coup commanded by General Qasim, who drew explicit parallels between the Iraqi Revolution and French Revolution in his speeches.[47] From the late eighteenth century onward, the French Revolution changed the mental mapping of empires and the role of their elites in the center and periphery. In the context of the Ottoman Empire, the impact of the French Revolution was not confined to Serbian, Greek, and Romanian independence movements. Contrary to the conventional views that prioritize the role of the peripheral elites in using the ideas of the French Revolution, the bulk of the importing was done by the Ottoman imperial elites for military and bureaucratic reforms: first to consolidate the authority of the sultan and later by the newly emerging bureaucratic class to limit the powers of the sovereign. The central elites faced the difficult task of modernizing the Ottoman Empire and at the same time maintaining maximum territory by accommodating the forces of nationalism and confronting the Russian Empire, which was the main supporter of the national movements in the Balkans, in numerous wars. However, rather than imitating the practices and concepts of the French Revolution, the imperial elites used them on an ad hoc basis. They borrowed and manipulated the ideas and achievements of the French Revolution for their strategic interests.[48]

One of the most important ideas of the French Revolution that was adopted by the Ottoman elites was the concept of patriotism and *patrie* or *vatan* in Turkish and *watan* in Arabic. Bernard Lewis argued that the roots of the word *patrie* go back to Greek and Roman times. "The sense of country, as the ultimate identity and loyalty, remained strong and became stronger" in European political culture after the decline of the Roman

Empire.⁴⁹ For Lewis, contrary to the Western understanding, in Arabic, Turkish, and Persian the word *vatan/watan* had never had any political meaning or implied loyalty to a territory. It "simply means one's place of residence, which may be adopted or temporary" and "had no more political significance than the English word home."⁵⁰ However, prominent scholars of nationalism, such as Ernest Gellner and Benedict Anderson, rejected the primordial understanding of nationalism that considers nations as a social reality dating back at least two thousand years. They both claimed that until the end of the eighteenth century, national loyalties were nonexistent in Europe.⁵¹ Likewise, the nationalist vocabulary emerged in French in the last quarter of the eighteenth century. In 1690, the *Dictionnaire Universel* of the Abbè Furetière defined *patrie* as "the country where one is born, and it refers to a particular place as much as to the province and the empire or the state where one was born ... the Romans and the Greeks were famous for their love of the patrie ... It is sometimes figuratively said that Rome is the patrie of all Christians. Heaven is our true patrie, a philosopher is everywhere in his patrie. Patrie is the place where one feels good."⁵² Still, at the end of the seventeenth century, patriotism was regarded as a sentiment characteristic of the ancients, and patrie had religious connotations. The word *patrie* acquired nationalistic meaning in the same dictionary in an edition published in 1777: "France is our patrie. Love of the patrie. For the good of the patrie. In the service of the patrie. To serve one's patrie. To defend one's patrie. To die for the patrie. The duty to the patrie is one of the primary duties."⁵³

Right from the beginning, Ottoman statesmen and diplomats were aware of the emergence of nationalism as a powerful idea in France. Ebubekir Ratib Efendi, the Ottoman ambassador in Vienna in 1792, was the first Ottoman diplomat who used the words *vatan* and *millet* in the modern sense in his treatise and travelogues.⁵⁴ During his five-month-long stay in Vienna, Ratib Efendi encountered the turmoil in Europe and particularly in French politics. He warned the Ottoman sultan not to consider France in a process of disintegration due to the civil war. He emphasized that "unlike [the] Habsburg Empire, France was united in a single religion, in a single nation, enjoying a common language."⁵⁵ Ratib Efendi argued that if the Jacobins took power, France would become a republic and export revolutionary ideology to other European monarchies. In his writings, Ratib Efendi used the concept of *kavim* (people) for Hungarians, Bulgarians, and Greeks. However, for France and Frenchmen he applied concepts of vatan and millet, and he was fully aware of the fact that a powerful nation-state with one nation and one homeland was emerging in Europe.[56] Ratib Efendi also noticed the alliance among the European monarchs against France based on their fears from "the new order" (*nizam-i cedid*) in the republican regime.[57]

Another Ottoman diplomat influenced by the developments in Europe at the end of the eighteenth century was Mahmud Raif Efendi. His book *Tableau des Nouveaux Règlements de l'Empire Ottoman*, published in 1798, was the first study written by a Muslim Ottoman bureaucrat in a Western language. Mahmud Raif Efendi wrote this book to inform European states about the reforms initiated by Sultan Selim the Third. Although his main focus was the military reforms to elevate the Ottoman Empire into "a respectable status" among European powers, there are important points in the book that reflect the ongoing modernization of the worldview of the Ottoman statesman.[58] In the first sentence of the book, Mustafa Raif Efendi emphasized a striking fact: "I desired to be beneficial for my Patrie since I was admitted into the Sublime Porte as an officer when I was very young."[59] Since Mahmud Raif Efendi wrote "Patrie" with a capital letter, he clearly understood the meaning and the power of the word.[60] Additionally, the comparison of the introduction of Mahmud Raif Efendi's book with İbrahim Müteferrika's *Usul el-Hikem fi Nizam el-Ümem*, which had been printed sixty-six years before, reveals a paradigm shift in the Ottoman mentality. Whereas Müteferrika praised God and the Prophet Mohammad in the introductory sentences of his book in line with the conventional invocation in Islamic writing, Mahmud Raif Efendi admired in an avant-garde style the patrie, the Ottoman state, and the sultan without mentioning God. Another important point brought up by Mahmud Raif Efendi was the changing geopolitical consciousness of Ottoman statesmen, who now viewed Russia as one of the most important threats to the empire's security. Previously, the Porte had considered the Dardanelles significant for the defense of Istanbul and neglected the Bosporus because the Black Sea was under the domination of the Ottoman Empire. Now, however, Mahmud Raif Efendi mentioned the new military fortifications on the Bosporus in response to increasing Russian power, which would become the most serious threat to the empire's territorial integrity in the next hundred years.[61]

Seyyid Mustafa Efendi's book *Diatribe Sur L'état Actuel de L'art Militaire, Du Génie et des Sciences à Constantinople* is another important study that identified European superiority with the development of scientific advancement. The book was written in 1803 in French and then rewritten by Seyyid Mustafa Efendi in Ottoman Turkish.[62] In the French version, he mentioned two times the word *patrie:* in the introduction and in the last paragraph. In the introduction, Seyyid Mustafa Efendi indicated that he was studying modern sciences and waiting for an opportunity to be sent by the Ottoman state to Europe. Sultan Selim the Third's project to open a new mathematics school changed Seyyid Mustafa Efendi's mind as "the idea to be able to be useful for patrie enchanted me and prevailed; I stayed."[63] In the last section of the book, he states that the Ottoman Empire had been a military state established based on the notion of conquest and the Islamic principle of fighting against infidels. According to Seyyid Mustafa Efendi, as a result of the corruption, local military authorities emerged and threatened the power of the sultan. He was very pleased with the reforms in the Ottoman army and reconsolidation of central authority: "I am very delighted of seeing my patrie in the state—I desired so ardently—enlightened by the torch of sciences and arts day by day and it was not possible for me to continue to be silent anymore."[64]

In light of these examples, at the end of the eighteenth century Ottoman bureaucrats and diplomats started to adopt the European concept of patrie and to use the word *vatan* in a similar way. This change in the meaning of vatan from a place where one was born and lives to a place for which one feels loyalty does not indicate that there now existed an imagination of national territory. The internalization and adoption of Ottoman patriotism as an ideology would happen after the Tanzimat Edict in 1839. These examples signify a shift from a pre-modern to a modern mode of legitimization of political power. To be more precise, Ottoman statesmen were aware of the fact that it was not sufficient to justify the political power of the sultan by basing it on divine right. During this period, one of the major challenges to the legitimacy of the sultan was Rhigas Pheraios and his revolutionary ideas about changing the Ottoman regime into a pseudo-Jacobin republic.⁶⁵ Rhigas called all Ottoman subjects from Bosnia to Arabia to revolt against the sultan. His revolutionary slogans, such as "freedom for all faith," "our hearts for our country," and "draw the sword for liberty," were condemned by the Orthodox patriarchate in Istanbul. In 1798 he was arrested by the Austrian police in Trieste, handed over to Ottoman authorities, and executed in Belgrade.⁶⁶ Rhigas's revolutionary ideas were some of the first harbingers of the national movements that would challenge the imperial elites in the nineteenth century. In parallel to the Ottoman Empire, other European monarchies had been experiencing similar crises of legitimacy: "Such traditional guarantors of loyalty as dynastic legitimacy, divine ordination, historic right and continuity of rule, or religious cohesion, were severely weakened. Last but not least, all these traditional legitimations of state authority were, since 1789, under permanent challenge. This is clear in the case of monarchy. The need to provide a new or at least a supplementary, 'national' foundation for this institution was felt in states as secure from revolution as George III's Britain and Nicholas I's Russia. And monarchies certainly tried to adapt themselves."⁶⁷

The Ottoman imperial elites not only suppressed the separatist national movement and demands for modernization but also used these new ideas to devise policies and "invent traditions" to strengthen the political power of the center and legitimize their positions.⁶⁸ However, constructing an Ottoman nation and patriotism to unite people from different ethnic and religious origins was a very difficult task. It was best described by Benedict Anderson as "stretching the short, tight, skin of the nation over the gigantic body of the empire."⁶⁹

The reforms of Sultan Selim the Third and the New Order ended as a result of the Janissary Revolt in 1807, in which Sultan Selim the Third and several reformers, including Mahmud Raif Efendi, were killed by Janissaries. The reactionaries were able to stop the reform process only for a limited time. As Ahmet Hamdi Tanpınar rightly put it, the reforms "did not wither as their seeds scattered into the life were nurtured by the exigencies."⁷⁰ Indeed, nineteen years after the revolt, the centuries-old Ottoman institution, the Janissary corps, was abolished by Sultan Mahmud the Second in 1826. The national uprising in Serbia between 1804 and 1817 and the independence of Greece in 1821 challenged the traditional millet system of the empire. Furthermore, the millet system became a tool for international powers such as Russia, Britain, and France to influence and manipulate the internal politics of the Ottoman Empire. Sultan Mahmud the Second and his bureaucrats tried to overcome these problems by constructing a new Ottoman state "composed of peoples of diverse nationalities and religions, based on secular principles of sovereignty as contrasted with the medieval concept of an Islamic empire."[71] The Tanzimat Edict that was proclaimed in 1839 was the culmination of these politics. The text of Tanzimat, which means literally "reorganization," was written by the foreign minister Mustafa Reşid Pasha and read in front of the ambassadors of European powers to influence them. The Porte officially notified the European states of the Tanzimat Edict.[72]

The Tanzimat stated that Ottoman subjects had inalienable rights and liberties that could not be revoked arbitrarily. The main objective was to acknowledge the legal equality of Muslims and non-Muslims and to unite them under the umbrella of Ottomanism. During Sultan Mahmud the Second's reign, symbols and ceremonies had been created to emphasize royal power and to establish a "national monarchy."[73] The creation of the first coat of arms for the dynasty, the composition of the first national anthem (the Mahmudiye march by Guiseppe Donizetti, who was later made a pasha), and the introduction of medals for service and loyalty to the state were examples of the glorification of the dynasty as a response to inflating nationalism. As Kemal Karpat argued, "these activities divested the dynasty of its traditional position as the absolute owner of the territory and all that lived on it and subordinated the dynasty to the state."[74]

In *Avrupa Risalesi* (The European Treatise), Mustafa Sami Efendi, a diplomat in the Ottoman embassy in Paris in 1838–1839, admired "the love of vatan" among French people.[75] In the last section of the book, Mustafa Sami Efendi attributed the progress of European civilization to the advancement of science. He underlined that by making science prevalent among the whole society, all Ottoman subjects would appreciate the significance of "vatan and millet."[76]

Ottoman statesmen realized the necessity of education in instilling a love of vatan among children in order to develop Ottoman patriotism. A couple of months before the Tanzimat Edict, a memorandum was published in Istanbul that was "the first definite initiative toward the reformation of the school system to a worldly-practical direction."[77] It is striking that the memorandum emphasized that "without science, the people cannot know the meaning of love for the state and vatan."[78] Similarly, it was the necessity of territorial loyalty to empower the authority of the sultan that was very well reflected in the text of the Tanzimat Edict: "If there is an absence of security with regard to property, everyone remains indifferent to his state and community; nobody deals with the progress of the public wealth, absorbed as he is in his own troubles and worries. If, on the contrary, he enjoys perfect security, he will not depart from the ways of loyalty and he feels each day to intensify his love for state and community, devotion to his vatan."[79]

Furthermore, military service was no longer presented as a religious obligation of Muslim subjects compelled to fight against infidels; it was regarded instead as the duty of all Ottomans compelled to defend the vatan: "The defense of the vatan is an important issue and it is a duty for all to provide soldiers for this purpose."[80] Two years after the Tanzimat Edict, *Ceride-i Havadis* (Journal of News), the first semi-private Ottoman newspaper, published an article about the importance of patriotism based on vatan for the state and sultanate: "The power of the state, the strength of the sultanate, and the prosperousness and prominence of the country stems from the endeavor for vatan. The endeavor for vatan means that people, who want their state to be in perfect order, regard the general interest as better than their self interests."[81] As emphasized by Ahmet Hamdi Tanpınar and Hilmi Ziya Ülken, this article promoting patriotism based on vatan was very innovative for that period.[82] What is more striking about this article is that there was not a single reference to Islam. Instead the author sets a Roman prince, who sacrificed himself for his people, as an example of the endeavor for vatan for Ottoman statesmen. Nevertheless, this secular and modern perspective of Tanzimat about patriotism based on vatan would be taken over by a more Islamic discourse in the second half of the nineteenth century.

PROMOTING AN IMPERIAL VATAN TO ENCOURAGE OTTOMAN PATRIOTISM

Promoting vatan as a territorial concept to secure the loyalty of subjects served as a modern political foundation for the Ottoman state. Attachment to Ottoman territory had significant value in political discourses involving the ruling elites during the second half of the nineteenth century. Contrary to the secular role of the patrie or fatherland in European political culture, in the context of the Ottoman Empire, loyalty to vatan was considered a part of the Muslim faith and culture and was used by both elites and intellectuals to establish a firm foundation for the ideology of Ottomanism. The Islamization of vatan intensified after the second half of the 1860s as a reaction to the privileged status of Christian millets and Balkan nationalism. Although the Tanzimat aimed to establish "an Ottoman nation" based on a common vatan, "in which subjects would benefit from identical civil rights," the author of the Tanzimat Edict, Mustafa Reşid Pasha, did not envision that the full equality of both Muslims and Christians would soon be realized.[83]

The first shift that changed the balance between the Muslim and Christian communities was the Anglo-Ottoman Commercial Convention of 1838. It allowed foreign merchants to participate in internal trade. This resulted in the abandonment of protectionism and with it the guild system. Non-Muslim Ottoman merchants who played an intermediary role between European markets and local Muslim producers benefited from expanded trade and foreign imports. This pattern ultimately eliminated Muslim merchants and improved the status of Christian merchants, who were preferred by European traders as partners in the empire, and secured for them a privileged legal status because of the capitulations granted to all European powers. The improved conditions of non-Muslim moneylenders "increased national awareness and exacerbated religious and ethnic tensions with grave consequences in the future."[84] The Islahat Edict in 1856, a result of European pressure, augmented the economic power of non-Muslim groups and contributed to the solidification of boundaries and identities. By declaring the Tanzimat Edict in 1839, the Porte acknowledged the equality of all Ottoman subjects regardless of religion, but owing to a lack of appropriate institutional support, this declaration could not be enforced. The Islahat Edict institutionalized the promise of Tanzimat by abolishing the head tax and by securing equality in the military as well as in education, justice, and government employment.[85] The resentment among the Muslim community after the proclamation of the Islahat Edict was best described by Ahmet Cevdet Pasha, a prominent Ottoman historian and statesman: "Many Moslems began to grumble: 'Today we lost our sacred national rights which our ancestors gained with their blood. While the Islamic nation used to be the ruling nation, it is now bereft of this sacred right. This is a day of tears and mourning for the Moslem brethren.'"[86] Nationalist uprisings in the Balkans also increased the resentment in the Muslim community. In 1859, Moldavia and Wallachia united and formed the autonomous Romania, which acted as a de facto sovereign state until it was awarded full independence in 1877. In 1862, clashes started in Belgrade between the Ottoman army and the local population. Under pressure from European powers and Russia, the last Ottoman soldier left Belgrade in 1867, officially bringing to an end the centuries-old Ottoman rule in Serbia. In addition to the de facto independence of Romania and Serbia, conflicts in Lebanon, Crete, Bosnia, and Montenegro in the 1860s precipitated the formation of a patriotic movement known as the "Young Ottomans," among the mostly Turkish-speaking Muslim intelligentsia. The avowed goal of the movement was to "save the empire." Its members were significantly influenced by the Carbonari in Italy and by other patriotic movements in Europe, such as Young Italy, Young France, and Young Germany.

Benedict Anderson considers the emergence of print capitalism as a crucial factor in the rise of nationalism because the expansion of books and newspapers throughout the country enabled people to see themselves as part of a national community and to better relate to their fellow citizens.[87] In the context of the Ottoman Empire, it is impossible to argue for the importance of the emergence of print capitalism in the 1860s, because the very low literacy rate made it difficult for entrepreneurs to start profitable print businesses. However, the establishment of the first private newspapers owned by Muslims played an important role in the emergence of patriotic movements, such as the Young Ottomans, among intellectuals and bureaucrats. Between 1729 and 1829, only 180 books were printed in the Ottoman Empire. This number increased to 6,357 between 1876 and 1892 and to 10,601 between 1893 and 1907. In 1875, the number of journals and newspapers was 87. This total grew to reach 144 in 1883, 226 in 1895, and 548 in 1911.[88] With the ever-increasing availability of printed materials, Ottoman intellectuals tried to address the fundamental challenge concerning the empire's survival: how to maintain social order while religious communities were transformed into political communities. In parallel with the official Ottoman patriotism developed after the Tanzimat by bureaucrats of the Sublime Porte, Young Ottomans sought to construct territorial patriotism as a constitutive common identity for all Ottoman subjects. They were challenged not only by nationalist movements in the Balkans but also by other Muslim intellectuals in Egypt and Lebanon, who developed local territorial patriotic movements that questioned the legitimacy of the imperial center.

Rifa'a al-Tahtawi (1801–1873) was one of the leading Middle Eastern thinkers who expressed the idea of territorial patriotism based on the Egyptian vatan. According to Tahtawi, *hubb ul-vatan*, which means "love of vatan," was the foundation of a society's solidarity. Duties of members of a society toward their country, such as sacrifice, unity, submission to law, and all rights to freedom, originate from love of vatan.[89] Tahtawi's Egyptian patriotism, which focused on Egypt's territory, was a clear break from the Islamic political concept of ummah. In his book *Manahij*, Tahtawi quoted the Prophet Mohammad's well-known hadith, "the Muslim is brother of the Muslim," and compared religious loyalty with patriotism (*wataniyyah*): "All that is binding on a believer in regard to his fellow believers is binding also on members of the same watan in their mutual rights. For there is a national brotherhood between them over and above the brotherhood in religion. There is a moral obligation on those who share the same watan to work together to improve it and perfect its organization in all that concern its honor and greatness and wealth."[90]

Another Arab thinker who referred extensively to vatan and territorial patriotism was Butrus al-Bustani (1819–1883). During communal violence in Lebanon in 1860, Bustani wrote eleven pamphlets in an effort to unite different religious sects. In these pamphlets, Bustani addressed members of the Syrian society known as "children of the vatan" (*Ya abna al-watan*) and signed each pamphlet simply as "the patriot" (*muhibb li'l-watan*).[91] A comparison of the patriotism of Fuad Pasha, who was sent to Lebanon by the Sublime Porte to suppress local violence, with Bustani's patriotism reveals significant differences between the central and peripheral elites of the empire. While both Fuad Pasha and Bustani underlined the importance of the love of vatan in overcoming differences between religious sects, these two individuals adopted completely different perspectives in terms of patriotism. While Bustani's patriotism envisioned active and equal subjects who "would have to transform themselves into citizens,"[92] Fuad Pasha's call for patriotism was paternalistic and aimed to strengthen the hierarchical relationship between rulers and ruled. He called for all Ottoman subjects to uncritically obey the orders of the sultan: "All people should act in accordance with the Sultan's benevolent wishes, and each class of the imperial subjects should embrace tightly the principles of unity, patriotism [*hubb ul-vatan*], and service to the nation by obeying imperial orders and by zealously fulfilling humanitarian obligations."[93] Fuad Pasha and the elites in Istanbul were aware of the developing patriotic consciousness among Arab thinkers. For example, Tahtawi's book *Takhlis al-Ibriz ila Talkhis Bariz* (The Extraction of Gold from a Distillation of Paris) was published in Turkish in 1839. Young Ottomans tried to counterbalance emerging local patriotic ideas and movements with Ottoman patriotism, which was called Ottomanism (*Osmanlılık*).

The intellectual foundations of the Young Ottomans were established by İbrahim Şinasi (1826–1871), who published the Ottoman Empire's first private newspaper, *Tercüman-ı Ahval* (Interpreter of Conditions). Şinasi truly believed in the modernization mission of the Tanzimat. The major difference between his viewpoint and that of his intellectual predecessors was that Şinasi realized the importance of the people's right to be informed of the workings of government. He considered journalism an important tool in providing such information to the Ottoman people. In the foreword of the first issue of *Tercüman-ı Ahval*, Şinasi explicitly associated the dissemination of ideas through written materials with the interests of vatan: "Since people who live in a society have a duty of loyalty to various official obligations, it necessarily follows that a part of their rights consists of the dissemination of verbal and written ideas to promote the interests of the vatan."[94] The influence of the ideas of the French Revolution on Şinasi's writing is obvious in his frequent use of the word "nation" and the phrase "the Great Ottoman nation." Nonetheless, it is not possible to label him an "Ottoman nationalist" because his line of thinking also reflected the universalist perspective of the French Revolution. In his article in the newspaper *Ceride-i Askeriye* (Newspaper of the Military) published on January 17, 1864, Şinasi defined the duty of the Ottoman nation as one whose aim was to "to enlighten and improve humanity." Şinasi also echoed Victor Hugo's universalist words "avoir pour patrie le monde et pour nation l'humanité" in one of his verses: *Milletim nev-i beşerdir vatanım rûy-i zemin*, which may be translated as "mankind is my nation and the Earth is my vatan."[95] Well-known Young Ottoman intellectuals, such as Namık Kemal and Ali Suavi, who were mentored by Şinasi, did not take the universalistic tone of Şinasi into consideration and instead employed Ottoman patriotism more vigorously in their writings.

Namık Kemal (1840–1888) is by far the most prominent figure of Ottoman patriotism. As a consequence of Namık Kemal's writings, the word *vatan* acquired political significance and came to be used extensively in Turkish literature.[96] Years later, his patriotic poems, plays, and articles became sources of inspiration for Turkish nationalists. After the First Battle of İnönü in 1921, in which national forces stopped the advancing Greek army in Anatolia, Mustafa Kemal labeled Namık Kemal "the guardian of our vatan overlooking from the heaven" and quoted from his well-known poem, *Vatan*: "[Namık] Kemal asked: 'In the heart of the vatan is the enemy's dagger; isn't there anyone to save the ill fortuned mother[land]?' Here, from this bench as the president of the sublime parliament, I state on behalf of each and every member of the parliament and the entire nation: So be the enemy's dagger in the heart of the vatan; there shall be definitely one to save the ill fortuned mother[land]."[97]

Today, Turkish primary school students still read Namık Kemal's poems and perform his well-known play, *Vatan, or Silistre* (*Vatan Yahut Silistre*). In Turkey, he is known as "the poet of the vatan" (*Vatan Şairi*). Without a doubt, the concept of vatan acquired significant patriotic meaning through Namık Kemal's writings. He transformed the meaning of vatan from a feeling of belonging to a birthplace into a feeling of loyalty toward a sacred territory.[98] According to Namık Kemal, vatan requires dedication and allegiance; in return, the love of vatan provides "glory and inner contentment."[99] He considered the defense of vatan as the most sacred duty of the Ottoman people.

Namık Kemal's patriotism was a response to the inexorable and ongoing disintegration of the empire. At the time, his goal was to prevent further loss of territory and maintain the empire's borders. His solution to reuniting diverse ethnic groups in the empire and resisting Russian expansion was a patriotic appropriation of space.[100] Namık Kemal employed ideological motivation and passionate discourse to make people conscious of Ottoman territories as sacred constituents of their lives. However, he was aware that drawing the borders of a common Ottoman vatan, which would also include peripheral regions, such as Tunisia and Yemen, and groups from different ethnic and religious backgrounds, would be very difficult. Consequently, his patriotic discourse on vatan was essentially an overly idealistic portrayal of several key themes. Namık Kemal explicitly said that the unity of the Muslim people could not be destroyed "by drawing lines on the map."[101] The main difference between the Ottoman patriotism of Namık Kemal and nationalist movements in Western Europe, particularly those in Italy and Germany, was the absence of clearly defined efforts to expand the borders of the Ottoman Empire. From this standpoint, there are similarities between Namık Kemal and Ernest Renan. For both, the fatherland was an emotional and sentimental concept, not a simple geographical unit with clearly defined borders.[102] In his article "Vatan" published on March 22, 1873, Namık Kemal rejected rationalistic conceptions of borders: "Imagination of vatan in the shape of borders or a map . . . A person loves his vatan, because it is not composed by the vague lines traced by the sword of a conqueror or the pen of a scribe. It is a sacred idea resulting from the coalescence of various emotions such as the nation, liberty, interest, solidarity, sovereignty, respect for one's ancestors, love of the family, and childhood memories . . . Therefore, in every religion, in every nation, in every culture, in every civilization love of vatan is the most important virtue and the most sacred duty."[103]

Similarly, in another article he said that "although vatan is an imagined concept, everybody agrees that it is much more effective to protect justice and general interest than fortifications made of iron and stone."[104] For him, the disintegration of the Ottoman vatan was incomprehensible, as different nations and religious sects benefited from sharing the same territory that organically constituted the Ottoman nation. Ruling elites and the Ottoman people had to be made aware that justice, liberty, and love of vatan were indispensable factors in protecting 600 years of Ottoman unity: "Nobody has either the right or the power to destroy [Ottoman] unity by reinforcing the Arabian, Tunisian, Egyptian or Yemeni identities."[105] To overcome differences among various religious and ethnic groups and to unite them under the umbrella of Ottoman identity, he proposed "establish[ing] schools, which would accept children from different religious and ethnic backgrounds." If "children of vatan" (*evladı vatan*) attended the same school, "it would be impossible [for foreign powers] to sow discord between them."[106]

Until the first half of the nineteenth century, only the ruling elites considered themselves as Ottomans. Namık Kemal believed that a societal Ottoman identity would be essential in bonding together the people of the empire; he finished some of his articles with the motto "long live the Ottomans" (*Yaşasın Osmanlılar*). Namık Kemal's play *Vatan, or Silistre*, which portrayed the sacrifice and heroism of Ottoman soldiers in their defense of the Silistre Fortress (in today's Bulgaria) against the Russian army during the Crimean War, generated patriotic euphoria among the public when it opened on April 1, 1873. The popular sentiment was so strong that in a week the theater was closed, the play was censored, and Namık Kemal and his friends were exiled by the government, which was afraid of a patriotic uprising.

There was a deliberate ambiguity in the thinking of Namık Kemal regarding how to define the Ottoman nation (*Millet-i Osmaniye*) and the Ottoman vatan. Sometimes, the Ottoman nation was defined as all individuals living in Ottoman territories regardless of religion and ethnicity. On other occasions, the Unity of Islam, namely, Muslims in the empire, was identified as the backbone of the Ottoman nation. In *Vatan, or Silistre*, the Balkans were labeled as the heartland of the Ottoman vatan and the River Danube was the "elixir of life." Therefore, "if Danube is lost, the vatan cannot survive, and nobody can live on." In his poem "Uproar" (*Vaveyla*), he defined the borders of the vatan by employing religious symbols: "Vatan, go to Kaaba, wrap yourself with black; put your one hand on the thumb of the Prophet in Medina; and your other hand on the thumb of Husayin in Kerbela; look to the universe with all your magnificence." It is clear that although the Balkans were portrayed as the indispensable center of vatan in the play, the poem "Uproar" defined vatan from a religious perspective and used the holy sites of Islam to give the concept a sacred connotation. The ambiguity and confusion over the concept of vatan in the writings of Namık Kemal and other post-Tanzimat intellectuals captures the zeitgeist of the second half of the nineteenth century. Although all were aware of a real Turkish ethnicity, which served as the foundation of the empire, it was impossible for them to advocate the idea of Turkish nationalism. As Hilmi Ziya Ülken correctly argued, "despite the fact that the empire was contracting, it was still surviving." Young Ottomans realized that the establishment of a national society in the future was inevitable. Nevertheless, because they remained imperial elites, supporting the idea of a national society would have been "self-denial."[107]

Young Ottomans developed two different ideologies to protect the unity of the Ottoman Empire: Unity of the Elements (*İttihad-ı Anasır*) and Unity of Islam (*İttihad-ı İslam*). Unity of the Elements was envisaged by Tanzimat bureaucrats and intellectuals as a means of maintaining the loyalty of ethnic religious groups toward the imperial center. Unity of Islam emerged as an ideology in the 1860s, when over a million Muslims were forced by Russia to migrate from the Caucasus to the Ottoman territories. Unity of Islam became the dominant ideology of the state after the 1877–1878 war with Russia, when the Ottoman Empire lost almost one-third of its territory and its Christian population decreased from 40 percent to 20 percent. Unity of the Elements and Unity of Islam were not considered competing ideologies by the Young Ottomans, who employed these terms interchangeably in their writings.[108]

Ali Suavi (1838–1878) was one of the first Ottoman intellectuals to use the concept of Turkishness in his writings. Although he was considered to be the first Turkish nationalist by Falih Rıfkı Atay and others, Ali Suavi was not exceptional among Young Ottomans in his efforts to maintain the integrity of the empire by developing the ideologies of the Unity of the Elements and Unity of Islam.[109] His main distinguishing feature was that he was not "unaware of the national consciousness."[110] Ali Suavi's article "Türk," which was published in the *Muhbir* newspaper in London, aimed to erase "the image of the vulgar and uncivilized Turk."[111] He examined the roots of Turks in Central Asia and sought to elevate the status of Turks by tracing their historical contributions to world civilization. Similar to Namık Kemal, Ali Suavi wrote about the concept of vatan extensively: "Retaining the possession of the territories outside of the homeland requires an extensive [military] force, which we cannot afford anymore. Thus, we should grant independence to the autonomous regions and create a strong Islamic state in Africa by helping Tripoli, Benghazi, and Egypt unite. The Ottoman Empire and this newly formed state would support each other. If there is an act of aggression against our territories in Africa, as was the case in Algeria, what can we do other than protest the aggressor? Our mother vatan then would consist of Rumelia and Anatolia, which includes Syria, Iraq and Palestine. This would be the homeland, where we would exercise our sovereignty."[112]

Ali Suavi criticized European intellectuals for their attempts to analyze Eastern civilizations by drawing upon Western standards. He asserted that the two worldviews were completely different. According to Ali Suavi, "a Frenchman cannot rise to the rank of minister under the English government. Likewise, an Algerian Arab can never enjoy the rights granted to [a] Frenchman. However, the question of ethnicity does not exist in the East."[113] In Ali Suavi's thinking, Turkism, Islamism, and Ottomanism could easily be combined. Rather than facing ethnic problems, in the Ottoman Empire all Muslims united under the Islamic ideology of tawhid. This unity became apparent in his conceptualization of Ottoman vatan and in his comparison with the French patrie: "For instance Frenchmen number only 30 million people, who support the case of Frenchness. However, Turks are 200 million people in their case of Islam. Ethnicity can perish. But Islam shall exist forever. Therefore Turks will not ever perish."[114] Far from arguing a nationalist worldview, Ali Suavi defended the imperial and Islamic vatan, in which Turks played a vital role as the key element of the Ottoman Empire. He looked down on Western nationalism and praised Islamic unity: "In Islam, if Islamic lands were attacked, it is the duty of every Muslim to defend it . . . We read in the books that this was not the case in France. Instead, they have 'amour de la patrie,' which means love of vatan. If the French patrie is attacked, all Frenchmen will defend the vatan. However, Prussian soldiers invaded France. The French newspapers sounded alarms for two months, trying to incite the French people to defend their vatan, but nobody revolted against the enemy."[115]

Young Ottomans were the ideologues of the Ottoman Empire. Their ideology was to "save the state" and to "awaken the nation." Because there were no intermediary institutions in the empire between the sultan and the people, Young Ottomans developed the idea of loyalty toward the vatan as a means of depersonalizing the authority of the Ottoman state. The young Ottoman sultan Abdulhamid II, who came to power because of a political coup d'état, used the devastating Russo-Ottoman war to strengthen his authority. He purged the major figures of the Young Ottoman movement, dissolved Parliament, and suspended the constitution.

During his extended rule from 1876 to 1909, Abdulhamid continued the reforms started in the Tanzimat era to modernize imperial institutions, such as education and transportation, with an emphasis on the centralization of power. The main difference between Tanzimat reformers and Abdulhamid was that he considered patriotism to be a major threat to his rule. He firmly declared the impossibility of ever constructing a "national consciousness" among the Ottoman people and instead employed Islam as an ideology to protect the territorial integrity of his empire:[116] "In their attempts to denigrate us, Europeans label us with the cliché of 'the dreadful fanaticism of Muslims.' With this phrase they refer to the so-called bloody atrocities we committed against people of other religions. But isn't this the same love with the one they name love of vatan in their case, which they refer to as fanaticism to describe our case? What they feel for their vatan is similar to what we feel for our religion."[117]

Abdulhamid used the office of the caliphate to influence Muslims outside of the Ottoman Empire, especially Muslims in the British and Russian empires. In so doing, he wished to strengthen his hand against the European powers. In turn, he believed that Britain was encouraging national uprisings in the empire in an attempt to dethrone him: "Certain young people, who received a little intellectual polish in Europe, deliver from time to time speeches concerning the love of vatan. However the love of vatan should not come first in our empire. The love of the faith and the caliph should be the first and then should come love of vatan. Is not that the case among the Catholics of Europe? The Christians first pay respect to the Catholic Church and the Pope, and then they consider their vatan in the second place. Britain has been spreading the idea of the vatan in the Islamic lands with the aim to undermine my authority. This idea has already made a considerable progress in Egypt. Egyptian patriots are unwittingly deceived by the British and undermine the power of Islam as well as the prestige of the caliphate."[118]

To weaken the attraction of nationalist movements among Muslims within the empire, Abdulhamid added a strong Islamic accent to his political regime, which may be termed Islamic Ottomanism. Abdulhamid reinvented traditions and ceremonies to establish a personality cult around the caliphate.[119] His greatest monument was the construction of the Hejaz railway from Damascus to Medina. The Hejaz railway facilitated the transportation of pilgrims to Mecca and was completed in 1908 using financial contributions and donations from Muslims all over the world. However, he also established a highly developed censorship mechanism to control opposition groups. Officials even condemned the use of the word *vatan* in printed materials as a potentially dangerous act. The exiled Namık Kemal removed the word from the title of his play and renamed it *Silistre* in order not to arouse suspicion.[120] Most of the leading figures that were opposed to the Hamidian regime escaped to Europe and continued their political activities, mainly in France. They formed secret committees and disseminated their journals and articles throughout the major cities of the empire with the objective of overthrowing the sultan and reinstating the constitution and Parliament. Although they shared a common enemy—namely, Abdulhamid—and therefore combined under the banner of the Young Turks, these intellectuals did not have a common agenda, because they were from different ethnic and religious origins and pursued various ideological and cultural priorities.[121]

RISE OF THE YOUNG TURKS: "SAVING THE VATAN"

The formation of the Ottoman Unity Society (*İttihad-ı Osmani Cemiyeti*) in 1889 is considered a foundational moment for the Young Turks. However, none of the founders of the Ottoman Unity Society were ethnically Turkish.[122] In the first meeting in 1889, there were debates about membership criteria, with some members arguing that only Muslims could join the organization. İbrahim Temo, who held membership ID number 1-1 (that is, the first member of the first division), rejected these proposals. Temo proposed that "every trustworthy Ottoman with goodwill be admitted to the organization regardless of his religion and ethnicity," and his proposal was accepted.[123] In 1895, the Ottoman Unity Society was renamed the Committee of Union and Progress (CUP; *İttihad ve Terakki Cemiyeti*), an organization that was to leave its mark on the next twenty-five years of the empire. Its leader, Ahmet Rıza (1857–1930), rejected the name Unity of Islam. Because there were various nations and religions in the empire, for Ahmet Rıza it was essential that the name of the committee embrace all Ottomans. Ahmet Rıza offered two alternatives, Unity of Ottomans (*İttihad-ı Osmani*) and Union and Progress (*İttihat ve Terakki*), and ultimately the latter was accepted.[124] While the word "progress" in the name of the committee referred to the modernization of political and economic frameworks, the word "union" signified the unity of every ethnic and religious group in the empire.

Between 1894 and 1896, there were Armenian rebellions and intercommunal conflicts in the Anatolian provinces and in Istanbul. During this turmoil, the CUP declared that its goal was to protect the unity of the empire through loyalty to a common vatan. One of the first pamphlets published by the CUP was entitled *Vatan Tehlikede* (Vatan Is in Danger). It was written by İbrahim Temo and his associates in response to the Armenian rebellions of October 1895, which took place a couple of months after the formation of the CUP. The authors used one of the slogans of the French Revolution, *La Patrie est en danger*, as the title of the pamphlet.[125] In the first two paragraphs of the pamphlet, the authors explained why they took the French Revolution as their model:

> A hundred years ago, during the French Revolution when France was attacked by foreign forces, a well-known individual unfurled the flag of patriotism and shouted "our vatan is in danger." Every Parisian old enough to be drafted into the army accepted this patriotic invitation and chose to serve and to sacrifice themselves for their vatan. Soon, the sacrifice that had started in the capital began to spread all over the country. Volunteer armies succeeded in saving their country from danger and in defending it against their oppressors. Even though this important event happened a hundred years ago in a foreign country, we draw parallels with our situation today. Our precious vatan has been in danger for some time. We reiterate the scale of this danger. Our goal is to find a solution together to save our common holy mother, our dear vatan.[126]

According to the CUP, the most important factor, "which put state, nation, and 600 hundred year old honor in danger," was the Armenian question. Although the CUP supported general reforms in the empire, it was against the preferential treatment of the Armenian community in six provinces, because this gave the impression that the empire had surrendered to pressure from European states. The authors rejected seeing the empire as the "sultan's ranch and the people as his slaves." According to them, the sultan should consider "the members of the nation as citizens and be just and fair to them."¹²⁷ In the last pages of the pamphlet, "all Ottomans" were called to act to "save their vatan" and to demonstrate in front of the palace in the hundreds of thousands so that the sultan would fulfill his duty toward the nation and reopen the Parliament, in which Muslims and Christians could be represented without ethnic and religious discrimination. The CUP warned all Ottoman people that if they hesitated in acting to save the vatan, it would be broken into pieces by foreign countries and all Ottomans would face misery.

The political ideal of "saving the vatan" had a remarkable impact on the generation of the Young Turks. A letter written by Greek-Ottoman citizen Lamçanti and published by the newspaper *Bedreka-i Salamet* in Filibe (Plovdiv in today's Bulgaria) in March 1897 reveals that the Ottoman patriotism based on Ottoman vatan was also embraced by non-Muslims. The editors of the newspaper praised the letter: "this young man is fulfilling his outstanding duty of loving vatan that dignified his religious sect and nationality and at the same time he is displaying his Ottomanness, which is a very honorable attitude in our opinion."¹²⁸ Lamçanti sent his letter to the newspaper in order to show "to his Greek-Ottoman co-religionists that to love the vatan by heart is a prime duty of each man regardless of his religion and ethnicity." Lamçanti also emphasized that in the ongoing war between Ottoman Empire and Greece, he was ready to fight in the Ottoman army as a volunteer to fulfill the "duty of defending the vatan."¹²⁹

Young Turks adopted the ideal of "saving the vatan" from the Young Ottomans, particularly from Namık Kemal. Under the repressive regime of Abdulhamid, Namık Kemal and his patriotism especially influenced students in the military and medical schools. When İbrahim Temo was a medical student, he was questioned by his professors about why he had hung pictures of Ali Suavi and Namık Kemal on the wall of his dormitory room. İbrahim Temo explained that he had these pictures because "the members of the nation should appreciate and respect these people." The professors then asked him "why he did not display pictures of the recent sultans." His answer was "because we were not taught about the sultans after Sultan Mahmud and we cannot even find their pictures." He was forced to take down these pictures, and his room was inspected regularly after the incident.¹³⁰ Resneli Ahmet Niyazi, who was a rebellious figure during the 1908 revolution and became a "hero of freedom," complained to his friends in military school about the lack of patriotism in their education: "We are raised as military officers to protect our vatan and destroy the invading enemy. Then why is there not a single course in our program about the love of vatan . . . The answer is 'for the sake of the Yıldız' [the name of the palace, where Abdulhamid resided]."[131] As one of the first members of the CUP, Kazım Nami Duru mentioned in his memoirs that in military school in Manastır (Bitola in today's Macedonia), he grasped the significance of Namık Kemal and his writings: "I was so excited after reading Namık Kemal that I imagined myself as an eagle flying around the summit of the mountain of freedom. I learned the vatan, the love of vatan, to defend the vatan, and the love of freedom from him."[132] Similarly, Yusuf Kemal Tengirşenk, who served as the minister of foreign affairs between 1921 and 1922 in the Ankara government, emphasized in his memoirs how Namık Kemal's works transformed his religion-based worldview to a patriotic one after primary school: "When I came from Boyabat [a small town in the Black Sea region], due to the religious environment in which I was raised in, I prayed, 'Dear God, martyr me for the sake of religion.' I did not have any commitment to the world. My sentiments to religion were transformed to the love vatan. To die for vatan was the highest rank to be reached for me."[133]

Thirteen years after the publication of the pamphlet *Vatan Is in Danger*, the CUP decided to act to save the vatan from the despotism of the sultan. The revolution of 1908 resulted in the restoration of the constitutional regime and the first general election since 1876. The composition of the new Parliament reflected the multicultural nature of Ottoman society. Out of a total of 288 deputies in the Parliament, there were 147 Turks, 60 Arabs, 27 Albanians, 26 Greeks, 14 Armenians, 10 Slavs, and 4 Jews.[134] Although the period after 1908 and the political regime of the CUP were considered by some scholars to represent the galvanization of nascent Turkish nationalism, the leaders of the CUP were well aware that they were ruling a multiethnic empire and not a nation-state.

Therefore, it is more appropriate to call them Ottoman patriots rather than Turkish nationalists, at least until the second half of World War I. Mehmed Reşid Bey's dispute with local Arabs in the city hall of Tripoli after the Revolution of 1908 revealed how a member of the CUP viewed a distant territory, namely, Libya, as part of the Ottoman vatan.[135] Local Arabs considered Ottoman patriots and Young Turks, who were exiled to Libya, as "nonbelievers," and they opposed the reforms of the Young Turks: "By declaring freedom [the Young Turks] want to turn us into infidels, make us embrace the customs of the heathen, coerce our women to walk naked in the streets, and force us to be brothers with infidels and Jews . . . They have to go back to their country. This is our country not theirs. We have inhabited here for centuries. Our ancestors have been buried here. [The Young Turks] are foreigners."[136] Reşid Bey's response was striking because it revealed that the dispute was between not Arab and Turkish nationalism but conservatism and modern Ottoman patriotism:

> First of all, this is not your country; it belongs to all Ottomans. The difference between us is that you consider only Tripoli as vatan, whereas we consider Anatolia, Rumelia, Arabia, and here as vatan, because all of the latter constitute the Ottoman Empire. You are so careless and irresponsible about the future and welfare of Tripoli, even though you consider it your vatan. We believe that it is our duty to sacrifice our lives for our vatan. If we had thought that vatan is the place where we were born and where we earn our living, we would not have left our family and our independence and we would not have come here.
> I stand up to you and tell you to your face that there is not even a single person among you that has worked as much as I have worked for this country in the last eleven years . . . You do not even know what the love of vatan means. Recently when the Italian navy threatened [Libya] and insulted our nation, you all kept quiet and did not do anything. If you had loved your vatan, you would have sent telegrams to Istanbul to obtain ammunition and you would have stated your willingness to be soldiers and defend our country. You would have affirmed that you are Ottomans and that you want to continue to be Ottomans. You would have expressed your readiness to sacrifice yourselves because you cannot tolerate our territory being invaded and our religion being mocked by the enemy.[137]

Some scholars portrayed Ottoman rule over peripheral regions, such as Libya, Yemen, or Lebanon, as "Ottoman Turkish" colonialism.[138] Nevertheless, there are striking differences between the patriotic vision of

Reşid Bey, and his embrace of Tripoli as a part of the Ottoman vatan, and British colonial officers' view of India or French colonizers' ambitions in respect to Algeria.[139] Two major problems can be identified in the context of labeling the Ottoman administration of peripheral regions as "colonialism" in a similar category to European colonial rule in Africa or in other parts of the world. First, the Ottoman Empire did not have economic ambitions for peripheral regions to develop industry and thereby compete with European powers. In the nineteenth century, the empire itself became a semi-colony of Britain and France.[140] Second, the crucial difference between Western colonialism and the Ottoman rule of peripheral regions was that the Ottoman rulers and the ruled shared the same religion.[141] Moreover, especially in the late nineteenth century, the center of the empire legitimated its rule over these territories by positioning the Ottoman sultan as the caliph and therefore the leader of all the Muslims in the world. The position of the Ottoman sultan vis-à-vis other Muslim rulers was further strengthened by the fact that in the late nineteenth century, the Ottoman sultan was the only Muslim sovereign ruler who could still play the custodian role for Muslims who were threatened by European colonial empires. The leaders of Muslim societies in such distant places as Aceh, Kashgar, and the Comore Islands approached the Ottoman sultan "believing rather naively that he possessed enough military and economic power to assure their independence and protect them against England, France, Russia, and so on."[142]

Another problem is the usage of the adjectival "Ottoman Turkish" to define the rule over non-Turkish Muslims and non-Muslims. According to Ussama Makdisi, "Ottoman Orientalism," which emerged after the loss of the Balkan territories in 1878, "reflected the rise of a specifically *Turkish* sensibility as the dominant element of a westernized Islamic Ottoman nationalism" (emphasis in original).[143] Makdisi used the terms "Ottoman Turkish rule," "Ottoman Turkish nation," "Ottoman Turkish elite," "Ottoman Turkish tutelage," "Ottoman Turkish press," and "Ottoman Turkish modernity" to underline the increasing Turkish nationalism in the last fifty years of the empire. He differentiated the last fifty years of the empire from its classical age, during which Islamic symbolism was used to legitimize sultans' rule. Makdisi specified "the facilitation and protection of the annual Hajj" as one of the important examples of Islamic symbolism during the classical age.[144] As mentioned above, long after the classical age, Islamic symbols were extensively used during Abdulhamid's reign to legitimize his rule. The grandeur of the construction of the Hejaz railway to facilitate pilgrimages was the zenith of this policy. Even though most Ottoman intellectuals, including Namık Kemal and Ali Suavi, were aware of the Turkish consciousness, neither they nor the ruling elite used Turkish nationalism as a political ideology until World War I. Even after 1908, when the CUP came to power, the ruling elite of the empire identified themselves as Ottomans and sought to protect the territorial integrity of the empire by emphasizing the common Ottoman identity and Ottoman vatan. Contrary to arguments that the Young Turks' main objective was the restructuring of the empire under Turkish hegemony, Young Turks aimed to "save the Ottoman vatan" by championing Ottomanism. In the first decade of the twentieth century, there were intellectuals, such as Yusuf Akçura (1876–1935),[145] who openly supported pan-Turkism against Ottomanism. But their ideas were not supported by the CUP and the majority of the Young Turks until the Balkan Wars of 1913.

Yusuf Akçura's revolutionary article "Three Political Ways" (*Üç Tarz-ı Siyaset*) has been called the "Manifesto of Turkish nationalism."[146] In it, Akçura compares Turkism with Ottomanism and Islamism for the first time as one of three viable ideologies for the Ottoman Empire. Akçura questioned the ideology of the Young Turks that was founded on the premise that reforming the Ottoman Empire's political system would protect its borders, territories, and multiethnic social structure. The majority of the Young Turks shared the political ideal of "saving the state" by creating an Ottoman nation with Ottoman statesmen, but both sides advocated different methods. While the Young Turks advocated for a constitutional monarchy, Ottoman statesmen defended the despotic regime of Abdulhamid, because they considered it the only way to suppress separatist movements. Akçura refused to idealize the notion of supranational Ottoman identity by asking this crucial question in his article: "Is the Ottoman Empire able to protect its present geographical borders with its existent forces?"[147] For Akçura, preserving the integrity of the Ottoman Empire by creating an Ottoman nation was a "futile mission."[148] While Akçura rejected the ideology of Ottomanism in the article, he implicitly hinted that in place of Islamism he favored Turkism, which he defined as a "newborn child," to guard the interests of the empire. According to Akçura, the main handicap of Turkism was that the empire would lose territories inhabited by non-Turkish Muslims.

After the publication of "Three Political Ways" in the journal *Türk*, two articles appeared in the same journal as responses to Akçura. Ali Kemal, a supporter of Ottomanism who later opposed the Kemalist movement and was killed by nationalists in 1922, argued that pan-Turkism was a fantasy for the Ottoman Empire: "Who are we unifying? Let's leave the history aside and look at the geography and the circumstances of the world. To unify the Turks, the whole world should be turned upside down . . . Think about how it would be possible to take pieces from the body of the colossal Russia."[149]

Ahmet Ferit's response to Akçura revealed that it was still too early for Ottoman intellectuals to accept Turkism as the dominant ideology of the state.[150] Ahmet Ferit accepted "the impossibility of protecting the current borders of the empire and the infeasibility of turning all people living within its borders into Ottomans and Turks." According to Ahmet Ferit, instead of abandoning the Ottoman ideal, the objective should be to use the ideology of Ottomanism "to maintain as many territories and people as possible."[151] Later, during the Balkan Wars, Ahmet Ferit changed his stance and asserted that a national state should be established in the north from Rize to Edirne and in the south from Kirkuk to the island of Rhodes.[152] Similarly, according to the memoirs of Ali Fuat Cebesoy, before the 1908 Revolution Mustafa Kemal argued that after taking power the CUP should liquidate the Ottoman Empire and establish a nation-state: "In Rumelia, we will keep the Western and Eastern Thrace. The border in the north of Edirne will be redrawn to Bulgaria's disadvantage . . . The islands close to the Anatolian coast will remain in the newly established Turkish state, the remaining islands will be transferred to Greece. In the south, we will keep Mosul, Aleppo, and Hatay; the rest will be left to the Arabs. There won't be any changes in the eastern and the northeastern borders. The Greek, the Bulgarian, and the Serbian minorities in the new Turkey will be exchanged with Turkish minorities, who will be left outside of our borders."[153]

The nationalist ideas of the Turkists were not favored by the majority of the CUP members, who refused to liquidate the empire to create a nation-state. They protested that such a move would lead to a loss of territory in Rumelia and Mecca, Medina, and Jerusalem in the Middle East, all of which were considered indispensable parts of the Ottoman vatan. Unionist leaders embraced the imperial discourse in opposition to a nationalist discourse. The manifesto, which was distributed by the CUP to European consulates (except Russia) in Manastır two months before the 1908 Revolution, was a clear example of imperial discourse as adapted by Unionists. The manifesto rejected the intervention of European powers in Macedonia and the appointment of a foreign governor to the region. According to the CUP, European intervention in the internal affairs of the empire would be collectively rejected by Muslims and Christians, who would act together to "defend their vatan from the foreign invasion and therefore decide to take over power from the current [Abdulhamid] regime."[154] The manifesto repeatedly underlined the solidarity between Muslims and Christians, based on the love of vatan: "In Macedonia and in other regions Muslims and Christians are children of the same soil and they are not so unwise as to fight their brethren, who are also captives of the despotic regime . . . Muslims are aware of the fact that their union with other citizens, who speak different languages and belong to different religions, will be crucial for the future of the vatan . . . Regardless of religion and ethnicity, all Ottomans are brothers. For the sake of vatan, the differences between Christian and Muslim communities disappear and Ottoman identity prevails."[155]

The Young Turks and the CUP had various reasons for adopting Ottomanism as their ideology. The primary reason was pragmatism. After taking power in 1908, they had to transform themselves from an intellectual movement into a political organization that could compete against other parties. As "empire savers," they had to find ways to maintain the balance between various ethnic and religious groups and to protect the territorial integrity of the empire.[156] The pan-Turkists were marginalized in the CUP in order to avoid offending Islamists and non-Turkish groups. The CUP adopted Ottomanism not only rhetorically but also idealistically. From the idealistic point of view, to create an Ottoman patriotism based on common vatan, history, and language was seen as the only viable alternative to pan-Turkism and pan-Islamism in order to overcome separatist tendencies in a multiethnic empire. The best example of this policy was the change of the mission of the Ottoman army from fighting on behalf of Islam to the patriotic defense of the vatan.[157] It must be emphasized that Ottomanism, pan-Turkism, and Islamism were not mutually exclusive political ideologies. Ottomanism was considered as an umbrella ideology, which included pan-Turkist and Islamist elements. Given the changing circumstances, the Unionists advanced either pan-Turkism or Islamism without downgrading Ottomanism from its central position. However, the infusion of patriotic elements in education, military, and politics caused negative reactions among non-Turkish communities. Ottomanist policies of the CUP were considered tools of Turkification.

When the CUP took power in 1908, the empire stretched from Libya to Yemen and from Basra to Kosova. According to the population census in 1906–1907, there were 15,508,753 Muslims (mainly Turks and Arabs); 2,823,063 Greeks; 1,031,668 Armenians; 761,530 Bulgarians; and 253,425 Jews in the Ottoman Empire.[158] In this chaotic, multiethnic, and multireligious environment, it would have been political suicide for the CUP to apply nationalist policies and a Turkification campaign toward non-Turkish groups. According to Şükrü Hanioğlu, "the available CUP documents reveal that only in very late 1917 did the CUP decide to totally abandon Ottomanism and pursue a Turkist policy."[159] Similarly, François Georgeon argued that "during the 1908 Revolution, the nationalist movement was nonexistent. There were no newspapers or organizations that supported [nationalist] ideas."[160] Ten years after the 1908 Revolution, there was a radically different tableau before the ruling elites of the empire. In the war against Italy in 1911–1912, the empire lost Libya, its last territory in Africa. In the Balkan Wars, the European heartland of the empire was invaded by the Balkan states. Except for the Edirne region, all of the European territories were surrendered. The dramatic loss of significant territories resulted in the dislocation of the imperial discourse.[161] In the case of the Ottoman Empire, the loss of territories in the Balkans and Libya caused Turkish and Arab intellectuals to question the validity of Ottomanism. Arab intellectuals also questioned the ability of the Ottoman state—due to its poor performance against Italy in Libya—to defend territories inhabited by Arabs in the Middle East against European powers. Similarly, Turkish nationalists argued that the Ottoman state and the army were too weak for imperial ambitions.[162] During World War I, when the Ottoman sultan's declaration of jihad to unite all Muslims against the empire's enemies was disregarded by most non-Turkish Muslims, pan-Turkist voices started to be heard more loudly, arguing that uniting all Turks would serve the empire's interests better than Islamism. In 1918, the empire was merely controlling territories where Turks and Kurds were the majority. The ideology of Turkish nationalism emerged as the dominant discourse on account of this dislocation.

CHAPTER TWO

From Imperial to National Vatan

IN 1913, when the Ottomans were fighting against the Balkan armies, a series of conferences was organized in Istanbul by Sati Bey (1880–1969), the director of the School of Education, about the defense of vatan. During the turmoil due to the loss of the Rumelia and the historic city of Edirne, Sati Bey undertook a comprehensive analysis of how to imbue citizens with Ottoman patriotism. These conferences were published in a book called *Vatan İçin Beş Konferans* (Five Conferences for the Vatan).[1] The titles of the conferences were as follows: (1) The Idea of Vatan, (2) The Education for Vatan, (3) The Duty for Vatan, (4) Defending the Nation, and (5) The Emergence of Prussia and the Speeches of Fichte. It must be emphasized that Sati Bey was born an Arab in Yemen in 1880 and became one of the founders of modern education in the Ottoman Empire.[2] The issues dealt with in these conferences and Sati Bey's thoughts revealed that as late as 1913, an Arab intellectual was truly committed to Ottomanism and considered it to be the only viable ideology for all Ottoman people.

In these conferences, Sati Bey complained about "the weakness of the love of vatan" among the Ottomans. For Sati Bey, the primary duty of the Ottoman state was to "strengthen the idea of vatan" among its people.[3] He criticized the supporters of Turkish, Arab, and Armenian nationalisms and their negation of Ottoman patriotism as a feasible ideology.

Sati Bey refused to imitate the European countries to construct an Ottoman vatan based on language or ethnicity, as there were various ethnic groups and a great number of languages dispersed in the vast territories of the empire. To overcome these differences, Sati Bey claimed that loyalty to the Ottoman vatan "has to be established on the basis of the Ottoman state and common history." According to him, Islam was the most important link among Ottomans, and it [the Ottomon state] was "the only Muslim state, which would be able to protect its sovereignty."[4] He emphasized the importance of symbols, such as the national flag, the national anthem, and the teaching of the "vatan's geography and history" for the development of Ottoman patriotism.[5] The Ottoman Empire and Sati Bey were not unique in an era that sought to solve the nationality problem in a multiethnic empire by promoting patriotism and loyalty to a common fatherland. In a comparably chaotic atmosphere, Josef Alexander Helfert (1820–1910), the undersecretary of the ministry of education in the Habsburg Empire, reacted similarly to the national uprisings in 1848.[6] For Helfert, as for Sati Bey, the solution for overcoming the national uprisings was to teach the history of the fatherland (*vaterländische Geschichte*) to the children and to imbue them with imperial patriotic feelings: "We saw everywhere nationalist extremists of different kinds among Germans in Vienna, Salzburg and Graz, among the Czechs in Bohemia and Moravia and among Hungarians in Hungary and Transylvania. The chance to learn more about our homeland and to love it seemed to have been lost everywhere. As soon as the days of temptation had come, those who lacked sound intuition allowed themselves to be drawn into shortsighted sympathies for narrow-minded tendencies of secession or into a fixation on a distant external attraction."[7]

Neither Sati Bey's nor Josef Alexander Helfert's views about imperial patriotism achieved wide-ranging support among the people in these empires. The Ottoman and Habsburg empires were unable to construct durable senses of patriotism and were therefore unable to maintain territorial integrity. The people in Ottoman and Habsburg lands lost confidence in the value of belonging to an empire. Rival nationalist ideologies, which aimed to create national territories, were much more powerful than imperial patriotism in creating physical boundaries, to unite and divide space and mental boundaries and to separate "us" from "them." The nation-state paradigm attributes great importance to the control over territory to legitimize the power of the state. Whereas the political structure of the empire consisted of heterogeneous units in which membership was organized hierarchically, the nation-state insisted on abolishing hierarchical belonging and replacing it with popular sovereignty, which belonged to a homogenous group of people.[8] Ernest Gellner explained how nationalism changed the political authority by comparing "two ethnographic maps, one drawn up before the age of nationalism, and the other after the principle of nationalism had done much of its work. The first map resembles a painting by Kokoschka. The riot of diverse points of colour is such that no clear pattern can be discerned in any detail, though the picture as a whole does have one. A great diversity and plurality and complexity characterizes all distinct parts of the whole... Look now instead at the ethnographic and political map of an area of the modern world. It resembles not Kokoschka, but, say, Modigliani. There is very little shading; neat flat surfaces are clearly separated from each other, it is generally plain where one begins and another ends, and there is little if any ambiguity or overlap."[9]

By constructing territories as the basis of identities, the nation-state provided an ontological security for its citizens. Boundaries played a crucial role in the process of institutionalizing territories as homelands. Therefore, territorial identities are socially constructed and historically contingent, which is revealed not only by the placement of a territory's boundary but also by the perception of its "natural" existence and its silencing of resistant forces. National identity essentialized itself by claiming to be in existence since ancient times. Although nationalism claimed the unchanging presence of the nation in the fullness of time, the nation is not a singular and static entity. It has various meanings "for different actors and in different contexts."[10]

In the case of Turkey, the analysis of the change from a heterogeneous imperial homeland to a homogenous national homeland illustrates how national discourses and practices nationalized education, politics, and daily life in order to maintain social integration and control. This was a very difficult process because it required not only the acceptance and internalization of significant territorial losses such as Rumelia, in which most of the founders of the Republic of Turkey were born, including Mustafa Kemal, but also the change of identity and belonging.[11] In order to establish a nation-state, the ruling elites had to transform the existing imperial consciousness to a Turkish national identity in an environment where "the borders were deprived of their essential character and the vast empire stood insecure against the outside world."[12] Indeed, the Sèvres Treaty and the occupation of Istanbul and other parts of Anatolia by European powers and Greece played a crucial role in the nationalist discourse during the War of Independence. A couple of months after starting "the National Movement" (*Hareket-i Milliye*) in Anatolia, Mustafa Kemal defined its main objective as "defending the miserable country and territories against the foreign and aggressive powers, who are seeking to invade and carve it out through the illegitimate policies of imperialism and colonization."[13]

In this chapter, I examine the nation-state building process in Turkey. An in-depth analysis of this process reveals that the imperial elites changed themselves and nationalized the political discourse, which defined sovereignty as "national sovereignty," the borders as "national borders," the Parliament as a "national assembly," and education as "national education." I will analyze how Turkish nationalism successfully adapted a territorial approach based on "national borders" and became the dominant ideology among the ruling elites and intellectuals by eliminating competing ideologies such as Ottomanism, Islamism, and pan-Turkism.[14]

BETWEEN OTTOMANISM, ISLAMISM, AND PAN-TURKISM

With the signing of the Treaty of Lausanne in 1923, the Republic of Turkey was established within the borders identified in the National Pact that was announced by the last term of the Ottoman Parliament in 1920, with some major exceptions, such as Western Thrace and the districts of Mosul and Iskenderun. In contrast to Germany, Austria, Hungary, and Bulgaria, who lost World War I and accepted the agreements enforced by the Entente Powers, the Turkish nationalists waged a war against the implementation of the Sèvres Treaty. Furthermore, Turkish nationalists' refusal to accept territorial losses in Anatolia and their signing of a new peace treaty as a result of a military victory in the National Liberation War was the crucial difference between Turkey and the Middle Eastern states, which gained their independence without a major military confrontation in the boundaries drawn by colonial powers.[15] This distinctive feature had a major impact on the politics of Turkey and on its foreign policy.

Turkish nationalism, which was shaped in the political and social context of the period after World War I, envisaged a homeland limited to Anatolia and Eastern Thrace. This territorial feature of Turkish nationalism played a major role in the creation of modern Turkey, and it signified a major break from pan-Turkist ideology, which advocated for the unity of all Turkic people in Eurasia. Yusuf Akçura (1876–1935) and Ziya Gökalp (1875–1924) were the two major ideologues of Turkish nationalism, and their thinking, which was considered the basis of the nationalist ideology's corpus, evolved from pan-Turkism to Turkish nationalism in the first quarter of the twentieth century.[16] Although both Akçura and Gökalp supported the Kemalist movement, there was an essential difference between their earlier view of nationalism that lasted until the end of World War I and their later view after the beginning of the national struggle in 1919. While they considered ethnicity to be the most important feature of the Turkish nationalism, which identified the unification of all Turkic groups as a political objective, Kemalist nationalism clearly rejected their expansionist worldview and restricted Turkish nationalism through national borders. As Ali Kazancıgil has rightly argued, "while Ziya Gökalp defined the nation as people with the same education, language and religion—but non-territorial, insofar as the Turks were part of Islam; Kemalist nationalism was above all territorial."[17]

The early Turkists' thoughts were too idealistic and romantic to define the territorial limits of the Turkish vatan. Yusuf Akçura's pioneering article "Three Political Ways" vaguely defined the geographical objective of the "Turkish Union," which "is not limited to the borders of the Ottoman Empire." According to Akçura, "the Turkish world" would emerge between the "white and yellow races" and would "unify all the Turks being spread over a great portion of Asia and over the Eastern parts of Europe." The area between these two races would be led by the Ottoman Empire, and it "could play a role similar to that which is played by Japan among the yellow races."[18] It is obvious that Akçura was not interested in devising a nationalist ideology for a Turkish nation-state. His vision was clearly expansionist, as he sought to develop pan-Turkism as the main policy of the Ottoman Empire. To put his vision into practice, Akçura came to Istanbul in 1908 and established the first Turkist institution in the Ottoman Empire: the Turkish Association (*Türk Derneği*).[19] The aim of the Turkish Association was to "study and teach history, language, and literature of all the Turks, to explore the geography of the Turkish countries and to develop our language so that it will be suitable for an extensive civilization."[20] In three years, almost all Turkist intellectuals, including Ziya Gökalp, Fuat Köprülü (1890–1966), Mehmet Emin (1869–1944), and Ahmet Ağaoğlu (1869–1939), came together in the journal *Türk Yurdu* (Turkish Homeland), which was led by Akçura.[21] *Türk Yurdu* would become one of the most influential publications of Turkish nationalism in the twentieth century.[22]

The agenda of *Türk Yurdu*, which was written by Akçura, was in favor of empowering Turkism in the Ottoman Empire and strengthening the relationship between the various Turkish groups in Eurasia: "The journal will not support any political party when it talks about the internal politics of the Ottoman state. However, it will defend the political and economic interests of the Turks. While it defends the interests of the Turkish society, it will refrain to cause conflict among different societies [in the empire] ... The main ideal of the journal in international politics is to defend the interests of the Turkish world."[23] Until the Balkan Wars, the journal was the major publication in the Ottoman Empire that explicitly supported Turkism against Ottomanism. It identified Turkism as the most suitable ideology for defending the interests of the Turks. In his article "In the Turkish World," Akçura held the Ottoman statesmen responsible for not developing the regions inhabited by Turks and for giving preferential treatment to areas inhabited by Arabs, Armenians, and Albanians: "It is those Turks who sacrifice everything their all own for this country and get nothing in return ... Listen, from now on Turks demand their rights and their legitimate status in the empire."[24]

Between the 1908 Revolution and the Balkan Wars of 1912–1913, the Unionists optimistically believed that maintaining the imperial political structure was in the interests of all Ottomans and therefore should be endorsed by them.[25] The general hatred toward the despotic regime of Abdulhamid disguised fundamental differences between various groups about the outlook of the empire. The Unionists disregarded the political and social developments in Europe during the nineteenth century and took the French Revolution as their political model. As Tarık Zafer Tunaya has convincingly argued, they "abolished the established political regime without any future plans by employing an outdated ideology borrowed from France that was forgotten even by her."²⁶ The Committee of Union and Progress (CUP) reasoned that Ottomanism and loyalty to the Ottoman vatan would be the glue to unify all Ottoman people (Figure 2.1). In fact, the Young Turk movement, which was formed by different ethnic groups from all over the empire, was more Ottoman than its predecessor, the Young Ottomans, which was restricted to Turcophile intellectuals in the imperial center.²⁷ According to the Young Turks, all ethnic groups had their "special vatans" (*vatan-ı hususi*), which were enclosed by the "general vatan" (*vatan-ı umumi*).²⁸ The interior minister Halil Bey (Menteşe), who was called as a part-time member of the triumvirate of Talat, Enver, and Cemal Pashas, rejected "the Turkification of Ottomans" and regarded such a policy as "destructive" for the empire: "The aim of the government in the internal politics is the union of all Ottomans. The objective of the policy of union is to convince all Ottomans that they will consider every part of the Ottoman vatan as their common vatan and with the same common love and affection they will see the Ottoman state as their own state."²⁹ A clear illustration of how the CUP embraced the policy of the "Unity of Elements" or Ottomanism was Sultan Mehmed Reşad's historic tour of Ottoman cities in the Balkans in 1911. The CUP meticulously organized parades in which Bulgarians, Greeks, and Albanians demonstrated their loyalty to the sultan.³⁰

Both CUP politicians and intellectuals such as Ziya Gökalp, who would be a leading Turkish nationalist after the Balkan Wars, were unable to decide between Turkism and Ottomanism until 1913. Ziya Gökalp defined the Ottoman Empire as "the free and progressivist America of the East."³¹ He used the term "Young Ottomans" instead of "Young Turks" to define the patriotic intellectuals: "Who are the Young Ottomans? Regardless of their [ethnic] identity, they are open-minded people, who adapted to the new life and the new civilization, seeking to save patriotism from the hegemony of one [ethnic] group and disseminate it to all citizens."³² Gökalp highlighted the fact that the Young Ottomans did not restrict themselves with the proclamation of the constitutional regime. Their two other crucial objectives were to realize "Ottoman Unity" and to establish "an advanced civilization" for the Ottoman society. According to Gökalp, members of the Young Ottomans referred to themselves first as Ottomans and then as Arabs, Turks, Armenians, or

FIGURE 2.1 One of the posters used during the 1908 Revolution. "Vatan" was written on the cow. Ottoman vatan was portrayed as an exploited cow. The flag in the hand of the female figure lists the four political concepts of the revolution: liberty, justice, equality, and fraternity. The phrase at the bottom of the poster reads "Here are some traitors of the nation exploiting and destroying the vatan." Just below the female figure, "traitors" are warned with the following sentence: "You traitors! Is it still not enough that you exploited the vatan during [the Hamidian] despotic era?"

Greeks, depending on their ethnicity. In 1909, Gökalp truly believed in the viability of the Ottoman nation, "which would exist forever in constitutionalism and friendship, and will always advance under the guidance of the Young Ottomans."[33] Two years later, in the article "The Resistance of the Old," Gökalp made a clear distinction between ethnicity (*kavim*) and nation (*millet*). Whereas Armenians, Turks, Greeks, and Kurds were different ethnicities, they together constituted the Ottoman nation, which had a political character: "An Englishman, a Frenchman, and a German belong to different political communities. All of them have a specific vatan. Like them, we belong to the Ottoman nation and the Ottoman vatan."[34]

While Ziya Gökalp still believed in the cosmopolitan ideology of Ottomanism, Akçura, Ağaoğlu, and other authors published in *Türk Yurdu* advocated for an ethnic Turkish nationalism to change the multiethnic political structure of the Ottoman Empire, and they severely criticized Ottomanism. In an article published in the journal, İsmail Gasprinski (1851–1914) denounced the Ottoman foreign policy in the post-Tanzimat period.[35] According to Gasprinski, the main objective of the foreign policy of the Ottoman Empire during this period was to "avoid the trouble" (*def'-i gaile*) by giving concessions to European powers. As a result of this policy, he continued, the empire had lost Crete, Bosnia, Egypt, Tunis, and Eastern Rumelia. He denounced the Ottoman sultans for not having an ideal, as they aimed only at maintaining their rule rather than at protecting the territorial integrity of the empire. Gasprinski argued that Germany and Japan had developed and expanded during the same period as a result of a nationalist ideal, whereas the Ottoman Empire was weakened because it ignored the Turks and their heartland of Anatolia: "How to calm down Albania and how to finish the war against Italy are today's problems. Their consequences are contingent upon present conditions. However, for Turkey the real problem of yesterday, today, and tomorrow is the question of Anatolia, which is the matter of life and death. The Anatolian question has to do with reviving Anatolia and recovering the Turks ... During the [last] sixty years, at a time when the Istanbul government was gradually being freed from the Rumelian burden on his back, if it had made any effort to revive Anatolia, things would have been quite different today."[36]

Likewise, Akçura analyzed the foreign policy of the Ottoman Empire from an ethnic perspective in his article published just after the beginning of the Balkan Wars. He defined the wars as "an offensive of the Slavic world against Turkishness."[37] According to Akçura, the major power behind the Slavic alliance was Russia, whose aim was to "drive out Turks and Germans from the Balkan peninsula and to subjugate Albanians, Helens, and Romanians to Slavic control." The war revealed the ignorance of high-ranking Turkish officials about the significance of ethnicity in politics, as they sought to "set up a Balkan Alliance under the auspices of the Ottoman Sultan" just before the conflict.[38]

The Balkan territories of the empire had a significant position in the eyes of the Ottoman ruling elite. The grand vizier Sait Pasha (1830–1914) argued in his report submitted to Sultan Abdulhamid that "the survival of this state depends on the continuation of our rule in the Rumelia region."[39] Indeed, the Balkan Wars were the turning point for the Ottoman Empire and the development of Turkish nationalism. Balkan countries such as Greece, Serbia, Montenegro, and Bulgaria formed an alliance against the Ottoman Empire and declared war in October 1912. Within a couple of months, the Ottoman army had lost battles on all fronts and retreated to its last defense line in Çatalca, 60 kilometers from Istanbul. The loss of all territories in the Balkans, including the historic capital city of Edirne, and the arrival of thousands of Muslim immigrants who fled in front of the advancing Balkan armies created a feeling of despair within Turkish society. The collapse of the imperial discourse was reflected remarkably in an account by Şevket Süreyya Aydemir (1897–1976):[40] "Eventually when the Balkan War broke out and the imperial armies lost all the Ottoman territories in Europe to the Balkan armies, which had been so despised before, everything became clear. This collapse was not simply a defeat of a state. It was the end of a groundless dream. It was a complete downfall of a spirit and mentality. A tale, an imperial tale was coming to an end. Apparently, what we considered as grandeur was just a sleep of negligence."[41]

Indeed, intellectuals and politicians described the situation in the empire after the first Balkan War as a "national disaster." Newspapers and journals published articles and conferences were organized to make the Turkish society conscious of the seriousness of the military defeat to an unprecedented degree. On April 12, 1913, Halide Edib (1884–1964)—a feminist political figure who later became very active in the National Liberation War in Anatolia—gave a speech with the title "Nations after

Disasters" to women at a conference in *Darulfünun* (the House of Multiple Sciences, which later became Istanbul University).[42] The language of her speech was passionately nationalistic. She frequently stressed the fact that Turks had never experienced such a disaster in Ottoman history. According to Halide Edib, the main difference between the war against Russia in 1877–1878 and the Balkan Wars was that for the first time "the nation carries the disaster in its heart. Today, vatan is not a territory, fortress or country separate from us. Today, vatan is a country lying in our heart and spirit."[43] Halide Edip argued that Italian unification had demonstrated that when a nation kept the love of vatan in its heart, it was impossible to destroy that nation. Therefore, she continued, Turkish mothers had to instill "the hatred against enemies" in their children. Halide Edib considered Bulgaria and the Bulgarian army, which captured Edirne, as the main threat to Turkish people: "'Bulgaria should be destroyed.' You have to blow this [idea] like a fire so that neither years nor death can kill it in your hearts. You have to inject [hatred] into your children's veins with the milk of your breasts."[44] The reason to carry hatred and the need for revenge to future generations was to realize the ideal of "establishing a strong and free Turkey and Turks."[45]

Fuat Köprülü criticized the prevalent feeling of desperation among Turks after the loss of Edirne. According to him, the Turkish youth should leave submissive thoughts aside and get ready for revenge: "If today's youth gradually instill the common people with the principles of nationality and revenge, there will be no need to fear the arrival of the Slav army at the gates of Çatalca."[46] In the same way, the speaker of the Parliament, Halil Bey, warned members of Parliament not to forget the loss of Rumelia: "Other nations do not forget the parts of their vatan they lost in wars, keeping them alive for future generations. In doing so, they protect the future from the disastrous consequences of the same causes. From this exalted pulpit, I recommend to my nation: Do not forget! Do not forget the beloved Salonica, the cradle of the torch of freedom and constitutionalism, green Monastir, Kosova, Shkoder, Ioannina, and all of the beautiful Rumelia. With their lessons, articles, poems, and all their spiritual influence, I hereby request our teachers, authors, poets, and intellectuals to keep alive for the future generations the fact that there are brothers and parts of vatan to be saved across the border."[47]

After the Greek army conquered Selanik, the leading authors of the journal *Genç Kalemler* (Young Pens), such as Ziya Gökalp and Ömer Seyfettin (1884–1920), came to Istanbul and joined other Turkists in the *Türk Yurdu*.[48] Ziya Gökalp, who truly believed in the viability of Ottomanism before 1912, made a dramatic change in his thought and declared the demise of the Ottoman unity. His article "Turkification, Islamization, Modernization," published by *Türk Yurdu* on March 20, 1913, bore a resemblance to Akçura's article "Three Political Ways," with one major difference. Whereas nine years before Akçura had analyzed and compared three different ideologies, namely, Turkism, Islamism, and Ottomanism, Gökalp refused to examine Ottomanism as a feasible ideology. For Gökalp, Turkishness should be the dominant ideology against the "cosmopolitan" ideologies of Islamism and Ottomanism.[49] He claimed that "Tanzimat [reformers] had faith in creating a voluntary nation out of an existing nation consisting of different ethnic and religious elements. With this conviction in mind, they attributed a new meaning to the historical 'Ottoman' concept that was entirely free of national colors. The painful past experiences proved that the new meaning of the term (Ottoman) was embraced only by pro-Tanzimat Turks."[50] According to Gökalp, because the twentieth century was "the century of nationality," the goal for Turks at this time should have been to construct a "modern and Islamic Turkishness."[51]

Before the Balkan Wars, there was a disagreement between the authors of *Genç Kalemler*, particularly between Ali Canip (1887–1967) and Fuat Köprülü, who was writing in the journal *Servet-i Fünun* (Wealth of Sciences), over the construction of a national language for Turks in the Ottoman Empire. The authors of *Genç Kalemler* argued that Ottoman Turkish was too complicated for the common Turkish people. For that reason, there was a need to reform the language and to replace Arabic and Persian words with native Turkish words. Ali Canip contended that while young writers in Istanbul such as Köprülü represented the cosmopolite "internationalism," the young people in Anatolia defended "the patriotism." According to Ali Canip, Köprülü would soon understand that his "cosmopolitism shall bring this poor vatan into terrible abyss."[52] Against the demands of Turkification of the language, Fuat Köprülü defended Ottoman Turkish. He refused to accept the "new language movement" because he believed that this new language was stillborn, like Esperanto. Köprülü blamed the authors of *Genç Kalemler* for "taking us [i.e., the Ottoman Turks] back to Karakorum," in Central Asia, which would "cause us to live similar to Oğuz Khan," who was the mythical founder of Hun Turks.[53]

After the Balkan Wars, as had happened with Ziya Gökalp, Köprülü's thought shifted in favor of Turkism. In his article "Turkism, Islamism, Ottomanism" in *Türk Yurdu*, Köprülü argued that "the development of Ottomanism and Islamism is only possible by awakening and advancing Turkism." Where he had previously objected to the formation of a national Turkish language a couple of years before, after the Balkan Wars Köprülü now considered the "national ideal" the only option for the survival of the Ottoman Turks: "The two important elements, which constitute nationality, are national history and national language. However, language and tradition lost their meaning [among Turks] and they have become the basis for decadence. National history has been forgotten to such a degree that the nation's name Turk has disappeared and the word Ottoman, which is a diplomatic concept, is used instead."[54] According to Köprülü, "the Ottoman state lost most parts of the vatan, because of the weakness of the Turkish core."[55] The military officials also deemed the lack of a national ideal as the major reason for the catastrophic defeat of the Ottoman army. Fevzi Pasha (Çakmak, 1876–1950), who fought in Kosova during the Balkan Wars and later became the field marshal in the Turkish army, analyzed the Balkan Wars in a conference in 1927. According to Fevzi Pasha, "Turkism as an ideal was nonexistent during the Balkan Wars . . . All other nations, which together constituted the Ottoman union, had different and conflicting religions, vatans, and ideals."[56]

As these examples reveal, nationalism became the central ideology among Turkish intellectuals, politicians, and military officials after 1913. However, there was disagreement and confusion among and within them whether to limit nationalism to the Turks living in the Ottoman Empire or to support pan-Turkist ideals for the unity of all Turkic groups in Eurasia. Whereas Yusuf Akçura and Ahmet Ağaoğlu had a clear pan-Turkist stance, Fuat Köprülü opted for developing the national consciousness among Ottoman Turks. Others such as Ziya Gökalp were undecided about whether to support pan-Turkism or Turkish nationalism. On the one hand, Gökalp was delighted with the idea of pan-Turkism, and he wrote poems about it. On the other hand, his articles admitted the impossibility of the unity of all Turks under one state. Gökalp popularized among the common people the "ideal of Turan," which played a compensatory role for Turkists in the declining years of the Ottoman Empire.[57] Gökalp defined the homeland for all Turks in his poem "Turan," published by the journal *Genç Kalemler* in 1911: "The vatan of the Turks is neither Turkey, nor Turkistan. Their vatan is a vast and eternal land: Turan."[58]

It must be emphasized that Gökalp used the concept of Turan as an imaginary ideal for Turks rather than as an immediate political objective for the empire. He later admitted that the unity of all Turkic people in the Eurasian continent would be possible only in the distant future. Turkish intellectuals rapidly appropriated the ideal of Turan because of its imaginary feature. Due to the significant territorial losses in the empire's heartland of Rumelia in the Balkan Wars, Ottomanism and its ideals had lost their appeal for intellectuals. These intellectuals considered the ideal of Turan to be the only panacea to alleviate the territorial losses in the last four decades and to expand the empire toward the east. The psychological condition of Turkish intellectuals was best reflected by Aydemir, when he defined his own state of mind after the Balkan Wars. According to him, Anatolia was too small to satisfy the ideals of the young people from Rumelia who dreamed of ruling the territories "from Danube to the Caucasus and from Africa to the gates of India."[59] Pan-Turkism presented a vast region for them to identify as their homeland: "But in the midst of all these turbulences, a new way of thinking was crystallizing in our minds. This was an understanding of a new vatan and a new nation. Accordingly, vatan was not anymore equal to the territories belonging to the state. That is, vatan was not simply the territories under the control of the army."[60] For Aydemir, "vatan meant anywhere inhabited by the [Turkish] nation. Regardless of the sovereign and the flag, the name of this vatan was Turan ... What is disappearing is only the Ottoman vatan. However, the vatan of the Turks covers the entire world. Because every place inhabited by Turks is the part of the Turkish vatan, no matter which flag it is under. The borders of this vatan stretch from Danube and Maritsa up to Altai Mountains, to the Great Wall of

China and even to the Yellow Sea. It extends from the deserts of Arabia and Himalayas to the North Sea."[61]

Various authors sought to define the borders of this new vatan, which was sometimes referred to as "Turkish homeland" and sometimes as "Turan." In the first issue of *Türk Yurdu*, Ahmet Ağaoğlu admitted that "there is nothing more difficult than drawing the real boundaries of the Turkish world, which is as large and at the same time as vague as imagination."[62] For him, the "Turkish world" could not include such regions as Hungary, Finland, North Africa, or remote regions in China, which had only historical links with the Turks. It should instead be composed of the regions that had been dominated by the Turks and Turkish civilization. Nevertheless, his vision of the Turkish world was expansive, reaching from Mongolia to the Balkan Mountains and from Syria to the Caspian Sea.

Halide Edip's utopian novel *Yeni Turan* (The New Turan), published in 1912, became a leading literary work following Gökalp's poem "Turan" and had a great impact on Turkish society. Due to the popularity of the novel, many cafes and restaurants named themselves after *Yeni Turan*.[63] The novel is based on a struggle between two political parties. The New Turan advocates for Turkish nationalism against an Ottomanist party, which suppresses Turkish nationalism for the sake of Ottoman unity. Although the title of the novel has a pan-Turkist connotation, Halide Edib imagined New Turan as an advanced Turkish country in Anatolia with modern institutions, such as railways and high schools. The main characters of the novel search for the imagined country and repeatedly ask the same question throughout the novel: "O! New Turan, dear country, tell me how can I reach you?" For Halide Edib, to realize the imagined New Turan the most important step was to develop strong territorial nationalism among Turkish people.[64]

The territorial losses also had dramatic effects on the political environment in the capital. When the military situation was desperate at the front, the Ottoman government decided to accept the armistice in December 1912. Diplomats convened in London to negotiate the terms of the peace agreement in January 1913, and the Ottoman government was pressured to accept the surrender of Edirne to Bulgaria. When the news reached Istanbul, the CUP leaders used the appeasing approach of the

Ottoman government as a justification to depose the government. Powerful Unionist politicians and army officers decided to launch a coup d'état, and an armed group headed by Enver and Talat raided the cabinet and killed the war minister. The CUP's rule, which would last until 1918, was further consolidated after Enver led the Ottoman army into Eastern Thrace and recovered the historic capital city of Edirne from Bulgaria. Aided by the military victory, the Unionists purged the leading members of the opposition. The CUP convened its fifth congress in this chaotic political environment. It transformed itself from an association to a party, and it decided to adopt a nationalist stance toward education and the economy. Yusuf Akçura fully supported this nationalist change in the CUP: "This year, the stance of the Central Committee of the Union and Progress towards the nationality question is coming close to a stage, which is considered ideal for nationalists. Türk Yurdu was born nationalist, because it was the product of the belief that considers the national idea the strongest impetus for Turkish awakening and development. We are pleased to see the very same line of thinking in the report of the Central Committee."[65]

Nationalism in the late Ottoman period evolved as a de facto ideology in response to wars, territorial losses, and large-scale migrations. Between the 1908 Revolution and the establishment of the Republic of Turkey in 1923, the ruling elite oscillated between Ottoman patriotism, pan-Turkism, and Islamism in order to develop the most appropriate ideology to prevent the disintegration of the empire and "to save the vatan." At the end of the Balkan Wars, since the empire had lost those territories where Christians were in the majority, ruling elites and intellectuals realized that there was no longer a need to employ Ottomanism, whose major objective was to maintain the loyalty of all Ottoman citizens regardless of their religion. Ziya Gökalp's response to an Armenian author who defended Ottomanism in his article published by Türk Yurdu illustrated that Gökalp favored Turkism and Islamism over Ottomanism. According to Gökalp, "an Ottoman culture" similar to "British culture" was not possible since the representatives of Armenians and Greeks were against the "education of all Ottoman people in the same schools."[66] In the same way, for Yusuf Akçura, the appearance of the Bulgarian army in the outskirts of Istanbul in 1912 signified the collapse of Ottomanism, which started with the Tanzimat and aimed to unite people from different ethnic and religious backgrounds around "the Ottoman state and the Ottoman vatan."[67]

The period between 1908 and 1918 has been called "the longest decade" within "the longest century" of the Ottoman Empire.[68] During this decade, the CUP was the most important political factor in sealing the fate of the empire. The Unionists faced large-scale territorial losses and massive migrations as a result of the wars against Italy, the Balkan states, and the Entente powers. Preventing the disintegration of the empire required the CUP to balance two clashing dynamics: while it sought to reform the political, economic, and military structures to fight wars on various fronts, it simultaneously had to transform itself and its policies according to the rapidly changing conditions in both domestic and international politics.[69] After the Balkan Wars, Turkish nationalism became one of the leading ideological trends among the Unionists. When World War I started, the CUP was aware of the fact that the empire had a considerable non-Turkish Muslim population, and it realized that their loyalty would play a determining role in the Middle Eastern front. Enver Pasha, who as minister of war had designed the military strategy of the Ottoman army, believed that the empire "would not last without taking the Caucasus and its oil reserves, and Egypt and its cotton."[70]

With the beginning of World War I, Ottoman statesmen started to advocate Islamism as a way of obtaining the support of non-Turkish Muslims. Sultan Mehmed Reşad's speech in 1914 at the inauguration of the Parliament warned all Muslims against the hostile policies of Russia, France, and Britain: "I invited all Muslims to the Jihad against these states and their allies."[71] In rallies in Istanbul at the beginning of the war, Enver Pasha was referred to as "Enver, who carries the Islamic flag in his hand with courage."[72] In February 1916, a couple of months before the Hashemite Revolt, which would incorrectly become known as the Arab Revolt in British propaganda, Enver Pasha toured the Middle Eastern front from Damascus to the Sinai Peninsula, Mecca, and Medina. His visit to Medina and the tomb of the Prophet Muhammad was identified as an "agent's account to the master about his duty, which was entrusted by the former from the latter."[73] Said Halim Pasha's (1865–1921) appointment to the grand vizierate in 1913 demonstrated that the CUP took the ideology of Islamism seriously into consideration to ensure the loyalty of Arabs to the center.[74] Said Halim Pasha, who was the grandson of Mehmed

Ali Pasha of Egypt and had connections with Arab intellectuals, served between the years 1913 and 1917. He became the longest-serving grand vizier in the last decade of the empire.[75] He believed that the Ottoman Empire was in "the age of stagnation" (*Devr-i Tevakkuf*), and during the world war its main consideration had to be to "protect the borders." He rejected the expansionist aspirations of Enver Pasha: "I beg you to abandon the conquest of Turan and Egypt and aspirations for Tripoli, Tunisia, Algeria etc."[76]

Whereas Islamism and "Grand Jihad" (*Cihad-ı Ekber*) were employed against the British Empire to obtain the support of non-Turkish Muslims, the aim of pan-Turkism was to unite the Turks in the Caucasus and Central Asia, inciting them to revolt against the Russian Empire. When the war on the Caucasus front started at the end of 1914, the CUP officials constructed road signs in Anatolian cities pointing toward the east and reading "the road toward Turan."[77] CUP's two-directional policy was best reflected in Gökalp's poem "Kızıl Destan" (Red Epic), which was published in the newspaper *Tanin* just four days after the signing of the Ottoman-German alliance. Gökalp identified the conquest of Turan as the main military objective for the Ottoman Empire: "The land of the enemy shall be devastated, Turkey shall be enlarged and become Turan ... The Altai homeland shall be the great vatan, and the sultan shall be the ruler of Turan."[78] Although scholars such as Bernard Lewis and Jacob Landau have extensively cited "Red Epic" to portray the pan-Turkist stance of the CUP, they have not noticed the unambiguous Islamist perspective of Gökalp.[79] In "Red Epic," Gökalp identifies the British Empire as the common enemy of all Muslims and calls on them to unite against the enemy:

> Englishmen captured the *Sultan Osman* [a warship]
> By using it they will control India and Amman! Islam identified
>   its enemy
> Soon there shall be a happy moment: Koran shall take the revenge
>   from the enemy.[80]

During World War I, Ziya Gökalp modified his pan-Turkist stance and put more emphasis on Islam and on the solidarity between Turks and Arabs. According to Gökalp, "the Ottoman state can be named a Turk-Arab state."[81] For Gökalp, there were three different vatans in the empire: the Turkish vatan, which was referred to as Turan; the Arabic vatan; and the

Islamic vatan, which encompassed all of the Muslims in the world. Gökalp emphasized that Turks' devotion to Turan did not imply that they disregarded "the lesser Islamic vatan" (the Ottoman country) and "the greater Islamic vatan."[82] In the same way, Ömer Seyfeddin identified three types of vatan for the Turks: (1) national vatan, which was Turan; (2) religious vatan, which was all the territories inhabited by Muslims; and (3) physical vatan, which Ömer Seyfeddin referred to as "Turkey" and included all of the Ottoman territories. According to him, Turks and Arabs shared the religious vatan, and it was their duty to liberate its occupied parts.[83]

In 1914, the CUP considered the support of the Arabs to be critical in the Middle Eastern front against the British Empire. Grand Vizier Said Halim Pasha's Islamist critical stance against nationalist imaginations about vatan signified that Islamism was the only contending ideology against Turkism. Said Halim Pasha truly believed in the internationalism of Islam, and he rejected the import of nationalism from the West and its adaptation in Muslim societies. According to him, a unified Islamic worldview should prevail in every Muslim country as "Islamic realities did not belong to a specific vatan." Islamic traditions and ideals, which together constituted the "spiritual vatan," were much more important than the physical vatan. For Said Halim Pasha "the vatan of a Muslim is the place where the Islamic law reigns."[84] The well-known Islamist intellectual Mehmet Akif (1873–1936), who was a member of the CUP and the author of the Turkish national anthem, also harshly criticized pan-Turkists. Mehmet Akif claimed that ethnic nationalism did great harm to the cohesive structure of Islam and divided Islamic society into various competing groups. In his poems, he accused pan-Turkists such as Ziya Gökalp of running after impractical ideas and therefore damaging the integrity of the traditional Islamic structure of the Ottoman Empire: "We acquired a myth named the 'County of Turan'; we considered this myth to be the cause and strived for it. But we lost many homelands to realize this cause; the lost ones are enough, feel sorry for the remaining homeland!"[85] In the same way, Islamist writer Ahmed Naim (1872–1934) accused pan-Turkists of turning from Kaaba to Turan and criticized their partitioning of the Ottoman Empire into three different vatans: "I beg you for Islam, for mankind, and for Turkism, about whose future I am afraid: Do not create two ideals for the people. There are some among you who want to have three different vatans. According to a Turkish saying, the fork cannot be put into a hole for a pole. How can you insert this fork-type ideal, namely three different vatans, into people? Do not deviate from the Islamic ideal."[86]

Both pan-Turkism and Islamism were employed by the CUP as ideological tools "to save the empire" from disintegration. In both ideologies, the purpose was to establish a "general vatan" for the unity of various groups living in a diverse geography rather than a national territory. Whereas the imagined vatan, namely, Turan, reached as far as the Chinese border, the spiritual Islamic vatan embraced all Muslims in the Middle East and North Africa. The CUP's vision was clearly imperial, and its recipe to prevent the collapse of the empire was to expand the borders.[87] For Unionists, the only way for the Ottoman Empire to escape its declining position in international politics was to return to Great Power status.[88] On September 11, 1914, one month after the signing of the Ottoman-German alliance, the Ottoman government unilaterally abrogated the capitulations that had transformed the empire into a colonial power in the nineteenth century. After the empire officially entered the war in November 1914, its first military objective was to wage an offensive on the Caucasus front against Russia. In the winter of 1915, the empire initiated another offensive against Britain to capture the Suez region. As mentioned above, politicians and intellectuals such as Said Halim Pasha and Yahya Kemal (1884–1958) openly criticized the offensive war objectives of the CUP and instead advocated for a defensive stance in the war. However, these dissident voices were disregarded and silenced by the authoritarian CUP rule during the war.

Contrary to expectations about the rapid breakdown of the Ottoman Empire on the various military fronts, its military performance in the Battle of Dardanelles and in Iraq against the British army was outstanding. However, what had been promising expectations turned ominous in 1916. The empire lost almost all of Eastern Anatolia to the Russian Empire. On the Middle Eastern front, two military campaigns to capture the Suez region ended without any success. Moreover, the call of all the Muslims to jihad against the British Empire was futile and did not have a major effect on the Arab people. Due to the Hashemite Revolt and the retreat of the Ottoman army on the Middle Eastern front, Islamism lost its appeal for the Unionists. The CUP perceived a Turkist and secular outlook in its congress of 1916.[89] In 1917, the war was called the "Independence War" in the Ottoman Parliament.[90] The gloomy outlook changed once again after the Russian revolution and the signing of the Treaty of Brest Litovsk in March 1918. Before the end of World War I, although the Ottoman army had retreated to Mosul and Aleppo, thereby losing almost all of its possessions in the Middle East, it had captured Tabriz and Baku on the Caucasian front. With the signing of the Armistice of Mudros in October 1918, the empire abandoned its territorial gains in the Caucasus, and all of the Ottoman garrisons outside of Anatolia were surrendered to the Allies.[91] After the establishment of the Republic of Turkey, the national discourse disregarded the Ottoman territorial gains in the Caucasian front, as the Kemalist regime clearly distanced itself from the expansionist pan-Turkist ideals. The Ottoman victory in the Battle of Dardanelles was a more suitable memorial for the defensive worldview of the Kemalist regime.

IMAGINING ANATOLIA AS A NATIONAL VATAN

Before World War I, Ottoman intellectuals such as Ahmet Ferit and Abdullah Cevdet advocated the creation of a national vatan in Anatolia and abandoned the imperial vision. During the Balkan Wars, Abdullah Cevdet emphasized the significance of Anatolia and identified it as the heartland of the Turks: "What frightens me is not the Bulgarian artillery . . . Do not tell me that we should not think about Anatolia when Çatalca and Edirne are in flames and the survival of the state is at stake. We take every second of our life from Anatolia. It is our heart, mind, and breath."[92] Although these Anatolianist views were in the minority before 1914, their voices were heard more loudly in 1918, when the empire lost all its territories outside Anatolia. The debate over Anatolia among the intellectuals was crystallized during the congress of the pan-Turkist institution of Turkish Hearths (*Türk Ocakları*) in June 1918. Members such as Halide Edib, Ahmet Ferit, and Nüzhet Sabit proposed changing the second clause of the charter of the Turkish Hearths. According to the proposal, "the objective of the Turkish Hearths is the cultural unity of the Turks and advancement of [Turkish] civilization. The field of activity of the Turkish Hearths is limited particularly with Turkey."[93] The words "particularly with Turkey" created a dispute among members. Hamdullah Suphi (1885–1966), who served as the chairman of the Turkish Hearths for thirty-four years between 1912 and 1966, suggested eliminating this phrase, since "it will offend our Turkish brothers, who are far from us and request our moral assistance." Nüzhet Sabit defended the proposal by stating that "while we support the great Turan ideal with hopes, we have to restrict our activity in the first instance to Turkey." Halide Edib addressed the members after Nüzhet Sabit, and she clearly took a pro-Anatolian stance against Turanism. She separated the members into two groups: (1) the romantics, who dreamed of conquering "the Caucasus and Turkistan" and could realize their dreams only in poems; and (2) the realists, who focused on Anatolia and sought to find ways to develop it.[94] After heated discussions in the congress, the members decided to eliminate the phrase "particularly with Turkey." This decision did not stop the argument between the two camps and did not overcome differences over whether to limit Turkism to Anatolia.

A couple of days later, Halide Edib wrote an article entitled "Let's Take Care of Our Own Home: The Field of Activity of Turkism" in the newspaper *Vakit*. Her article was one of the first written works to call for the attention of all Turkish intellectuals in order to face Anatolia's desperate condition. According to Halide Edib, Turkish engineers, doctors, and military officers who went to war with imperial ideals had to face reality and develop a new task for Turkism to save the country and its people. She argued that Turkism should focus on "young Turkey" instead of the "newly established Turkish republics" in Eurasia. She openly advocated for territorial nationalism rather than one based on ethnicity: "Today, races are hypothetical concepts and nations are facts. A nation, which seeks to exist, should first match its field of activity with its countries' borders ... At present, young Turkey is desperate to get service and care of its children. Every Turk who carries his energy and service outside of young Turkey puts himself in the position of one robbing his own mother and his own home."[95]

Just four days after the appearance of Halide Edib's article, Ziya Gökalp responded to her with an article entitled "Turkism and Turkeyism." Gökalp made an unambiguous distinction between these two terms. Whereas "Turkism" referred to ethnicity and promoted solidarity among the Turkish societies in Eurasia, "Turkeyism" described the territorial patriotism of all ethnic groups in Anatolia. Gökalp compared these two terms with "Germanism" and "Prussianism." For him, in order to create a unified and advanced country in Eurasia similar to Germany in Europe, Turkism should prevail over other nationalist movements in Azerbaijan, Crimea, Kazan, Uzbekistan, and Kashgar, similar to Germanism's success against Prussian, Saxon, and Bavarian movements in the nineteenth century: "Our nation's borders are not limited with the borders of state, ummah, and race. A nation is completely different from these categories and instead, it is a cultural category. As culture's characteristics are language and religion, our nation is comprised by Turkish speaking Muslims."[96] According to Gökalp, the definition of the Turkish nation included Azerbaijani, Crimean, Kazan, Turkmen, Sart, Uzbek, Kirgiz, and Kashgar people in addition to Turkish-speaking Muslims in Anatolia.

Fuat Köprülü, who had held an Ottomanist stance before the Balkan Wars and had accused Turkists in that period of "taking us back to Karakorum," also criticized Halide Edib's Anatolianism in his article "The Aims of Turkism," published by *Vakit* on July 16, 1918. Like Gökalp, Fuat Köprülü argued that a "Turkish nation" was creating a "Turkish world" in Eurasia similar to the German union and the German nation: "Today the local interests and needs of Istanbul, Bursa, Aydın, and Konya together constitute the general and common interests of Turkey. Likewise, the interests of Crimea, Turkistan, Kazakhstan, and north Türkeli [Turkistan] together constitute the common interests of the Turkish world."[97] According to Köprülü, Turkism emerged against the Ottomanist conviction of "restricting our operations within our borders and disregarding our compatriots living outside of our borders." Both Gökalp's and Köprülü's articles were written in a period when the Ottoman Empire had captured Tabriz, Kars, and Tbilisi by taking advantage of a military power vacuum in the Caucasus that had emerged as a result of the Soviet revolution. During the summer of 1918, the "Army of Islam" was established by Nuri Pasha, Enver Pasha's stepbrother, to take over Baku.[98] Fuat Köprülü wholeheartedly supported the Caucasus campaign of the army. He argued that "our negligence of our compatriots in Russia can lead to the devastation of that world by the new Russian force formed in the future that can destroy us easily."[99]

Although the military situation in the Caucasus seemed promising, there were fewer than 8,000 soldiers available to defend Istanbul against the advancing Allied armies led by French general Louis Franchet d'Esprey in the Balkans, which defeated the Bulgarian army and forced Bulgaria to sign the armistice agreement on September 29, 1918.[100] As the military situation disintegrated on the western and southern fronts and the railway link between the Ottoman Empire and its allies Germany and Austria-Hungary was blocked in the Balkans by the Allied armies, the Unionist government resigned on October 13, 1918. The new Ottoman government formed by the respected general Ahmet İzzet Pasha asked the Allies for an armistice to save the capital and the sultan from the assault of the Allied army stationed in Eastern Rumelia and Western Thrace.[101] Before the Ottoman delegation left Istanbul for negotiations on the Aegean island of Limnos, the sultan instructed them on two principal points on which he would not compromise: (1) the Ottoman family would continue to retain the titles of the caliphate and the sultanate to rule the Ottoman Empire; (2) the empire would grant administrative autonomy to a number of provinces. However, it would refuse to recognize the status of political autonomy, as this would pave the way for the independence of these provinces. The sultan did not mention the self-determination of the Turkish nation or protecting the national borders. As late as 1918, the Ottoman sultan Vahdettin and his entourage considered Islam and therefore the preservation of Ottoman sovereignty over the Holy Places of Mecca and Medina the only way to ensure the continuation of the Ottoman Empire.

The signing of the Armistice of Mudros on October 30 was welcomed by the ruling elite in Istanbul as an optimistic step taken to protect the territories where Turks were in the majority. According to Rauf Bey, the head of the Ottoman delegation, places such as Kars, Batum, and Adana would not be occupied: "This was more than we had hoped for the Armistice. The independence of the state, rights of the sultan and national pride have been entirely saved."[102] A speech by British prime minister Lloyd George in the House of Commons on January 5, 1918, and Woodrow Wilson's Fourteen Points, declared on January 8, 1918, were the two important references for the optimistic perceptions of the Ottoman ruling elite about the vague clauses of the Mudros Armistice. They believed that these vague clauses would not be used by the Allies "to annihilate Turkism."[103] Lloyd George emphasized in his speech in the British Parliament that Britain was not at war "to deprive Turkey of its capital, or of the rich and renowned lands of Asia Minor and Thrace, which are predominantly Turkish in race."[104] Three days later, United States president Woodrow Wilson declared his Fourteen Points in a joint session of the

Congress. Point 12 recognized the right of self-determination for Turkish areas: "The Turkish portion of the present Ottoman Empire should be assured a secure sovereignty, but the other nationalities which are now under Turkish rule should be assured an undoubted security of life and an absolutely unmolested opportunity of autonomous development, and the Dardanelles should be permanently opened as a free passage to the ships and commerce of all nations under international guarantees."[105]

The grand vizier Ahmet İzzet Pasha and other statesmen considered Wilson's principles a last chance not only to preserve Ottoman rule in Anatolia but to get back Western Thrace, since Turks were in the majority in this region. They aimed to maintain the Ottoman territories in the Middle East by granting autonomy to Arabs, hoping that Wilson's Fourteen Points would annul the secret agreements signed between the Allies during World War I to partition the empire's Arab territories.[106] In a move that ran counter to Ottoman statesmen's optimism, immediately after the armistice of Mudros, British and French armies started to occupy places such as Mosul, Iskenderun, Antep, Maraş, Mersin, and Adana, which were in the possession of the Ottoman armies before the armistice. Against the Ottoman protests, the Allies argued that these places were parts of Cilicia, Syria, and Mesopotamia and therefore, according to clause 16 of the armistice, had to be surrendered by Ottoman armies.[107] Britain and France stretched the meanings of geographical and historical terms such as Cilicia, Mesopotamia, and Syria, which did not exist in the administrative system of the Ottoman Empire, and used them to occupy these cities.[108]

Mustafa Kemal analyzed the emergence of the national struggle against the Allies in his six-day-long speech delivered in October 1927. According to the official discourse, which was based on Mustafa Kemal's point of view, the national struggle started with Mustafa Kemal's arrival in Samsun on May 19, 1919, to organize the Turkish people in Anatolia to "save the vatan from the enemies." The official discourse disregarded the roles of the members of the Istanbul government, other leading figures, and intellectuals in the national struggle. Contrary to the official discourse, during the eight months between the signing of the Armistice of Mudros and the Paris Peace Conference in June 1919, three important developments occurred that formed the basis of the national liberation movement in Anatolia: (1) the establishment of Defense of

Rights organizations in Thrace, the Aegean region, and Eastern Anatolia; (2) the occupation of Izmir by Greece and large-scale protest meetings in Istanbul; and (3) the Ottoman government's memorandum to the Allies in the Paris Peace Conference about the borders of the empire.

When Mustafa Kemal arrived in Samsun on May 19, 1919, there were a number of Defense of Rights organizations in Anatolia and Thrace that aimed to resist Armenian and Greek territorial demands at the regional level. The most significant ones were in Thrace, Trabzon, Erzurum, Kars, and Izmir. The organizations in Erzurum and Kars were formed against the Armenian territorial demands on Eastern Anatolia. The ones in Trabzon, Izmir, and Thrace were organized to fight against the Greek occupation of these regions. As Turks formed a majority in all these regions, the Defense of Rights associations based their claims of self-determination on the twelfth article of Wilson's principles. For the first time in the Ottoman Empire, independent and isolated organizations were established to defend the "national" rights of the Muslim people in Anatolia and to defend the national vatan against the occupying forces. Most of these organizations—for example, the Trabzon Defense of National Rights Society, the National Rejection of Annexation Society in the Aegean Region, and the National Government of the Southwest Caucasus—had the word "national" (*milli*) in their names or had "national manifestations" included in their agendas. Nevertheless, there was not enough cooperation between these various organizations, which were founded autonomously in different cities, to organize a national movement to defend all of Anatolia.

After the Mudros Armistice, British and French army units landed in coastal towns of Anatolia, including Adana, Mersin, Iskenderun, and Çanakkale. As these army units consisted of only a couple hundred soldiers, they were considered to be temporary by local people and therefore did not incite large-scale protests. However, the Greek occupation of Izmir on May 15, 1919, was the turning point for the national struggle. Just two days after the Greek occupation of Izmir, 75,000 people attended a protest meeting in Istanbul organized by Turkish Hearths and the Karakol Association. Throughout the following week, leaflets were distributed to call people to a meeting on Friday, May 23, 1919. Both religious and national notions were used to incite patriotism: "Muslims! This coming Friday is the day of the official prayer. On that day, after the Friday prayer in the Fatih, Beyazıt, and Sultanahmet mosques, special prayers will be recited for the liberation of the Muslim and Turkish homelands ... Your beloved vatan is being broken up. Lethal disasters are coming over on us ... Keep your eyes open; think about your enemies and your nation! Learn about the tragedies in Izmir. Anatolia is also waiting for your decision. Cry out against the injustices. Rally to defend your vatan, which is being carved up, as well as your rights with a passion appealing to the conscience of the world."[109] The organizers of the meeting accentuated the partition of the vatan, which was identified as Anatolia. The call to defend the vatan brought about the largest meeting in Ottoman history. There were 200,000 demonstrators in Sultanahmet Square who were stirred up by the passionate speeches of nationalist poet Mehmet Emin and Halide Edib.

The occupation of Izmir and the mass protests that followed drove the sultan and the Damat Ferit (1853–1923) government into a corner. The sultan had kept the Ottoman Parliament closed from the end of World War I by postponing elections.[110] Sultan Vahdettin and Grand Vizier Damat Ferit decided to convene an "Assembly of the Sultanate" during this political turmoil in the capital to share the responsibility of forming the strategy for the conference, which would be pursued by the Ottoman delegation in the coming peace conference in Paris. On May 26, 1919, over 130 dignitaries attended the meeting at the Yıldız Palace. Besides ministers, ambassadors, and journalists, representatives of the National Rights Societies from Trabzon, Izmir, Thrace, and Eastern Anatolia also attended the Assembly of the Sultanate. In the opening speech, the sultan emphasized that the dignitaries were convened to save "the Ottoman state from its difficult situation by urgently determining the necessary actions."[111] Although the subject matter of the meeting was the occupation of Izmir, the delegates deliberated on how to defend the rights and interests of Turks at the Paris conference. The majority of the dignitaries agreed that the Ottoman delegation would have to base its argument on the right of self-determination of the Turks, who were "in the majority from Edirne to the East of Anatolia."[112]

Three weeks after this important meeting, the Ottoman delegation headed by Damat Ferit arrived in Paris. Damat Ferit submitted a detailed memorandum on June 23 to the Allies represented by the U.S. president Woodrow Wilson, British prime minister Lloyd George, and the French prime minister Georges Clemenceau. This memorandum was decisive in terms of demarcating the territories in which Turks were the majority. As Damat Ferit was labeled a traitor by Mustafa Kemal, the memorandum's importance in the context of the National Liberation War was completely ignored by the official national discourse. For the first time, an official Ottoman delegation had defined the boundaries of the Turkish vatan in an international conference (see Figure 2.2):

> The Ottoman Empire's legal sovereignty over its Turkish elements can only be ensured by protecting the national unity and political independence of the regions inhabited by Turks. Thus, it is indispensable to establish a Turkish vatan subject to the conditions of full independence and territorial integrity. Its western boundaries shall be the pre-Balkan War Turkish-Bulgarian border including the district of Gümülcine [Komotini]. The northern boundary shall be the Black Sea. To the east it shall start from the south of Poti and comprise all the territories inhabited by Turks including the Three Provinces [Kars, Ardahan, Batum], and be subsequently demarcated by the future Turkish-Armenian border and the historical boundary with Iran. Starting from the district of Kirkuk, the southern boundary shall be the Turkish-Arab national border line that follows Mosul, Ra's al-'Ayn, Aleppo and ends at the Mediterranean Sea, at Ibn Hani point located to the north of Lattakia. Together with Istanbul, which is the seat of the sultanate, the territories falling within these borders shall be the vatan of Turkish national sovereignty on the basis of the Wilson principles.[113]

In the memorandum, Damat Ferit proposed an exchange of the Muslim population in Greece and the Caucasus with the Greek and Armenian population in Anatolia. Four years later, at the Lausanne Conference, the Turkish delegation insisted on a population exchange with Greece in parallel with the Ottoman delegation's memorandum at the Paris Peace Conference. Moreover, the Ottoman memorandum stressed the new political situation in the Middle East and proposed maximum autonomy for Syria, Iraq, Palestine, Hejaz, and Yemen. The islands adjacent to Anatolia were also claimed by the Ottoman delegation due to their strategic

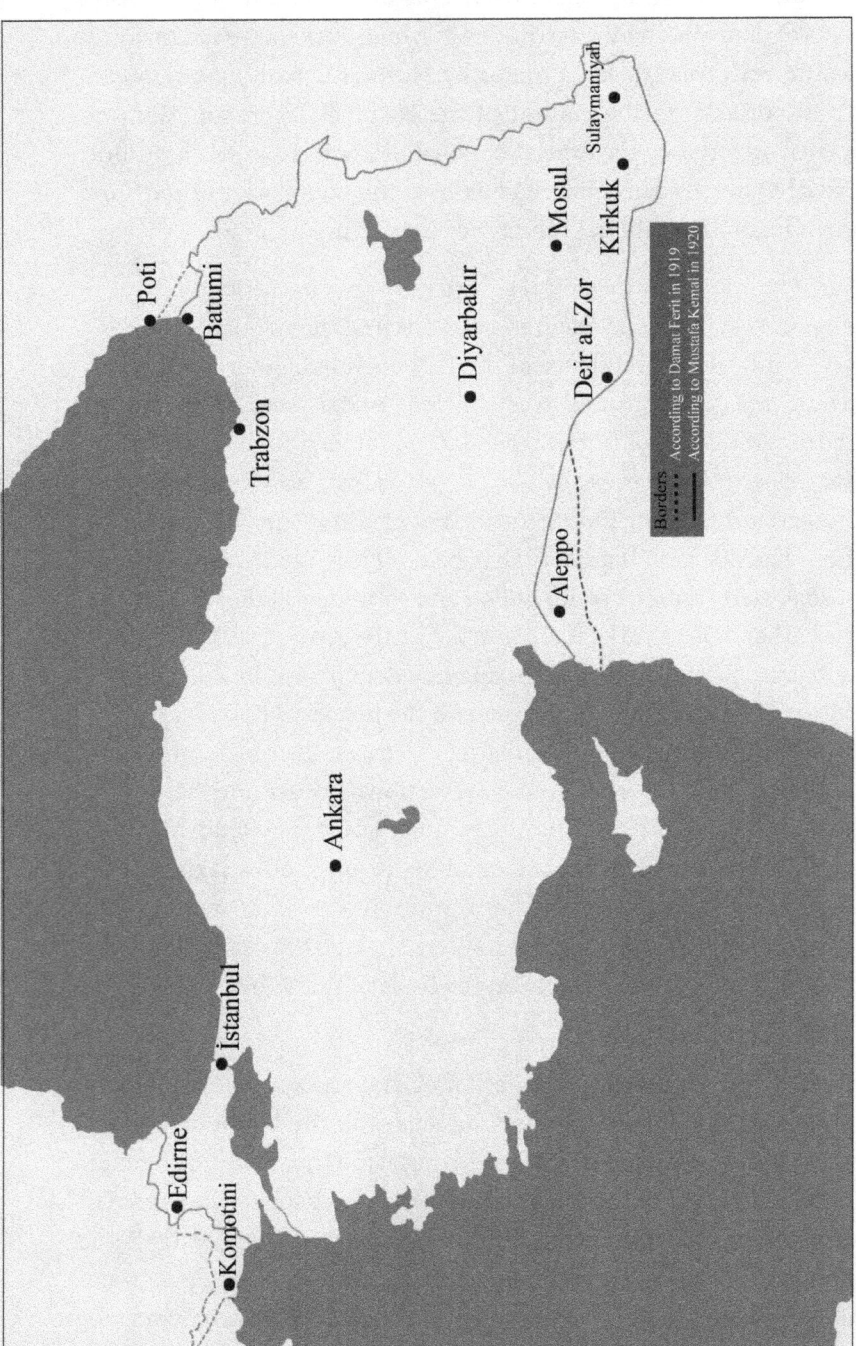

FIGURE 2.2 This map shows the borders of Turkey as suggested by Damat Ferit at the Paris Peace Conference of 1919 and later by Mustafa Kemal in 1920. Note that both proposals included the mainly Kurdish-populated northern Iraq within Turkey's borders. Nevertheless, there are three important differences between the two: Damat Ferit included Aleppo, the area between Poti and Batumi, and Western Thrace, while Mustafa Kemal did not.

importance. The Ottoman delegation also protested the occupation of Izmir, Mersin, Antalya, Konya, Adana, and Karesi and insisted on an immediate withdrawal of the Allied armies. Furthermore, the termination of the capitulations was considered indispensable for "the financial and economic independence of Turkey." The last section of the memorandum argued that "the [Ottoman] government believes that should these demands be met, a new independent Turkey aspiring for modernization shall be established." Not only the new Turkish state but also Turks would be indebted to the Western powers and they would be a "peaceful and hard-working nation deserving to be a member of the League of Nations."

The borders of the Turkish vatan explicated by the Ottoman delegation in Paris became the boundaries of the Republic of Turkey at the Lausanne Conference three years later, with four major differences: (1) the Batum district, (2) the Iskenderun district, (3) Western Thrace, and (4) the Mosul district. These four districts, which were announced as parts of the Turkish vatan—first by Damat Ferit, then in the National Pact by the Ottoman Parliament, and later by the Ankara government and Mustafa Kemal—were ceded by the Ankara government to the Soviet Union, to the French mandate of Syria, to Greece, and to the British mandate of Iraq, respectively. The Ankara government's decision to cede these territories faced severe opposition in the Parliament and had and continue to have an important impact on the foreign policy of Turkey.

Two weeks after the Ottoman delegation submitted its memorandum and its dissemination to the Turkish media, the delegates of the eastern Anatolian cities convened in Erzurum under the leadership of Mustafa Kemal. The second article of the conclusions of the Erzurum Congress, which brought delegates only from the Eastern Anatolian cities, declared that the objective of the "National Forces" was "to protect the integrity of the Ottoman vatan." The sixth article mentioned the boundaries of the vatan without going into the details: "We insist that, within the boundaries specified in the Armistice signed by the Allied powers on October 30, 1918, like in all parts of the country, those areas of East Anatolia in which Muslims live and where Muslim culture and economic dominance has existed must remain within our borders. There can be no dividing; our national unity, historic rights and traditions and religion must continue, and all efforts against this must not succeed."[114]

The uncertainty about the boundaries continued at the Congress of Sivas, which was held in September 1919 with delegates from all over Anatolia. The declaration of the congress argued that territories "within the boundaries specified in the Armistice signed on October 30, 1918" were inseparable from each other and from the Ottoman state. The vagueness of the decisions of both congresses was not a result of an unintentional mistake on the part of the leaders of the national movement. Mustafa Kemal acted pragmatically and did not make a clear announcement about the boundaries, which would have been a binding reference point in the future for the national movement. However, in his meetings with National Rights Societies and in his communications with leading figures, Mustafa Kemal hinted that it would be impossible to include in the national vatan some of the territories in which Turks and Muslims had a majority. He clearly separated the defense of Eastern Thrace from that of Western Thrace. In his meeting with the delegates from Thrace in Istanbul, Mustafa Kemal argued that Eastern Thrace was an indispensable part of the Turkish vatan. He defined Western Thrace as "an abandoned part of vatan," since it was ceded to Bulgaria after the Balkan Wars: "To state the unification of the Eastern and Western Thrace is not right for Ottoman diplomacy. Eastern Thrace is an unequivocal part of the Ottoman country. Western Thrace was an abandoned part of vatan, which was ceded with an agreement once upon a time."[115] Another problematic region was the Three Districts, namely, Batum, Kars, and Ardahan. Although the Muslims and the Turks were the majority in the Three Districts, from the legal point of view their inclusion in the Turkish vatan would be a thorny issue, as they had been ceded to Russia in 1878. In the Erzurum Congress, Mustafa Kemal detached the issue of the Three Districts from the defense of Eastern Anatolia, and he did not allow the participation of the delegates from this region in the congress. Furthermore, the first article of the decisions of the Erzurum Congress argued that the cities of Eastern Anatolia, namely, Trabzon, Erzurum, Sivas, Bitlis, Van, Diyarbakır, and Ma'muretül-Aziz, "are an inseparable whole which cannot be separated from one another and from the Ottoman community."[116] It was striking that the cities of Kars, Ardahan, and Batum were not mentioned as part of Eastern Anatolia in the decisions of the Erzurum Congress.

The National Pact, which was the manifesto of the National Liberation War, was announced by the Ottoman Parliament on February 17, 1920. In the introductory section, the National Pact emphasized the fact that "the independence of the State and the future of the Nation can be assured by complete respect for the following principles, which represent the maximum of sacrifice and which can be undertaken in order to achieve a just and lasting peace."[117] The first article of the National Pact defined the boundaries of the Ottoman state without going into the details. The National Pact acknowledged that the destiny of Ottoman territories, which were peopled by an Arab majority and were under Allied occupation, would be determined by a plebiscite of all inhabitants. With reference to the rest of the territories, it made a significant departure from the decisions of the Erzurum and Sivas congresses: "The whole of those parts whether *within or outside the said armistice line* which are inhabited by an Ottoman Muslim majority, united in religion, in race and in aim, imbued with sentiments of mutual respect for each other and of sacrifice, and wholly respectful of each other's racial and social rights and surrounding conditions, form a whole which does not admit of division for any reason in truth or in ordinance"[118] (emphasis mine). It was clear that the members of the last Ottoman Parliament did not restrict the boundaries of the Ottoman state to the Armistice line. Although Mustafa Kemal and Kazım Karabekir objected to the word "outside" in the text, by adding it to the National Pact, the members of the last Ottoman Parliament claimed that the districts of Aleppo, Kirkuk, and Sulaymaniyah, which were beyond the Armistice line but not inhabited by the Arab majority, were indispensable parts of the Ottoman state. After the establishment of the Republic of Turkey, textbooks, and other written materials omitted the word "outside" from the text of the National Pact. Furthermore, the second and third articles claimed that to integrate the Three Districts into the Caucasus and Western Thrace into the Ottoman state, the Ottoman Parliament was ready to accept holding referendums in these regions.

The National Pact prioritized the territorial principle of "geographical unity" (*vahdet-i coğrafiye*) to draw the new borders. This principle was first coined by the newspaper *Minber*, which was founded by Mustafa Kemal and Fethi Okyar in Istanbul on November 1, 1918. The editorial

"Our Geographical Unity," published on November 8, 1918, argued that "there isn't any vatan in the world that is inhabited by only one nation. Therefore if the nationality principle is implemented as the only legitimate criterion, there won't be any state left on earth."[119] According to the editorial, the districts of Izmir and Aydın could not be separated from the Ottoman vatan, even if it was assumed that Greeks were the majority in them, because such a policy would be detrimental to the "whole of national vatan and geographical unity." During the National Liberation War, the Ankara government claimed the sovereignty of Turkey over the regions in which the Kurds had a majority by proposing the principle of geographical unity.[120] Moreover, during the negotiations with France over the border between Syria and Turkey in June 1921, the Turkish delegation based its claims regarding districts, such as Iskenderun, on the principle of geographical unity.[121]

After the proclamation of the National Pact, the Allies decided to occupy Istanbul officially. The Allied forces closed the Ottoman Parliament and arrested its members. On April 23, 1920, a new Parliament opened in Ankara, and on that day, for the first time Mustafa Kemal explicitly defined the "borders of our vatan" in his speech at the Parliament by referencing the decisions of the Erzurum Congress instead of the National Pact: "Consider the Eastern boundary by including the Three Districts. The Western border passes through Edirne, as we know. The greatest change occurred in the Southern border. It starts to the south of Iskenderun and follows the line between Aleppo and the Katma [train] station extending to Cerablus Bridge. The eastern part includes the Mosul province and the surrounding areas of Kirkuk and Sulaymaniyah. Gentlemen, this border was not simply drawn by military considerations; it was defined to be the national border . . . However, do not think that Islamic communities within this border consist of a single nation. Within this border, there are Turks, Circassians, and other Islamic communities. This border is a national border of fellow nations, which live in a united way and joined all their ideals."[122]

The need to defend the national vatan was a building block beneath the decisions made by the Erzurum and Sivas congresses and the National Pact. The comparison of these texts with the Ottoman delegation's memorandum at the Paris conference reveals that whereas the nationalist forces in Anatolia emphasized Ottomanness and Islam, the Ottoman delegation used Turkishness against the Allied powers in Paris to defend Anatolia and Thrace. While the Ottoman memorandum used concepts such as "Turkish vatan," "Turks," "Turkish-Arab border," and "Turkish national sovereignty," nowhere in the texts of the decisions of the congresses and the National Pact was there any reference to the Turkish vatan or Turkishness.[123] Anatolia and Thrace were identified as the "Ottoman vatan," and the people who inhabited these territories were jointly called the "Ottoman society." These texts employed Islam rather than ethnicity as the main point of reference. They argued that because the majority of the people in Anatolia and Thrace belonged to the same religion, they formed a whole and did not admit of divisions of these territories for any reason. Furthermore, during the National Liberation War, Mustafa Kemal argued that the "national border" did not refer only to Turks: "During the demarcation and fixing of the borders, we claimed that our national border runs to the south of Iskenderun, and includes Mosul, Kirkuk, and Sulaymaniyah by extending to the east. This is our national frontier line! Nevertheless, there are Turks as well as Kurds living in the North of Kirkuk and we did not discriminate them. Therefore, the nation, which we are seeking to defend, does not consist of a single [ethnic] element, but of various Islamic groups. Each Islamic group constituting this society is our fellow brother and our citizens with whom we share common interests."[124]

The Ottoman delegation in Paris highlighted the Turkish ethnic element, since they believed that it was impossible to maintain the Ottoman rule in Anatolia and Istanbul through an armed struggle against the Allies. According to Sultan Vahdettin and his grand vizier Damat Ferit, the only way for the Ottoman Empire to survive was for it to base its claims on the right to self-determination of the Turks, which was also recognized by Wilsonian principles. Mustafa Kemal and his supporters believed that the armed struggle against the Greek and Armenian armies was inescapable if they wanted to save Anatolia. Contrary to the Turkish official discourse, which depicted the National Liberation War as a number of wars waged against the major European powers, the Turkish army under the leadership of Mustafa Kemal fought only against Greece and Armenia, not against Britain, Italy, and France.[125] In his speech in the

Erzurum Congress on July 10, 1919, Mustafa Kemal stressed two important points about the international balance of power that would have a great impact on the national liberation movement: (1) the Allies would not act against the "national will" of the Anatolian people; and (2) the Allies would not be able to unite, due to their conflicting interests, to fight a war against the national forces in Anatolia.[126]

The national liberation movement headed by Mustafa Kemal combined concepts such as "Ottoman vatan" and "Ottoman society" in its discourse with nationalist terms such as "national borders," "national pact," and "national parliament." However, its understanding of Ottomanness was clearly different from the concept of Ottomanism, which was championed by ruling elites since Tanzimat. Mustafa Kemal and his supporters imagined a national Ottoman unity that was geographically limited to Anatolia and did not have any imperial ambitions. Expansionist policies of pan-Islamism and pan-Turkism were clearly rejected by Mustafa Kemal: "Gentlemen, we drew the enmity and hate of the entire world towards this country and nation, since we have chased great fantasies, which are in reality unattainable. We did not pursue pan-Islamism. We perhaps stated 'we are pursuing or we will pursue.' Then our enemies said 'let us kill them right away so that they will not pursue.' We did not pursue pan-Turanism! We said that 'we pursue, we are pursuing, we are going to pursue' and yet they again said 'let us kill them' . . . Instead of bringing more enemies and pressure upon ourselves by running after ideas, which we did not and cannot realize, we should return to the natural borders, to the legal borders."[127]

In this imagination of Turkey, there was no place for Christian groups in Anatolia, namely, Greeks and Armenians, who were in any case not interested in joining to the national liberation movement. There was not a single representative of the Greeks and Armenians at the Grand National Assembly in Ankara. Until 1921, Mustafa Kemal and other leaders pragmatically did not put forward the Turkish ethnicity in the national liberation struggle. Instead, they adopted a territorial approach and used the concept of the "common vatan," namely, Anatolia, to obtain the support of all Muslim groups for the armed struggle against the invading forces. However, the territorial approach adopted by the National Pact was unprecedented. For the first time in Ottoman history, it separated the destiny of the Muslim people in Anatolia from that of the Arabs.

The response of the Allies to the National Pact was the Sèvres Treaty, signed on August 10, 1920, between the Allies and the Ottoman Empire. The Sèvres Treaty partitioned Anatolia and Thrace, in which Muslims were in the majority, among Armenia, Greece, Britain, France, and Italy. Eastern Thrace, including Edirne, was given to Greece. Moreover, Greece would have administrative and military control over the Izmir district, whose status would be determined after five years using a plebiscite. Armenia obtained northeastern Anatolia, including Trabzon, Erzurum, Van, and Bitlis. According to the treaty, the boundary between Turkey, Armenia, and the autonomous Kurdish region would be designated by President Wilson. The Straits would be governed by an international commission. The rest of Anatolia was divided between Britain, Italy, and France into zones of influence. Before signing the treaty, the Grand National Assembly rejected the Sèvres Treaty, and the Council of Ministers declared Damat Ferit and other Ottoman statesmen who participated in the negotiations to be "traitors." In reality, apart from the Greek Army in Anatolia, neither the Allies nor the Ottoman government in Istanbul had enough military resources to implement the terms of the Sèvres Treaty. This situation was best described by Secretary of State for War Winston Churchill's confidential memorandum sent to all the members of the British cabinet: "Are the Allies, thus weakened at the very centre of their influence upon Turkey, nevertheless to persist in a Treaty which they have no power to enforce, with the consequent condemnation to anarchy and barbarism for an indefinite period of the greater part of the Turkish Empire?"[128] The signing of the treaty by the Ottoman government was disseminated to all those in Anatolia via the newspapers. The Istanbul government lost all its credibility in the eyes of the Turkish people, and the authority and legitimacy of the nationalist movement in Ankara was further entrenched.

The concept of defense of vatan was employed intensely not only at the congresses in Anatolia, in the official declarations of parliaments, and in speeches made by Mustafa Kemal and other leading figures of the Ankara government but also in articles and poems written by intellectuals who supported the national struggle. During the National Liberation War, *Hakimiyet-i Milliye* (National Sovereignty), the official newspaper of the Ankara government, publicized the views of Kemalists to obtain the support of people in Anatolia and Istanbul and also to influence public opinion in European countries. The newspaper was established in January 1920, a couple of weeks after Mustafa Kemal arrived in Ankara. Between 1920 and 1922, *Hakimiyet-i Milliye* published numerous articles about the borders and how to form a national vatan in Anatolia. Analysis of these articles reveals that Kemalists did not push for Turkish ethnicity in 1920 and the first half of 1921. Instead, they employed Islamic notions to obtain the support of non-Turkish Muslims, such as Kurds, Circasssians, and Lazes. Nonetheless, after winning the Second İnönü Battle in March 1921, Kemalists and intellectuals supporting them modified their discourses and emphasized the significance of Turkish nationalism in the defense of the "national" vatan and the formation of the new "national" state.

The article "The Border Problem," published by *Hakimiyet-i Milliye* on January 24, 1920, openly rejected the creation of a common vatan with Arabs in Iraq and Syria. It also refused the establishment of a mandate of a European power over Anatolia, Syria, and Iraq that would integrate these regions with each other: "Succumbing to a protectorate or mandate in order to include Arabia and Iraq within the borders would destroy the future of Anatolia at a stroke . . . Given that every nation has the right to determine its own destiny according to these [Wilsonian] principles, Arabs are also entitled to have a voice in the issues of their very own existence and future."[129] The article argued that the new border passed "from the south of Iskenderun, north of Aleppo and between Aleppo and Katme and leaves the Cerablus Bridge, Deir al-Zor and Sulaymaniyah district in our side. To the south of this border, language, civilization and society are predominantly Arab."[130] Another article published by *Hakimiyet-i Milliye*, "Britain's Politics of Islam," put together Kurds, Circassians, and Turks under the title of "Muslims of Turkey" and invited them to establish a common front against the invaders to defend Islam. Still another article, "Anatolia," argued that a new ideology was born in Anatolia after the Mudros Armistice.[131] This ideology was very similar to the Monroe Doctrine; its motto was "Anatolia belongs to Anatolians": "Today, Anatolia is not anymore a simply geographical designation; it started to refer to an idea . . . Anatolia constitutes a political entity. It is such a political entity that it is independent from the outside and free on its own."[132]

During the National Liberation War, some well-known Turkists such as Ziya Gökalp and Hamdullah Suphi, who had refused to limit Turkism in Anatolia in 1918, adjusted their views regarding the changing conditions and wholeheartedly defended the national movement in Ankara that rejected expansionist imperial policies and restricted its objectives to the liberation of Anatolia. Ziya Gökalp, who had announced in 1911 that "the vatan of the Turks is neither Turkey, nor Turkistan, their vatan is a vast and eternal land: Turan," modified his concept of vatan in 1920 in his poem "Shepherd and Nightingale." It is remarkable that Ziya Gökalp depicted the nightingale, traditionally a symbol of a lover in classical Ottoman literature, as a figure speaking on behalf of vatan: "Shepherd said: Although all countries forsake me, Anatolia does not secede from me. Nightingale said: Although the enemy envies me, the voice of the Turk will be heard in Istanbul . . . Shepherd said: From Edirne to Van and to Erzurum, all belong to me. Nightingale said: Izmir, Maras, Adana, Iskenderun, and Kirkuk are all purely Turkish."[133]

Similarly, Hamdullah Suphi, who had rejected the idea of limiting the field of activity of the Turkish Hearths to Turkey in 1918, since it would have offended the Turks outside of Anatolia, labeled the Anatolian unity as the unconquerable in his speech in the Parliament in Ankara in 1920: "The combat forces will surface from the Anatolian heartland . . . Therefore to prevent it, they [the enemies] will seek to destroy the heart of Anatolia. There is not a single piece of our territory which is immune from this threat."[134] The Turkish national anthem, "Independence March" (İstiklal Marşı), written by Mehmet Akif and officially adopted by the Parliament in Ankara on March 12, 1921, was a remarkable example of how Islam was the dominant factor in the national discourse during the first years of the National Liberation War. While there was not a single word about Turks, Turkey, or Turkishness in the national anthem, which is comprised of ten long stanzas, there were repeating references to Islam and God. Similarly, Mehmet Akif's imagination of vatan in the national anthem was more religious than national.[135] He elevated vatan to a sacred territory that should be defended by the "God-worshipping nation." The fifth, sixth, seventh, and eighth stanzas of the national anthem particularly sanctified the homeland:

> O my friend! Do not let the villain desecrate my land
> To curb this indecent incursion, do make thyself a shield
> For soon shall rise the sun of the promise of Heaven
> Maybe tomorrow, who knoweth? Maybe sooner even!

Do know that the ground thou treadest is not mere soil
Do think about the thousands lying in graves without veil
Thou art the son of a martyr, do honor your sire
Never cede this vatan, even with the promise of the whole sky

For this heavenly vatan, who would not lay down his life?
Should one squeeze the soil, martyrs would burst, sure enough
Of my soul, my beloved, of all what I have, May God me deprive
But not separate me from the only vatan I need to survive

O Lord, here is the sole wish of my pain-stricken heart
Let no heathen hands ever touch my shrine's chest
These adhans, witnessing the pillars of my faith
Should be heard upon my immortal homeland day and night

After winning the defensive battles of İnönü and Sakarya against the Greek army on the western front in 1921, the Islamic tone of the national struggle was lessened and the nationalization of the vatan was intensified by the Kemalists. Other important developments were the defeat of the Armenian army in eastern Anatolia and the signing of the Treaty of Moscow with the Soviet Union in March 1921, through which the Kemalists reached their territorial objectives on the eastern front except for the Batumi district, which was ceded to Georgia. Furthermore, the local armed struggle against the French troops in the southeast also ended in March 1921. As a result of these military and diplomatic successes, the Ankara government entrenched its authority in the east of Anatolia, where the Kurds were the majority. The support of the Kurds for the National Liberation War was not as noteworthy as it had been two years before. As the national forces were prepared for a final assault to oust the Greek army from Anatolia, the focal point of the national discourse moved from Turkeyism to Turkish nationalism, which gave special importance to the Turkification of the vatan rather than emphasizing the harmony of different Islamic ethnic groups inside the borders announced by the National Pact. Moreover, Mustafa Kemal started to identify the national liberation war as an anti-imperialist struggle against European powers.

Before 1921, Mustafa Kemal refrained from using terms such as "Turkish nation" in his speeches and preferred phrases like "people in Turkey." His discourse changed in 1921, and he started to emphasize

Turkish nationalism in his addresses in addition to the geographic unity of different ethnic groups in Anatolia. In his statement to the Associated Press in August 1921, Mustafa Kemal proclaimed that "Turkey belongs to Turks." According to him, this was "the motto of nationalists."[136] Starting in the winter of 1921, Mustafa Kemal depicted the "invasion of the Turkish homeland by Greek forces" as "the imperialist desire of Britain." In his speech in the Parliament on January 29, 1921, about the forthcoming negotiations in London with the Allied forces, Mustafa Kemal identified "the imperialist and capitalists forces" as one of the main threats to the nation: "Imperialist power considered our nation as a flock of animals deprived of justice, honor, and independence. This line of thinking follows that such a vast and valuable country, enjoying plenty of natural resources, cannot be left to the hands of such a flock."[137]

In the same way, intellectuals who supported the national forces started to underline Turkish nationalism in their writings after 1921. Ruşen Eşref (1892–1959) compared the area between Bursa and Eskişehir, in which national forces were fighting against the Greek army, with the Hedjaz region, which included sacred cities of Islam in Mecca and Medina. He named the area between Bursa and Eskişehir "the sacred house of the Turks."[138] According to him, this invasion was completely different than the previous military losses in the Balkans, in which only the conquered territories had been lost. This time the invaders were taking control of "Turkish districts, Turkish architecture, Turkish capitals, Turkish honor, Turkish tradition, and Turkish religion." Ruşen Eşref argued that "the remaining vatan" without Bursa, Edirne, and Istanbul was so small that "there was not a single sultan tomb in it." Even the grave in Gallipoli of Namık Kemal, "the poet of vatan," was surrendered to "the infidels." For him, "to own the vatan, we should all be a part of the vatan."

According to Falih Rıfkı (1894–1971), because of the heroic resistance of the national forces during the Sakarya Battle, the name of the river Sakarya had moved "from national geography to national history." Falih Rıfkı claimed that "by carrying the Greek blood to the sea for seven days, the river Sakarya prevents our territories from being desecrated."[139] In another article, he argued that Mustafa Kemal was taking Turks to "the promised land." However, "the promised land" was neither the Caucasus nor Central Asia. For Falih Rıfkı, "the promised land is the land of unity and freedom for Turks. In this promised land, Turks are going to meet with themselves, they are going to work for themselves, they are going to live for themselves, and they are going to die for themselves. This promised land is 'the national vatan.' "[140]

Yahya Kemal, who criticized the expansionist policies of the CUP during World War I, enthusiastically supported the national forces' defense of Anatolia against the invading armies. In his article "Our Notion of Independence," Yahya Kemal compared the National Liberation War with the Polish struggle for independence: "The notion of independence has been dormant in the hearts of Turks for centuries like a sacred fire under ashes. When it realized that it was going to be extinguished, it sparked furiously."[141] For Yahya Kemal, the heroic Turkish resistance to invaders vindicated Namık Kemal's dictum that "in each part of our territory, there is a lion waiting."[142] As a result of the victories of Turkish armies, "the map of Armenia, which includes the area from Sivas to Adana, and the map of Greece, which encircled all the ports and coasts of the Western seas [Aegean Sea], were left on the walls." In another article, "The New Turkish Spirit," Yahya Kemal argued that in the fifty years between Namık Kemal and Mustafa Kemal, a "new Turkish spirit" had surfaced and reached its zenith in the national struggle in Anatolia. The major characteristic of this "Turkish national spirit" was that whereas before Namık Kemal the "love of vatan" had consisted of only misery and melancholy, after Namık Kemal it had become a passionate and encouraging ideal. For Yahya Kemal, "the last three years of Anatolia illustrated the new Turkish spirit even to those who were not willing to realize it."[143]

Ziya Gökalp, who had supported Turanism and the expansionist policies, became an ardent anti-imperialist during the National Liberation War. In his poems, he argued that the Greek invasion of Anatolia had been planned by Britain and not by Greek statesmen. Therefore, Gökalp considered Greece to be Prime Minister Lloyd George's puppet: "Lloyd George deceived Greece once again . . . Our hatred does not consider Greece as the enemy; it is you [Lloyd George] who had this slave [i.e., Greece] revolt; after a few slaps he shall regret, but you [Britain] are the one against whom we bare the eternal grudge."[144] Similarly, in his poem "Beware of Britain," Gökalp identified Britain as the main threat for vatan: "[Britain] destroyed all vatans, it took over a hundred states, it drowned the freedom, it enslaved this nation . . . All the world is now its slaves. Only Anatolia remains as a free country. [Anatolia] is the one waging the holy war against oppression. It is our duty to come to its rescue."[145]

Mustafa Kemal wrote a declaration after the national forces drove all Greek forces out of Anatolia as a result of the final assault, which started on August 26, 1922, and ended within two weeks. He addressed all the people in Turkey as the "grand and noble Turkish nation."[146] One month after the military victory, Mustafa Kemal told the American news reporter Richard Danin that in the war, the Turks ceded "Macedonia and Syria. But, now we demand every place and everything left behind that is solely Turkish. We are determined to recover them and we will." Mustafa Kemal emphasized that he was not going to stop until he had saved all the Turkish territories, including "Istanbul and Thrace until the Maritsa River in Europe; Anatolia, the territories of Mosul, and half of Iraq in Asia."[147] Indeed, the Turkish delegation to the Lausanne Conference and its head, İsmet İnönü, were instructed by Parliament not to make any concessions on the issue of national borders. There were fourteen articles in the ordinance prepared by the cabinet. About two articles in particular, the delegation was instructed to leave the conference if the Allies would not accept Turkey's terms. These were Article 1, which dealt with Turkey's eastern borders and rejected the establishment of an Armenian state in Eastern Anatolia; and Article 8, in which the delegation demanded an abrogation of the capitulations.[148] Article 2 dealt with the Iraqi border, which claimed to take back Sulaymaniyah, Kirkuk, and Mosul. Article 3 was about the border with Syria and called for a change that would transfer the cities Harim, Meskene, and Müslimiye between Aleppo and the current border and Deir al-Zor to Turkey. According to Article 4, the delegation should insist on regaining the Aegean islands close to the coast. Article 5 accepted the 1914 border of eastern Thrace, which left Edirne to Turkey. According to Article 6, there should be a plebiscite about the status of Western Thrace.

During the first part of the Congress of Lausanne that ended in February 1923, after three months of intense negotiations between the representatives from Turkey, Britain, France, and Italy, the Turkish delegation realized that reaching the borders announced by the National Pact was impossible through the peace negotiations, as France and Britain were not willing to give control of the districts of Iskenderun and Mosul to Turkey.

During this period, there were also passionate debates in the Grand National Assembly in Ankara. The majority of the members of the Parliament seemed to stand firm about the territorial objectives proclaimed in the National Pact. Some of the members of Parliament even argued that they preferred to continue to fight against the enemies rather than to accept a humiliating peace agreement.[149] After breaking off the negations in Lausanne, the Turkish delegation returned to Ankara and its head, İsmet İnönü, encountered a Parliament eager to insist on the terms of the National Pact. Mustafa Kemal and İsmet İnönü, two leading politicians, decided to change their strategy of saving all the Turkish territories in order to Turkify those territories that would be left to Turkey through the peace agreement.

İsmet İnönü's speeches in the Parliament after the breaking off of the diplomatic negotiations revealed that Mustafa Kemal and İsmet İnönü preferred to sign the peace agreement and consolidate their political status in Turkey rather than compelling European powers, if necessary militarily, to agree to cede the Mosul and Iskenderun districts to Turkey. On February 27, 1923, İsmet Pasha emphasized that Turkey would give some concessions on territorial issues to obtain the abrogation of capitulations: "A greater vatan does not necessarily secure our life. Thus, the point here has to do with living as a nation in the Turkish vatan, wherever it is going to be. We committed to uphold this principle and told the Allies that in terms of the territorial issues, we will satisfy the Allies by finding a position reconcilable with the National Pact . . . This is the decision we have taken."[150] İsmet İnönü told members of Parliament that if the Mosul issue was not resolved in the negotiations between Britain and Turkey, the League of Nations would decide on the status of the district (Fig. 2.3). Members of Parliament reacted to this decision by exclaiming that "we are ceding Mosul."[151]

While some scholars criticized the Turkish delegation in Lausanne, as "Turkey" lost the districts announced by the National Pact—namely, Mosul—and accepted the international regime of the Straits, some others applauded İsmet İnönü for securing the abolition of capitulations and the population exchange, which ended with the expulsion of 1.5 million Greeks from "Turkey." However, both of these analyses were anachronistic, because the Turkey that included Mosul and Iskenderun or the Turkey with a 1.5 million Greek population in Anatolia never existed. Indeed,

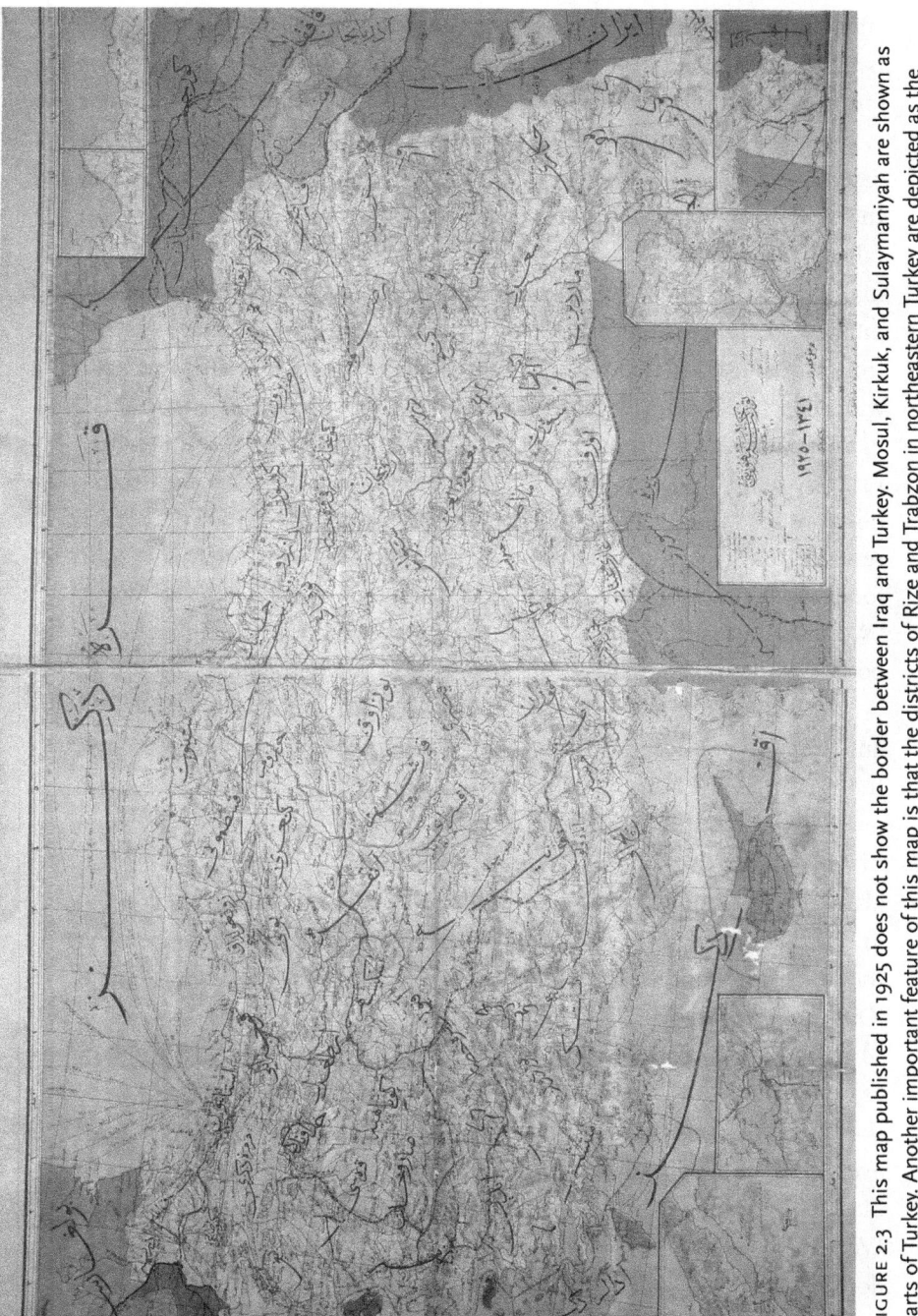

FIGURE 2.3 This map published in 1925 does not show the border between Iraq and Turkey. Mosul, Kirkuk, and Sulaymaniyah are shown as parts of Turkey. Another important feature of this map is that the districts of Rize and Trabzon in northeastern Turkey are depicted as the "Lazistan" region. Although ethnic designations were often used for regions in the Ottoman maps, they were never used in the Turkish maps published after the end of the 1920s.

the Republic of Turkey was established on October 29, 1923, three months after the conclusion of the Treaty of Lausanne. After signing the treaty, İsmet İnönü announced in his speech in Parliament that as a result, "we found a radical remedy for the malady that our goodwill has been unable to overcome for centuries. What we have accomplished is that the Anatolian homeland has become an almost homogenous vatan."[152] According to İnönü, Turkey would not have a significant Christian minority, what he called a "state within a state."[153] In the last part of his speech, İnönü "summarized" the achievements of the Treaty of Lausanne, calling the new republic "a homogeneous and unitary vatan within which we are exempt from unnatural restrictions and internal concessions resembling a state within a state. An unconstrained vatan free from unnatural financial obligations, enjoying absolute right of defense and ample resources: this vatan is named Turkey."[154] İnönü's arguments for legitimizing the national vatan, which was significantly smaller than the imperial version, revealed that the concept of vatan had changed radically for İnönü, who fought as a colonel in the Ottoman army in Yemen during World War I: "We all know that the sons of vatan, who were not able to defend even our borders and our vatan, had been squandered outside of vatan."[155]

In his speech in the Parliament on August 13, 1923, Mustafa Kemal analyzed the political outcome of the National Liberation War. For him, the Ottoman Empire ended when Istanbul was invaded by the Allies on March 16, 1920. Since then, the "national state" had been established in Anatolia on the basis of "national sovereignty." It formed a "national army" to expel the invading armies from the "Turkish vatan." According to Mustafa Kemal, the new Turkey faced difficulties and problems during the peace negotiations due to the "bad inheritance from the 400-years-old [Ottoman] period." As with İnönü, in the concluding part of his speech, Mustafa Kemal sanctified the vatan: "Gentlemen! Let us leave the details aside and look at the sacred entity of vatan from a general point of view. We would then see that simply a piece of black soil, which is devoid of everything needed to live and to attain [modern] civilization. Under the black soil there are treasures, and on it, a noble and brave nation exists. We have endured all these long and painful struggles . . . for the freedom and inviolability of vatan and nation."[156]

CONCLUSION

In this chapter we have seen how the spatial consciousness of the Ottoman ruling elites was changed from an imperial vatan to a national one between 1908 and 1923. The loss of territories had a deep impact on the imagination of physical and mental boundaries of the vatan. During this turbulent era, three different ideologies—Islamism, Ottomanism, and pan-Turkism—challenged each other to become hegemonic in politics, with the objective of maintaining the Ottoman Empire. Although there were major differences between them, they all had imperial visions about vatan. With the occupation of various parts of Anatolia and the victory of the national struggle, a fourth ideology—Turkish nationalism—emerged with a completely different objective of establishing a "national state," which would be governed by a "national assembly" and protected by a "national army." Turkish nationalism overcame the major predicament of Islamism, Ottomanism, and pan-Turkism of how to save the Ottoman state and vatan by imagining a new state and a national vatan. In so doing, it gradually disqualified the three other ideologies and became hegemonic when the war ended in 1922.

It is important to emphasize that at the beginning of the national struggle, the goal of defending the vatan against "the enemies of Islam" who had invaded Anatolia formed the building block of the coalition of various groups led by Mustafa Kemal. With the consolidation of their power, Kemalists started to put more emphasis on the Turkishness of the vatan. Turkish nationalism determined the "general condition of the modern body politic" after the creation of the Republic of Turkey, with its distinct and innovative form of territoriality, which combined "material and emotional powers of space."[157] However, the new Turkish vatan and Turkish identity, like any other constructed national homeland and identity, were far from "homogenous and stable," as claimed by İsmet İnönü after the Treaty of Lausanne. Their physical and conceptual borders have been contested by various political and social groups since 1923. The next chapter analyzes the quest of the Turkish ruling elites for the creation of a uniform and homogenous nation within the territory of the Republic of Turkey.

CHAPTER THREE

From Geography to Vatan

REMZI OĞUZ ARIK'S ARTICLE "From Geography to Vatan," published by the journal *Millet* in 1942, exemplified the Kemalist elites' efforts and policies to nationalize the territories within the boundaries of Turkey after the proclamation of the Republic in 1923.[1] According to Arık, the main difference between geography and vatan was that the former was simply an area where certain physical actions were performed, whereas the latter was a sanctified territory that had a venerated value for those who act within it. For Arık, "at first glance, the geography of a country seems to be miserable and inferior."[2] It is merely soil on which "enemies and friends trampled carelessly." This "inanimate geography" turns into "a vatan" when people share miseries and victories in it and act together for a common cause. From then on, "man and territory take each others' names. Hereafter, if the man attacks or is attacked, he will act in the name of a 'particular' society and its homeland. That is how vatan was born."[3] Arık identified all other non-Turk civilizations in Anatolia—which he named "mother vatan"—including "Byzantium, the Roman Empire, Greece, Iran, Asur and Hittites," as "exploiters." After sweeping away all the alien entities in Anatolia, however, Turkic tribes unified it by founding their own vatan. Arık argued that Turks lost centuries by devoting themselves to religious and imperial vatans, namely, "Islamic internationalism and the Ottoman Empire." Turks regained their national features

102

with the establishment of national vatan in Anatolia at the end of the National Liberation War.

Remzi Oğuz Arık was truly devoted to the ideology of nationalism, which insists on an isomorphism between place and ethnicity and considers the linkage between citizens of states and their territories as natural. In the nationalist imagination, the concept of homeland is the dominant symbol that portrays the contested and unfixed association between people and place as obvious, commonsensical and agreed upon. The representation of the world to schoolchildren as a collection of nation-states in a multicolored school atlas entrenched the nationalist rationale that Turkey is where the Turks live, while Germany is where the Germans live, and so forth.[4] As Gupta and Ferguson rightly put it, as a result of commonsense nationalist ideas, "space itself becomes a kind of neutral grid on which cultural difference, historical memory, and societal organization are inscribed. It is in this way that space functions as a central organizing principle in the social sciences at the same time that it disappears from analytical purview."[5]

After the establishment of the republic in 1923, the state played a crucial role in the formation of the Turkish nation and homeland. As mentioned in the previous chapter, securing the "national borders" announced by the National Pact was the foremost objective of the national liberation movement in Anatolia. After achieving this objective with the Treaty of Lausanne, Kemalist elites sought to institutionalize the territories within the "national borders" as national homeland and conceptualize them as sources of identification for people in Turkey. The national discourse of the newly established republic had temporal and spatial dimensions. The temporal dimension constructed a narrative of a Turkish nation that established an uninterrupted link between Turkish people in Anatolia and ancient civilizations in Central Asia. Furthermore, the race-based "Sun Language Theory," supported by Mustafa Kemal in the 1930s, argued that all human languages descended from the Turkish language of Central Asian tribes. The natural outcome of the "Turkish Thesis of History" was that because Turks established the first civilization on earth, the Sumerians and Hittites, who inhabited Anatolia before the ancient Greeks and Armenians, had Turkish origins.[6]

Whereas the temporal dimension legitimated the Turkish national identity by tracing back to a fictional common past, the spatialization of the Turkish nation was another key element in the national discourse that tied territory with national identity. Kemalist elites established inclusive and exclusive forms of territoriality to promote Anatolia as the national homeland. Indeed, the representation of Anatolia as the homeland of Turks played an essential role in the homogenization of various ethnic groups in Turkey.[7] One of the first articulations of the Turkification of Anatolia was İsmet İnönü's speech at the Turkish Hearths in 1925. İnönü gave this nationalist speech after the suppression of the Şeyh Sait Revolt in the Diyarbakır region, in which Kurds were in the majority: "We are openly nationalists . . . and nationalism is the only element for our unity. As Turks are in the majority, other [ethnic] groups do not have any power. Our mission is to Turkify non-Turkish groups in the Turkish vatan. We are going to extirpate groups, who oppose Turks and Turkishness. The primary criterion we seek for those who are going to serve this country, is to be a Turk."[8] Most scholars, intellectuals, and journalists supported the Kemalist policy of homogenization and the assimilation of non-Turkish ethnic groups in order to create solidarity inside the Turkish vatan. Like İnönü, Remzi Oğuz Arık was very aggressive about non-Turkish groups in Anatolia: "Those who want to come to this vatan and join this nation have to accept and appreciate the conditions that were considered necessary by the founders of the vatan."[9]

Turkish nationalism constructed the meaning of homeland set against the "Others." These "Others" were sometimes identified as internal enemies in Anatolia, and other times they were identified as external enemies. However, contrary to most of the other European nation-states, which presented minorities as the "Other" and identified them as the main enemy, non-Turkish ethnic groups in Turkey were actively forgotten by ruling elites. For example, the word "Kurd" became taboo in Turkish political discourse and was not mentioned by the majority of politicians and intellectuals until the 1980s. During the Cold War, right-wing parties and politicians readily labeled left-wing opposition groups as internal enemies and accused them of working in the interests of the Soviet Union. The relationship between the Turkish homeland and the external Others was also problematic. The national discourse identified European imperial powers, which had sought to partition the Turkish homeland after World War I, as external enemies. Nevertheless, to realize Mustafa Kemal's objective of "elevating Turkey to the level of contemporary civilization," the Turkish state had to consider the external enemies, namely, European countries, as its model. This dilemma still carries a heavy burden in Turkish politics, as its secular and pro-Western military-bureaucratic elite considers reforms, which are necessary for Turkey's full accession to the European Union (EU), as threatening to national security.

Nationalism not only shaped the political and social life in Turkey after 1923, but it also increased the presence of the state in daily life. National identity, which stipulated that citizens define themselves as Turks, became prevalent against other individual identifications, such as gender, religion, and class. In the two decades after 1923, the state increased its authority all over Anatolia. It cultivated and disseminated Turkish national identity by establishing modern institutions in the media, transportation, and education. In 1927—five years after the British Broadcasting Corporation had started radio broadcasting—two radio transmitters began broadcasting in Istanbul and Ankara. In 1935, in the Fourth Great Congress of the Republican People's Party (RPP), radio was announced "as a valuable instrument to educate the nation culturally and politically."[10] Indeed, radio as a key media institution became the "lips of the state and ears of citizens," as the number of radio receivers increased from 1,178 in 1927 to 180,000 in 1946.[11] In terms of transportation, Anatolia experienced a railway revolution in the first twenty-five years of the Kemalist regime. The young republic inherited 4,559 kilometers of railway lines from the Ottoman Empire. With the objective of transporting goods in the most efficient way, Kemalists made railway construction an industrial priority, and by 1940 the railway network was almost doubled, reaching 8,637 kilometers.[12] The Tenth Year Anthem, which was written in 1933 and is still sung at many national holidays and celebrations, announced the success of the regime in transportation with the following line, which was added by Mustafa Kemal: "We have covered the motherland with iron webs from one end to another."[13]

While radio and railways became effective state institutions in the legitimation of the newly established Turkish state, another institution, education, was the central mechanism of the state for the Kemalist regime to enter the daily life of citizens in order to establish a "natural" link between the national homeland and its people. Kemalists modernized and reformed mass education to inculcate the national identity and the

Turkish homeland in the young, so that, eventually, all individuals would presuppose that they were part of the Turkish nation and the Turkish homeland. In March 1923, just after the end of the National Liberation War, Mustafa Kemal launched a war in education: "During the war, schools offered the educated and sophisticated youth to the vacant officer ranks in the front. Following an era of peace and stability, where these qualified people will return to the classroom in schools and transform munitions into maps and books, national education shall rise as an invincible bastion against ignorance. The future shall be conquered and captured from this bastion."[14]

In this chapter, I take up a concept Susan Schulten has repeatedly explored—"how geography has mediated the world for us, and how it has concretized the abstract"—analyzing this in the context of the evolution of Turkish national/territorial identity.[15] It examines how nationalist discourse became prevalent in educational materials and particularly how state education implanted national ideals into geography textbooks and promoted Turkish national identity and the country's spatial and cultural features. Anssi Paasi employed the term "pedagogy of space" to describe "the role of school geography in the creation of spatial representations, regional narratives, knowledge, images and stereotypes regarding the 'national character,' cultures or identities of 'we' and 'them.'"[16] A comparison of the "pedagogy of space" in Turkey before and after 1923 reveals that the newly established Turkish state effectively used education in geography to construct spatial consciousness about the national homeland and to popularize collective national duties. A comparison of geography textbooks published before and after 1923 illustrates how education became an important tool in the nationalization of space and everyday life by the state. The spatial representations used in geography textbooks, including maps and images, changed dramatically with the establishment of the republic. The analysis of this transformation reveals that the nationalist ideology used various forms of exclusion, active forgetting, and images of the Other to unite people inhabiting the territories saved from "foreign invaders" and identifying them as "Turks," whose national duty was to defend the Turkish vatan. The objective of this chapter is to analyze the nationalist representation of space in Turkey and the production of geographical knowledge by the Turkish state to justify its own power and authority over its citizens.[17] Instead of considering national essences as commonsensical and matters of fact, I seek to deconstruct them to reveal processes of power. Processes rather than essences invent national homeland and national boundaries and treat them as meaningful.

GEOGRAPHY EDUCATION DURING THE LATE OTTOMAN PERIOD

Geography as a science had attracted the attention of Ottoman intellectuals, such as Piri Reis and Katip Çelebi, since the sixteenth century. However, they produced books and maps for a small ruling elite, namely, statesmen, scholars, high-ranking military officers, and sea captains. Whereas Ottoman elites were kept apprised of recent developments and discoveries made by European geographers, the general public, which had a literacy rate of about 2 or 3 percent, did not have any geographical information about the empire's vast territories. As a result of Tanzimat reforms, educational institutions developed both qualitatively and quantitatively. The number of schools increased dramatically during the nineteenth century, which resulted in the expansion of public education and the rise of the literacy rate to 15 percent by the end of the century.[18] In 1853, the Ottoman state decided to open 25 high schools (*Rüşdiye*) in major cities. At that time, there were only 12 high schools in Istanbul. This number increased to 70 in Istanbul and to 619 throughout the empire by the end of Abdulhamid's rule in 1908, and the number of pupils attending elementary school was about one million in a total population of 37 million people.[19]

Geography courses were compulsory for high school students for all classes and ranged from one to three hours per week. Selim Sabit Efendi (1829–1910) was one of the first instructors who employed pedagogical tools in education, such as maps and the abacus.[20] By introducing students to maps, Sabit Efendi and other lecturers in high schools caused an uproar among conservatives, who considered maps blasphemous drawings, using this as an excuse to destroy them.[21] The minister of education advised Selim Sabit Efendi that he should be "progressing step by step, not straight away."[22] Indeed, a decade later educational reforms were firmly established, and maps became an indispensable part of geography education. In 1874, Selim Sabit Efendi instructed teachers about geography classes in his book *Instructions for Teachers*: "In geography [classes] five continents should be presented to students on the map and on the terrestrial globe. They should be taught about how to draw maps."[23]

Maps of the Ottoman Empire in textbooks were cartographic images of Ottoman territories. Ottoman scholars adapted these maps from Western European models, which divided the earth into continents and represented each continent on a separate map and therefore did not reflect the fact that the Ottoman territories extended over three continents—Asia, Europe, and Africa—in a unified way.[24] Furthermore, since all Ottoman territories were on the edge of three continents, these maps gave readers the impression that the empire was marginalized in Europe, Asia, and Africa. One clear exception to this trend was the map in Selim Sabit Efendi's *Short Book on Geography*, first published in 1870, that showed Ottoman territories in Europe, Asia, and the north of Egypt together.[25] Although it did not include the Ottoman territories of Yemen, Hedjaz, and Tripoli, a map appeared in a textbook that showed the territories of the Ottoman Empire in three continents in a unified way for the first time (see Figure 3.1).

This book included six more maps: a world map and five maps of Asia, Europe, North and South America, Oceania, and Africa. In these maps, Selim Sabit Efendi imitated British cartographers and marked the Ottoman territories in pink. During that era, coloring Ottoman territories in pink became a tradition among Ottoman cartographers, and the practice would continue until the disintegration of the empire. In Selim Sabit Efendi's book, the map of the European continent included the Ottoman territories in Asia in its lower right corner. Whereas the Ottoman territories in Europe were marked with the color pink, Anatolia, Syria, and upper Mesopotamia were left uncolored. In the same manner, the map of Africa did not mark Ottoman territories in Asia, and the map of Asia left the Ottoman territories in Europe and Africa uncolored. Moreover, in the map of Asia, Yemen and Hedjaz were not shown as part of the Ottoman Empire (see Figure 3.2), and in the map of Africa, Egypt was shown as a British colony despite the fact that it belonged to the Ottoman Empire at the time. These inaccuracies about the Ottoman territories demonstrated that even such an avant-garde Ottoman scholar as Selim Sabit Efendi did not have a clear image of the geo-body of the Ottoman Empire when adapting European maps, which did not respect the territorial integrity of the Ottoman Empire.

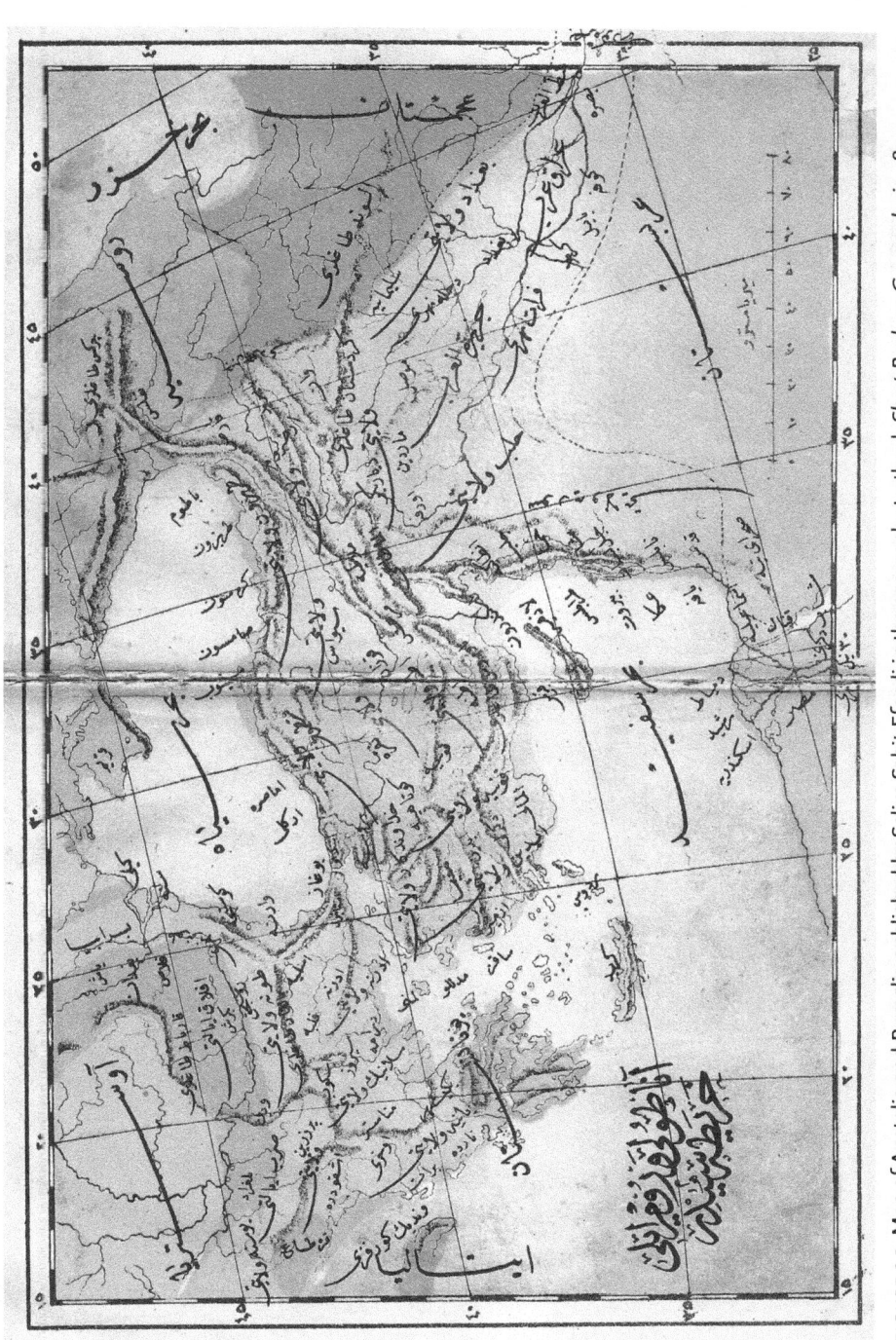

FIGURE 3.1 Map of Anatolia and Rumelia published by Selim Sabit Efendi in the geography textbook *Short Book on Geography* in 1874. The mountains in the Hakkari region were marked as the "Kurdistan Mountains."

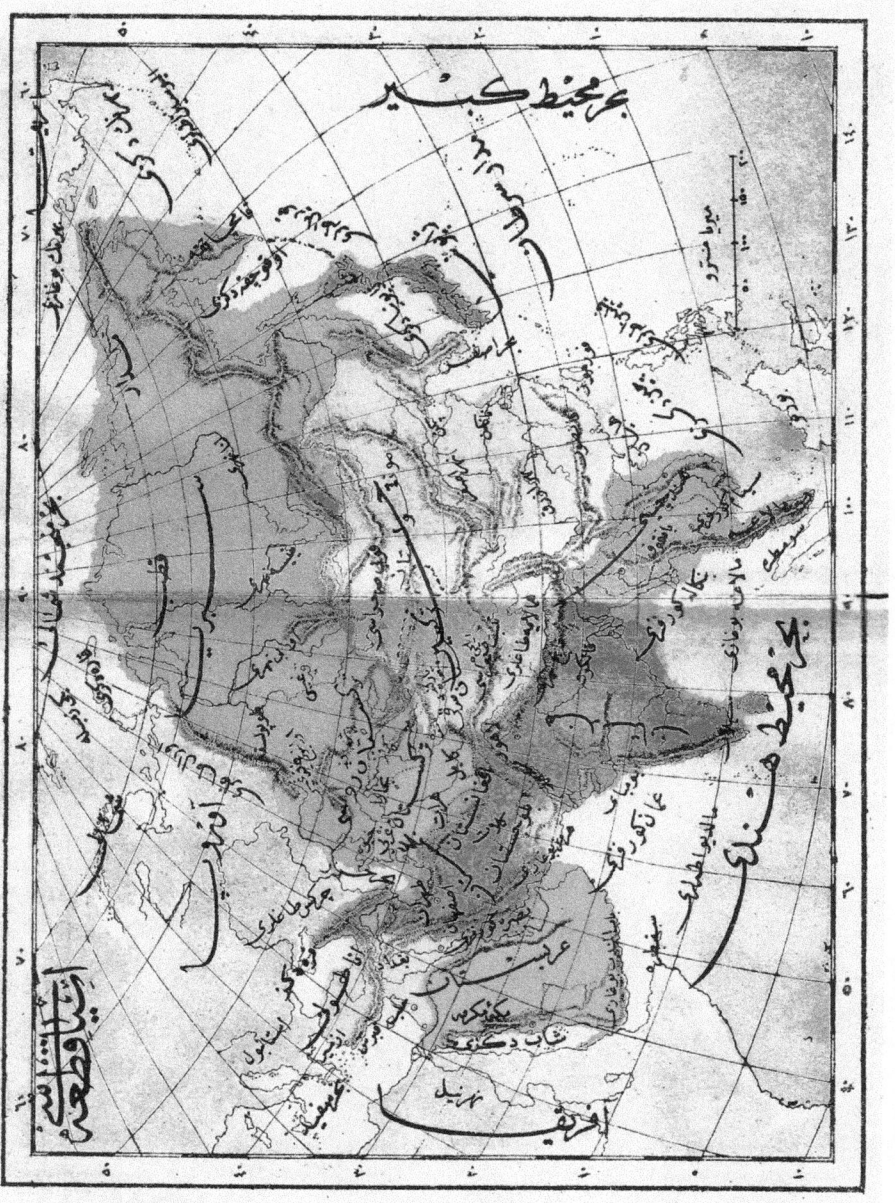

FIGURE 3.2 Map of Asia published by Selim Sabit Efendi in the geography textbook *Short Book on Geography* in 1874.

All of the geography textbooks published in the late Ottoman period divided the empire geographically into three parts: (1) Ottoman Europe (*Avrupa-yı Osmani*), (2) Ottoman Asia (*Asya-yı Osmani*), and (3) Ottoman Africa (*Afrika-yı Osmani*).[26] However, there was no consensus among the authors of these textbooks about how to subdivide the three continental parts of the empire. Selim Sabit Efendi divided Ottoman Asia into two parts: Anatolia and Arabia. According to him, whereas the "Country of Anatolia" included regions such as Baghdad, Basra, Aleppo, and Damascus, the "Country of Arabia" consisted of the regions of Hedjaz, Yemen, and Nejd.[27] Ahmet Cemal divided Ottoman Asia into six parts in his geography textbook written for military school students: (1) Anatolia; (2) the Aegean Islands; (3) Kurdistan; (4) Al-Jazeera, Iraq, and Al-Hasa; (5) Syria and Palestine; and (6) Hedjaz and Yemen.[28] The Kurdistan region included the cities of Erzurum, Van, Diyarbakır, Beyazıd, Erzincan, Harput, Mosul, Kirkuk, Sulaymaniyah, and Urfa.[29]

Geography textbooks published before the 1908 Revolution consisted of factual information about the Ottoman Empire and the continents, such as size, population, rivers, and mountains. Geography was defined as "a science, whose education is indispensable" for "people, who are in the service of the state."[30] Therefore, statesmen had to be educated about the Ottoman territories, "which spread into three continents."[31] Indeed, Mehmed Hikmet argued that, because of its geographic location, the Ottoman Empire was "in the center of world trade."[32] Whereas geography textbooks published before 1908 did not seek to promote patriotic loyalty to the homeland, nation, and state, this would become one of the most central themes in geography education after 1908. There was not a single reference to Ottomanism and Islamism, which were the two prevailing ideologies during Abdulhamid's reign. Another important characteristic of the geography textbooks published before 1908 was that students were not informed about the loss of Ottoman control over regions such as Bosnia, Tunis, Bulgaria, and Egypt. Although Bosnia was occupied by the Austro-Hungarian Empire in 1878, Tunis was lost to France in 1881, Britain became the de facto ruler of Egypt in 1882, and Bulgaria took control of Eastern Rumelia in 1885 and became a de facto independent state, these countries were still considered Ottoman possessions like any other.[33] However, students noticed the weakness of the Ottoman state in daily life when they read newspapers and realized that the vision of the grandeur of the Ottoman Empire presented in textbooks was an exaggeration. Hüseyin Cahid Yalçın (1875–1957), a well-known political journalist from the 1908 Revolution to the early 1950s who studied in military school in Serres and high school in Istanbul in the 1890s, stated his disappointment about Bulgaria's de facto independence: "We fooled ourselves by still referring to the 'Prince of Bulgaria' and the 'Governor of Eastern Rumelia.' In our schools we had our children read, 'Bulgaria is ours.' Bulgaria had been long gone."[34]

The content, approach, and even the title of textbooks changed dramatically with the 1908 Revolution. After the Young Turks' rise to power, geography education became an essential tool of "state patriotism," which aimed to create "a civic-territorial, indeed revolutionary-democratic, Ottoman political community by promoting an identification with the state and the country through the sultan and instituting representative government."[35] The objective was to imbue students with a sense of devotion to the Ottoman vatan. Maps and textbooks were the predominant educational means for promoting among students a sense of belonging to the Ottoman territories.[36] Young Turks sought to maintain the authority of the center against the rising local elites and secessionist national movements through education, which aimed to establish an imperial territorial consciousness for the Ottoman people. Geography education thus turned into one of the main instruments of Ottomanism and Ottoman patriotism.

After the revolution, Ali Tevfik revised his book *Geography of Ottoman Domains* and republished it in 1909. To instill Ottoman patriotism in students, he argued that "the people of Ottoman Asia were composed of various groups such as Turks, Tatars, Kurds, Circassians, Arabs, Lazes, Greeks, Armenians, and Jews. They are all united under the name of Ottoman and proud of it."[37] Behram Münir's geography textbook, published in 1912 before the Balkan Wars, had the title *Sacred Vatan or the Geography of Ottoman Domains*. Throughout the book, Behram Münir sought to impress Ottomanism and "Ottoman brotherhood" upon the students. In the introductory pages, he exalted the Ottoman territories in which "the first achievements of the civilization had appeared." Furthermore, the Ottoman Empire was located "in the most important part of the world and it possesses the most beautiful and exceptional regions of nature."[38]

Behram Münir analyzed demographic characteristics of the empire and classified the population according to ethnicity and religion. He classified all ethnic groups together as "Ottomans" and emphasized that the multiethnic character of the Ottoman population was a boon for the empire: "[The Ottoman Empire] should have advanced because it was composed by different nations. However, today, it is in a regrettable condition."[39] For Behram Münir, the reasons for the decadence of the empire included "heavy despotism, lack of patriotism in education, the influence of foreign countries on some sections of the society that caused these sections to act against the interests of vatan, the feeling of hatred among various groups that emerged because of history, and some people who worked for the interests of their ethnic groups that harmed other groups."[40] Although the empire was in a desperate situation, he recommended that students be hopeful about the future, because the establishment of a constitution in 1908 would restore the "Ottoman brotherhood" and the empire would soon advance.

Another radical departure from the traditional geography education was the emphasis put on the Turkish element in the empire. The language of the geography textbooks for primary school students started to use first-person plural constructions, "we" and "ours," when talking about Ottoman territories and wars. The tragic defeat of the empire in the Balkan Wars and the CUP's rise to power in 1913 had a crucial impact on textbooks. The CUP considered geography an educational tool to build social consciousness about patriotism and a sense of belonging to Ottoman territories among students. Mehmet Ali Tevfik (1889–1941), who was a leading member of Turkish Hearths as well as a member of the Unionist intellectual entourage, elaborated the theoretical framework of the patriotic geography education in a conference called "New Life, Spiritual Homeland," organized by the CUP in Thessaloniki on January 18, 1912.[41] Mehmet Ali Tevfik's speech was published by the journal *Genç Kalemler*.[42] A couple of months later, he published another article with the title, "Once Again Spiritual Homeland."[43]

According to Mehmet Ali Tevfik, there were two types of vatan: (1) physical vatan, and (2) spiritual vatan or spiritual homeland (*yurt*).[44] He argued that, since primitive times, human beings had a sense of loyalty to their native place or physical vatan where they were born. In modern times, patriotism and a sense of loyalty had developed among European peoples and now attached to a spiritual homeland. This spiritual homeland "connects present people with people who lived in the past, psychologically. As soon as memory and tradition mix with the ideas about vatan, physical vatan turns to spiritual vatan."[45] Mehmet Ali Tevfik claimed that the "Turkish nation and Turkish vatan should be constructed by learning Turkish ethnography, Turkish geography, Turkish history and a Turkish source of pride."[46] The major obstacle for "constructing Turkish vatan" was the "apathy of the youth towards its vatan."[47] Therefore, by using "methods in education," the youth would be indoctrinated with patriotism based on the concept of vatan. After the Balkan Wars, Mehmet Ali Tevfik identified geography education as the building block for raising a patriotic young generation who would be aware of "the lost territories [in the Balkans] up to the smallest villages."[48]

After 1908, geography not only became a central instrument for patriotic education in primary and high schools, but it was also institutionalized as a modern science in academia.[49] For modern geography professors such as Faik Sabri, Ali Macid, and Selim Mansur, all of whom trained in France, geography was not limited to the practice of enumerating districts and places. According to Faik Sabri, geography should analyze the influence of natural factors on people. However, Faik Sabri rejected the crude determinism of geography over politics. He argued that humans could overcome nature's power by using their intelligence:[50] "As a result of a remarkable transformation in the last years, geography's nature is not the same as it was thirty years ago. Geography [teaching] should leave aside the knotty and useless rigmaroles. In classes, students should not be forced to memorize names. Instead, geography should leave traces in the minds of students by teaching them unforgettable memories. Geography is constituted by reasons, ideas, and observations, not by spiritless names."[51]

After 1912, the promotion of revenge for the lost territories increased significantly in Turkish Ottoman textbooks. Textbooks published maps about the territories lost in Rumelia. Students read the dramatic stories of the migrants who escaped from the advancing Balkan armies. They were admonished not to forget Rumelia. The primary school geography book *Geography Stories for Children*, written by Saffet Bey (Geylangil, 1875–1944) and published in 1916, displayed "the map of revenge," which showed the territories lost by the Ottoman Empire in the Balkan Wars:[52]

"My dear sons, you all know this deplorable memory... They [Balkan states] took the beautiful Rumelia from us. Look at the map of revenge, which shows the places we lost... Do not forget this tragic disaster... Do not fail to remember their revenge even for a second" (see Figure 3.3).

A similar book, written by Faik Sabri (Duran, 1882–1943) with the title *Geography Reading for Children*, reminded students about the lost territories through a conversation between two children named Ferit and Reşit: "Reşit said: As you see Ferit, our country is located on three continents. We possess few places in Europe. However, in the past we had more territories. In the end, we lost all of them including the enormous region of Rumelia. In Europe, only Edirne and Istanbul remained in our hands... Ferit: We are not going to forget Rumelia, are we my brother? Reşit: You are right Ferit. We are never going to forget these places. We should always remember our defenseless coreligionists, who remained

FIGURE 3.3 "Map of Revenge," which displays the area lost by the Ottoman Empire during the Balkan Wars. It was published by Saffet Bey in the textbook *Geography Stories for Children* in 1916.

there."[53] Saffet Bey also analyzed the lost territories in the Balkans region by region in the textbook *Ottoman Geography*, published for high school students in 1916. He argued that "we have to teach our lost territories to the young generations, so that they won't be brought up without having a feeling of vatan."[54]

Ahmed Cevad's book *Talks on Vatan*, published in 1916 for secondary school students, is a prime example of the nationalist agitation at that time over the lost territories in the Balkan Wars. The dramatic conditions of refugees and the desperate situation of Muslim people in Rumelian cities captured by Balkan armies were narrated in detail. The author asked the question "Why were Turks and Muslims sacked from all parts of Rumelia by Bulgarians, Greeks, Serbs and Montenegrins?" The students were told that "because they are all our enemies and they all covet our vatan."[55] Ahmed Cevad classified vatan into two parts: (1) captured vatan, and (2) the remaining vatan, which was exposed to threats and attacks. For Ahmed Cevad, the only way to resist the enemies was that every person from the ages of 19 to 60 should be a soldier defending the vatan. He referred to children as "small soldiers" and advised them "to prepare themselves for the military service."[56]

In summary, there was a significant difference between textbooks printed before and after 1908. Whereas the former sought to conceal the deterioration of the empire, the latter repeatedly emphasized the territories lost by the Ottoman Empire since the end of the eighteenth century. Before 1908, students were taught about the Ottoman armies fighting in the center of Europe to capture Vienna and about the Ottoman navy controlling the Mediterranean and turning the Black Sea into an Ottoman lake.[57] Subsequently, they were instructed about how the empire had suffered defeats and had failed to maintain its control of Libya, Bosnia, Rumelia, Crimea, Egypt, Algeria, and Tunisia. Nevertheless, to prevent an inferiority complex in relation to the West among students, the remaining parts of the empire were compared with European countries in terms of territorial size. In *Ottoman Geography*, Saffet Bey told students that Anatolia was as big as France, Upper Jazeera and the Erzurum Plateau were larger than the sum of Romania and Montenegro, Al-Jazeera and Iraq were as large as Romania, Greece, and Bulgaria combined, Syria and Palestine were larger than Italy, and Ottoman Arabia was larger than the total of all Balkan states.[58]

The authors of geography textbooks argued that the existence of the Turkish element was essential for continuing the multiethnic structure of the empire. In the textbook *Sacred Vatan or Geography of Ottoman Domains*, Behram Münir argued that "Turks formed the Ottoman government and they stay away from acts which are harmful for others." He called "the existence of Turks as God's grace" as they "prevent the enmities among other groups."[59] In another textbook written by Saffet Bey, students were told that the total number of Turks was between eleven and twelve million and that they were "the constitutive part of the population in Anatolian cities."[60] As Turks were employed in the military and bureaucracy, Saffet Bey continued, they left economic activities to other ethnic groups. According to him, Turks had always respected the rights of other ethnicities, and if the Turks had not existed, other ethnic groups "would have slaughtered each other."[61] While Faik Sabri called Anatolia "the Turkish homeland" in his geography textbook, Mehmet Asım and Ahmed Cevad, in *The Book of the Anatolian Child*, called Istanbul "the head of vatan and Anatolia as its body" in a section entitled "Turkey."[62] Furthermore, students were introduced to the ethnic map of Anatolia (see Figure 3.4). The map divided the Anatolian population into four groups and gave the number of each population: Muslims (13,559,786), Greeks (1,614,981), Armenians (1,214,453), and other millets (226,006). In an earlier version of the same book, a map with the title "From Turan to Anatolia" was presented to students.[63] In it Turan was defined as "the vatan of old Turks"[64] (see Figure 3.5).

Ottoman geography textbooks also included information about other ethnic groups, including Arabs, Kurds, Greeks, and Armenians. An examination of more than twenty textbooks published between 1874 and 1919 did not reveal any derogatory expressions about other ethnic groups. Generally, the authors of these books presented students with factual information about various ethnic groups. Usually Arabs were praised and called an "intelligent" nation, and Kurds were identified as a tribal society. The authors emphasized that whereas Kurds and Arabs were concentrated in particular regions, Turks, Armenians, Greeks, and Jews were dispersed all over the empire.

Almost all of the geography textbooks published after the Balkan Wars put a special emphasis on Anatolia and identified it as the "homeland of the Turks." However, there was an indistinctness about the geographical

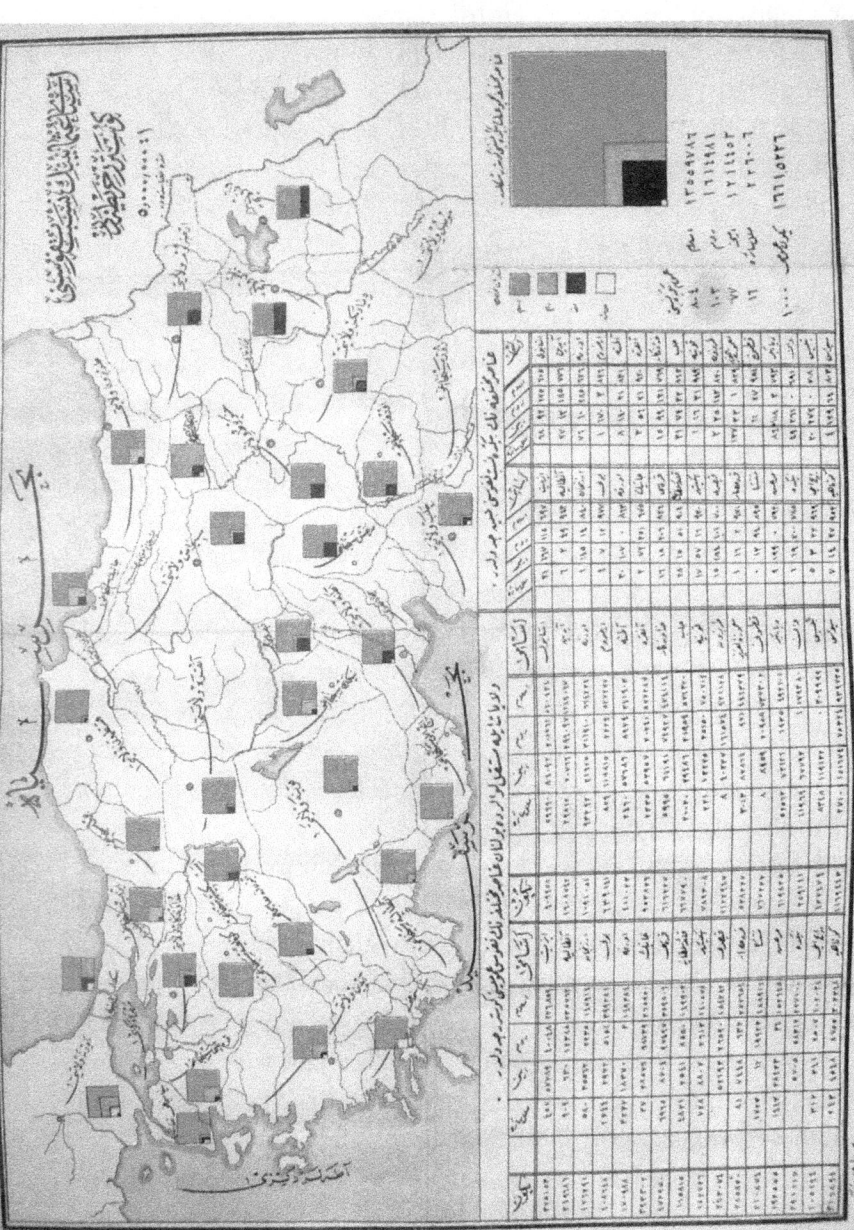

FIGURE 3.4 "The Map Showing the Distribution of Population in Ottoman Asia," published by Mehmet Asım in the textbook *The Book of the Anatolian Child* in 1919. In squares, dark gray illustrates the proportion of the Muslim population, light gray shows the proportion of the Greek population, and black shows the proportion of the Armenian population. It is striking that the map is organized according to the Ottoman millet system although it was published as late as 1919.

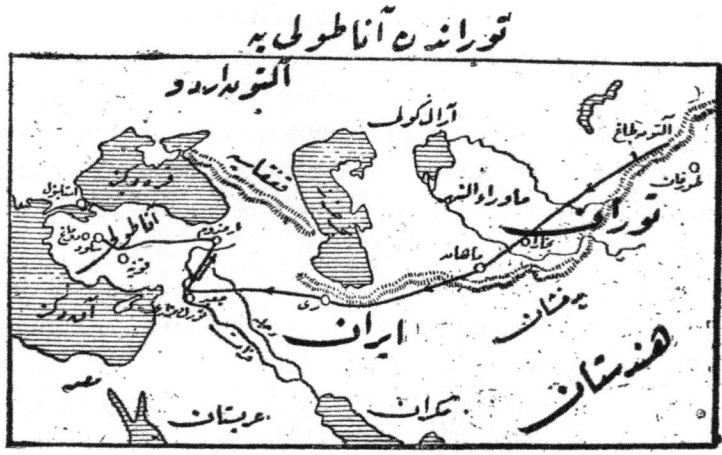

FIGURE 3.5 "From Turan to Anatolia," published by Mehmet Asım in the textbook *The Book of the Anatolian Child* in 1917. By marking the area east of the Caspian Sea as "Turan," this map seeks to concretize the idealized concept of Turan. The Russian territories in the north of the Black Sea are marked as Golden Horde. Moreover, the migration path of the Turkish tribes starts in the map from Altundağ (Golden Mountain or Kin Shan) in Central Asia and continues to Bukhara, Mahan, Rey in Iran, the Tomb of Ja'bar, and Erzurum, and ends in Söğüt in Western Anatolia.

borders of Anatolia in most of the textbooks. Anatolia did not include cities such as Erzurum, Van, and Diyarbakir, in the region of Upper Jazeera. Indeed, the two leading geographers, Faik Sabri and Saffet Bey, claimed that the area of Anatolia was 501,000 square kilometers, which was 254,868 square kilometers less than the current area of Anatolia.[65] Although Anatolia had a special status in geography textbooks, this did not mean that authors did not consider other regions a part of the Ottoman vatan. In the geography textbook *Geography Stories for Children*, students were encouraged to travel to all Ottoman territories: "The Ottoman Empire is so beautiful that our vatan should be traveled in order to appreciate these beauties."[66] Saffet Bey told the story of a teenager who traveled from Zonguldak, located in the western Black Sea Coast, to Yemen. During the journey, students were informed about Ottoman cities Izmir, Beirut, Mecca, and Jeddah, which were all considered indispensable parts of the Ottoman vatan.

After 1912, paralleling the political developments, students were told detailed ethnic information about Turks. Almost all of the textbooks published at this time claimed that Turks belong to the Turanic race. Maps about Turan were published in order to visualize the journey of Turks from Turan to Anatolia. Between 1919 and 1923, because of the occupation of various regions of Anatolia and the National Liberation War, very few geography books were written and published. Those published during this period were new editions of older books. With the establishment of the republic, the content and discourse of the textbooks changed fundamentally once again.

TURKIFICATION OF GEOGRAPHY AFTER THE ESTABLISHMENT OF THE REPUBLIC

As examined in the previous chapter, the discourse of the ruling elite during the first two years of the national liberation struggle was based on the unity of all Muslim ethnic groups in Anatolia. The leading political figures emphasized Turkeyism rather than Turkish nationalism. After decisive victories against the Greek and Armenian forces, the discourse of national struggle started to change, and Turkish nationalism came into prominence. Rıza Nur (1879–1942), who served as the minister of education in the first Ankara government in 1920 and was, after İsmet İnönü, the second-most important member of the Turkish delegation at the Lausanne Conference, published an article entitled "The Character of Our State and Its National Name," in the journal *Türk Yurdu* in November 1924. He argued that the ancient nations of Anatolia, such as "Urartu, Elam, Sumer, Tobal, Hittite, and Kumak" all belonged to the Turan family.[67] These were later assimilated by Greeks, Romans, and Byzantines and lost their Turanic characters. According to Rıza Nur, with the arrival of Turks in Anatolia in the eleventh century, Seljuks turned the assimilated people of Anatolia back to their original roots, and thus did Anatolia become "a new Turkistan or a new Turan."[68] Although Rıza Nur was exiled less than one year later after the publication of this article due to his opposition to Mustafa Kemal and İsmet İnönü, Kemalists envisaged a geography and history that were very similar to Rıza Nur's nationalistic worldview. At the end of the article, Rıza Nur compared a number of names, such as the Turkish state, the Anatolian state, the Turkmen state, and Turkey for the newly established republic. He argued that the name "Turkey" was the best alternative as "we are Turks of Turkey within the great Turkish family."[69]

In November of 1925, Mustafa Kemal stated in his speech before the Ankara Law School that the cement that kept the nation together for centuries had changed with the establishment of the republic: "Instead of religious and sectarian relationships, people are united with the cement of Turkish nationality." On April 26, 1926, Mustafa Kemal told the delegates of Turkish Hearths that "we are explicitly nationalist and Turkish nationalists. Our Republic is founded on the Turkish nation. If the members of this society are molded with Turkish culture, the Republic, which is based on this society, will be stronger."[70] In accordance with the rising nationalistic political discourse, the Third Congress of the Republican People's Party set forth as part of its program a definition of vatan that regarded the remnants of ancient Anatolian civilization as a part of Turkish national heritage: "Vatan is the historical vestiges of the Turkish nation that are under the soil [of Anatolia] and at the same time it is the homeland within our current borders."[71]

According to Bernard Lewis, the major obstacle for Kemalists was that "the loss of Empire was recent, and still rankled with many, to whom the idea of a comparatively small nation-state seemed unsatisfying and unattractive."[72] Instead of supporting pan-Turkist ambitions for a Turkish Empire, which would unite all Anatolian and Central Asian Turks in one state, Kemalists initiated a campaign of territorial nationalism. This territorial nationalism would strengthen the Turkish people's national psyche, which had been undermined by uninterrupted military defeats and territorial losses since 1774: "Kemal sought to adapt and inculcate the new idea of an Anatolian Turkish fatherland. His aim was to destroy what remained of the Islamic and Ottoman feelings of loyalty, to counter the distractions of pan-Islamic and pan-Turkist appeals, and to forge a new loyalty, of the Turkish nation to its homeland."[73] Lewis argued that Kemalists chose history as an instrument to raise a new patriotic generation, who "considered Turkish Republic as the final fruition of land and people." Although teaching history was a decisive instrument in inculcating Turkish people with territorial nationalism through the republican educational institutions, another discipline, geography, was also considered by Kemalists as a valuable instrument to realize their objectives, and geography played an important role in the nationalization of the territory of the republic.

The change of the political discourse about the vatan also affected the textbooks printed after 1923. One of the first textbooks published after 1923 was *Information about Vatan*, written for primary school students by Muhiddin Adil, who was a professor of law.[74] Students were told that vatan was "the territories, sea, and air that belong to us and to our ancestors."[75] Muhiddin Adil argued that there were two types of vatan. While physical vatan included "territories owned by us, ideational vatan is larger than this. Every place in which Turks live and Turkish is spoken belongs to ideational vatan."[76] The book also praised Mustafa Kemal and the National Liberation War. Mustafa Kemal was identified as a "chieftain" who "sought to strangle the enemy in the center of the mother vatan."[77]

Between 1928 and 1932, two fundamental reforms drastically changed the cultural life of Turkish society. The first was replacing the Arabic script with the Latin alphabet in 1928. Mustafa Kemal himself was involved in teaching the new alphabet by traveling to various Anatolian cities and encouraging everyone to learn the new letters. As Feroz Ahmad has argued, the alphabet revolution, "more than virtually any other, loosened Turkey's ties with the Islamic world to its east and irrevocably forced the country to face west."[78] The success of the alphabet revolution encouraged the Kemalist elite to remove all Arabic and Persian words from the Turkish language. In a couple of years, they had created a pure Turkish language by reintroducing words from Turkic dialects in Central Asia and ancient literary sources.[79]

The second reform was the construction of the Turkish Historical Thesis in the years 1931 and 1932. According to the thesis, Central Asia, which was the ancient homeland of the Turks, was the cradle of civilization. Due to drought, Turkish tribes had migrated to other parts of Eurasia and formed new civilizations in Mesopotamia, Anatolia, and Europe. By stating that Hittites and other ancient Anatolian societies were part of Turkish civilization, Kemalists sought to prove that "Anatolia had been a Turkish country since time immemorial, thus extending the roots of the citizens of the republic in the soil they inhabited."[80]

The Turkish Historical Thesis influenced geography textbooks published after 1932, which analyzed Central Asia thoroughly since it was considered "first and oldest vatan of Turks."[81] In the textbook *General Geography* written by Saffet Geylangil, Turks were defined as "the oldest nation in the world. They have thousands years of history. These distinguished people had created empires in China and Central Asia and contrary to the claims of Europeans they did not arrive in Anatolia only a few hundred years ago. Presumably they had come [to Anatolia] a couple of thousand years ago, established powerful states, and left traces of their civilization." Under the influence of rising racism in 1930s Europe, textbooks published maps of Eurasia that divided the continent according to races (see Figure 3.6). Students were told that "the great Turkish block lives in vast territories . . . larger than 5 million square kilometers" and stretching from China to Bosnia.[82] In examining the neighboring regions of Turkey, all the geography textbooks stressed that these countries had been ruled by Turks during the long Ottoman times. To make up for the possible disappointment among students who might think that Turks were squeezed in Anatolia due to the loss of vast territories, the textbooks had a specific chapter about other "Turkish" groups outside Turkey. The textbook *New Geography Lessons* written by Besim Darkot and Cemal Arif Alagöz had a chapter titled "Turks on the Earth." According to the authors, the "Turkish nation differs from other nations with its ancient history and the large space it occupies in the world." The chapter studied the Turks according to their geographic locations in Eurasia: "Turks in Turkey, Caucasian Turks, Turks in Iran, Turks in Romania, Northern Turks, Central Asian Turks, and Turks in Northern Asia"[83] (Figure 3.7). Similarly, in his textbook *Geography*, Faik Sabri devoted a chapter to "Turkish Countries," which divided Central Asia into two parts: "Turkistan," under Soviet control, and "Turkeli," which is the present-day Xinjiang region of China. Students were introduced to these "Turkish Countries" via photos depicting daily life in Central Asian societies that emphasized "the Turkishness" of these people (Figure 3.8).[84]

In 1929, less than a year after the alphabet revolution, Faik Sabri wrote the first geography textbook in Latin letters with the title *The Geography of Turkey*.[85] The book was printed by the state press in Istanbul and had excellent print quality. Faik Sabri argued that Turkey was located "in a prominent place of the Earth."[86] This was also illustrated with a map, which showed Turkey in the center of Asia, Europe, and Africa. Indeed, Faik Sabri used spatial representations such as maps, graphics, and figures throughout the book to demonstrate to the students that they belonged to a country that was larger than its neighbors and that occupied one of the most important places on earth. One figure compared Turkey's

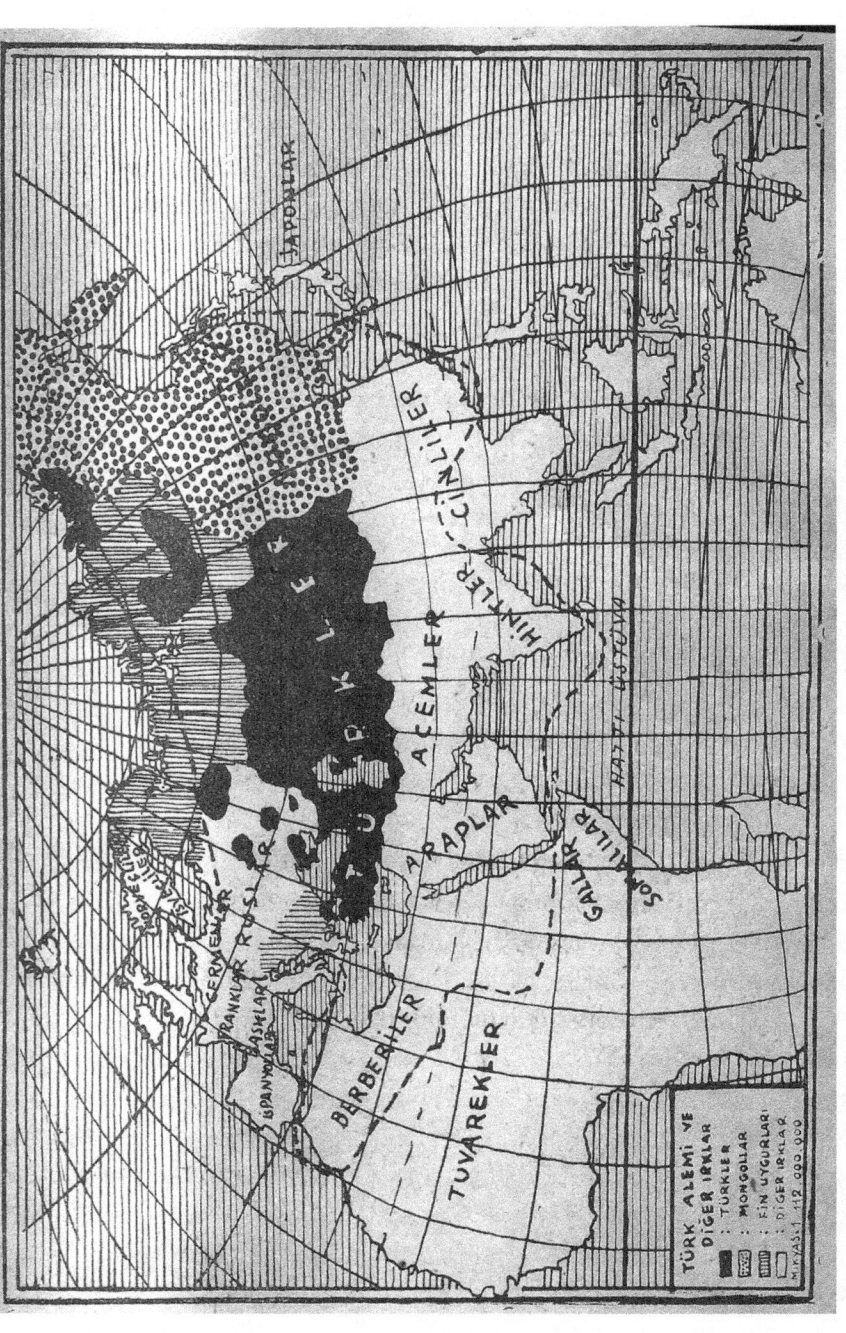

FIGURE 3.6 Map of races published in the *General Geography* in 1938 by Saffet Geylangil. It is important to note that during the 1930s, geographers in Turkey tended to see the world as divided into races. Black indicates the distribution of the "Turks." Interestingly, the author included Mongols (the dotted area in eastern Asia) and Finno-Uighur elements (vertically striped areas in northern Asia and the Balkans). The names of the non-Turkic races, including Iranians, Russians, Germanic people, Arabs, Indians, and Chinese, were also indicated.

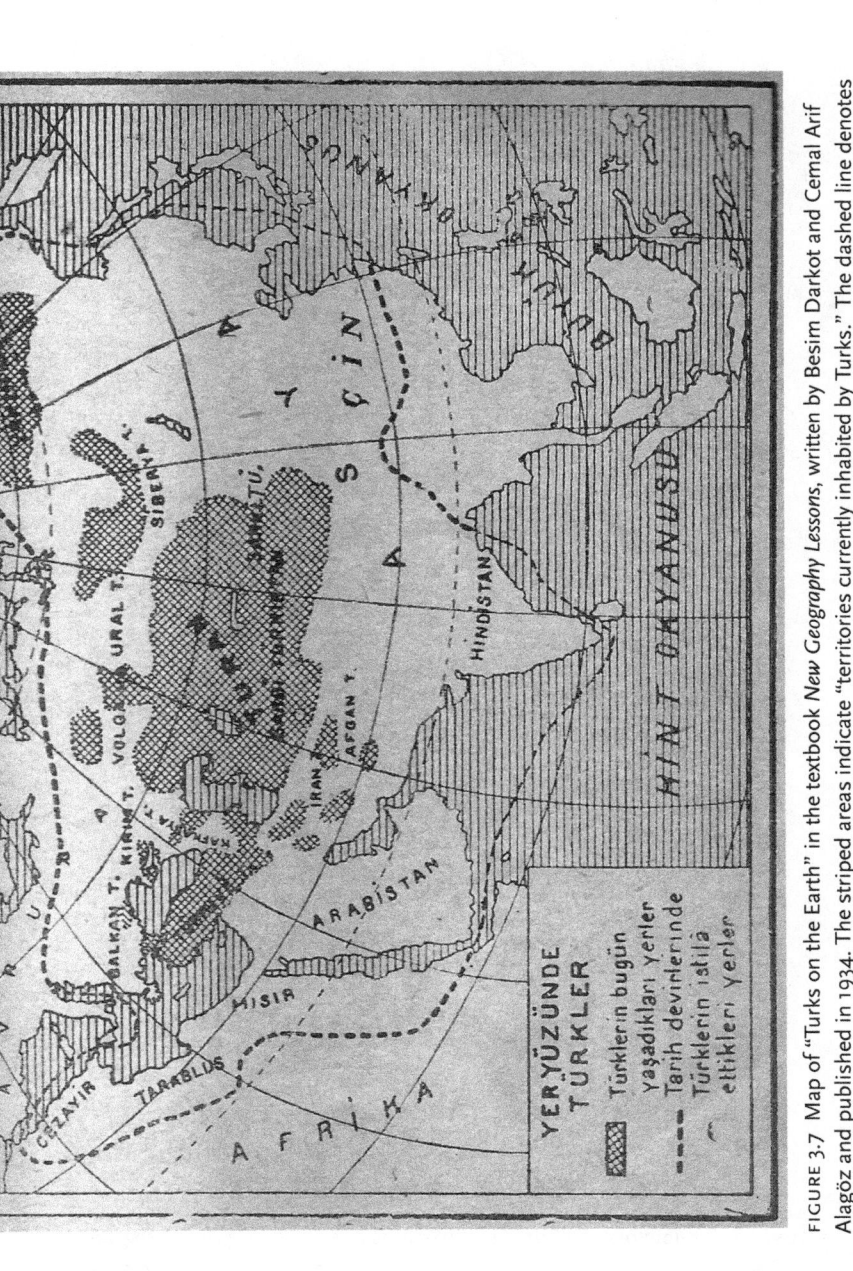

FIGURE 3.7 Map of "Turks on the Earth" in the textbook *New Geography Lessons*, written by Besim Darkot and Cemal Arif Alagöz and published in 1934. The striped areas indicate "territories currently inhabited by Turks." The dashed line denotes the boundaries of "territories invaded by Turks throughout the historical ages." Note that the area east of Aral Lake is shown as "Turan." Other Turkic groups, such as Balkan Turks, Iranian Turks, and Caucasian Turks, are also indicated on the map.

Türk Anayurdunun bugünkü sakinlerinden: Yarkent'li genç kız. Anadolu çocuklarına nekadar benzediğine dikkat ediniz.

FIGURE 3.8 A photo of a girl from Central Asia as published in 1932 in *Geography*, by Faik Sabri. The legend under the photo emphasizes the similarity between people in Anatolia and Central Asia: "A current resident of the Turkish homeland: Young lady from Yarkant [in Xinjiang]. Please note how similar she is to Anatolian children."

territories with Balkan countries and confirmed that Turkey was larger than the sum of Romania, Yugoslavia, Bulgaria, and Greece. In another figure, students were informed that Turkey's population was larger than that of all of its neighbors. In order to prove this, Faik Sabri displayed Armenia and Georgia instead of the Soviet Union, despite the fact that these two countries were not independent at that time and were parts of the Soviet Union. Furthermore, while the citizens of all other countries were represented by ethnic clothes, residents of Turkey were represented by an apparently Western man with a hat, jacket, and tie (see Figure 3.9).

Similar to geography books published after 1912, Faik Sabri's book included a number of maps that showed the territories lost by the Ottoman Empire in the last two centuries. However, the major objective of the author was not to inculcate vengeful ideas among students about

FIGURE 3.9 Comparison of Turkey's population with its neighbors', in Faik Sabri's book *The Geography of Turkey* published in 1929. Interestingly, although Turkey was represented by an apparently Western man with a hat, jacket, and tie, all of Turkey's neighbors, including Greece and Bulgaria, were represented with figures wearing ethnic clothes. The countries from left to right are Bulgaria, Greece, Turkey, Iran, Iraq, Syria, Georgia, and Armenia.

these lost territories. Rather, Faik Sabri sought to justify the establishment of the new Turkish state, as Turks became an ethnically homogenous society in Anatolia as a result of a centuries-old retreat from the Balkans, the Caucasus, and the Middle East (Figure 3.10): "Finally Turkey has become a politically and ethnically unified country in a territory that is inhabited only by Turks . . . The Republican government was established and a new Turkey was born within the national borders."[87] Faik Sabri claimed that as a result of the National Liberation War, "non-Turks and those who are foreign to Turkishness either remained out of the vatan or were removed from it and by doing so the national unity was accomplished."[88] In a section titled "The People and the Government of Turkey," students were introduced to non-Turkish Muslim groups, such as Kurds, Circassians, Bosnians, Albanians, and Georgians. However, the author argued that these non-Turkish Muslim groups were "eventually Turkified." There was also information about the non-Muslim groups of Greeks, Armenians, and Jews.[89]

In the secondary school geography textbook *Geography Courses*, written by one of the prominent geographers of the republic, Hamit Sadi (1892–1968), Turkey was defined "as the name of the new state established by the Turkish nation after the disintegration of the Ottoman reign."[90] Students were taught about the main difference between the Ottoman Empire and Turkey: "Unlike the [Ottoman] empire, this state [Turkey] does not include various nations and countries. It forms a unity with the nation and the country. As a geographical term, Turkey represents the national territory of the newly established Turkish state."[91] In the section "Population and Administrative Sections," non-Turkish groups were specified as Greeks, Armenians, and Jews. According to the author, the non-Muslims in Anatolia, whose population was less than 400,000, "mushroomed" in Anatolia during Ottoman rule. Furthermore, students were told that "there are around one million Kurdish-speaking people." Whereas geography textbooks published until the first half of the 1930s emphasized the existence of non-Turkish groups, such as Greeks, Armenians, Jews, and Kurds, textbooks published after the 1940s did not even mention the names of these groups. For example, the geography textbook *The Geography of Turkey*, written by Besim Darkot, analyzed the characteristics of the population of Turkey. The author told the students that there were "foreign ethnic groups" in the Ottoman Empire, such as "Arabs, Albanians,

FIGURE 3.10 This map published in Faik Sabri's book *The Geography of Turkey* shows the territories of the Ottoman Empire in the seventeenth century, before the Balkan Wars and the Republic of Turkey. The author depicts the far-stretching Ottoman borders anachronistically as "Turkish borders."

Serbians, Greeks, Armenians and Bulgarians."[92] Darkot emphasized various factors that contributed to the establishment of a homogenous society in Turkey: (1) the countries populated by these ethnic groups had seceded; (2) Greeks had migrated to Greece as a result of the population exchange; and (3) Armenians had left Anatolia. As a result of these factors, "the population of Turkey consists of only Turks."[93] There was not a single reference to the existence of Kurds in Turkey in this textbook, as was the case in textbooks published after the 1940s.

Another key characteristic of the textbooks published after 1928 was their extensive use of maps in order to imbue the students with awareness of the "geo-body" of the newly established Turkish state. As Thongchai Winichakul has stated, "a map merely represents something which already exists objectively. In the history of the geo-body, this relationship was reversed. A map anticipated a spatial reality, not vice versa. In other words, a map was a model for, rather than a model of, what it purported to represent. A map was not a transparent medium between human beings and space. It was an active mediator."[94] In the case of Turkey, the use of various maps contributed to the construction of the narrative of the nation and the naturalization of the borders of the republic. The first print edition of Mustafa Kemal's famous six-day-long speech, delivered in October 1927 to the Republican People's Party congress, included the map of Turkey according to the Sèvres Treaty. Mustafa Kemal analyzed the accomplishments of the National Liberation War by comparing the borders of Turkey drawn by the treaties of Sèvres and Lausanne. Consequently, textbooks published after 1928 used maps to compare the borders of Turkey according to the Sèvres Treaty and the Lausanne Treaty. In this way, the establishment of the Republican regime was justified in the eyes of students, as Mustafa Kemal, the founder of the republic, was portrayed as a savior who had liberated the invaded parts of the Turkish homeland. Mümtaz Soysal, who served as the foreign minister of Turkey in 1994, argued that the textbooks constructed a collective "Sèvres syndrome" for all Turkish people: "The map of 'Anatolia according to Sèvres' remained in the pages of schoolbooks as a symbol of hostile intentions on the last piece of land left to Turks at the end of their historic adventure from the steppes of Central Asia to the center of Europe. The memory of the map is always very vivid in the minds of all those who have gone through the republican educational system and still influences the thinking of both civilian and military cadres, creating a suspicious attitude toward any suggestion of encouraging regionalism or establishing an independent Kurdish state, even outside the present borders of the Republic."[95]

In the textbook *The Geography of Turkey*, Faik Sabri published two maps of Turkey (see Figures 3.11 and 3.12). The first map shows the borders of Turkey according to the Sèvres Treaty. According to this map, Izmir was given to Greece, Erzurum and Trabzon were given to Armenia, and an autonomous region was established in the east, which "was prepared for a probable independence."[96] The map also shows the Italian, British, and French zones of influence. Only the remaining white area in the center of Anatolia was left to Turkey. The other map showed the borders of Turkey after Lausanne and the demilitarized zones in the Straits and in Thrace. Moreover, in the text attached to the maps, students were told how the Turkish nation under the leadership of "the savior"—that is, Mustafa Kemal—had repelled the enemies: "The Lausanne Treaty was a glamorous political success that defends the independence and the interests of Turkey. If this map is compared with the map of the Sèvres project on the opposite page, it is easily realized that national struggle achieved great results. Except for Turks living in Mosul, Iskenderun, and Antakya, Turkey assured the national borders, which include all the regions in Anatolia that are inhabited by Turks."[97]

Another textbook, *Geography for Secondary Schools*, written by Abdülkadir Sadi and published in 1935, displayed a similar map, with the caption "Sèvres is Death, Lausanne is Life; Sèvres belongs to the Sultanate, Lausanne belongs to the Republic."[98] The author also exalted Mustafa Kemal, whose success was "to take the Turkish nation from the abyss of Sèvres to the zenith of Lausanne" (Figure 3.13).[99]

GEOGRAPHY EDUCATION AFTER WORLD WAR II

İsmail Habib Sevük (1892–1954), a journalist and ardent supporter of Kemalism, published an account of his travels throughout Anatolia in a book entitled *Writings from the Homeland*.[100] When the book was published in 1943, two decades had passed since the establishment of the republic, and Kemalist policies were entrenched in political institutions and social life. In the introductory pages of the book, Sevük emphasized that there had been apathy among intellectuals about Anatolia before 1923. In a similar way, Şevket Süreyya Aydemir, who was born in Rumelia, admit-

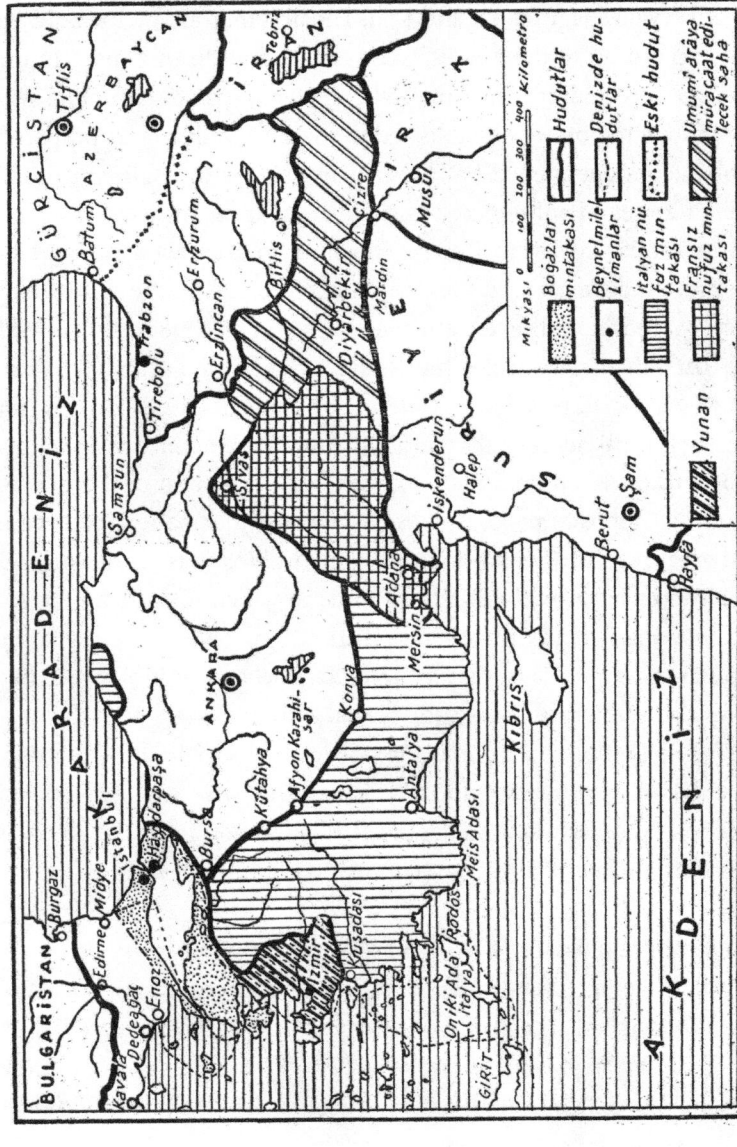

FIGURE 3.11 Map of Turkey according to the Sèvres Treaty as published by Faik Sabri in the textbook *The Geography of Turkey* in 1929.

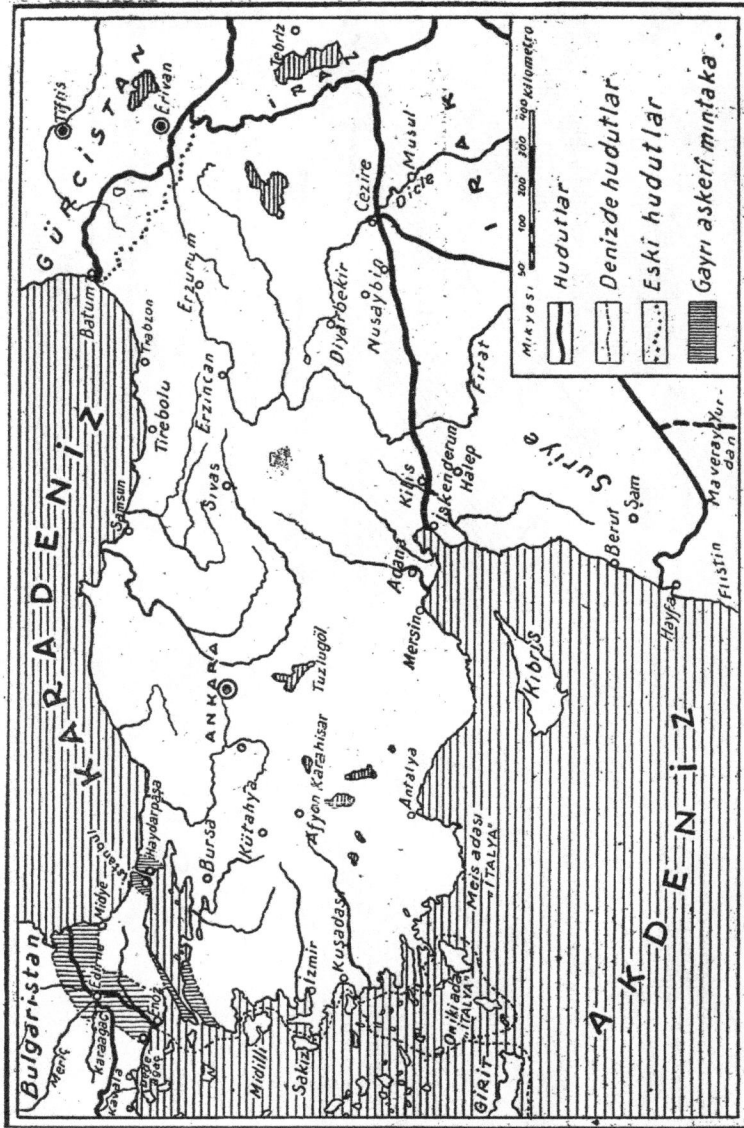

FIGURE 3.12 Map of Turkey according to the Lausanne Treaty as published by Faik Sabri in the textbook *The Geography of Turkey* in 1929.

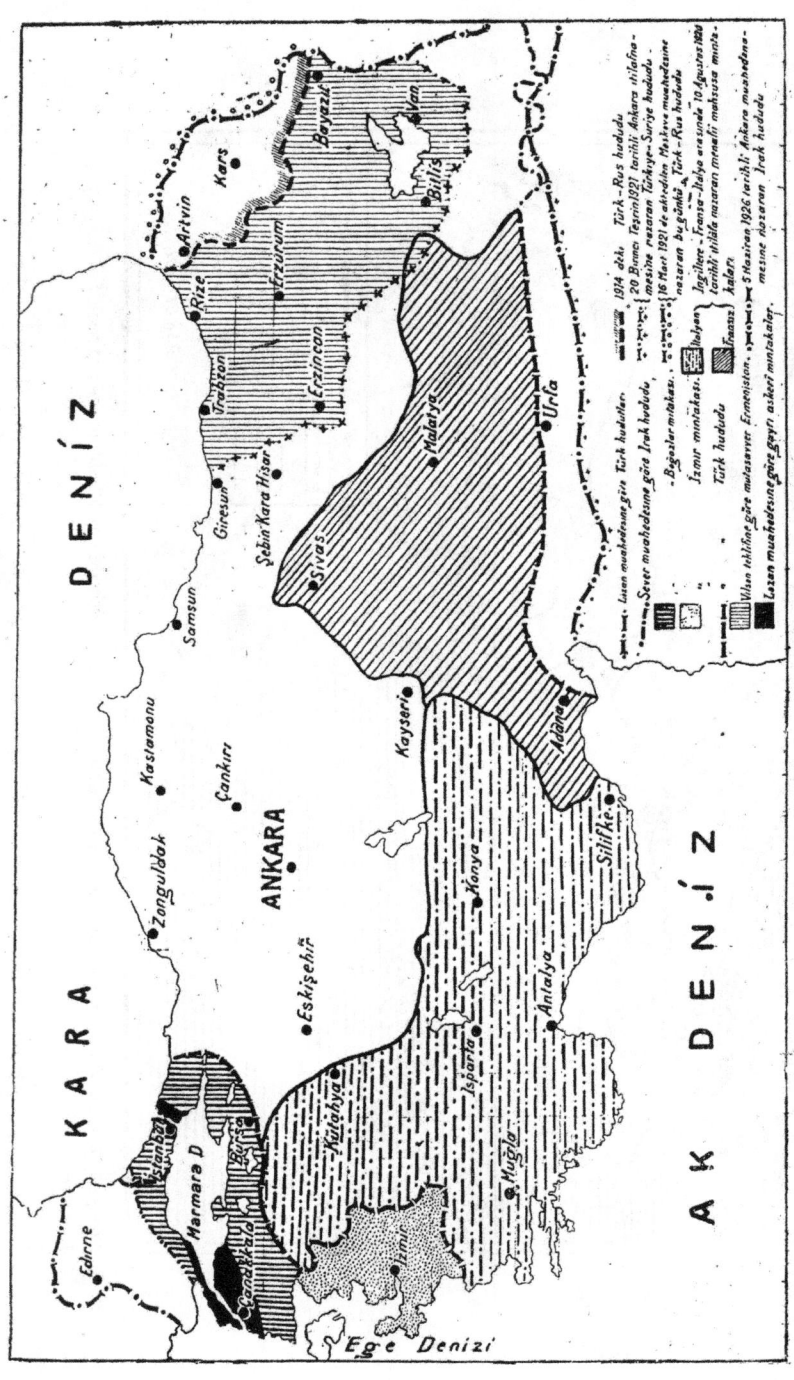

FIGURE 3.13 This map indicates the differences between the borders of the Sèvres and Lausanne treaties. Based on the Sèvres Treaty, the map shows Izmir and the Straits region outside of Turkey. The part of the eastern Anatolia from Trabzon to Van is depicted as Armenia. The other two regions were French and Italian influence zones. Turkey's borders based on the Lausanne Treaty are shown with the dotted lines and include all areas lost with the Sèvres Treaty. This map was published by Abdülkadir Sadi in the textbook *Geography for Secondary Schools* in 1935.

ted that children of Rumelia knew nothing about Anatolia other than what they had imagined: "We had realized that the real Anatolia had been totally different from our imaginations and desires. This had been the biggest disillusionment of our life and I believe that we were totally committed to Anatolia because of this disillusionment."[101] Similarly, Sevük argued that "vatan was disintegrating because of our lack of information about vatan." Anatolia had remained a backward country during the six-century-long Ottoman rule, Sevük continued, because Turks wasted the inexhaustible power of Anatolia in faraway countries.[102] However, the establishment of modern Turkey signified the end of the unfortunate fate of Anatolia. Throughout the book, Sevük sought to familiarize Anatolia to the readers as if it had been an unknown country. For example, the river Euphrates filled the hole opened in the consciousness of Turks due to the loss of the Danube. Sevük talked to the Euphrates: "For me you became a Danube."[103] Sevük further argued that after winning the national struggle, Kemalists started to wage an industrial war to make Anatolia an advanced country. The nationalization of the coal mines in the Zonguldak region was labeled as "İnönü and Sakarya" wars of national development.[104]

Alan K. Henrikson has argued that "one of the first steps of a newly independent country is often to commission a national atlas, to print stamps with a map of the country's outline on them, and otherwise to use the emblem of the map to assert the country's new identity in a new setting—a new pride of place."[105] In the same way, Kemalists were waging another war in geography education in order to create a national homeland in Anatolia. In June of 1941, the First Geography Congress brought together all prominent geographers of Turkey, such as Faik Sabri Duran, Saffet Geylangil, Besim Darkot, and Hamit Sadi Selen, under the leadership of the minister of education, Hasan Ali Yücel. President İsmet İnönü also visited the congress and was debriefed about the recent developments in the discipline of geography. In the opening speech of the congress, Yücel defined the mission of geography education: "The primary subject of geography is [to study] every region and aspect of our vatan, Turkish country, and Turkish nation. Our mission is to examine the Turkish vatan—we sacrifice our life in order to defend it and we are ready to sacrifice everything we own—from the perspective of science and train the future generations with the same perspective."[106]

The congress's major task was to divide Turkey into geographic regions and to identify their borders. Geographers categorized Turkey into seven regions: (1) the Marmara, (2) the Aegean, (3) the Mediterranean, (4) the Black Sea, (5) the Inner Anatolian, (6) the Eastern Anatolian, and (7) the Southeast Anatolian.[107] Geographers preferred to use the names of the seas for the coastal regions. Inner regions were named according to their locations in Anatolia.[108] Geographers were hesitant to use regional names such as Lazistan and Kurdistan, which were widely used during Ottoman times, as they had ethnic connotations.

One of the most important consequences of the First Geography Congress was the institutionalization of geography education in secondary and high schools. Geography courses became compulsory for all students from the sixth to eleventh grades for two hours per week. The congress decided to organize geography education into three different categories. In the sixth and ninth grades, the objective was to teach about general geography. Whereas seventh and tenth grades' geography education was about countries and continents, in the eighth and eleventh grades students were taught about Turkey's geography.[109] Moreover, the Ministry of Education established a strict monitoring mechanism over geography textbooks and teaching materials.

Five years after the First Geography Congress in 1946, the RPP decided to end the one-party regime, and in 1950, the Democrat Party took power after free elections. Political parties, which controlled the National Education Ministry after 1950, changed the textbooks according to their worldview. An examination of geography textbooks published after World War II reveals that the content of the textbooks was heavily influenced by the changes in the domestic and foreign politics of Turkey. During the thirty years between 1950 and 1980, center-right parties dominated Turkey's politics except for short periods after military coups in 1960 and 1971. As these parties wholeheartedly supported Turkey's relations with the North Atlantic Treaty Organization (NATO), geography textbooks published during this period gave special emphasis to Turkey's role in the "Western Bloc." Furthermore, as the center-right parties embraced nationalism and conservatism, textbooks published after 1950 had a clear nationalist perspective. The military coup in 1980, which was initiated after long and bloody conflict between leftist and rightist groups during the 1970s, resulted in a complete change in geography education.

Textbooks inculcated students with the worldview of the military, which imagined Turkey surrounded by "internal and external enemies." Students were disciplined and trained as soldiers of the Turkish nation who should be prepared to sacrifice themselves to save their homeland. After the second half of the 1990s, various civil and political actors challenged the political discourse based on national security. For example, the Turkish Industrialists and Businessmen's Association (TÜSİAD) supported a complete reform in education and published alternative textbooks in history, geography, and philosophy.

The content of the textbook *The Geography of Turkey*, published in 1950, reflected Turkey's changing perceptions about international politics. At the beginning of the book, there was a map that showed Turkey in the center of the earth. Authors identified Turkey "as the real bridge between Asia and Europe" (Figure 3.14).[110] By showing the world map centered on Turkey to students, the authors aimed to demonstrate the primary importance of Turkey's geopolitical position.

According to the authors, the current borders of Turkey were shaped as a result of a centuries-old political struggle, as the Republic of Turkey was established on the territories that "had been the center of the Ottoman Empire and the origin of its power."[111] As mentioned earlier, unlike textbooks published in the 1930s, non-Turkish ethnic groups were not mentioned throughout the book: "First of all our borders are national. Within our current borders, the number of non-Turkish citizens is negligible (just 2 percent of the whole population of the country); and they are concentrated in a couple of large cities (especially in Istanbul). Nevertheless, the percentage of minorities is very high in our neighbors. For example, minorities in Greece constitute 8 percent and in Bulgaria 15.6 percent of the population. On the other hand, outside of our state borders, there are a significant number of Turks who remained in the neighboring countries."[112] Indeed, the subject of the Turks living outside of the borders of Turkey was one of the most prevalent subjects in the textbooks published after 1950. Whereas detailed information was given to the students about Turks in Greece, Bulgaria, Soviet Union, Iraq, Syria, and Iran, non-Turkish ethnic groups in Turkey remained a terra incognita for students.

Geography textbooks published during the Cold War attached special importance to Turkey's membership in NATO. The textbooks *Geography of States* and *The Geography of Turkey*, written by Sırrı Erinç and Sami

FIGURE 3.14 The world map in the textbook *The Geography of Turkey*, written by Sırrı Erinç and Sami Öngör and published in 1950. Turkey is shown disproportionately larger and in the center of the world.

Öngör and published in 1975 and 1976, respectively, informed students in their introductory chapters about political developments after World War II.[113] The authors examined states in three categories based on economic and political characteristics: (1) capitalist countries, (2) socialist or communist countries, and (3) nonaligned countries. Students were given detailed information about the international organizations NATO, the Central Treaty Organization (CENTO), the Southeast Asia Treaty Organization, the Warsaw Pact, the European Economic Community, the Council for Mutual Assistance, and the Council of Europe.[114] Turkey's membership in the Western Bloc was also displayed with maps (Figure 3.15). The authors defined

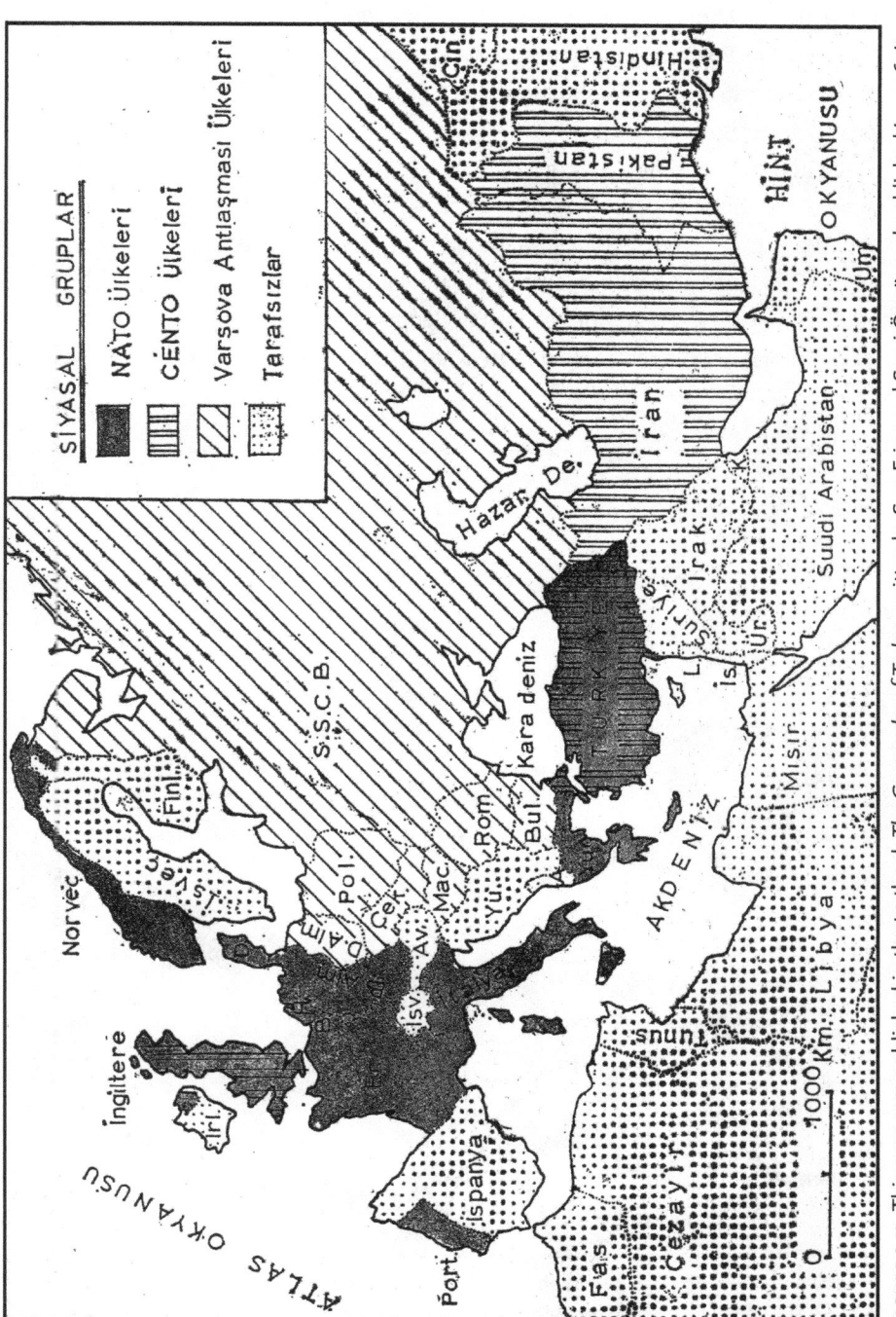

FIGURE 3.15 This map was published in the textbook *The Geography of Turkey*, written by Sırrı Erinç and Sami Öngör and published in 1976. It shows NATO countries, CENTO countries, Warsaw Pact countries, and neutral countries. Turkey was the only country that was a member of both NATO and CENTO.

Turkey as the "only European country in the Middle East."[115] They underlined the fact that although just a small portion of Turkey's territories were on the European continent, "close cultural, political and economic relations with Europe established after 1923" confirmed Turkey's "Europeanness" (Figure 3.16).[116]

There was a major change in the content and structure of textbooks after the military coup of 1980. To begin with, the name of the course in the sixth and seventh grades was changed from "Geography" to "National Geography." The subjects of the books were also modified according to the requirements of "National Geography." Textbooks published after the 1980s divided the earth into continents and analyzed the lead-

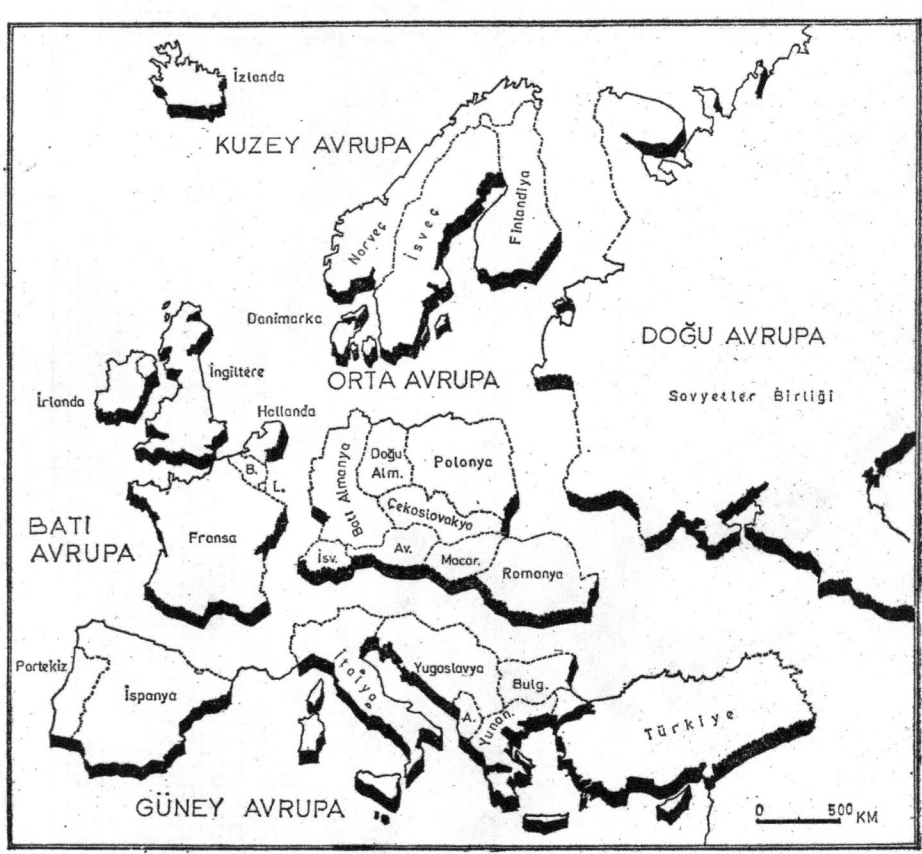

FIGURE 3.16 This map was published in the textbook *Geography of States*, written by Sırrı Erinç and Sami Öngör and published in 1975. Turkey is shown in the region of southern Europe to underline Turkey's "Europeanness."

ing countries of each continent. They studied the continents under the title "The Geographic Distribution of Turks in the Earth."[117] For example, the textbook *National Geography* for sixth-grade students analyzed Asia in terms of "countries and regions of Asia, in which Turks live." The Soviet Republics of Kazakhstan, Uzbekistan, Turkmenistan, Kyrgyzstan, and Tajikistan were collected under the title of "West Turkistan."[118] The Xinjiang region of China was named "East Turkistan." Azerbaijan, Yakutistan, Afghanistan, Iran, Iraq, Syria, and Cyprus were also examined in detail and identified as countries that had a significant Turkish population. For the European continent, the textbook gave information only about Bulgaria, Greece, Yugoslavia, and Romania, which all had a significant Turkish population. The textbook did not have any information about other European and Asian countries, such as Britain, Germany, India, or Japan. Textbooks educated students about continents from a purely ethnic Turkish perspective. The crystallization of this policy came after the disintegration of the Soviet Union, when the Ministry of National Education required that in the disciplines of geography, history, and literature, each primary and high school textbook must have as its last page the map of the "Turkish World" (Figure 3.17).

Another crucial change in the geography education was that national geography textbooks for seventh-grade classes published after the second half of the 1980s included a chapter about "Turkey's Strategic Situation."[119] This chapter began with a definition of geopolitics: "Geopolitics is the science, which studies a country's status in world geography and its relations with neighboring countries."[120] There were four subcategories in the chapter: (1) Turkey's geopolitical importance, (2) its internal enemies, (3) its external enemies, and (4) love of homeland. Students were taught about how Turkey was a geopolitically important country in the world. According to this rationale, as Turkey was geopolitically very important, it was surrounded by internal and external enemies: "The unique geographical location of Turkey attracted the interest of states, which aim to establish their authority in the world and especially in the Middle East. Those who sought to capture our Straits during the First World War and destroy our country with the Treaty of Sèvres endeavored to take advantage of our country's geographical status. If a state rules our country and the Straits, it will control the routes and trade between Europe and Asia. It will also benefit from the oil fields in the Middle East.

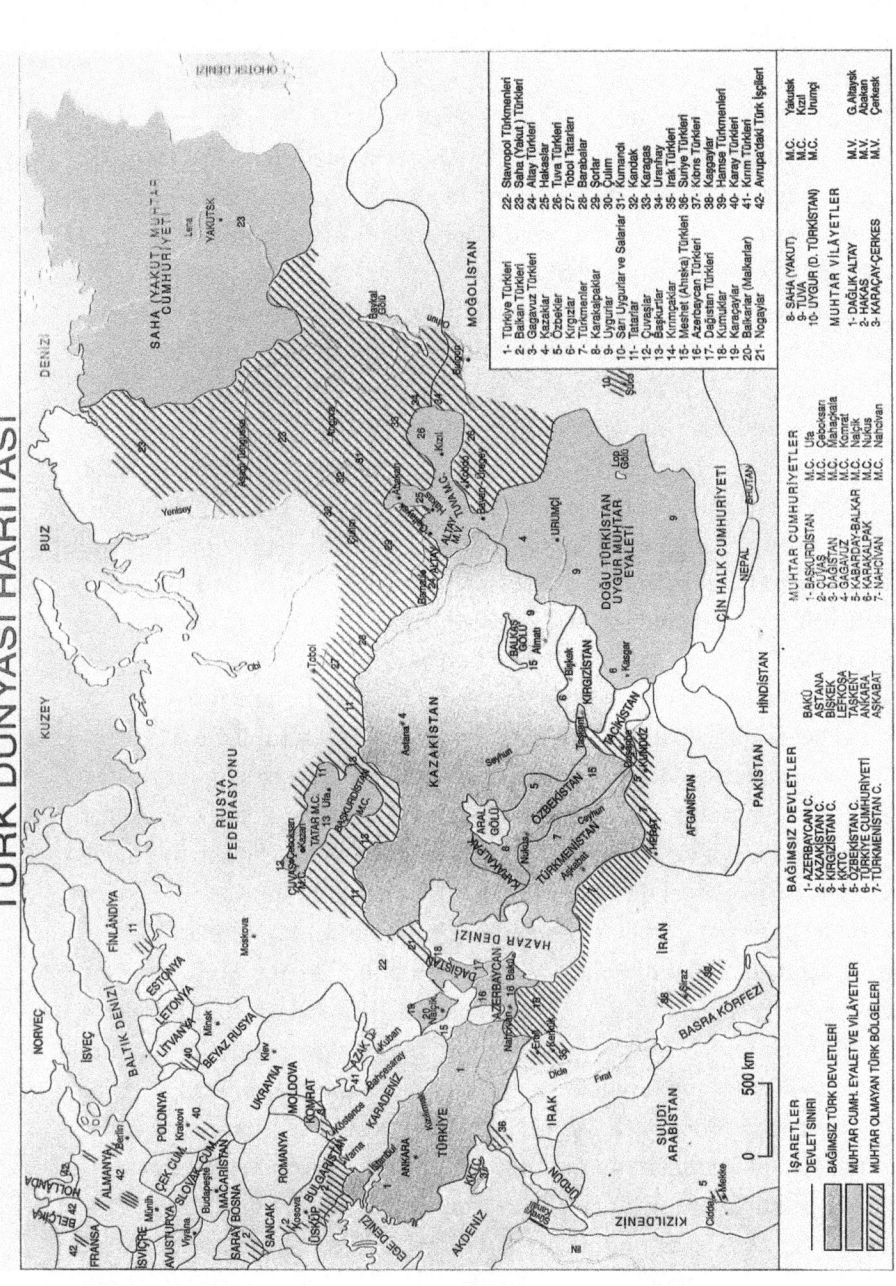

FIGURE 3.17 "Map of the Turkish World." After the disintegration of the Soviet Union, it became compulsory for primary and high school textbooks in social sciences to have this map on their last page. On the map, the light grey signifies "independent Turkish states" and "autonomous Turkish republics, states and districts." The dark shaded areas are "non-autonomous Turkish regions."

Some countries still seek to realize these types of objectives openly or secretly."[121]

Although the section on internal enemies did not name any group or ideology specifically, it was clear that armed Kurdish insurgents and left-wing opposition groups were considered the main threats to national unity. In the next section, Syria and Greece were identified as the primary external enemies of Turkey. Against these enemies, students were advised to love their homeland and defend national unity. Sam Kaplan, author of the book *The Pedagogical State: Education and the Politics of National Culture in Post-1980 Turkey*, attended a geography class in a school in the small town of Yayla. As the class was about the geopolitical situation of Turkey and threats to national unity, it is worth quoting Kaplan at length:

> In the lesson on Turkey's geopolitical situation, which I attended, the instructor wove his religious nationalist views into the reading passages. Through his performance of the text in class, the instructor not only articulated reasons for his political beliefs but also actualized them. An outspoken supporter of the Turkish Islamic Synthesis, he took advantage of his role as teacher to explicitly link foreign ideologies to Marxism-Leninism. In class, he asserted that the internal threat was none other than those atheistic leftists who served in the interests of Moscow and were intent on "weakening the Turkish people's religious unity" and "creating divisions among the people with their materialist ideologies." He concluded the lesson by reminding pupils that they were "permanent soldiers on duty" who must keep alert to dangerous, subversive atheists.[122]

Indoctrination of students with Turkish nationalism was not only limited to secondary schools and high schools. Even the books studied in universities did not question the official ideology of the state and did not recognize the existence of Kurds as a different ethnic group. In addition to the policy of omitting the words "Kurds" and "Kurdistan," university textbooks also argued that Kurds were of debased Turkish origin and were therefore referred to as "Mountain Turks." The textbook *The Cultural Geography of Turkey*, written by Hayati Doğanay for university geography departments in 1994, argued that as 99 percent of Turkey's population was constituted of Turkish Muslims, Turkey's national solidarity was much more powerful than that of the United States and Russia: "There does not exist any minority in Anatolia called Kurds. Although it is believed that they speak a different language, this language is a degenerated version of Turkish. They are Turkish Kurds like Kirgiz, Turkmen, Azeri, and Uzbek Turks. If they had been a different nation, they would have had a separate state in the past."[123]

CONCLUSION

With the establishment of the Republic of Turkey, geography education changed in order to raise citizens who would be loyal to the Turkish homeland and nation. This was the main dividing line between the late Ottoman and republican geography education. Ottoman textbooks published after 1908 emphasized Turkish people as the backbone of the empire. However, they also informed students about other ethnic groups in the empire, such as Kurds, Armenians, Greeks, and Arabs. Geography textbooks published after 1923 adapted the national discourse of the newly established republic and aimed to inculcate students with loyalty to the national homeland. Whereas textbooks published between 1923 and the early 1930s mentioned non-Turkish ethnic groups, those published after the second half of the 1930s completely omitted the names of non-Turkish groups, such as the Kurds. Nationalist discourse became even more entrenched in geography textbooks after the 1940s, as "the republic that evolved became a Republic of Turks at the end of various policies of homogenization of the population via exclusionary as well as assimilation policies."[124]

During the Cold War, geography education integrated the changing foreign policy preferences of the Turkish state. Students were trained about Turkey's special relations with the Western military institutions of NATO and CENTO. Furthermore, during this period, textbooks started to allot more space to Turks living in neighboring countries. After the military coup of 1980, there was a radical change in the content of geography education. The name of the course was changed to "National Geography" for sixth and seventh graders, and textbooks portrayed Turkey as a country located in one of the most important regions on the earth and therefore surrounded by internal and external enemies. By doing so, geography education legitimized the military's strong presence in Turkish politics in the eyes of students, and at the same time, it encouraged "a passive citizenry burdened with duties to protect national unity and the indivisibility of the country."[125]

In the last twenty years, new substate and nongovernmental actors have emerged and become increasingly vocal in Turkish politics as a result of economic and political liberalization that was also reinforced by the developing relations between Turkey and the EU. When Turkey became an official candidate to join the EU at the Helsinki Summit in 1999, the disagreement between these new actors and the military-bureaucratic elite crystallized over the adoption of international societal norms, such as cultural pluralism and linguistic rights for ethnic groups and the rejection of the traditional national security discourse. Education in general, and geography education in particular, became one of the contested issues between pro-EU actors and Eurosceptics. In 2002, TÜSİAD published an alternative geography textbook.[126] In the introduction, its authors emphasized that "instead of imposing to young individuals a feeling of loneliness and isolation in the world and in his/her region," the book sought to assist students in embracing "a citizenship based on global and democratic values."[127] The authors divided the textbook into three sections: the earth, Europe, and Turkey. Whereas the textbook prioritized European politics and Turkey's relations with the EU, it notably ignored analyzing the Middle East and the Caucasus. In accordance with TÜSİAD's policy of promoting liberalism in Turkey, the authors portrayed "the United States as the single superpower and liberal democracy as the single political model."[128] The first decade of the twenty-first century revealed that the Turkish state's hegemony over education has been seriously challenged by nonstate actors. They reject the isolationist understanding of Turkey as surrounded by enemies and thus the resulting belief that in this dangerous geography the only choice for Turkish people to survive is to have a strong military and state. On the contrary, they support the integration of Turkish people into global politics and culture by radically changing the Turkish education system.

CHAPTER FOUR

Vatan and Turkey's Foreign Policy

TURKEY'S FOREIGN POLICY DISCOURSE generated specific systems of meaning, common sense, and regimes of truth in order to legitimize the Turkish state as a political unit. By using representations of threats and dangers to vatan, ruling elites formed a historical bloc to discipline Turkish people and eliminate other antagonistic groups that challenged their power and hegemony. As David Campbell rightly put it, "Foreign Policy is a discourse of power that is global in scope yet national in its legitimation. Foreign Policy is a number of discourses of danger circulating in the discursive economy of a nation state at any given time . . . But in the context of the modern nation-state, Foreign Policy has been granted a privileged position as the discourse to which we should turn as the source of the preeminent dangers to our society and ourselves."[1]

Turkey's foreign policy discourse has not embodied uniform characteristics since 1923. There have been three distinct periods, separated by radical breaks, *"a creatio ex nihilo."*[2] In the first, between 1923 and 1939, anti-imperialism and anti-colonialism weighed considerably in Turkey's foreign policy. During this period, Turkey was meticulous about not entering into the orbit of any of the Great Powers, and it sought to form regional alliances against revisionist powers. In the second, during the Cold War, anti-communism and association with the Western camp against the Soviet Union shaped Turkey's foreign policy. In the third period, after

1991, coinciding with the end of the Cold War and the disintegration of the Soviet Union, integration in the EU became the main point of reference for groups competing for hegemony in the foreign policy arena.

Since 1923, two significant dislocations—World War II and the emergence of a bipolar structure in world politics after it, and the disintegration of the Soviet Union—triggered political developments that could not be represented, symbolized, and integrated within the hegemonic foreign policy discourses.[3] During these two dislocations—the years between 1939 and 1952 and between 1991 and 2004—various political groups in Turkey competed fiercely against each other for hegemony in politics and foreign policy. While the first antagonistic struggle ended in 1952 with Turkey's entry into the North Atlantic Treaty Organization (NATO), the second culminated in 2004 when the EU decided to start accession negotiations with Turkey.

Since the collapse of the Soviet Union, scholars in the discipline of international relations have increasingly explored the shifts in Turkish foreign policy.[4] The prevalent, unquestioned assumption in these studies emphasizes that because Turkey is centered in a strategically critical region, its geography determines its foreign policy and security decisions. In addition to their assumptions of geographical determinism, these studies have been ideologically driven, extremely politicized, and based upon the functional principle of the "production of knowledge to aid the practice of statecraft and further the power of the state."[5] The Cold War geopolitical paradigm still significantly influences scholarly analyses of Turkey's foreign policy. It can be best summarized with Nicholas Spykman's dictum that "geography does not argue; it just is."[6] As this approach considers geography as a permanent, fixed, unchanging factor in international relations, the obvious outcome is that Turkey's geographic demands have remained the same for centuries.

In a related vein, William Hale explained, "for a state of its size and strength, Turkey had to deal with an extraordinary wide range of international questions, mainly due to its geographical location."[7] This allows Turkey to "extract some strategic rent" from the Great Powers, but it also heightens Turkey's chances of being attacked by any of the Great Powers that have aspirations in the Balkans, the Middle East, or the Caucasus.[8] Similarly, Meliha Benli Altunışık and Özlem Tür concluded that among the many factors influencing Turkey's foreign policy, "geopolitics has been the most constant theme."⁹ For them, geography is an inescapable reality for Turkey, making it a pawn of the Great Powers, especially in the nineteenth-century conflict between Britain and Russia, and after World War II, between the United States and the USSR (the Union of Soviet Socialist Republics).¹⁰ Mümtaz Soysal, former foreign minister of Turkey, presented a similar perspective in the article "The Future of Turkish Foreign Policy," stressing the factors of Turkey's location "at the center of the world" and the consequences of this "precarious geostrategic position." Soysal wrote, "Few states have a more multifaceted historic destiny and geographic position than the Turkish Republic."¹¹ Turkey has been primordially concerned for "national defense and security considerations" due to the competition among the big powers, with the risk of involving Turkey "in their violent clashes." So many other countries desire Turkey's territory, Soysal explained, because of "the value of its position."¹²

A methodological problem of these studies is that they seek to produce analyses and policies founded on timeless geographical truths. While such a method assumes these geographical realities as the raison d'être of Turkey, scholars cannot ignore that "the realness of this real" is constructed by a nation's political and social culture.¹³ They turn their subjective interpretations into undeniable and objective facts by examining the "geographical realities" of Turkey. By underlining the significance of enduring geopolitical oppositions (e.g., East and West, Islamic World and Europe) in Turkey's foreign policy, scholars seek to bring to light the deep truths and secrets veiled by the quotidian practices of foreign policy. Gearóid Ó Tuathail, among the leading critics of geographical determinism, called this line of reasoning "Cartesian perspectivalism." Tuathail argued that the geographer, by employing "Cartesian perspectivalism," can act "like the detached observer of a distant battle" and "can see the world as it really is, can narrate the truth of things, [and] can effectively represent the complex way things objectively are."¹⁴

In this chapter, I critically denaturalize social constructions in Turkey's foreign policy discourse, such as threats and dangers to Turkish vatan. Furthermore, in terms of their changes, I see the social constructions within these discourses as products of specific social practices in specific historical conditions. In the first section, I examine Turkey's foreign policy between 1923 and 1939. During this period, Turkey's foreign policy was based upon the notion of nonalignment. To protect the territorial integrity of the Turkish vatan, the Kemalist regime sought to establish alliances with other states in the Balkans and the Middle East against the aspirations of revisionist powers, particularly Italy. Until 1939, the Soviet Union was considered a friendly regime by Ankara, an acknowledgment of the military and financial assistance during the period of national struggle. In the next section, I analyze Turkey's foreign policy during the Cold War through two case studies. The first is focused on relations between Turkey and the Soviet Union after World War II, and the second concerns Turkey's participation in the Korean War. In each case, the representations of threats and dangers to Turkish vatan played an important role in determining foreign policy and constructing notions of national interests. The last section of the chapter is an analysis of how the traditional Turkish foreign policy discourse toward the Cyprus question has been challenged and transformed by new internal players and globalized dynamics after the end of the Cold War.

NONALIGNED FOREIGN POLICY AGAINST EUROPEAN IMPERIALISM FROM 1923 TO 1939

Jawaharlal Nehru, a founder of the Nonaligned Movement, praised the nationalist and anti-imperialist character of the Kemalist regime in Turkey in his book *The Discovery of India*, written during World War II, when he was in a prison camp operated by the British colonial regime: "Kemal Pasha was naturally popular in India with Moslems and Hindus alike. He had not only rescued Turkey from foreign domination and disruption but [also] had foiled the machinations of European imperialist powers, especially England . . . The old pan-Islamic ideal had ceased to have any meaning; there was no Khilafat and every Islamic country, Turkey most of all, was intensely nationalist, caring little for other Islamic peoples. Nationalism was, in fact, the dominant force in Asia as elsewhere, and in India the nationalist movement had grown powerful and challenged British rule repeatedly."[15]

The National Liberation War had a distinct anti-imperialist and anti-colonialist character that continued to be the backbone of Turkey's foreign policy from the establishment of the republic up until the end of the 1930s. Another factor shaping Turkey's anti-colonial attitude arose from the fact that the new republic was surrounded by great European powers to the south. While Iraq was under British control, France established mandatory rule in Syria, and fascist Italy was Turkey's southwestern neighbor, with the Dodecanese Islands belonging to Italy from 1912 until the end of World War II. The Italian threat was one of the reasons that influenced Turkish leaders' decision to choose Ankara as the capital of the republic. Compared with other cities in Western Anatolia, Ankara could not be reached by Italian warplanes stationed in military bases on the Dodecanese islands.[16] After the rapprochement with Britain in the 1930s, even though Kemalists toned down their anti-colonialist rhetoric, Turkey was still one of the few European countries to resist the demands of revisionist dictators, particularly Mussolini. This unique feature of Turkey's foreign policy was echoed in reports by George Orwell, who observed, "In the years 1935–39, when almost any ally against Fascism seemed acceptable, left-wingers found themselves praising Mustafa Kemal."[17]

During the national struggle, Mustafa Kemal denounced "the whole capitalist and imperialist world" as the enemy of the nation. In July 1922, he once again emphasized that Turkey's fight for independence was undertaken by the nations of the East: "Today, if Turkey's struggle was limited with its interests, it would be easier and less sanguinary to accomplish its objectives. Turkey is making a supreme effort, because it is defending the interests of all aggrieved nations and the case of the whole East. Until it accomplishes its objectives, Turkey is certain of the support of all eastern nations unto itself."[18] During the war against Greece and proxy wars against Britain, France, and Italy, the Soviet Union was the main supporter of Kemalists. As George F. Kennan postulated, the friendly attitude of the Soviet regime toward Turkey was "a forerunner of the tolerance which Moscow was to show on so much a wider scale in later decades for nationalist regimes in non-European countries whenever these latter were animated by anti-European sentiments and policies."[19]

The first official contact between Kemalists and the Soviet Union came in Moscow in the summer of 1920. Before leaving Turkey, Mustafa Kemal instructed the Turkish delegation, then led by Foreign Minister Bekir Sami Bey, to inform Soviet leaders that "Turkey is ready to unite its destiny with the destiny of the Soviet Union."[20] In Moscow, the Turkish delegation met with Vladimir Lenin and Georgy Chicherin, then the

Soviet foreign minister. The negotiations were deadlocked when the Soviets insisted on returning the districts of Muş, Van, and Bitlis to Armenia. Although Mustafa Kemal told Bekir Sami Bey that Kemalists could not even consider the Soviet demands as an issue in the negotiations, he advocated for continuing to normalize relations between the two countries, as the Kemalists and the Bolsheviks signed the first treaty at Moscow in March 1921. Earlier, Mustafa Kemal had sent a telegram to Lenin in January 1921, identifying "the destruction of the western imperialism" as "the common objective" of both nations.[21] Correspondingly, the introductory portion of the Treaty of Moscow indicated that Turkey and the Soviet Union shared "the principles of liberty of nations and the right of each nation to determine its own fate." Furthermore, both nations emphasized their "common struggle undertaken against imperialism."[22] In the first clause of the treaty, the Soviet Union recognized the territories defined by the National Pact as Turkey. According to the fifth clause, the status of the Straits would be determined by "a conference composed of delegates of the littoral States" of the Black Sea, provided that the decisions of the conference would not diminish the full sovereignty of Turkey or the security of Istanbul. In the eighth clause, the countries announced they would not tolerate organizations and associations within their territories "whose aim is to wage war against the other State."

During the Lausanne Conference, contrary to the terms of the Moscow treaty, Turkey was forced by the European powers to discuss the status of the Straits with non–Black Sea states, including Britain, France, and Japan. Moreover, although the Soviet Union supported Turkey's full sovereignty over the Straits, the Turkish delegation, pressured specifically by British resistance, compromised on this issue and accepted the jurisdiction of the international commission over the Straits. Nevertheless, cordial relations between the two countries, tinged by a shared animosity toward the Western powers, continued after the Lausanne Conference.

On another sensitive issue, namely, the status of the Mosul district, the Soviet Union supported Turkish claims against Britain. Soviet Foreign Minister Chicherin stated in 1924, "It is absolutely clear that Turkey will not abandon an important part of its people because the English capitalists and other capitalists want to take petrol from Mosul."[23] Just one day after the League of Nations decided to award the Mosul district to the British Mandate of Iraq by refusing Ankara's claims, Turkey signed a treaty of friendship and neutrality in December 1925 with the Soviet Union in Paris. The Turco-Soviet treaty aimed not only to counterbalance Britain but also to deter Mussolini's expansionist policies over Anatolia. During the Mosul crisis, Italy was waiting for the Kemalist regime to disintegrate as a result of an armed conflict between Britain and Turkey, occurring simultaneously with an insurgent uprising in the Kurdish-populated areas of Eastern Anatolia.[24] As reported in *The Times*, the British position was greatly strengthened by Mussolini's speeches, which focused "on the necessity for the Italian people of expansion overseas combined with the recovery of Greece to discourage even the most Chauvinist Turkish politicians from regarding the moment as propitious for an aggressive adventure."[25] Italian military intelligence opened new centers in Cairo, Rhodes, and Piraeus to survey the Anatolian coast for a possible military operation in the summer of 1926.[26] Foreign Minister Tevfik Rüştü Aras met with his counterpart Chicherin at Odessa in November 1926 and sought to obtain Soviet support against the growing Italian threat.[27] As Dilek Barlas observed, "the handling of the Mosul issue by the Great Powers convinced the Turkish political elite that these powers could, at any time, form a coalition against Turkey."[28] Plans to partition Anatolia as laid out by the same European powers during World War I still remained vivid in the Kemalist elite's memory.

In March 1928, for the first time after the signing of the Lausanne Treaty, Turkey participated in an international disarmament conference with Soviet support. Litvinov, the Soviet representative, emphasized the significance of Turkey's participation, because of the "Republic of Turkey's important role in world politics and its geographic location."[29] In April 1932, Prime Minister İsmet İnönü and Foreign Minister Tevfik Rüştü Aras visited Moscow, just a couple of months before Turkey joined the League of Nations, of which the Soviet Union was not a member at the time. Aras conditioned Turkey's entry into the League as a concerted effort of support with the Soviet leaders.[30] Ankara notified Moscow that if the League of Nations decided to take hostile action against the Soviet Union, Turkey would not consider itself bound by Article 16 obligations of the covenant requiring the cooperation of League members against aggressor states.[31]

From the establishment of the republic in 1923 to Turkey's entry into the League of Nations in 1932, the Turkish ruling elite's priority was to consolidate the Kemalist regime with social and political revolutions. At the same time, they sought to suppress large-scale revolts in Eastern Anatolia and to purge strong political and military leaders such as Rıza Nur, Kazım Karabekir, and Ali Fuat Cebesoy, who did not support radical revolutionary programs. During these turbulent years, in addition to political and social problems Kemalist elites had to confront deteriorating economic conditions resulting from the Great Depression that began in 1929. Hence, during the first decade of the republic, ruling elites concentrated on domestic political circumstances and challenges and pursued an isolationist foreign policy. An important feature of Turkey's foreign policy during Mustafa Kemal's presidency was Tevfik Rüştü Aras's thirteen-year tenure at the helm of the Ministry of Foreign Affairs. Aras, who still holds the record as Turkey's longest-serving foreign minister, was a principal architect of the Kemalist foreign policy of nonalignment. Aras left his post November 11, 1938, just one day after Mustafa Kemal's death; he was one of two ministers left out of the new government, which was established immediately after İnönü was elected Turkey's second president. İnönü sent Aras to London as ambassador in 1939, and after World War II, Aras became one of İnönü's most significant opponents, accusing him of abandoning Mustafa Kemal's nonaligned foreign policy.

During the first decade of the republic, relations with the Soviet Union comprised the cornerstone of Turkey's foreign policy and remained as such throughout the 1930s. However, given the hostility of the European powers toward Turkey and the Soviet Union, the cordial tone of their relations arose from pragmatic concerns and self-interests rather than ideological affinities. Although both Kemalists and Bolsheviks established their respective regimes as a result of anti-imperialist struggles, they differed significantly in terms of social and economic policies. Mustafa Kemal never considered communism a suitable ideology for Turkey, remaining meticulously vigilant about not turning his country into a Soviet satellite. In a Parliament address on January 3, 1921, Mustafa Kemal emphasized that communism did not determine or define Turkey's relations with the Soviet Union: "In our relations with Russians, communist principles, which are against capitalism, were not even mentioned. To establish relations, nobody told us that 'you should be communist' or 'you have to become communist.' We never said that 'in order to be your friend we decided to become communist.'"[32] Although the Kemalist regime openly rejected communism and outlawed the communist party, the Soviets continued supporting them militarily, politically, and economically. In the years following the worldwide economic collapse in 1929, the Soviet Union was alone in extending eight million dollars of interest-free credit annually to Turkey for twenty years.[33] A clear example of Turkey's balanced attitude toward the Soviet Union was Mustafa Kemal's decision granting political asylum to Leon Trotsky, Stalin's political enemy, from 1929 to 1933.[34] The editorial comment published by *The Times* just after Turkey became a member of the League of Nations summarized succinctly Turkey's foreign policy between 1923 and 1932: "For some time after the foundation of the League Turkey remained aloof, apparently one of the countries least likely to associate with its activities. The first impulse of the new State created by Ghazi Mustapha Kemal Pasha seemed to be to break away from Europe and European institutions, and the country with which it cultivated the closest relations was Soviet Russia. The Ghazi soon made it plain, however, that Turkey intended to establish a form of government copied from no other country, but suited to the characteristics of Turkish race and to the demands of modern life. Gradually the national movement was seen to be by no means anti-European, but rather an adaptation of European methods, an extension, as it were, of Europe into Anatolia."[35]

The tenth-anniversary celebrations of the republic in 1933 symbolized the consolidation of the Kemalist regime in Turkey. The striking characteristic of these celebrations showed how the ruling elites preferred to portray material achievements—such as the construction of railways, factories, and bridges—as the major achievements of the young republic.[36] On October 29, 1933, all newspapers devoted their entire front pages to illustrations depicting these material achievements of the regime. The celebration committee organized a ceremony in which small amounts of soil collected from the central squares within every district of the country were presented to Mustafa Kemal as a precious gift, signifying the unity of the Turkish homeland. During the celebrations in Istanbul, Cevdet Kerim, the chief administrator of Istanbul, established a clear and direct link between vatan and the Turkish nation: "All of the great characteristics and virtues of Turks, which is the greatest nation in the east, derives from its attachment to the territory and love of homeland ... Now the nation is presenting a gift to the great chief and savior. This gift is the soil, which is the Turkish nation's beloved and strongest attachment."[37]

With the regime's entrenchment bolstered by material and ideational achievements in the first ten years, the Kemalist elite's main concern in foreign policy shifted from sustaining Turkey's survival to becoming a regional power and establishing coalitions in the Balkans and the Middle East with the larger aim of resisting territorial ambitions of revisionist powers. And, similarly to the foreign policy–making approaches of most European nations in the 1930s, Turkey's authoritarian regime did not tolerate any opposition or divergent opinion challenging the state's exclusive authority in determining its external orientation. Prime Minister İnönü, Chief of Staff Fevzi Çakmak, and Foreign Minister Aras worked closely with Mustafa Kemal in monopolizing Turkey's foreign policy discourse, based upon principles of inviolable independence, territorial integrity, absolute priority of national interests, and mutual respect among nations.[38] These central foreign policy architects succeeded in restoring Turkey's sovereignty over the Straits with the completion of the Montreux Convention in 1936 and in annexing the Alexandretta district in 1939.

After 1933, the Turkish political elite's perception of Italy as a threat to Turkey's territorial integrity shaped the direction of foreign policy. Mussolini's announcement of the Four Power Pact in March 1933 convinced Turkish leaders about the formation of a Great Powers bloc to harmonize their competing interests at the expense of other European states. Mussolini, holding a hostile attitude toward the League of Nations, envisioned a new Concert of Europe between Britain, France, Germany, and Italy, which would divide Europe into respective spheres of influence. To counterbalance a possible alliance in the Balkans between Italy and Bulgaria that advocated revising treaties signed after World War I and modifying boundaries, in February 1934 Turkey, Romania, Yugoslavia, and Greece signed the Balkan Entente to guarantee mutually the inviolability of the existing boundaries and to consult with one another in the face of any act of aggression. The coalition of Balkan states was a stunning success of Turkish diplomacy considering that the same Balkan countries had united just two decades before to carve up Ottoman territories in Europe. As Turkey had demonstrated its commitment to a nonaligned foreign policy since 1923, the Balkan states were convinced that Ankara would not act with any of the European Great Powers to resurrect old imperial ambitions.

Just a month after the conclusion of the Balkan Entente, Mussolini announced Italy's "historical objectives" that further deteriorated Turkish-Italian relations: "The historical objectives of Italy have two names: Asia and Africa. South and East are the cardinal points that should excite the interest and the will of Italians. There is little or nothing to do towards the North and the same towards the West, neither in Europe nor beyond the Ocean. These two objectives of ours are justified by geography and history. Of all the large Western Powers of Europe, Italy is the nearest to Africa and Asia. A few hours by sea and much less by air are enough to link up Italy with Africa and with Asia."[39]

In the eyes of the Kemalist elite, Turkey's suspicions about Italy's ambitions were justified by Mussolini's speech, as it was obvious that with "Asia" he meant Anatolia, particularly the Antalya district, which was occupied by Italy after World War I. With the Italian invasion of Abyssinia in October 1935, the British and French policy of appeasement toward Mussolini alarmed Turkish diplomats about the validity of the collective security regime as documented in the League of Nations articles. In the spring of 1936, Ankara decided to act more decisively in the Mediterranean, informing the signatories of the Lausanne Treaty in writing that the existing demilitarized regime of the Straits did not guarantee Turkey's security. Ankara was "ready to undertake negotiations which would lead, in a short time, to the conclusion of new agreements for regulating the status of the Straits, with conditions of security necessary for maintaining the inviolable and indivisible character of Turkish territory."[40] During negotiations in Montreux, Turkey's draft convention had been used as the basis for discussion, with Turkey insisting on the unconditional militarization of the Straits and abolition of the International Straits Commission as well as freedom of passage and navigation for merchant vessels. Turkey also proposed limitations on the passage of warships, suggesting a maximum allowable tonnage for warships in the Straits of the non-Black Sea countries of 14,000 tons and for riparian states at

25,000 tons. The Soviet Union supported Turkish claims on militarization and reestablishment of Turkish sovereignty by abolishing the International Committee. However, it insisted on the unrestricted passage of warships carrying the flags of Black Sea states. Although Britain was the principal in imposing the internationalization and demilitarization of the Straits in the Lausanne treaty, it was careful not to reject Turkish claims because it believed that a hostile Turkey with the support of the Soviet Union would harm British interests in the Mediterranean. The Montreux Convention, signed on July 20, 1936, restored Turkish sovereignty over the Straits and allowed Turkey to militarize the region. The Soviets also reached their goals by restricting the passage of warships of non–Black Sea states through the Straits. Although the Convention could have been regarded as a retreat for Britain, gaining Turkey's friendship and preventing an alliance between the Soviet Union and Turkey played an important role in Britain's conciliatory approach.[41]

Another successful example of Turkey's diplomacy during this period was the annexation of the Alexandretta district. Turkey exerted diplomatic pressure upon France by using the deteriorating political situation in the eastern Mediterranean resulting from Mussolini's aspirations. On the eve of World War II, obtaining Turkey's support against Italy and Germany was much more important for France than continuing its mandatory obligations in Syria. Consequently, it accepted the cessation of the Alexandretta district from Syria.[42] The Montreux Convention and the annexation of Alexandretta showed that Turkish leadership did not prefer to solve foreign policy problems through unilateral actions as was the case for Germany's militarization of the Rhineland or for the annexation of Sudetenland. Turkey was the first state to employ peaceful and legal methods to revise the Lausanne treaty, specifically concerning the Straits issue.[43]

With these diplomatic successes, Turkey, as a nonaligned country, could play an important role in world politics and protect its national interests. Turkey accomplished almost all of its objectives in Montreux without going into an alliance with a Great Power. Defending Turkey's interests in the international arena by taking a nonaligned position defined Turkey's foreign policy during Mustafa Kemal's presidency, but this approach would be abandoned immediately after his death in 1938. A conversation on June 17, 1934, between Mustafa Kemal and Sir Percy

Loraine, then the newly appointed British ambassador to Ankara, revealed how Mustafa Kemal considered Turco-Soviet relations and rapprochement with Britain mutually exclusive issues. Mustafa Kemal left no ambiguities in articulating Turkey's serious intentions not to let Britain or any other European state interfere with its foreign policy. Loraine recounted their discussion:

> The Gazi [Mustafa Kemal] said he had the greatest esteem for England and that he wished for friendship with England. Why could we not come closer together? Did England attach no value to Turkey or her friendship? . . . I myself saw no reason why England and Turkey should not be good friends; we had certain interests in common, there were no questions of any gravity dividing us, and our relations were already good. I must, however, say one thing in this connection, and I wished His Excellency to hear me out. Turkey's most immediate friend today was Russia, whereas our relations with Russia, if correct, were certainly not close . . . The Gazi then held up his hand to check me and said, "Ah! if that is so, then very well." I sensed that this was the crucial point in the conversation, and his meaning seemed obviously to be that if we thought Turco-Russian intimacy a bar to Anglo-Turkish friendship, it was no use pursuing the latter question any further.[44]

According to the Russian scholar Boris Potskhveriya, because of the aggressive Italian foreign policy in the Mediterranean between 1934 and 1936, Turkey offered the joint defense of the Straits with the Soviet Union during wartime and emphasized that it was ready to close the Straits to other powers if the Soviet Union entered a war.[45] During these two years, although Moscow was hesitant to establish a binding military relationship with Ankara, it changed its position during the Montreux Convention. During the negotiations in Montreux, this time Soviet Foreign Minister Litvinov privately proposed to Foreign Minister Aras the joint defense of the Straits. However, Ankara sought to adapt a more balanced policy between Britain and the Soviet Union. Aras rejected Litvinov's offer since joint defense of a portion of Turkey with a Great Power would have contradicted Kemalist principles of full sovereignty and independence.[46]

Between 1923 and 1939, although Kemalists highly valued Soviet friendship, they were judicious about sustaining relations within the context of two equal sovereign states. During these years, the Turkish political leadership scrupulously avoided entering into alliances with the Great Powers. Instead of following a Great Power in international politics, Kemalists prioritized collective security and collaboration with Turkey's neighbors. So they initiated regional pacts, such as the Balkan Entente and Sadabad Pact with Iran, Iraq, and Afghanistan. However, Mustafa Kemal even questioned the necessity of the regional pacts, suspicious about any potential political and diplomatic damage to Turkey's nonaligned foreign policy. Hasan Rıza Soyak, Mustafa Kemal's general secretary after 1934, wrote in his memoirs about how Mustafa Kemal wrestled with his conscience after the completion of the Balkan Entente. Mustafa Kemal told Soyak he was restless during the night, worrying about changes in Turkey's foreign policy: "As you know, until today we have been busy with our own internal and external problems and have pursued an independent diplomacy. But now we are entering into the arena of international politics and we have new responsibilities. I have been pondering what will be the possible outcomes for us and therefore I could not sleep."[47]

The consensus among Turkey's top-level statesmen ended in 1937 as İnönü and Mustafa Kemal disagreed publicly over Turkey's foreign policy orientation. In 1937, the Turkish delegation under the leadership of Foreign Minister Aras participated in the Nyon Conference with other European countries to discuss responses to the increasingly frequent attacks by Italian submarines. Mustafa Kemal instructed the Turkish delegation to allow French and British forces to use Turkish ports. Although Prime Minister İnönü resisted cooperating with Britain and France against Italy, because he believed that such a policy would bring Italy and Turkey to the brink of war, the Turkish delegation followed Mustafa Kemal's instructions, and the Turkish Parliament approved the Nyon Treaty on September 18, 1937. Both leaders also disagreed on the diplomatic approach with France concerning the Alexandretta district. While Mustafa Kemal advocated for an unconditional position against France and did not rule out military intervention if necessary, İnönü preferred a more conciliatory approach to sustain French-Turkish relations. At the end of September 1937, Mustafa Kemal asked for İnönü's resignation as prime minister and appointed Celal Bayar to the post the following month.

In 1938, with Mustafa Kemal's health deteriorating, leading members of the Kemalist elite devised plans for a presidential succession that would keep İnönü's still-dominant political influence in check. In the cabinet, Prime Minister Bayar, Foreign Minister Aras, and Interior Minister Şükrü Kaya were seen as legitimate candidates to succeed Mustafa Kemal, as was Fevzi Çakmak, the chief of general staff. Although Çakmak was not a politician, he was the only marshal after Mustafa Kemal, and as head of the Turkish army since 1924, he held the potential to change the political balance against the mighty İnönü.[48]

Bayar and Çakmak were not eager about opposing İnönü, who had been prime minister for twelve years and had maintained total control over Parliament, key bureaucrats, and party members. Aras and Kaya, the two leading members of the anti-İnönü camp, sought to remove İnönü from the political scene by exiling him to the United States. In his memoirs, İnönü wrote that Aras had offered to appoint him as Turkey's ambassador to the United States at a 1938 meeting.[49] Aras also stated in an article, published by the daily *Milliyet* less than a year before his death, that he planned to send İnönü to the United States in order to "calm down both Atatürk and İnönü."[50] İnönü fiercely rejected Aras's plans: "I raised hell. I yelled at him that if he attempted to do such a thing, I would bring the world down upon his head."[51] On November 10, 1938, Mustafa Kemal died, and a day later, İnönü was elected as the second president of the republic, garnering 348 out of a possible 387 votes. The remaining thirty-nine votes were abstentions, in a silent parliamentary protest guided by Aras and Kaya. Shortly thereafter, Bayar announced the new cabinet without Aras and Kaya, both of whom had served the government for more than a decade. In less than thirty-six hours after Mustafa Kemal's death, İnönü had carried out a carefully orchestrated plan to win the presidency and eliminate his two strongest opponents with stunning clockwork efficiency. Ironically, Aras, who had sought to send İnönü to the United States as ambassador, lost his seat in the cabinet and was appointed by İnönü as the ambassador to London in January 1939. In the same month, Prime Minister Bayar resigned, and Refik Saydam became the fourth prime minister of the republic.

With İnönü's ascendancy to power, "the political atmosphere became more illiberal."⁵² As Selim Deringil observed, "the system was as hierarchical as it was authoritarian; the authoritarian principle permeating all levels of the İnönü government. İnönü himself, as the authoritarian head of an authoritarian government, was at the pinnacle of power and the focal point of all this centralization."⁵³ After Mustafa Kemal's death, İnönü removed all other strong statesmen from the political scene and ensured there was no power vacuum. Unlike Mustafa Kemal, who also was authoritarian but kept many associates and advisers in his circle, İnönü refused to allow anyone to come close to him. As Frederick Frey rightly argued, "İnönü had no İnönü."⁵⁴ During World War II, an already authoritarian regime morphed into a dictatorial one under İnönü's leadership. The style, tone, and content of Turkey's politics, along with its foreign policy, changed with İnönü's presidency. Despite İnönü's dictatorial tendencies, the opposition front was intact even if it was in a silent mode of dormancy during the war. Contrary to the official history, which characterized İnönü's succession to Mustafa Kemal as a smooth political transition, İnönü rose to the presidency as a result of a power struggle against Aras, Kaya, and some other members of the Kemalist elite. The silenced opposition resurfaced immediately after the end of World War II and resumed its vocal challenge to İnönü's leadership.

THE COLD WAR: PROTECTING VATAN FROM COMMUNISTS

The declaration of a mutual assistance pact between Turkey and Britain on May 12, 1939, was a turning point in Turkey's foreign policy. Prime Minister Saydam told the Parliament that Turkey's neutrality, the most important characteristic of its foreign policy since 1923, had ended with the signing of the declaration:

> You know that political events have lately occurred with lightning speed and have seriously occupied the attention of those burdened with the responsibilities of Government. At first, this Government decided that Turkey's best course was to remain neutral, but when events involved the Balkan Peninsula and raised the question of security in the eastern Mediterranean

we were faced with a situation pregnant with danger making it impossible for us to remain neutral. It is our conviction that the Mediterranean should be free to all nations on an equal footing, and that any attempt to interfere with that freedom would endanger Turkish security. Believing that this danger now exists, we have made up our minds to cooperate, and, if necessary, to fight with those equally anxious to preserve peace.[55]

Five months after the Anglo-Turkish declaration, Britain, France, and Turkey agreed to the Tripartite Treaty, indicating that if Turkey was attacked by a European power, Britain and France would provide mutual assistance to the nation. Conversely, if France and Britain entered into a war as a result of events in the Mediterranean region or as a result of their guarantees to Greece and Romania, Turkey would assist them. However, Turkey could remain neutral if Britain and France entered into a war because of events outside of the Mediterranean region. The Anglo-Turkish Declaration and the Tripartite Treaty were devised as a hedge against Italian aggression in the Mediterranean, and the Turkish government considered the Italian invasion of Albania in April 1939 as the first step of Mussolini's general offensive in the Balkans.

During this period of strained relations between Turkey and Italy, the Turkish press started to publish articles about the Italian aggression in southeast Europe.[56] The booklet *Do Not Touch This Lion*, published in 1939 by Faruk Gürtunca, one of the first publishers of Turkish comic strips and children's magazines in the 1930s, had a notable influence on Turkish society.[57] The booklet's unprecedented impact in the republic arose from Gürtunca's use of maps and images to influence public opinion against Italy.[58] On the cover were a lion statue, a Turkish flag, and a map of Turkey, carrying the tag "do not touch this lion" (Figure 4.1). On an inside page, a Turkish soldier standing on the map of Turkey faced the Dodecanese Islands, which then belonged to Italy (Figure 4.2). Gürtunca intended the book to reach as wide an audience as possible and kept the language simple and frequently coarse. Throughout the book, the conquest of Italy by Attila and the Huns and the Ottoman naval victory against the Christian Alliance in the Battle of Preveza in 1538 were illustrated extensively with iconic images, with the purpose of fomenting

FIGURE 4.1 The cover of the booklet *Do Not Touch This Lion* published in 1939 to counteract the "Italian threat." The lion represented Turkey, and the link between lion and Turkey was established through a map, which has the title of the booklet on it.

FIGURE 4.2 A Turkish soldier facing the Dodecanese islands, which belonged to Italy in 1939. *Do Not Touch This Lion* was one of the leading publications to use a map to create an image of the "enemy" in the public imagination.

nationalistic agitation against Italy and creating public support for the government's foreign policy (Figure 4.3). After World War II, similar publications were extensively used to manipulate public opinion and suppress opposition in other landmark foreign policy issues, such as the conflict with the Soviet Union after 1945, the Korean War, and the Cyprus conflict.

At various times during World War II, Turkey's political leaders reiterated the nation's position of "active neutrality" toward the Allies and the Axis powers. Turkey was the only ally of France and Britain to sign nonaggression and friendship agreements with Germany and the Soviet Union. Turkey's friendly stance toward Germany until 1944 was criticized as immoral by British and American policymakers and media. Against these criticisms, Turkish politicians defended themselves, stressing that the objective of active neutrality was to protect Turkey's territorial integrity. Unspoken, of course, was the strategy's effect in sustaining İnönü's political domination.

REPRESENTATION OF THE SOVIET UNION AS A THREAT TO VATAN

Most scholars who analyzed Turkey's foreign policy after the end of World War II accepted uncritically the Cold War thesis that the Soviet Union was preparing for an offensive war against Turkey to acquire the Kars and Ardahan districts in 1945 and 1946. Therefore, they claimed, the threat of "Soviet expansionism" had a tremendous impact upon Turkish policymakers and compelled Ankara to join the Western camp against Moscow in order to protect its territorial integrity.[59] The conventional assumption in these studies suggests that Soviet "demands" and "threats" formed the organizing principle of Turkey's foreign policy during the Cold War. William Hale explained that, just after World War II, "Turkey's territorial integrity and its future as an independent state was gravely threatened by a resurgent Russia, and that Turkey urgently needed to find allies to fend it off."[60] Hale argued that Turkey's decision to join the anti-Soviet Western alliance was unavoidable as "Turkey was forced into the Western camp in the Cold War because it was directly threatened by the Soviet Union."[61] Likewise, Kemal Karpat asserted that "it was the immensity of Soviet military power and her insatiable ambition for territorial and ideological expansion in 1946, which forced Turkey to seek full

FIGURE 4.3 Another image in *Do Not Touch This Lion* used for nationalist agitation. It shows the map of Italy invaded by Turkish cavaliers.

affiliation with the West almost at any price, and embark at the same time upon a policy of identification with the West in the economic, social, political and cultural fields. Probably at no time in history was the Westernization of Turkey so intensive and one sided as in the period after WW2, and this thanks to the pressure coming from the Soviet Union."[62]

Not only scholars but also right-wing, conservative-nationalist politicians considered the Soviet "demands" as a constituent factor in Turkish politics and foreign policy. Mehmet Keçeciler, who was a member of the Islamist National Salvation Party before the 1980 military coup and served as minister in cabinets of the center-right Motherland Party in the 1980s and 1990s, argued that Soviet "demands" shaped the Turkish right during the Cold War: "During the Stalin era, because USSR demanded Kars and Ardahan, and base at the Straits from Turkey, Turkey was forced to enter NATO. It forced Turkey to ban the communists party ... From the beginning the Turkish right was nationalist and therefore it had positioned itself against communism. Communism was considered as a threat, because people believed that if it spread to Turkey, the strategy that wants to grab our districts from us would prevail. It was perceived more than an ideological threat. The struggle [with communism] was against the disintegration of Turkey and against grabbing territories from our country."[63]

Namık Kemal Zeybek, who also served as a minister in the Motherland Party cabinet at the end of 1980s and was a member of the Nationalist Action Party (NAP) before 1980, underlined the importance of Soviet "demands" for the Turkish right: "In Turkey the fear was whether 'Turkey would become a satellite or a region of the Soviet Union and lose its flag and independence.' This fear was not unjust when the Soviet Union was using communism as an ideological weapon. Stalin's threats after the Second World War were very interesting. He threatened Turkey openly. It is a fact that he demanded a base at the Straits, as well as Kars and Ardahan ... Turkey was afraid of [the Soviet Union] since it will use its military power to capture Turkey. Was it unwarranted? No. Many people in Turkey developed their thoughts based on this justified fear."[64]

If we analyze the notorious private talks between Soviet Foreign Minister Molotov and the Turkish ambassador Selim Sarper in June 1945, we realize that Molotov insisted on three conditions if Turkey wanted to renew the Treaty of Friendship and Non-Aggression that would end after November 7, 1945. The Soviets proposed for a bilateral agreement to revise the Montreux Convention, establish Soviet military bases in the Straits for joint defense, and cede the Kars and Ardahan districts in northeastern Anatolia to Soviet Armenia and Soviet Georgia, respectively. In August 1946, the Soviet Union, without mentioning any territorial demands, proposed the joint defense of the Straits and a new Straits regime between Turkey and other Black Sea states. The Soviet proposals were seen as an existentialist threat against Turkey by President İnönü, Prime Minister Saraçoğlu, and other leading statesmen as well as the media. To Turkey, the proposals, which were often described as demands in the press, verified that the Soviet Union expected to finally realize the imperial ambitions of the Russian tsars in the Straits and Turkish territories. Much of the academic literature on this subject suggested that by articulating the "demands" about the Straits and northeastern Anatolia in 1945 and 1946, the Soviet Union changed sentiments among Turkey's leaders who were then forced to make alliances with the Western Bloc.

Between the two world wars, when relations between the Soviet Union and Turkey were friendly, Soviet leaders had put forward similar proposals about the Straits and Eastern Anatolia. Before negotiations during the summer of 1920 in Moscow, Mustafa Kemal instructed the Turkish delegation to tell the Soviets that Turkey accepted rights of free passage for the Black Sea states. In addition, Mustafa Kemal indicated that Turkey was ready to defend the Straits together with the Black Sea states.[65] During the talks, the Soviet Union proposed returning the districts of Muş, Bitlis, and Van to Armenia.[66] Although the Soviet proposals were rejected by Ankara, Turkey's leaders did not change their stance toward Moscow and continued their diplomatic initiatives to establish friendly relations with the Bolsheviks. During the negotiations at Montreux in 1936, Soviet Foreign Minister Litvinov asked Aras, his Turkish counterpart, whether Turkey would consider defending the Straits jointly with the Soviet Union. Even though Aras told Litvinov that Turkey was not interested in joint defense of the Straits and rejected the Soviet offer, Ankara did not see the proposal as a threat to Turkey's sovereignty. While Turkish statesmen did not consider Soviet proposals about the Straits and the territorial concessions as threats to Turkey's territorial integrity during the interwar period, their position changed after World War II, when similar proposals were now seen as encroachments on Turkey's independence and sovereignty and the Soviet regime was publicly identified as Turkey's greatest enemy.

I refuse to attach an ontological status to the "Soviet danger" in Turkey's foreign policy, explaining instead that terms like "danger," "security," and "threat" are not objective entities existing "independently of those to whom it may become a threat."[67] Their meanings are contingent upon the contemporary dynamics of foreign policy discourses. The construction of dangers is central for the architects of foreign policy to control and discipline the political struggle and eliminate any oppositional groups. Therefore, Turkey's foreign policy during the Cold War cannot be understood comprehensively by considering the prior existence of a "Soviet danger" to the territorial integrity of Turkey, as suggested by Hale, Karpat, and other scholars.

After World War II, Molotov articulated territorial concessions privately with the Turkish ambassador Sarper, adding that this was a precondition if Turkey wanted to renew the friendship and nonaggression treaty. This issue was raised by Molotov during the Potsdam Conference:

> The Turkish government showed initiative and suggested the Soviet government should sign an allied treaty. The Turkish government put this question first before our Ambassador in Ankara, and then, later in May, through the Turkish Ambassador in Moscow. In early June I had two meetings with Sarper in Moscow. Asked by the Turkish government about an allied treaty, we responded that the Soviet government does not object to concluding such a treaty on certain conditions. I gave instructions that when concluding an allied treaty we should settle mutual claims. We have two questions to be settled. Conclusion of the allied treaty means that we should jointly protect our borders: the USSR not only its own but Turkish ones as well; Turkey not only its own but Soviet ones as well. However, in some parts, we consider the border between the USSR and Turkey to be unfair. Indeed, in 1921, a territory was annexed from Soviet Armenia and Soviet Georgia. This includes the areas of Kars, Artvin and Ardahan.[68]

The second issue was the revision of the Montreux Convention. Molotov said that according to the Montreux Convention, "the rights of the Soviet Union are similar to those of the Japanese Emperor": "The Turkish government said that if it was ready to settle basic disputed issues, we are ready to sign an allied treaty after their resolution. In saying so, we expressed our willingness to settle the issues put forward by Turkey. We added that if the Turkish government considers it inadmissible to resolve both issues, we were ready to reach an agreement on the Straits only."[69]

Although Molotov explicitly stated to his British and American counterparts in Potsdam and to the Turkish ambassador Sarper two months before the conference that territorial changes were a precondition for an alliance between Turkey and the Soviet Union, Turkish politicians and the media exaggerated the situation as if Soviets were preparing to annex these districts, if necessary by deploying military force. Turkish politicians and journalists identified the Soviet Union and, therefore, communism as the greatest dangers to Turkish vatan. Soviet proposals were not only used as a foreign policy means to justify Turkey's entry into the Western camp against the Soviet Union but also as a rational excuse to silence the opposition. During the crucial period between 1945 and 1950, when political parties had risen against the Republican People's Party (RPP) and its leader, İnönü, the Republicans categorized all left-wing groups as well as those criticizing the government in any way or form as being tied directly or indirectly to communism and the Soviet Union. By doing so, they established strict control over the opposition and outlawed any political group challenging the government, depicting them as enemies of the Turkish nation and as traitors to vatan. What David Campbell said about the politics of the United States after World War II was valid for Turkey as well: "Danger was being totalized in the external realm in conjunction with its increased individualization in the internal field, with the result being the performative reconstitution of the borders of the state identity. In this sense, the cold war needs to be understood as a disciplinary strategy that was global in scope but national in design."[70]

Even long before the Soviet proposals were articulated by Molotov in 1945, at the fifth session of the Supreme Soviet on October 31, 1939, the same Molotov publicly denied that "the USSR demanded the transfer of areas of Ardahan and Kars." According to him, these allegations were "fabrication and lie."[71] Nevertheless, during World War II, Turkish diplomats were deliberating about the Soviet "threats" and "territorial demands." As early as July 1940, the Turkish ambassador in Moscow Haydar Aktay sent a report to Ankara that Soviets would demand "from both Turkey and Iran frontier rectification."[72] According to the Turkish consul in Batum, there "were persistent rumors here that Russians are about to seize Kars."[73] In the same way, the Turkish ambassador in Washington Münir Ertegün asked questions about Soviet demands in his report sent to Ankara in March 1943: "Do Russia's real desires extend no further than effective control on the Dardanelles, exercised in conjunction with ourselves and purely in the interests of her security? Or are they aiming at the acquisition of Istanbul, the Straits, and other portions of our territory?"[74] In October 1943, the Japanese ambassador mentioned in his report sent to Tokyo that Turks were concerned about the annexation of Kars and Erzurum districts by the Soviet Union.[75] However, according to Hughe Knatchbull-Hugessen, the British ambassador in Ankara, Turkish concerns about the Soviet invasion of Eastern Anatolia were groundless in 1943. Hugessen believed that Turkish foreign policy circles were in a "national psychosis." He criticized Turkish concerns about the Soviet threat and identified Turkish fears as "simply idiotic" and an "insane Russian complex."[76]

Turkish fears were manipulated by British and American newspapers and magazines in order to influence Turkish foreign policy according to the interests of Britain and the United States. On February 28, 1943, the *New York Times* published an article carrying the headline "Russia's Ambitions Are Secrets of Kremlin."[77] The article stated that at the end of the world war, the Soviet Union "will insist on control of Europe as far as the Adriatic, ownership of the Hellespont and the Dardanelles or all of Scandinavia or of all Iran, and possibly Afghanistan." In the Middle East, the article continued, "there is some possibility that the Turco-Russian parleys now taking place may involve Soviet demands on former Russian regions surrounding Kars and Ardahan."[78] On July 12, 1943, *Time* magazine published a cover article with the title "Choice."[79] The article praised Turkey's neutral policy as directed by Prime Minister Şükrü Saraçoğlu since the beginning of the world war. However, the *Time* correspondent added that Turkey had to enter the war with the Allies in order to have "a strong voice at the peace table." The correspondent explained that Şükrü Saraçoğlu "would easily find a place for himself in the rough-and-tumble political arena of the US. He likes America, Americans and things American—automobiles, cigarets [sic], architecture, movies, industry, government." In the last section of the article, Turkish politicians were warned about the Soviet danger that would threaten Turkey after the war: "Probably the most powerful trump card Allies can play is the prospect of furnishing postwar influence for Turkey against Soviet Russia. Despite the 'series of most advanced treaties' which Saraçoğlu announced as having consolidated the Turkish rapprochement with Russia, Russian postwar aims remain Turkey's greatest fear. Control of the Dardanelles, Russia's only outlet to the southern waterways, has been a sore point between the two nations for decades; Turkey's control of it today hinges on the Montreux Convention of 1936. The Government's fear of Communism is another stimulant to Turkish suspicion."[80]

Although the American press asserted as early as 1943 that the Soviet Union would be a crucial threat for Turkey's security in the postwar era, Aras, Turkey's former foreign minister who resigned in 1942 from the ambassador's post in London and had returned to Turkey, supported Soviet policies in Eastern Europe, according to an interview published by the *New York Times* on December 25, 1943.[81] Aras emphasized that the Soviets carried the burden of the war alone in the last two years in Europe against Germany and, therefore, that they had the right to support friendly governments along their boundaries: "It was Russia that, before the war, incessantly advocated collective security, but to no avail. The Russians are aware that hostile neighbors and an inimical world hoped that Germany would destroy the despised Soviet regime, but fate willed differently. Today the hitherto loathsome Russians are cheered as great heroes who helped to save Britain, and the Red Army is still fighting with fervor to drive out the invaders, thus helping to free the European Continent from the German yoke."[82]

In the summer of 1943, an unprecedented political dispute erupted in Turkey between left-wing and ultranationalist groups as they published journals and pamphlets vehemently accusing each other of being puppets of Nazi Germany and the Soviet Union. Since the start of World War II, the activities of pan-Turkist groups had increased dramatically in Turkey as they publicly endorsed Turkey's entry into the war on the side of Germany against the Soviet Union "in order to fulfill their irredentists' visions."[83] Émigrés from Crimea, Tataristan, and Azerbaijan—such as Zeki Velidi Togan, Mehmet Emin Resulzade, and Ahmet Caferoğlu—actively disseminated their anti-Soviet and pan-Turkist views through publications. They supported the formation of fighting units in the Nazi army among the Turkic prisoners of war in German camps. There also were high-ranking military officials in the Turkish army—such as General Ali Fuad Erden, General Cemil Toydemir, retired General Hüseyin Hüsnü Erkilet, and Nuri Pasha, the stepbrother of Enver Pasha—who supported pan-Turkism and Nazi Germany. After Germany's attack on the Soviet Union in 1941, Erden and Erkilet visited Berlin and the eastern front in October of that year. They met Hitler and other high-ranking German officials and discussed Turkey's participation in the war against the Soviet Union, and after returning to Ankara, Erden reported to İnönü, Çakmak, and Saraçoğlu in a meeting lasting six hours.[84]

The counterpoint to pan-Turkists sentiments came in *The Greatest Danger*, a pamphlet published by Faris Erkman in May 1943.[85] Erkman accused pan-Turkists of racism, condemning their irredentist policies and explaining that when the Soviet armies retreated against Nazi Germany on the eastern front, pan-Turkists started to dream about ministerial posts in the pro-Nazi governments that would have been established in Azerbaijan and Crimea by Germany. He rejected the pan-Turkist vision of a Turkish Empire that ran against Kemalist foreign policy principles: "Anti-imperialist Turkey, which waged a national liberation war against foreign domination to free itself from the semi-colonial status during the War of Independence and Republican Revolution, does not have any expansionist objective."[86] The pamphlet had a significant impact on Turkish politics. Leading pan-Turkists—including Nihal Atsız, Reha Oğuz Türkkan, and Orhan Seyfi Orhon—responded with their own publications, defending pan-Turkism and depicting communism as "the greatest danger."[87] Erkman's pamphlet caught the attention of Parliament, with Foreign Minister Numan Menemencioğlu openly rejecting pan-Turkism on the parliamentary floor: "We could only wish happiness and well-being for Turks, who are outside of our borders. Our policy and our Turkism are limited with the Turks living within the borders of this vatan."[88] In having the foreign minister and not the interior minister make the statement for the formal parliamentary record, the government made clear that pan-Turkism was significant not only as a domestic issue but, even more so, as a foreign policy one.[89]

In March 1944, Radio Moscow broadcasted Nazi activities in Turkey and gave a list of Turkish people who supported Nazi Germany.[90] İnönü, who had been impartial between left-wing and pan-Turkist groups until then, decided to suppress pan-Turkist activities in 1944 as the likelihood of the Allies' victory became increasingly evident in Europe. İnönü's speech on May 19, 1944, signaled that he had changed his stance toward pan-Turkists, accusing them of being in the service of foreigners and portraying them as detrimental to the Turkish youth: "Turanism is a harmful and sick demonstration of the latest times."[91] Well-known pan-Turkists—including Nihal Atsız, Zeki Velidi Togan, Reha Oğuz Türkkan, and several army officers such as Alparslan Türkeş—were arrested, and pan-Turkist newspapers and journals, which supported the destruction of the Soviet Union by Nazi Germany and advocated the unity of all Turks, were closed. Eventually, in March 1945, pan-Turkists were sentenced from one to ten years in jail. However, as tension with the Soviet Union increased after the summer of 1945, the court revoked the sentences and all pan-Turkists were released from jail. It is striking that just a month after İnönü's attack on pan-Turkists, the president forced Numan Menemencioğlu, who was considered pro-German but, in fact, was a key architect of Turkey's "active neutrality" policy, to resign from his post as minister of foreign affairs. By doing so, İnönü vindicated himself in the eyes of the Allies, scapegoating Menemencioğlu as the primary Turkish politician who advocated and coordinated plans to build friendly relations with Nazi Germany.

In the second half of 1944, criticisms against İnönü and particularly his stance on foreign policy increased in the Turkish press and Parliament. Bayar, who had been silent since resigning as prime minister, criticized the government's economic policies in May 1944 during budgetary sessions in the Parliament. Aras started to write critical articles in the Turkish newspapers, *Tan* and *Vatan*, which opposed İnönü's authoritarian policies. In the article "Our Great Neighbor and Friend," published by *Vatan* on June 13, 1944, Aras wrote that Turkey and the Soviet Union should enter into an alliance.[92] For Aras, a Soviet-Turkish alliance was a necessary element for establishing security in the Mediterranean. Two weeks later, Aras wrote another article with the title "I Am Going to Say More Clearly," in which he indicated that if there was a conflict between the Soviet Union, the United States, and Britain after the end of the war, it would be very damaging for the whole of humanity.[93] Aras stressed that Turkey, already an ally of Britain, could play an important role in preventing future conflicts among the Allies if it entered into an alliance with the Soviet Union. In concluding, Aras asked: "To establish security in our region after the end of the war, is there a better and more stable way than Turkish-Russian friendship as it had been in the past?"[94] Aras's articles, in stressing the significance of the alliance between Turkey and the Soviet Union, had widespread repercussions in Turkish and foreign papers.[95] Ahmet Emin Yalman and other columnists debated about how such an alliance would be possible if there was a disagreement between Anglo-Saxon powers and the Soviet Union over the future of Europe. As early as 1944, Aras stated that in a conflict between Anglo-Saxons and the Soviets, Turkey should avoid becoming an Anglo-Saxon outpost against the Soviet Union as advocated by some policy experts, because such a decision would create risky and dangerous conditions for Turkey's foreign policy.[96]

In August 1944, Turkey broke off relations with Germany and, six months later in February 1945, declared war on Germany and Japan in order to join the United Nations Conference in San Francisco. Although the Soviet Union rejected the participation of neutral states such as Spain and Portugal in the conference, it did not reject Turkey's participation. Nevertheless, in March 1945, the Soviet Union notified Ankara that it would terminate the Treaty of Friendship, which had been in effect since 1925, because it "no longer corresponds to new conditions and needs considerable improvement."[97] Three months later, Molotov laid out the conditions essential to renewing the twenty-year-old treaty: revise the Montreux Convention, allow Soviet Union bases in the Straits, and cede the Kars and Ardahan districts to Soviet Armenia and Georgia.

Russian scholars Zubok and Pleshakov have argued that Stalin "raised territorial demands only as a bargaining chip; he dropped them in August 1946."[98] In his last years, Molotov also admitted that the territorial proposals were "ill-timed and unrealistic."[99] Strangely enough and contrary to the Turkish newspapers' claims, almost all of the Turkish politicians realized that the Soviets' main objective was to acquire political and military privileges in the Straits and that they were not serious about territorial proposals. Ambassador Sarper sent a telegram to Ankara after his talks with Molotov that was made public by Turkey's Ministry of Foreign Affairs in 1973. Sarper claimed that the Soviets put forward the territorial proposals to strengthen their position on the issue of the Straits: "They are not going to cut off the talks. I sensed that Molotov brought up this issue [i.e., the territorial proposals] in order to obtain compromises on other issues."[100] Moreover, Sarper also emphasized that although the Soviets seemed to be firm on the issue of Soviet bases in the Straits, they would accept a joint defense formula of the Straits during wartime.[101] Fevzi Çakmak, who was forced by İnönü to retire as chief of general staff in 1944, explained at the time why he could not understand the worries about Turkish-Soviet relations: "Even Stalin's proposal did not make me anxious. In my opinion, we have to talk with the Soviets. There is no need to be angry about their erroneous demands. On the contrary we have to sit at the table and explain their mistakes to them . . . During the Liberation War, there were some disagreements between the Soviets and us. However, we talked about them. In the end, we not only solved our problems but also established a friendship with them . . . Now they demanded the three districts. There is no need to worry. When they realize they made a mistake, they will give up this zeal."[102]

Saffet Arıkan, who served as Turkey's ambassador in Berlin between 1942 and 1944, considered the Soviet proposals as a bluffing tactic, explaining that there was no reason to be "afraid of Russians. They are exhausted and tired."[103] In April 1946, Bayar, interviewed by a North American Journalists Association correspondent, was asked about the Soviet proposals. He said that these were only rumors and that he did not take them seriously: "Soviet Union and Republican Turkey had solved all the problems—inherited from Tsarist Russia and the Ottoman Empire—in a friendly atmosphere. There is no issue in dispute between us. I personally participated in official negotiations and agreements. The private conversations should be considered as small talk and should not be taken seriously. As someone who closely witnessed the coherent Turkish-Russian relations, I cannot accept the opposite argument."[104] Similarly, in August 1946, Fuat Köprülü, among the four founders of the Democrat Party, said the ruling party was fabricating rumors about the external threats in order to preserve its power: "In my opinion our current foreign situation is not as dangerous as the government believes or as it sought to make the nation believe in order to influence the elections."[105]

Three weeks after the Molotov-Sarper talks in Moscow, İnönü came to Istanbul for two meetings with high-ranking military officials and bureaucrats about the recent developments in Soviet-Turkish relations.[106] The first meeting took place with military officials on July 8, 1945, in the suburb of Istanbul, Hadımköy. On the next day, İnönü met with bureaucrats in Dolmabahçe Palace. Although both of these meetings were closed to the press, İnönü's speeches were published in 2003. İnönü's speeches during these two meetings were landmark events reflecting the ruling elite's state of mind after World War II. After summarizing the Soviet proposals, İnönü, not expecting a Soviet military attack, told the high-ranking military officials that "the situation is not serious" and that there was no need for a military mobilization.[107] He believed the Soviets would not dare take such a grave step just after the San Francisco Conference, at which fifty nations mutually pledged respect for the territorial integrity of others. İnönü added, "Russians will not look for a new adventure after tremendous sufferings" during World War II.[108] İnönü asked the meeting participants: "If they [the Soviets] are not going to attack us right away, why did they put forth secret aims and ideas?" For İnönü, the Soviet proposals were intended to ignite consternation in the Turkish public and military as a pretext for the eventual disintegration of the political regime in Turkey.

During these meetings, İnönü stressed democracy's importance for Turkey's postwar development. But he also said it is necessary to "guide" Turkish democracy in order to avoid dangerous political factions, which supported friendly relations with the Soviet Union and which could prove disruptive to the nation's internal integrity and stability. The real risks for Turkish democracy, İnönü continued, were pro-Soviet groups that would hijack the newly established opposition party, transforming it into a communist party commanded by the Soviet Union.[109] To eliminate the "communist threat," the president demarcated the limits of

Turkish democracy, which remained valid until the disintegration of the Soviet Union in the early 1990s. Turkey's political system during the Cold War was, for all intents and purposes, a "guided democracy."

Toward the end of World War II, domestic and international pressures compelled the Republican ruling elites to establish a multiparty democracy. At the San Francisco Conference in 1945, Turkey accepted the United Nations charter, committing itself to liberalizing the political regime at home and setting the stage for opposition political parties to arise. From the spring of 1945 onward, the opposition's voice in and out of the RPP also grew steadily in volume and tone. Within the RPP, the opposition was galvanized around four members of Parliament: Celal Bayar, Fuat Köprülü, Refik Koraltan, and Adnan Menderes. In June 1945, they proposed three basic democratic reforms: restoring the National Assembly's power to control the government, granting individual political rights, and establishing a multiparty regime.[110] Outside of Parliament, the left-wing newspaper *Tan* became the gathering place for intellectuals including Zekeriya Sertel, Sabiha Sertel, and Behice Boran as well as politicians who were purged by İnönü, such as Aras and Cami Baykurt. Although these intellectuals and politicians condemned the right-wing posturing of the leading Republicans like Hüseyin Cahit Yalçın, they stepped gingerly to avoid explicit criticism of İnönü's policies.

In opening the parliamentary session on November 1, 1945, İnönü declared that an opposition party was needed for Turkey to establish a multiparty democracy: "The only thing we lack is an opposition party confronting the party in government."[111] However, İnönü did not imagine a full-fledged multiparty democracy representing the whole range of political factions. As Kemal Karpat rightly observed, "İnönü had in mind, at this stage, a rather limited democracy that would not challenge the Republican Party's rule."[112] In the second half of 1945, leading opposition figures such as Bayar, Sabiha Sertel, Aras, Baykurt, and Köprülü met several times before forming a political front against the RPP.[113] As a first step, they agreed on publishing their political views in a newly established journal *Görüşler* (Views), whose premier issue was published on December 1, 1945. The first cover depicted a theatrical stage and a partially opened curtain revealing three men symbolizing the "fascism, profiteering, and corruption" prevalent during İnönü's rule.[114] There also were photos of Bayar, Aras, Köprülü, Menderes, Sabiha Sertel, and Baykurt on the front page, presented to readers as the journal's staff of contributors. Sabiha Sertel, who owned the journal, later recalled that Bayar, Menderes, and Köprülü were unable to write for the first issue because they were engulfed in establishing the new Democrat Party. Sabiha Sertel's opening article for the journal, headlined "Enchained Freedom," accused Turkey's rulers of blocking democratic reforms. Sertel detailed the group's objective in forming a new Turkey that would recognize individual rights and freedoms: "Turkey should be a free vatan in the free world . . . This vatan does not belong to people who live on top of us. It is a vatan in which we will work with machines and share the collective sufferings and troubles. We are going to turn it into a utopia. Should the occasion arise, we will die for it. But we are going to love it as a vatan of free and unprivileged people."[115]

The opposition bloc, including well-known politicians who had served as prime minister, foreign minister, and interior minister as well as respected leftist intellectuals, alarmed Republican political circles with their vigorous campaign. İnönü permitted an opposition in order to save Turkey from being isolated in the international arena and to rehabilitate his public image domestically and internationally, especially as American and British diplomats considered İnönü an authoritarian leader who had flirted with the Nazis during the war. However, the opposition, seen by some as a stalking-horse party in a guided democracy, challenged İnönü by demanding free press, land reform, individual rights, the formation of trade unions, the right to strike for workers, and other substantive democratic reforms. Soviet proposals and the communist "threat" were used by the Republican elite as bogeymen to suppress the opposition and their democratic demands. They branded any critic against the government as participants in communist activity and therefore labeled their opponents outright as Soviet agents. For them, the means of communism were designed to realize much older territorial ambitions as the Soviet Union had inherited tsarist Russia's drive to the warm seas. Accomplishing such an objective would require the formation of left-wing groups targeted toward transforming Turkey into a Soviet satellite. In 1945, government-controlled newspapers initiated a political campaign against the opposition by exaggerating the Soviet territorial demands, identifying left-wing activists as "traitors to vatan" because they supported friendship with the Soviet Union and thus the destruction of Turkish vatan through territorial concessions.

Hüseyin Cahit Yalçın, a Republican member of Parliament and editor-in-chief of the newspaper *Tanin*, openly attacked the new opposition in an article headlined "Rise up the Sons of Vatan," published on the front page on December 3, 1945.[116] It was striking that Yalçın borrowed the headline from Namık Kemal, who had used it against the despotism of Abdulhamid. Yalçın wrote that the opposition, which came together at the *Görüşler* journal, was totally subordinate to Moscow, a de facto fifth column of the Soviet Union. For Yalçın, the opposition's emergence after the articulation of territorial "demands" by the Soviet leadership substantiated Soviet ambitions regarding Turkey. Against these "threats," he called for the creation of a nationalistic "front of vatan."[117] Yalçın was concerned that this anti-leftist thinking, prevalent in the Turkish political discourse during the Cold War, sought to validate communism as an internationally acceptable ideology, anticipating the unity of all workers around the world. More directly, Yalçın explained that all Turkish leftists were disloyal to the Turkish vatan. As leftists did not have any patriotic feelings for Turkish vatan, they were indifferent toward Soviet territorial "demands" and uninterested in the defense of Turkey's territorial integrity.[118] Yalçın's impassioned defense for nationalism, which considered any critic against the government as treasonous to vatan, was an iconic snapshot of the hegemonic political discourse during the Cold War. Hence it is worth quoting at length his article published just one day before the destruction of the *Tan* newspaper office by a mob of students:

> For centuries, this country defended itself against attacks from the north with its blood, spirit and army. Our nation's being was molded by these sufferings and disasters. This time, territories from the mother vatan and bases on the Straits have been demanded, which would end Turkish independence. Our National Chief [İsmet İnönü] reflected the nation's spirit when he said that we are going to live as a proud people and we are going to die as a proud people. However, the enemy has started infiltrating us in the form of communist propaganda. The

publications of Yeni Dünya and Görüşler removed any doubt on this subject. The situation is clear: The fifth column is working and has started the offensive ... The voice of the great patriot Namık Kemal is today's slogan: Rise up, oh! Sons of vatan! The struggle is beginning. We have to start. We cannot let the furious and merciless propaganda destroy Turkish citizens with its devastating and disheartening poison. Every Turk, who wants to own a vatan and to live freely and independently within this vatan, has to resist this propaganda and to make his own propaganda against it.[119]

Other pro-government journalists such as Asım Us and newspapers like *Vakit* and *Tasvir* joined this propaganda campaign and started to level frequent volleys in print against the leftist groups.

On December 4, 1945, a mob of students, organized by the Istanbul branch of the RPP, looted the *Tan* newspaper and other leftist publishers.[120] During the unrest, the police were present but did not stop the violence as students carried posters of İnönü and anti-Russian banners and shouted slogans such as "down with communists."[121] With the "Tan Raid" one of the most vigorous segments of the opposition was silenced by the Republicans. Afterward, the Soviets sent a written note to Turkey's foreign ministry stating, "The Soviet government cannot ignore these provocative actions against the USSR and as such, declares the Turkish government is responsible for these actions."[122] According to *Pravda*, "fascist riots in Istanbul" were "thoroughly planned and organized by local authorities," and similar anti-Soviet demonstrations occurred in Izmir and Bursa.[123] An article headlined "Our Legitimate Claims from Turkey," written by Georgian professors S. Janashia and N. Berdzenishvili, was published first by the Georgian newspaper *Kommunisti* on December 14, 1945, and immediately afterward by *Pravda* and *Izvestiya*.[124] The article was a historical analysis of northeastern Anatolia, and both authors concluded that this portion of Anatolia had belonged "rightfully" to the Georgian nation since the second millennium B.C. They argued that Turkey had harmed the anti-Hitler coalition during World War II by "siding with Fascist Germany ... The districts of Ardahan, Artvin, Oltu, Tortum, İspir, Bayburt, Trabzon, and Gümüşhane" should be returned to Georgia.[125]

Turkish newspapers started their own campaign against the Soviet Union following the controversial article's appearance in the Moscow media. Newspapers including *Tanin* and *Ulus* published photographs of Trabzon, Artvin, and Kars and announced slogans on their front pages to agitate the public opinion, such as "the Turkish vatan is indivisible" and "Our nation is ready to sacrifice in order to live."[126] Although, considering the strict centralized control over Soviet media, it would have been impossible for Georgian professors to publish their article in two prominent Soviet newspapers without the approval of Soviet authorities, similar articles had been published during World War II by pan-Turkist journals such as *Gökbörü*, *Bozkurt*, *Çınaraltı*, and *Orhun* that openly promoted territorial ambitions in the Caucasus and Central Asia. These publications had been tolerated by the İnönü regime until 1944.

In early February 1946, Gürtunca, who wrote the provocative booklet *Do Not Touch This Lion* in response to Italian territorial ambitions in 1939, published a similar one against the Soviet Union with the title *Do Not Touch This Vatan*.[127] For Gürtunca, the booklet was a "reply to Muscovites," full of militaristic and nationalistic illustrations and poems. The Turkish soldier who faced Italy in the previous booklet was now confronting Russia (Figure 4.4). While the author recounted the invasion of Russia by the "Hun Turks" from the Urals to the Volga, he also offered a humiliating reminder to the Georgians about their concubines being the most desirable women in the Ottoman harem. In addition to the historically steeped warnings, the booklet contained writings from nationalistic poets about the defense of the Turkish vatan: "Mother vatan, use your chest as a shield against weapons; the bullets cannot hurt you as they could not for years; my dear mother vatan: Spread thunderbolts from your chest; the Reds should understand the sacredness of the independence!"[128]

In the middle of the anti-Soviet and anti-communist propaganda war during the first winter following the end of World War II, the Democrat Party was established under the leadership of Bayar, Menderes, Koraltan, and Köprülü on January 7, 1946. Although Aras, who wrote articles about the necessity of the Turkish-Soviet friendship, participated in founding the Democrat Party, he was excluded from it by Bayar after the Tan Raid. With the escalating propaganda war in the Turkish press and political forums, Bayar decided to distance himself and the party

FIGURE 4.4 A map used in the popular booklet *Do Not Touch This Vatan*, showing a Turkish soldier facing the "Russian threat." It should be noted that one foot of the Turkish soldier is on the Straits region and the other on Kars.

from the left, which the ruling elite had associated with "Soviet aggression."[129] Nevertheless, Democrats could not avoid being denounced as "communists" and "Moscow's pawns" by Republican politicians and journalists whenever they criticized the İnönü regime. The Democrats' criticisms about the government's poor economic performance, suppression of the press, and irregularities in the 1946 elections were deemed "communist tactics" by Republican circles. To silence these criticisms, Republicans leveled barbs upon the Democrat Party, suggesting they were being "directed from Radio Moscow" and "financially supported by Bolsheviks."[130] Furthermore, in order to influence Turkish public opinion and American and British officials, Republicans argued that if Democrats won the elections, there would be a regime change in Turkey similar to those that had occurred in Bulgaria, Poland, Romania, and Albania.[131] On January 29, 1947, Şükrü Sökmensüer, the interior minister, spoke at length about "communist activities" in Turkey.[132] According to Sökmensüer, while the Republicans sought to establish closer relations with Britain, Fevzi Çakmak and Democrats argued that it was necessary to "come to an agreement with the Soviets in order to save the country and strengthen national independence."[133]

Between 1945 and 1947, the Republican ruling elites successfully exploited the Soviet territorial proposals to establish a "guided democracy" in Turkey and to situate an opposition that did not threaten İnönü's and his party's power. They linked substantial critiques against the government with perceptions of communist "threat" and treason to vatan in order to discredit the opposition. During this period, the state authorities tolerated and, even in particular cases, supported civil disobedience and vandalism against left-wing publications and institutions. In terms of creating an anti-communist rhetoric in politics, there were striking similarities between Turkey and the United States, where McCarthyism was beginning to cast a shadow over the American political discourse. This period played a significant role in the formation of the hegemonic Cold War political discourse, with the "communist threat" to the Turkish vatan functioning as a nodal point. In 1948, the Democrat Party's leading figures realized that the "communist threat" was a powerful tool for them to eliminate their opponents within the party. In 1948, some Democrat parliamentary members harshly criticized the Democrat leadership for using an authoritarian model in the party hierarchy. In return, the

Democrat leadership said that "the Red Danger" was seeking to infiltrate the party and characterized the opposition within the party as "Moscow's collaborators."[134] Bayar, accused by Republicans of collaborating with the Soviets, employed the same tactic to neutralize opposition, successfully forcing his critics to resign from the party. Even İnönü was not immune from accusations of being Moscow's pawn. Before the general elections in 1965, İnönü announced that the RPP had positioned itself to the "left of the center," a move sharply criticized by the right-wing Justice Party and conservative members of the RPP. The slogan "the left of the center is the road to Moscow" was frequently deployed during the election campaigns to damage İnönü's public image among nervous voters.

Turkey's anti-Soviet stance after 1945 left deep marks on the nation's foreign policy during the Cold War. Although Soviet proposals about the Straits and Eastern Anatolia in the interwar period—when Turkey considered the USSR a "friendly regime"—did not harm the close relations between the two countries, similar proposals in the postwar era represented grave threats to Turkey's territorial integrity and were consequently manifested in the hegemonic foreign policy discourse positioning the Soviet Union as Turkey's "enemy." Furthermore, after 1945, Turkish foreign policymakers based their rationale for establishing closer relations with Britain and the United States upon the increasing Soviet threat, and Turkish public opinion was swayed by the political discourse suggesting that Anatolia was under siege. Therefore, the general public accepted Turkey's entry into the Western camp as a symbolic liberation from the "communist threat," and most Cold War scholars accepted the conventional explanation that Soviet proposals compelled Turkey's integration into the Western sphere and NATO. Kamuran Gürün believed that Turkey would have continued its nonaligned foreign policy had the Soviet Union not insisted on territorial "demands" and the establishment of bases in the Straits.[135] Similarly, Duygu Bazoğlu Sezer observed, "had the Soviet Union not pushed Turkey into the western fold with her demands in 1945–1946, the same balance might have been maintained without Turkey's participation, and she might then have enjoyed the benefits of peace without having to choose between the two poles."[136]

While Western and Turkish scholars generally agree that Soviet proposals confirmed the Soviet expansionist push toward the south, revisionist scholars such as Melvyn Leffler, Thomas Paterson, and Haluk Gerger have criticized the entrenched Cold War rhetoric and its commonsense arguments.[137] Leffler explained: "Soviet demands on Turkey had a substantial defensive component," and they sought to control the eastern Mediterranean and Persian Gulf in order to defend their industrial areas and oil fields in the Caucasus against prospective military attacks originating in these regions. American strategic defense planners wanted to capitalize on the Soviet Union's extreme vulnerability in the region by establishing military bases in Turkey.[138] Bruce Kuniholm described Turkey's pivotal role in NATO as "bottling up the Soviet navy in the Black Sea, tying up Warsaw Pact forces along NATO's southern flank, and serving as a staging ground for a counterthrust against the Soviet Union."[139] In order to realize these objectives, NATO and American bases were established in the cities of Adana, Diyarbakır, İzmir, and İzmit.[140]

While Turkey, in 1945 and 1946, had vehemently refused official Soviet proposals concerning the joint defense of the Straits as encroachments upon its sovereignty and independence, the same Turkey, several years later, allowed the establishment of U.S. and NATO military bases in its territory, saying that these were necessary for the defense of the nation's territorial integrity. Nonalignment, which had been the backbone of Turkish foreign policy between 1923 and 1939, was considered "as dangerous as communist influence" by the prime minister Menderes.[141] It also was clear that Stalin overestimated his capacity to change the regime of the Straits and transfer Kars and Ardahan districts to the Soviet Union.[142] This hard-line Soviet policy toward Turkey as directed by Stalin and Molotov played an important role in the Turkish leadership's capacity for demonizing the image of the Soviet Union as a fatal enemy. Two months after Stalin's death in March 1953, the Soviet Union sent a written note to Turkey renouncing the territorial claims and the proposals for bases in the Straits. However, the Soviet policy shift toward Turkey did not challenge Ankara's allegiance to NATO nor its distrustful stance toward Moscow. Soviet proposals were not a real threat for Turkey's territorial integrity, but they did serve as an effective excuse for Turkish leaders to integrate the nation into the Western camp. İnönü's statement about Turkey's foreign policy in 1948 confirmed this stance: "Even if the Soviet Union had reversed its claims, I still would have preferred to collaborate closely with the United States."[143]

THE KOREAN WAR: A FIGHT FOR VATAN AGAINST COMMUNISM

The USS *Missouri*'s visit to Istanbul in April 1946 signified the establishment of close relations between Turkey and the United States. According to Nikolai Kochkin, Soviet diplomats considered this visit as "a military and political demonstration against the Soviet Union." It increased the importance of the Straits for Moscow. The issue of how to control the entrance into the Black Sea became much more significant than the question of how to ensure the Soviet Union's exit to the warm seas.[144] Afterward, proclamation of the Truman Doctrine in March 1947 and the subsequent aid package of $100 million for Turkey indicated the extent to which Washington considered Turkey an indispensable ally in its global struggle against communism. Later, Joint American Military Mission for Aid was created to administer American aid to Ankara, and by May 1948, 350 American personnel were deployed in Turkey to examine the national army's needs for modernization. With the inclusion of Turkey in the Marshall Plan, the number of American personnel administering economic and military assistance to Turkey increased to 1,644 in 1952 and to 5,000 in 1955.[145] Although military and economic relations with the United States warmed significantly after the *Missouri*'s 1946 visit to Istanbul, Ankara's diplomatic campaign to join NATO, launched in April 1949, was rejected initially by the United States, which hesitated to expand its military commitments outside of the Atlantic region, as well as by Britain, which was more willing to cooperate with Turkey in the Middle East than in Europe.

The general elections on May 14, 1950, resulted in the Democrat Party's victory with an overwhelming parliamentary majority. Bayar was elected by the Parliament as the third president of the republic while Menderes and Köprülü were appointed prime minister and foreign minister, respectively. Unlike Mustafa Kemal and İnönü, Bayar, Menderes, and Köprülü had no military background. On June 25, 1950, just one month after the Democrats came to power, North Korean armies crossed the Thirty-Eighth Parallel and invaded South Korea. Turkey was among the first countries to respond positively to the United Nations' call for assistance. Foreign Minister Köprülü, in briefing the Parliament on the conflict in the Korean peninsula and the United Nations' role, told members, "Turkey had communicated to them its willingness to execute loyally the engagements that it had entered into as a member of the United Nations."¹⁴⁶ On July 25, 1950, after an extraordinary meeting of the cabinet, Turkey offered a brigade of 4,500 soldiers to the coalition forces, its first involvement in an international military conflict since the end of the National Liberation War in 1922.

Of the twenty-one nations that participated in the Korean War, Turkey was the only Muslim country and the fourth largest military unit after the United States, Britain, and Canada.¹⁴⁷ Based on official statistics, up until the armistice in July 1953, 14,936 Turkish soldiers served in Korea. Of a total 3,277 Turkish casualties, there were 721 killed in action, 175 missing in action, 234 prisoners of war, and 2,147 wounded.¹⁴⁸ At 22 percent, the Turkish casualty rate in the Korean War was exceeded only by the United States. Turkey and the United States were the only two countries within the United Nations command to have more than 700 fatalities in the war.¹⁴⁹

What seemed striking about the government's decision to participate in the Korean War, in a distant part of Asia, was the lack of parliamentary debate. Although Article 26 of the Turkish constitution stipulated that "the power to declare war and participate in a war as well as to declare peace belongs to the Grand National Assembly of Turkey," the Democrat Party government did not even seek parliamentary counsel in its decision to enter the war.¹⁵⁰ By acting rapidly without consulting the Parliament and the opposition parties, the Democrat leadership anticipated that Turkey's decision to side with the United States in Korea would lead quickly to Turkey's entry into NATO. American Senator Harry Cain echoed these sentiments in a press conference in Ankara on July 25, 1950: "I can say we are going to be much more sympathetic in helping those who helped most in Korea, [and] we want all of our friends tied together as free nations militarily, economically and politically."¹⁵¹ Turkey submitted its formal proposal to join NATO just one week after its decision to send Turkish soldiers to Korea.¹⁵² The Democrat leadership wanted to "prove that this new government could succeed where the legendary İsmet İnönü, Atatürk's confidant and successor president, had failed just several months ago."¹⁵³ As expected, the Korean War played a decisive role in Turkey's admittance to NATO in 1952.

Following Köprülü's announcement about Turkey's readiness to fulfill its obligations to the United Nations, a nationalistic and anti-communist environment took hold in Turkish society. Newspaper editorial writers and columnists enthusiastically supported sending troops to Korea. By fighting against communism in a distant land, Turkey would demonstrate its determination to the Russians, who also had "threatened Turkey" with the invasion of northeastern Anatolia after World War II.[154] In the war euphoria, the only critical voice about sending troops to Korea came from the Turkish Association of Peace-Lovers, which was founded in May 1950 by a left-wing intellectual group led by Adnan Cemgil and Behice Boran. The group distributed 25,000 copies of an antiwar brochure in Istanbul, suggesting that the Menderes government had decided to send troops as a result of American pressure, directed by Senator Cain, who came to Turkey on July 23 and had met with the foreign minister and chief of staff. The brochure's authors argued that instead of participating in the Korean War, Turkey should offer peace and ceasefire proposals, like Indian Prime Minister Jawaharlal Nehru had done, to end the "internal war" in Korea.[155] After the mass brochure drop, the association cabled Parliament to ask its members to reverse the government's decision because it was illegal and because any war declaration came under jurisdiction of Parliament, not the executive cabinet.[156]

At a July 28, 1950, press conference, Prime Minister Menderes responded to the accusations of the Turkish Association of Peace-Lovers, alleging that the group was supported by external powers. Menderes told reporters, "while Turkey was preparing to counter the communist attacks in Korea, the objective of a similar provocation inside our nation was being realized by Turkish public opinion."[157] Furthermore, Menderes said that communists had been patronized by leading statesmen during the previous Republican governments, adding that the Democrat government would continue to fight against communism. Menderes defended the government's decision to send Turkish soldiers to Korea by stressing that "the independence and existence of the states could not be maintained by defending only their own geographical borders."[158] Just two months before this press conference, Menderes had stated that he was staunch in the struggle against "leftism," which he considered more dangerous than racism.[159] Likewise, Foreign Minister Köprülü described the antiwar activities of the Turkish Association of Peace-Lovers as "communist propaganda." The objective of the association, Köprülü added, was "to destroy the nation's power of resistance in order to turn it into a slave of foreign ideologies."[160]

Mainstream newspapers joined in the government's anti-communist rhetoric to silence the single opposition group regarding Turkey's participation in the war. Ali Naci Karacan, a columnist in the daily *Milliyet*, labeled members of the association as "red agents" and called for immediate governmental action against the group: "In a situation of war, the fifth column, which is the enemy's hand within Turkey's borders, cannot be allowed to pursue this type of provocation and defeatism."[161] The government subsequently outlawed the Turkish Association of Peace-Lovers, and its leaders Boran and Cemgil were arrested, tried in a military court, and sentenced to jail for up to three years.[162] The association's closing and the arrest of pro-peace academics and intellectuals "established a pattern of political repression by the Democrat Party, which had come to power on a promise of ending political repression."[163]

Even amid nationalist euphoria concerning Turkey's mobilization for the war, the Democrat leadership realized that the positive atmosphere inevitably would dissipate as soon as news about Turkish casualties appeared on newspaper front pages. In order to legitimize the decision to send Turkish soldiers and to counter anticipated criticisms and objections, Turkish leaders framed the Korean crisis as a religious war to defend Turkish vatan against atheist communists in a distant land. In August 1950, Ahmet Hamdi Akseki, the head of the religious affairs directorate, announced, "the mightiest weapon to defy communism is the power of faith and spirit. It is out of any reasonable question for a true believer to get along well with communist ideas."[164] The directorate published a book entitled *The Religious and Political Necessity of Our Participation in the Defense of Korea*, justifying Turkey's participation in the Korean War from a religious perspective. In defining "the road to Korea as Allah's road," the book positioned the war as a jihad, and those who died in Korea would be regarded as "martyrs."[165] With the Korean War, Turkish political discourse, which had been scrupulously secular since 1923, amalgamated anti-communism and nationalism with religious and Islamic sentiments. An icon of this change was the photograph published by the daily *Hürriyet* showing General Tahsin Yazıcı, the Turkish brigade commander in Korea, kissing the Koran before he left Turkey.[166]

After Parliament opened on November 1, 1950, Turkey's role in the Korean War was challenged in debates among the parties and newspaper columnists. Although the opposition of the RPP and the Nation Party did not object to sending troops to Korea, they accused the government of not consulting Parliament on such a grave matter of life or death. For the opposition and İnönü, the "problem was not 'why,' but rather 'how,' "[167] and both called for the Menderes government to resign. Opposition leaders equated Turkish troops' participation in Korea to a formal declaration of war and said that the Menderes government had acted unconstitutionally by subverting parliamentary approval. Replying to the parliamentary inquiry, Prime Minister Menderes accused the opposition of initiating a defamatory campaign with the intention of rendering the Democrat government disreputable in the eyes of the Turkish people. He emphasized that the government had responded properly to the United Nations' appeal and said that the decision of sending Turkish soldiers to Korea could not be regarded as a declaration of war. However, in the last portion of his speech, Menderes invoked a nationalistic tone, stressing that the Turkish nation had already rendered a decisive response to the parliamentary inquiry: "Today our country is once again experiencing the spirit of the National Forces. It is enthusiastic. Dear Friends, 4,500 sons of vatan that we sent there [to Korea] have established a new vatan with their blood."[168] Deputies of the Democrat Party reiterated the prime minister's words, accusing the opposition of generating polemics to impair the government while Turkish soldiers were dying in a heroic war against communism. Hamdullah Suphi Tanrıöver, who had played a key role in Turkish nationalism after the Balkan Wars, explained that the threat Turkey faced in the Caucasus and the disaster encroaching on Korea were directed from the same center: "Poor Turkish nation. After thousands of disasters, the Turkish nation is still continuing to raise heroes, who are fighting a battle far away from the Turkish vatan. That war is also my war. All the Asian territories are the vatan of ancient Turks."[169] Tanrıöver proposed leaving aside internal problems and disagreements and bringing together all the parties and factions against "the worldwide danger" as it had occurred during the National Liberation War.[170] After this steady stream of nationalistic speeches, the parliamentary enquiry was rejected by the Democrat deputies. Until the armistice in 1953 and well into 1954, the Democrat leadership continued to use the Korean War as a political tool against the RPP and İnönü, the party's leader. Fevzi Lütfi Karaosmanoğlu, minister of the interior, criticized İnönü's foreign policy during World War II, disparaging the country's former neutrality and championing the Democrat Party's pro-war foreign policy. Karaosmanoğlu said that İnönü "killed the country's masculinity and bravery" by staying neutral during World War II, adding that the Democrat Party had proved to the whole world that "our masculinity and bravery is still alive."[171]

After the Battle of Kunu-ri in November 1950, when Turkish soldiers broke the Chinese army's circled barrier with a bayonet attack, leading columnists in Turkish newspapers bolstered the government's nationalistic rhetoric, fully supporting its pro-war stance. On December 3, 1950, Hüseyin Cahit Yalçın wrote: "Turkish soldiers are fighting for Turkish vatan and at the same time for the dignity and salvation of humanity ... This is what is going to happen: As a result of the enemy's defeat in Korea and China, the enemy's forces, which are directed also for an attack against Turkey, will be reduced in size. The victorious United Nations' army in Korea will prevent the invasion of Turkish vatan. After all if Turkey is attacked, Turkey's companions at arms in Korea—Americans, British and other United Nations' forces—will come to destroy the Reds on Turkish soil. From now on, there is only one front in the world: civilization versus barbarity."[172]

The nationalistic sentiments bubbled over not only in the national dailies but also on the front pages of regional newspapers. Mehmet Tuncer, a columnist at the newspaper *Yeni Asır*, published in Izmir, characterized the Turkish soldiers' fight in Korea as "a defense of this vatan that is taking place in a distant land from the territories of this vatan."[173] Tuncer wrote that Turkish soldiers were going to be victorious in Korea because they knew exactly what they were fighting for: "[The] Turkish soldier was conscious of what he is going to fight for when he left vatan's soil. He carried the whole vatan in his heart. This is the reason for his defense of Korean soil inch by inch as if it was part of the soil of his vatan."[174]

The Democrat Party continued to play up Turkey's presence in Korea as a political instrument to attract voter interest and disparage the opposition parties. Before the 1954 general elections, the party published two booklets about Turkey's entry into NATO and Turkey's participation in the Korean War.[175] The first booklet, *Turkey and the Atlantic Pact*, was based on the well-established Cold War thinking of geographical determinism: "Our sacred vatan is located at the meeting point of Europe and Asia that is strategically very important."[176] The party authors explained that although the Turkish nation had defended its homeland against its enemy, namely, Russia, in the last centuries, "today it is very difficult to defeat the enemy with its satellites, whose population is fifteen times, territory thirty times, and economy approximately twenty to thirty times larger than ours."[177] The natural outcome of this dangerous geopolitical situation, the booklet continued, was Turkey's integration into the Atlantic Pact: "Our admittance to the Atlantic Pact hit Soviet imperialism like a thunderstorm. The Straits, the deep blue waters of the Mediterranean, and historic Istanbul—targets of centuries-long aspirations—became an unapproachable dream. These national objectives of Russia were buried in the true history."[178] The second booklet, *We Countered the Enemy in Korea*, sought to legitimize the extent of Turkish casualties in the Korean War. The booklet indicated that, in 1953, while approximately 1,300 people died in traffic accidents in Turkey, the total number of Turkish soldiers who died in the Korean War was less than 1,000. In return, the party authors wrote, Turkey had become a member of NATO and the Soviets renounced their demands on "the Straits, Kars, Ardahan, and Artvin."[179]

It is worth reiterating in the conclusion of this section that at the beginning of the Korean crisis, the Democrat leadership did not consider the North Korean invasion as a first step to worldwide communist expansion. In a meeting on June 28, 1950, Turkish Foreign Minister Köprülü conveyed this belief to General Horace McBride, the head of the U.S. military mission to Turkey: "The impression was left that the Turkish authorities considered this more or less a local affair and that it would not spread beyond the Korean area."[180] However, the government and mainstream newspapers represented the Korean War as a substantiation of "Soviet imperialism," identified as the most serious threat to Turkish vatan since 1945. The anti-communist and nationalist rhetoric of the government was so influential that even Turkish soldiers regarded Korea as part of their vatan in the same vein as their fathers, who had fought in the Ottoman armies in Yemen and Galicia and considered these countries as parts of their imperial vatan.[181] However, right from the start of the war, the government's main objective was to pave the way for Turkey's membership in NATO. To realize this objective, the Democrat leadership repressed any opposition to sending Turkish soldiers to Korea and used effectively the notion of vatan by linking criticism of the war effort to "traitors to vatan."

CYPRUS: FROM BABY-VATAN TO A GANGRENOUS PROBLEM

No other issue than the Cyprus question better indicates the transformation of Turkey's foreign policy and political discourse after the Cold War. Starting in the early 1950s, Cyprus had been represented as a baby-vatan (*yavru-vatan*), and its unification with the mother-vatan, Turkey, was perceived as the crucial national cause by the ruling elites. However, this well-established foreign policy stance toward Cyprus changed dramatically in the new century. At the European Union's 1999 Helsinki Summit, Turkey officially began the candidacy process for EU membership, but the Cyprus problem needed to be settled as a precondition for Turkey to start negotiations for full membership.[182] Turkish foreign policy decision makers, including the National Security Council and large segments of Turkish society, from business associations to trade unions, formed an unprecedented coalition to realize the objective of integrating Turkey into the EU, considered as the only viable option for a better future for the nation's people. They now regarded the Cyprus issue as a gangrenous problem threatening Turkey's Europeanization, one that should be surgically excised; doing so represented a sine qua non for Turkey's EU integration. In 2004, the Turkish government's acceptance of the Annan Plan as the basis of a settlement in Cyprus was the turning point in Turkey's foreign policy. The historical bloc eliminated the opposing nationalist groups and actors, foremost the veteran Turkish Cypriot leader Rauf Denktaş, who had actively participated in the struggle against Greek Cypriots since the 1950s and described the Annan Plan as "the annihilation plan for Turkish Cypriots."[183]

This section documents how Turkey's integration into the EU became a hegemonic project in foreign policy discourse, replacing the traditional national cause of integrating the baby-vatan, Cyprus, into Turkey with the more urgent need of solving the Cyprus problem so that Turkey's membership in the EU could proceed.[184] However, this shift cannot be analyzed by isolating it from recent Turkish and global social, economic, and political transformations. In the last three decades, while democratic reforms changed Turkey from a country ruled by military junta in 1980 to a viable candidate for the EU that met the Copenhagen criteria, the unprecedented efforts of liberalization and privatization converted the Turkish economy from import substitution industrialization based on strict government control to an export-oriented structure aimed at integrating Turkey with the global markets. As a result of these revolutionary changes, the platform upon which state-society relations were based shifted from an authoritarian tone to a democratic one. Interest groups and nongovernmental organizations (NGOs) with no say in the foreign policy–making process during the Cold War started to influence and shape Turkey's relations with the external world. Turkey's new foreign policy stance toward Cyprus in the 2000s—predicated on settling the Cyprus question according to an internationally supported plan involving the United Nations, United States, and the EU—became the archetype for this transformation.

Cyprus, which was transferred to British rule in 1878, was not considered part of the Turkish vatan in the National Pact announced in 1920. During the Lausanne Conference, Britain insisted that Turkey renounce all rights with regard to Cyprus and recognize the annexation of the island by Britain.[185] After World War II, when the British colonial empire started to disintegrate, Greek Cypriots, led by the communist Progressive Party of Working People and Archbishop Makarios of Cyprus, raised their demands for self-determination and Enosis—that is, the unification of the island with Greece. Until 1954, when Greece asked the UN to apply the self-determination principle to Cyprus, Turkey occasionally indicated that it preferred continuing British colonial rule on the island. On January 23, 1950, a couple of months before the Democrat Party's rise to power in Ankara, Turkey's Foreign Minister Necmettin Sadak announced, "There does not exist any problem called the Cyprus question. I told this to journalists explicitly some time ago. Today, Cyprus is under the sovereignty and control of Britain and we firmly believe that it will not transfer Cyprus to any other country."[186]

Ankara's pro–status quo policy about Cyprus continued with the Democrat Party government. On April 1, 1954, Turkey's foreign minister

Fuat Köprülü, when asked by a parliamentary member about the Turkish government's attitude on Cyprus, said, "There has never been a conversation or negotiation with our Greek allies and friends over Cyprus because the island is a British possession and it would be improper to discuss the subject with Greece. No Cyprus question exists for the Turkish government. But if a day arrives when the fate of Cyprus becomes a matter for discussion with Britain, naturally the presence of an important Turkish minority on the island will defer to Turkey the right to have her say."[187] Turkey's support for British colonial rule in Cyprus coincided with Turkey's pro-Western foreign policy stance in the 1950s. Along with Britain and the United States, the Menderes government condemned the nationalization of the Suez Canal by the Egyptian leader Gamal Abdel Nasser.[188] Contrary to Greece, which supported self-determination movements in Asia and Africa with the Afro-Asian bloc in the UN, Turkey sided with France and "voted in favor of the French position at the UN GA [General Assembly] regarding the independence of Algeria, Tunisia, and Morocco in the 1950s."[189]

Although the Turkish government sought to refrain from making assertive declarations about Cyprus in the first half of the 1950s, nationalist groups and newspapers, backed by the government against the "communist threat" since 1945, embraced the Cyprus issue and started to mold public opinion about it. During the 1950s, the newspaper *Hürriyet* took the lead, and Sedat Simavi, its editor-in-chief, published articles about Cyprus and advised the Turkish people and government to react against Greek ambitions aimed at turning Cyprus into another Crete by expelling all Turks from the island. As the political situation became exacerbated on the island, *Hürriyet* accused Istanbul's Greek minority of assisting Greek insurgents on Cyprus and laid the groundwork for the pogroms against the Greek minority on September 6–7, 1955.[190] Another important player was the National Students Federation of Turkey declaring the Cyprus question as the "national cause of the Turkish youth" as early as June 1953.[191] Strikingly, just three weeks after Foreign Minister Köprülü's statement indicating that there was no Cyprus question for Turkey at this time, the student group countered by declaring, "Cyprus is an indivisible part of mother-vatan."[192]

From 1954 on, Turkey's hegemonic political discourse identified Cyprus as the baby-vatan, and its eventual unification with Turkey was embraced by governments and newspapers as a national cause. In August 1954, immediately after Greece's application to the UN for a self-determining rule of Cyprus, the "Cyprus Is Turkish Committee" was founded by the National Students Federation of Turkey, and more than one hundred branches throughout the country opened in less than a year. As a result of establishing close contacts with Cypriot Turks, Fazıl Küçük, the leader of the Cyprus Turkish National Party, changed his party's name to "Cyprus Is Turkish." In the 1950s, the Cyprus issue became the predominant playground for nationalists and pan-Turkist groups in Turkey. They gave up their unification hopes with the Turkic groups in the Caucasus and Central Asia because of the Soviet Union's postwar consolidation in the region. While these nationalist groups fiercely rejected the Greek Cypriots' aspiration for Enosis, they advocated, oxymoronically, the counterargument for the Turkification of the island through Turkey's annexation. According to these groups, the "red danger" of the north sought to encircle Anatolia by establishing a communist regime in Cyprus under the leadership of Makarios, whose pro-nonaligned stance was seen as a serious threat to Turkey's well-being. As early as 1950, Ahmet Emin Yalman stated, "We are encountering a sabotage of Moscow" in Cyprus.[193] In the second half of the 1950s, nationalist publications illustrating Cyprus as a "baby-vatan" for the benefit of moving Turkish public opinion expanded rapidly in circulation.[194] As the general Turkish public did not have any notions about Cyprus because there was no information about the island in Turkish schoolbooks, the nationalistic publications employed maps to create the compelling image of Cyprus indelibly tied to Turkey. Among the most prominent examples was of the *Cyprus Is Turkish* publication, with a front-page map showing Cyprus chained to Turkey (Figure 4.5).[195]

As a result of increasing nationalistic sentiments in Turkish society and the beginning of the National Organization of Cypriot Fighters' armed struggle to unify the island with Greece, the Turkish government realized its status-quo policy in Cyprus had to change in anticipation of Britain's eventual withdrawal from the island. In August 1955, Turkey and Greece were invited to the Tripartite Conference in London to discuss Cyprus, thus legitimizing Turkey as an official player in the Cyprus question. Just a day before the Turkish delegation left Istanbul for the London conference, Adnan Menderes clarified the Turkish thesis: "The Turkish Anatolian

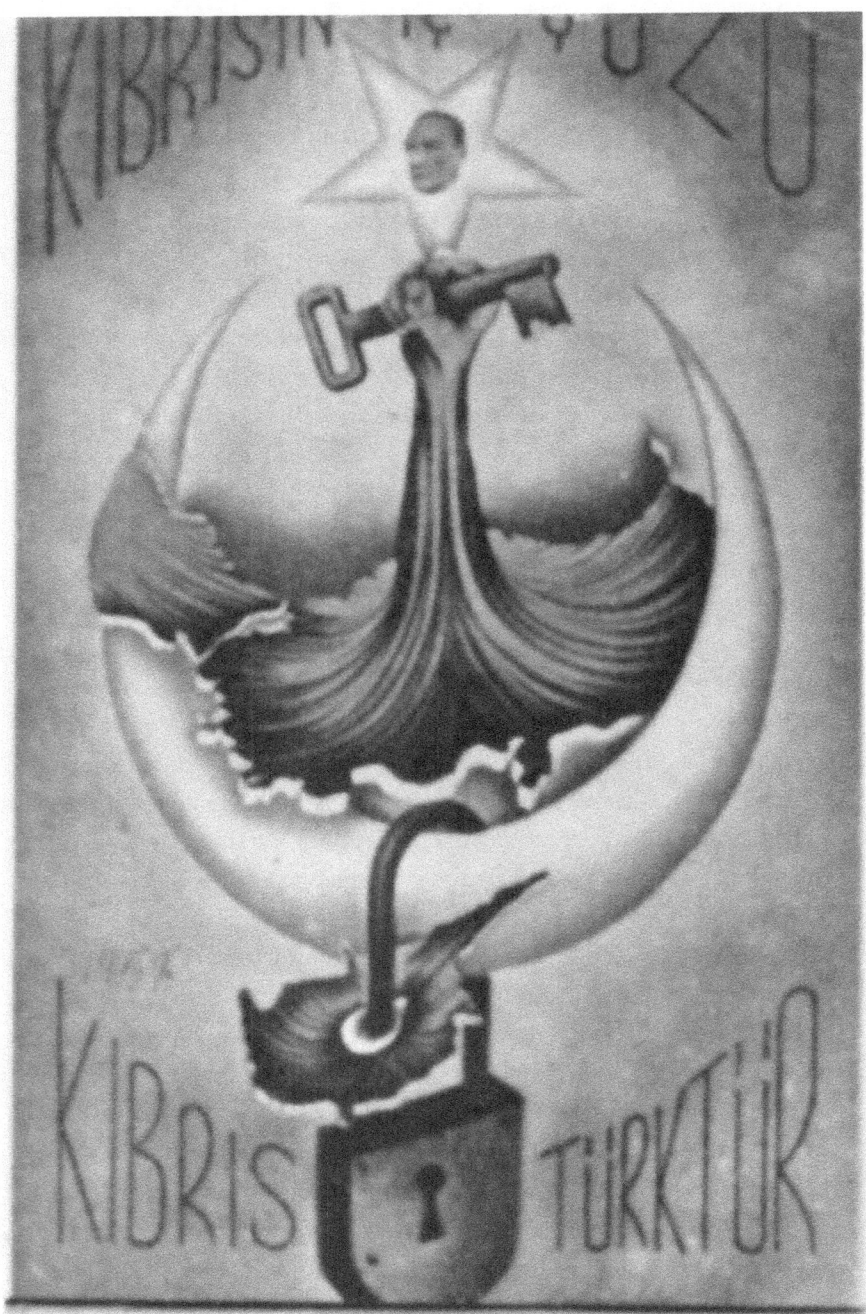

FIGURE 4.5 The front cover of the booklet *Cyprus Is Turkish* published in 1958. The map of Cyprus is chained to a crescent encircling the map of Turkey. Note the photo of Mustafa Kemal Atatürk in the star on the top of the page. This pictorial image was widely used in the late 1950s at mass rallies in Turkey and Cyprus.

coast is today surrounded by the advanced posts of a foreign country [Greece] and Cyprus is the only area free from this danger. Consequently, the Turkish thesis which will be put forward at the London conference is to sustain the status quo, the minimum threshold acceptable to Turkey; in the event of the island's changed status, Cyprus should be returned to Turkey."[196] In line with the nationalist rhetoric that "Cyprus is Turkish," Menderes predicated his declaration upon the geographic proximity between Cyprus and Anatolia, thereby defining "Cyprus as an extension of Anatolia." It was striking that Menderes rejected partitioning the island into two ethnic states, a position that would define Turkey's foreign policy regarding Cyprus after 1957. Menderes explained, "Vatan is not a piece of fabric in the hands of a tailor, who can cut it at his own will. It is a geographic entity constituting a geographic, political, economic, and military unity and whose borders are defined as a result of historical events."[197] Similarly, in July 1956, the Democrat Party's parliamentary group announced, "Cyprus is part of the mother-vatan and belongs to Anatolia from all geographical and historical points of view and [the island] is vital for Turkey's security."[198]

The Turkish government soon realized that its objective of reunification was not feasible, because Turkish Cypriots constituted only 20 percent of the total population. On December 28, 1956, Menderes reversed Turkey's stance toward Cyprus, declaring, "we are in favor of the partitioning of the island."[199] The move was crucial for Turkish political leadership not only for the protection of Turkish Cypriots but also for strategic reasons: "It is a piece of land that guards the security of 25 million people. We believe it is absolutely necessary to establish an advanced post there."[200] The partitioning (*taksim*) of the island into two ethnic states was accomplished in 1974 when Turkey intervened militarily. The impulse of partitioning had rooted itself deeply in the minds of the Turkish people and Turkish Cypriots with the slogan "partition or death" extensively used in mass demonstrations during the late 1950s and throughout the 1960s.

The Cyprus Republic was established in 1960 following the 1959 conferences in Zurich and London. Its political system arose from a power-sharing federation between Turkish and Greek Cypriots, with Turkey, Greece, and Britain acting as guarantor powers. In accepting the republic's existence, while Turkey seemed to back away from the partition thesis, the

Turkish and Turkish Cypriot political leaders never abandoned the goal of forming an independent Turkish state in the island's north sector. In 1964, after skirmishes erupted between Turkish and Greek Cypriots, Prime Minister İsmet İnönü stressed, "officially, we promoted the federation concept rather than the partition thesis so as to remain within the provisions of the Treaty."[201] After the ultranationalist military coup which was backed by the Greek military junta and attempted to unify the island with Greece, Turkey physically and ethnically divided the island as a result of two military operations in July and August 1974. In 1983, the Turkish Republic of Northern Cyprus (TRNC) was established in the north of the island, controlling 36 percent of Cyprus's total territory. While the UN Security Council denounced the formation of the TRNC as "legally invalid," only Turkey formally recognized the island republic, a country that was totally dependent upon Turkey.

Although Turkey justified the "Cyprus Peace Operation" as restoring the rightful independence and constitutional order of the Cyprus Republic, the establishment of an independent Turkish state, which involved expelling nearly all Greek Cypriots living in the north and the continuing presence of 30,000 Turkish military personnel, contradicted the military operation's declared peaceful objectives. Politicians and military officials never considered Turkish military personnel and garrisons in Cyprus as temporary presences that would be removed from the island as soon as Greek and Turkish Cypriots reached a settlement. Since 1974, the Turkish military operation has been represented as a campaign to recover the baby-vatan from Greek oppression. Bülent Ecevit, Turkey's prime minister in 1974, who ordered the landing of Turkish troops in Cyprus, became a national hero and was hailed as "the Conqueror of Cyprus," reminiscent of Mehmet the Conqueror, who vanquished Istanbul in 1453, thus ending the Byzantine Empire. Rauf Denktaş, who served as the president of the TRNC from its establishment until 2005, always believed it was impossible for Greek and Turkish Cypriots to live together peacefully. Emphasizing the unfeasibility of the Cypriot identity, Denktaş stated, "The only true Cypriot is the Cypriot donkey."[202] Accordingly, in all negotiations with the Greek Cypriots after 1974, Denktaş insisted on conditions of establishing a confederation or loose federation based on two sovereign states that would legalize the island's partitioning and would, therefore, pave the way for the independence of Turkish Cypriots.

Between the Helsinki Summit in 1999 and the Annan Plan referendum in 2004, Turkey's traditional foreign policy toward Cyprus, based on defending the baby-vatan as a separate Turkish state, dramatically changed. Eager to dispense Cyprus as a national cause, Turkey now considered it the main barrier to its EU membership. In Helsinki, the EU conferred Turkey's official status for EU candidacy, adding that its progress was contingent upon a satisfactory settlement of the Cyprus question. By doing so, the EU hoped the Turkish political leadership would pressure Denktaş, the Turkish Cypriot leader, to negotiate a compromise with Greek Cypriots. Consequently, the high-level debate emerging between the anti-EU and pro-EU camps ostensibly over Cyprus expanded into public ponderings about Turkey's future and whether it would become a democratic country fully integrated into the globalized world through the EU or an isolated country resisting "the transformation brought about by the process of globalization."[203]

The pro-EU actors, namely, TÜSİAD, liberal and social democrat columnists and newspapers, civil society organizations, Kurdish intellectuals, and the Justice and Development Party (JDP), which rose to power after the 2002 general elections, stressed that Turkey should solve the Cyprus issue by revising its traditional national security discourse and employing all possible means to become a member of the EU. In 2001, Turkey experienced one of its most severe economic crises since 1923 as Turkish currency plunged more than 50 percent, hundreds of thousands lost their jobs, and nearly a dozen private banks owned by Turkish conglomerates declared bankruptcy. During this economic downturn, Turkey's largest industrialists and large capital owners decided to intervene in Turkey's foreign policy, issuing press releases and mass media publications urging the settlement of the Cyprus question as the essential pretext to clearing the way for full EU membership and recovering from the economic crisis. In November 2001, TÜSİAD highlighted the significance of resolving the Cyprus question for Turkey's future: "Our country's primary national interest is to realize the objective of EU membership. For this reason, it is essential to handle the Cyprus issue in a way that it would not become an obstacle barring Turkey's membership to the EU and would not generate serious crises within the EU. It should not be forgotten that a deadlock on the Cyprus issue would result in a breakdown of Turkey-EU relations and, in the larger perspective, of Turkey's full membership status. Therefore its historical and social responsibility would be very heavy."[204] In 1974, the same TÜSİAD had supported the Turkish military operation in Cyprus and declared at that time that it was its national responsibility to contribute to the military operation by investing in the economic sphere.[205] Sabancı Holding, one of the largest conglomerates in Turkey, and its bank Akbank donated 1.5 million Turkish liras to the military immediately after the beginning of the military operation.[206] Nevertheless the TÜSİAD's statement in 2001 revealed the fact that Turkish industrialists had changed their political stance completely about the Cyprus conflict.

Almost a year after this announcement, the JDP came to power amid a landslide victory in the 2002 general elections, winning 363 of 550 seats in Parliament. However, Tayyip Erdoğan, JDP's leader, was barred from participating in the elections because of a 1998 conviction for inciting hatred on religious grounds after reading in public a poem. At that time, Erdoğan knew he would not have a political future in an undemocratic Turkey controlled by the military bureaucratic establishment that was cut off from the EU. Immediately after the general elections, Erdoğan campaigned for Turkey's EU membership, declaring himself committed to solving the Cyprus problem. Erdoğan endorsed the Annan Plan as a basis for negotiations:

> According to our point of view, the Cyprus question should not be a matter weakening Turkey any further. Therefore, we are ready to negotiate. We are not in favor of using the established status quo language regarding the Cyprus question. We think it necessary to find a solution to the forty-year-old Cyprus question. Both sides in Cyprus should refrain from accepting deadlocked negotiations as a kind of politics. According to our point of view, the plan presented to both sides on the island by United Nations Secretary-General Kofi Annan is a viable basis for negotiation. Some circles claim the plan is non-negotiable. They are wrong. No one can give up Cyprus or underestimate it. We propose to act reasonably by participating

in the negotiation process and by taking into consideration the mutual future of Turkey and the self-declared Turkish Republic of Northern Cyprus.[207]

Erdoğan's remarks about the Cyprus question not only represented a significant shift from Turkey's traditional Cyprus policy but also contradicted the then vision of Ahmet Davutoğlu, who served as the chief advisor to Erdoğan from 2003 till 2009 and later became the minister of foreign affairs. In his bestselling book, *Stratejik Derinlik*, which had been published only two years before Erdoğan's speech, Davutoğlu expressed his strategy about Cyprus very clearly: "Even if no single Muslim Turk had ever lived there, Turkey would have had a Cyprus issue. No country can remain indifferent towards an island located at the heart of its living space. Just like the continuing importance of the Dodecanese [for Turkey] which currently does not contain any significant Turkish population, and the direct US interest in Cuba and other Caribbean islands despite the lack of any social ties, Turkey needs to be interested, not only socially but also strategically, in Cyprus."[208] Davutoğlu's vision, which was very much in line with the conventional Turkish stance, would change dramatically, and he also became one of the strongest advocates in favor of solution in Cyprus.

On the other side, there were Eurosceptics, namely, the conservative military officials and bureaucrats, nationalists, and political parties such as the RPP and NAP. They insisted on supporting the long-standing national cause, refusing to compromise. They described any move to reestablish a common state between the Turks and Greeks in Cyprus as "selling vatan to Greeks." As negotiations between Turkish and Greek Cypriot leaders continued in New York City, General Hurşit Tolon, commander of the Aegean army, stated, "We quickly forgot the territories, which were flooded by the blood of martyrs. This country brought up beautiful people. But now it is also raising traitors. Is someone not a traitor who says 'give and get rid of it?' Are we going to leave our ethnic and religious brothers to the enslavement of Greeks? . . . The children of this nation are not going to abandon even a small stone."[209] In the Turkish media, a peculiar alliance emerged among newspaper columnists, who fiercely refused the settlement of the Cyprus question by way of Turkish concessions. Oddly, the debate brought together columnists such as

İlhan Selçuk, a Cold War–era left-wing intellectual who fiercely criticized right-wing governments during the 1960s and 1970s; Emin Çölaşan, who vehemently criticized right-wing politicians; and columnists in nationalist and Islamic newspapers such as *Tercüman*, *Milli Gazete*, and *Vakit*, which supported NAP and the Felicity Party, the main voice of Islamic fundamentalism in Turkey. They accused the JDP government and Prime Minister Tayyip Erdoğan as well as other supporters of the Annan Plan, such as TÜSİAD, of "selling vatan's soil."[210] Moreover, by associating Cyprus with Crete, which had become a Greek island as a result of a decades-old struggle against the Ottoman Empire, they labeled any compromise for the settlement of the Cyprus problem as "treason to vatan."[211]

İlhan Selçuk criticized Tayyip Erdoğan's policies in an article headlined "Baby-Vatan was Lost. Is Mother-Vatan going to be lost too?," published by *Cumhuriyet* on March 5, 2004. After accusing Erdoğan of exploiting religion for his political interests, Selçuk called upon Rauf Denktaş to save Turkey from Erdoğan: "Rauf Denktaş, the leader of Cyprus, is seeking to save the 'baby-vatan' from Ankara. But he is not able to save it. At least he has to come here and save the 'mother-vatan.' Turkey needs a real leader."[212] In articles published in the newspaper *Hürriyet*, Emin Çölaşan also criticized the political leadership for supporting the Annan Plan, explaining that the pro-EU camp aimed to integrate Turkey into the EU by advocating the campaign of "give and get rid of it." Çölaşan identified the pro-EU camp as "inclined to sell vatan's soil."[213] Similarly, Özgen Acar, a columnist at *Cumhuriyet*, labeled the business world, ruling elites, and the majority of the media in Turkey and Cyprus who supported the settlement as "give and get rid of it" actors and urged the readers to consider the fundamental question: "Under these conditions who is the traitor to vatan? Denktaş, who is at the negotiating table, or masochists who are shouting to Annan and Greeks to 'go ahead.' "[214]

Nearly every opposition party went up against the government's conciliatory approach that TÜSİAD and other leading NGOs supported. Deniz Baykal, the leader of the main opposition party of RPP, criticized Erdoğan's statement suggesting a specific amount of Cyprus territory could be ceded. Baykal said, "a dangerous crack and submission is emerging in Turkish foreign policy."[215] Devlet Bahçeli, the NAP leader, also condemned Erdoğan's foreign policy, explaining that Erdoğan was ignoring Turkey's forty-year-old struggle in Cyprus. Bahçeli added, "If the government gives Cyprus and saves itself, it will not save itself from the [Turkish] nation."[216] Bülent Ecevit, the leader of the Democratic Left Party who had been hailed as the "conqueror of Cyprus" since 1974, considered "the government as a serious threat not only for the regime, but also for the satisfaction of national unity."[217]

Prime Minister Erdoğan responded against these accusations, saying "no one has the right to claim that he loves his country more than any other person . . . We will achieve nothing by accepting the stalemate as a solution, pursuing passive wait-and-see policies, producing paranoiac fears and isolating ourselves from the world."[218] Hadi Uluengin, a columnist in the daily *Hürriyet*, criticized Eurosceptics, emphasizing that no one had the right to claim a monopoly over vatan and patriotism: "Traitor to vatan. This is the most delicate part of the matter. One who has the right to speak loudly and is able to pound the table vigorously thinks 'vatan' belongs only to him. He knows everything. Others with different opinions are seen as traitors who are selling Cyprus."[219] Similarly, Cüneyt Ülsever, another liberal columnist at *Hürriyet*, wrote that some high-level military officials and bureaucrats seemed to inhabit the syndrome of "what would vatan do without me? They inextricably identified themselves with their positions [in the state institutions]. In the end, they gradually become vatan and vatan becomes them . . . According to them, anybody who does not agree with them is a traitor to vatan."[220]

Although the Eurosceptic and pro-EU camps debated about Cyprus, the disagreement in reality became a testing ground involving two irreconcilable worldviews about Turkey's future. Eurosceptics considered giving concessions for a settlement in Cyprus as the first step of revitalizing the Sèvres project by the European powers. The Eurosceptics explained that if Turkey retreated in Cyprus, this would be followed by democratic reforms for the Kurds, thus ending the Turkish state's unitary structure, which would consequently end with the state's disintegration. Even unprecedented large-scale privatizations after 2002 were regarded as "selling vatan" to foreigners by this opinion camp.[221] Their solution to defend Turkey's independence and integrity against the offensive of EU and global economic forces and their "collaborators" within Turkey was outright isolation.

In line with the isolationist's worldview, some high-level military officials in the Turkish army, who staunchly supported Mustafa Kemal's goal since the republic's founding of achieving eventual parity in civilization with Turkey's continental neighbors, advocated breaking off relations with the EU. In March 2002, Tuncer Kılınç, secretary-general of Turkey's National Security Council and a four-star general, said, "the EU had taken an unfavorable stance" regarding Turkey's application for membership and, therefore, "Turkey should pursue closer ties with Iran and Russia without compromising its relations with the United States."[222] Although opponents of the Annan Plan—in particular, Rauf Denktaş, the Turkish Cypriot leader—embraced the generals' publicly stated position, Hilmi Özkök, the chief of general staff and presumably the most democratic general in the army in Turkey's modern history, declared that the military would not be involved in the political negotiations process being pursued by the Turkish government. Furthermore, the National Security Council press release in January 2004 indicated, "Turkey continues to support the goodwill mission of the UN secretary general and reiterates its political determination to reach speedily a solution through negotiations in line with the realities on the island as based on the Annan Plan."[223] This statement took a swing at the Eurosceptics, who anticipated that the Turkish military would never allow the Annan Plan to be implemented.

The pro-EU actors rejected this isolationist approach, arguing that Turkey's national interests necessitated integration into the EU, and they welcomed globalization and its effects such as the free movement of capital and goods, privatization, foreign direct investment, and participation in supranational institutions. The fierce debate over Cyprus ended with the pro-EU camp's victory when Turkey gave the green light to the Annan Plan, which was then put in referendum in the Turkish and Greek parts of Cyprus on April 24, 2004. While Turkish Cypriots overwhelmingly backed the Annan Plan (65 percent saying yes), it was not implemented, as the Greek Cypriots rejected it with an even more overwhelming majority (76 percent voting no). Nevertheless, in December 2004, the EU decided to initiate accession talks with Turkey largely due to Ankara's collegial approach toward settling the Cyprus issue.

Last of all, the Turkish Cypriots' will and conviction to change the status quo and unify Nicosia, the last divided capital in the world, was crucial in fundamentally changing Turkey's previously uncompromising stance toward Cyprus. In 2000, an extraordinary meeting in the Turkish Republic on the island brought together forty-one NGOs and trade unions with two opposition parties in a platform headlined "This country is ours," under which large-scale demonstrations were organized in favor of a Cyprus settlement. Platform organizers accused Denktaş of advocating Turkey's strategic interests over those affecting the future of Turkish Cypriots. The general elections in December 2003 turned into a referendum for the Annan Plan. Opposition parties, which supported the settlement against the status quo, won 51 percent of the votes, a major blow for Eurosceptics in Turkey. The disappointment was reflected strikingly in a *Star* newspaper article after the elections: "Honey [*Yavru-m*] Vatan . . . Apparently one part of Cyprus known as baby-vatan by us seems to have been so enthusiastic about Greeks for years now. They want to have a Greek leader. We learned this grim reality as election results were announced."[224] The pro-settlement groups in northern Cyprus replied to these accusations, labeling them as unpatriotic, by citing Nazım Hikmet's well-known poem "Traitor to Vatan," a personal response to his citizenship being stripped in the 1950s because of political views considered treasonous to vatan by the Menderes government.[225] Nazım Hikmet criticized the undercurrent of patriotism, dominated by the hegemony of ruling elites, writing, "Yes, I am a traitor, if you are a patriot; if you are a defender of our homeland, I am a traitor to my homeland; I am a traitor to my vatan." In quoting the poem and supporting unification, Turkish Cypriots turned against national dogma, which had suggested that living peacefully with the Greek Cypriots was incomprehensible and the only way for them to survive was to establish and protect their independent nation-state.

CONCLUSION

With the establishment of the Republic of Turkey in 1923, the Kemalist leadership employed a modern territorial approach to organize the new state's borders, institutions, citizenship, everyday life, education, and foreign policy based on the national vatan. As their imagined national sense of vatan based on territorial sovereignty radically differed from the imperial vatan in late Ottoman times, new political norms—such as anti-imperialism, anti-colonialism, nonalignment, and, most important, absolute independence—gradually came to dominate in Turkey's foreign policy during the 1920s and 1930s. Although the European Great Powers in Lausanne recognized Turkey's sovereignty, the Kemalist leadership did not trust these powers, believing they were waiting for an opportunity to resurrect the Sèvres project. Furthermore, Kemalists were aware that the National Liberation War would be a model for other Eastern nations in their struggle against European colonialism and that, because of this, they would be isolated by the European powers in the international political arena. To overcome this seclusion, Kemalists cooperated with the Soviet Union and established regional pacts in the Balkans and the Middle East to resist the revisionist powers' ambitions. Another important characteristic of Turkey's foreign policy during the 1920s and 1930s was that as Kemalists expelled all the members of the Ottoman dynasty and purged all of their opponents, they did not need to create "external threats" in order to sustain their hegemony in domestic politics. Instead their spatial imagination was centered upon "rebuilding the vatan and becoming the owner of the sovereignty in order to live happily and freely in it."[226]

With İnönü's rise to power in 1938, Turkey's foreign policy changed significantly. In 1939, the İnönü regime put an end to the Kemalist principle of nonalignment and allied with Britain and France. Another important change was that pragmatism and the preservation of political power rather than the pursuit of ideology defined the focal points for İnönü and his colleagues in foreign policy.[227] For example, at the beginning of World War II, Turkey was the ally of Britain and France and had a friendship agreement with the Soviet Union. Later, it signed a nonaggression pact with Berlin and exported crucial raw materials, such as chrome, to Nazi Germany until 1944. Although Turkish foreign policymakers promoted such a policy as active neutrality, it was more appropriate to characterize it as "chameleon neutrality."[228] The lack of distinct ideology and chameleon neutrality was manifested because İnönü never sensed he was secure enough in his political power. Although the official history portrayed İnönü's succession of Mustafa Kemal as an abrupt shift in consensus among the Kemalist elite, there were other leading politicians, such as Tevfik Rüştü Aras and Şükrü Kaya, who contested İnönü's leadership. However, this power struggle did not manifest fully until the end of World War II. As the opposition became better organized in the second half of 1944, İnönü realized he would face a difficult future on the domestic and international political scene as he was perceived by the Allies as authoritarian and unreliable because of his earlier foreign policy stance toward Nazi Germany.

Soviet proposals in 1945 gave a much-needed lifesaver to the İnönü regime intent on staying in power and suppressing the opposition. In representing the Soviet proposals as an "imminent threat" to Turkish vatan, the İnönü regime created a paranoid political environment in which major opposition political figures were seen as the fifth column of the Soviet Union and were labeled as communist traitors to vatan. Communism as a "threat" to Turkey's territorial integrity became a fulcrum in Turkey's political discourse during the Cold War. Reflecting, in part, Owen Lattimore's comment about the Great Wall, which "was more a product of the kind of state created within China than kind of pressure against China from the steppe," Turkey's foreign policy after 1945 based on defending vatan against communism was more a product of the Turkish ruling elite's mindset than the Soviet Union's stance toward Turkey.[229] Moreover, the "communist threat to vatan" became a crucial territorial component of Turkish national identity, which was employed by the political leadership for the purposes of maintaining a cohesive society and eliminating the opposition. The Democrat Party leaders, who also had been accused of adopting communist tactics before coming to power in 1950, soon realized the "communist threat to vatan" was a powerful political tool to exorcise any criticism against the government. During the Cold War, this "threat" successfully legitimized crucial foreign policy decisions such as sending Turkish troops to Korea, represented subsequently as a defense of vatan against communist expansionism in a remote part of Asia. In the 1950s, even the Greek Cypriots' political project of Enosis was described as a communist encirclement of Turkish vatan.

The Cold War's end dramatically affected Turkey's foreign policy. In addition to the disappearance of the Soviet "threat," Turkey's liberalization and integration into the world meant that the long-standing foreign policy discourse as based on 'threats' to vatan became meaningless. The change of Turkey's stance toward Cyprus in the 2000s exemplified this transformation. New political actors emerged and defended Turkey's membership in the EU as the only viable option for the country's future. They challenged Turkey's traditional foreign policy toward Cyprus, which had represented the island as a baby-vatan and had previously rejected any compromise by labeling it a betrayal. Now, the new generation of political actors saw that continuing this stance would risk isolating Turkey from the world. These shifts in the foreign policy attitude toward Cyprus and the acceptance of the Annan Plan suggested that representations of vatan were not static and, most important, were not being hegemonically directed by the ruling political elite as they had been during the Cold War. Instead, representations of vatan were continuously contested and dynamically evolving on a stage of new global and local political actors.

Conclusion

IN 1951, geographer Jean Gottmann raised a question far more profound and beyond the theoretical importance of his discipline: "if the earth's surface had been as even and uniform as a billiard ball, would it have been divided into so many political compartments?"[1] Gottmann was not quite sure about the answer at the time, but in an article published in 1978, he had concluded that "Geographical partitioning is fundamentally rooted in the minds of men."[2] The state-centered system of territories essentially defines how we understand the world and how our geopolitical imagination of the world is produced, organized, and used in constructing the nation-state system. State territoriality necessitates that all individuals belong to a nation and each "state presides over, maintains, and is identified with, one kind of culture, one style of communication, which prevails within its borders."[3] This rationale is pertinent to formulating our worldviews and identities.

Kemalist reforms were unprecedented in terms of combining Turkish identity with territoriality. Mustafa Kemal's notion of modernization was fundamentally different from all previous interpretations during the late Ottoman period. Mustafa Kemal rejected all forms of ambiguous nationalism, such as pan-Turanism and pan-Turkism, in favor of making Turkey an independent and territorially based state. With the establishment of the Turkish state, a sense of nationalism substituted servitude to the sultan with loyalty to the homeland. During the War of Independence and the reform period after 1923, not only was the Turkish state but the very idea of Turkish nation was "imagined."[4] Nevertheless, Kemalism, with its emancipating discourse, was an authoritarian ideology aimed at establishing hegemony over the society, politics, and economy. Ernesto Laclau's judgment about the antagonism between egalitarian and authoritarian tendencies in Jacobinism, taken as a model by Mustafa Kemal and other leading politicians, rightfully applied to Kemalism. On the one hand, Kemalism was, in every sense, revolutionary by establishing a Turkish nation with the motto that "sovereignty rests unconditionally with the nation." On the other hand, it became authoritarian as a result of "the dissolution of the plurality," "the affirmation that society must be radically reconstituted from a single political point," and an apodictic stance claiming "for itself an incontestable 'rationality.'"[5] Like any other nation-state in the twentieth century, the Turkish nation-state, which formed with the intention of unifying the society within a politically and ethnically homogeneous vatan, became like "a vortex sucking in social relations to mold them territorially."[6]

Vatan, far from a static territorial structure as suggested by nationalist ideology, has been continuously deterritorialized and reterritorialized by the hegemonic political discourse as internal and external conditions have changed. After World War II, because of the change from a one-party system to a multiparty one and as a result of Turkey's industrialization, new political parties and social classes emerged, demanding a more egalitarian political and economic system. However, the Cold War's dichotomous international structure allowed the ruling elites to contain the competition over politics and economy at high levels by restricting comprehensive democratic participation. Vatan, represented under the "threats and dangers" associated with Turkey's "fixed" geographic characteristics, significantly justified the bureaucratic-military establishment's capabilities to maintain its political influence as well as the refusal of the politicians in power to reform Turkey's "special" democracy. Up until the Soviet Union's collapse, left-wing groups and intellectuals were accused of working as the fifth column of communism in Turkey and were labeled as traitors to vatan. Turkish soldiers sacrificed their lives defending the same vatan in Korea against communist "expansion," and in Cyprus, a baby-vatan was born, whose protection became the Turkish people's national cause.

Strikingly, almost a century ago, Süleyman Nazif, an Ottoman writer and statesman, criticized militarist understandings of vatan and patriotism: "If we had loved our vatan properly, its mountains would not have been so bone dry, its rivers would not have been so miserable, its forests would not have been so looted, its coasts would not have been so empty and its plains would not have been so desolate. Briefly its territory would not have been so wretched and its people would not have been so ruined ... Vatans should not be protected only during war times and against external enemies. During peace times people's duty is much more important and difficult: to save the country from misery and to bring prosperity and happiness to today's ramshackle places."[7]

The fading of Cold War antagonisms has stirred up new discourses on vatan. The ruling elites no longer have hegemony over constructed mental maps, imposing order and identity in a way that made the world understandable for Turkish people. In line with Süleyman Nazif's ideas, today the meanings of territory and nation in Turkey are challenged under the strong currents of globalization by new internal players, including industrial regions, business associations, and civic organizations. They cooperate and compete with global and external actors, such as the EU, the International Monetary Fund, global financial institutions, and multinational companies, to influence how the Turkish vatan is remade. Although the Turkish state continues to be the main player within the vatan, these substate and suprastate actors continuously challenge the territorialization of social relations based on a national scale. They not only decenter but also seek to reconfigure the Turkish state, which is no longer able to stabilize social order and maintain the welfare system and, thus, must strive to establish a democratic political system and liberal economy amenable to attracting transnational capital. Even the Turkish military, once considered the ardent defender of the nation-state and vatan, has not been excluded from this transformation. On the one hand, the Turkish military continues to rely on the slogan "everything is for vatan," proclaiming it on garrison walls and putting it on the mountains of Eastern Anatolia, where it has been fighting against the Kurdish insurgency for more than two decades. Turkish soldiers still shout out the well-known motto "vatan, I am ready to sacrifice myself for you" every morning in their warm-up exercises. On the other hand, the military operates the Armed Forces Mutual Assistance Fund (OYAK), one of the largest industrial conglomerates in Turkey with a total of $8 billion under its control. The Turkish military benefited from the liberalization of the Turkish economy by selling OYAK's bank. OYAK bought the bank for $36,000 in 2001 and then sold it to the Dutch ING Bank for $2.7 billion in 2007.[8] Editors for the *Milliyet*, a Turkish daily newspaper, ridiculed the OYAK bank sale in an article headlined "The Soldiers' Bank Has Gone to Foreigners," especially because Coşkun Ulusoy, OYAK's chief executive, had criticized past transfers of large-scale state economic enterprises to private foreign companies in the name of "Turkey's strategic importance."[9]

Vatan continues to be the nodal point of Turkey's political discourse as it is for any other country. It was somewhat remarkable that U.S. Senator John McCain used the slogan "Country First" in his 2008 presidential campaign and Egypt's former President Hosni Mubarak defended his authoritarian rule against determined popular protests and pressure in February 2011 by arguing that "I never wanted power or prestige, and people know the difficult circumstances in which I shouldered the responsibility and what I have given to the watan during war and during the peace."[10] Today, such questions as "where is vatan" and "against whom should we defend vatan" are debated by different groups and are much more difficult to answer straightforwardly than they were two decades ago. However, one thing is certain: neither the Turkish nor any other state have a monopoly over its territory in the Weberian sense.

NOTES

INTRODUCTION

1. Hans H. Gerth and C. Wright Mills, eds., *From Max Weber: Essays in Sociology* (New York: Oxford University Press, 1958), 78.
2. Neil Brenner, Bob Jessop, Martin Jones, and Gordon Macleod, eds., *State/Space: A Reader* (Oxford: Blackwell Publishing, 2003), 2–3; John A. Agnew, *Geopolitics: Re-Visioning World Politics* (New York: Routledge, 1998), 51.
3. James Anderson, "Nationalist Ideology and Territory," in *Nationalism, Self-Determination and Political Geography*, ed. R. J. Johnston, David B. Knight, and Eleanor Kofman (New York: Croom Helm, 1988), 18.
4. According to Thongchai Winichakul, "the geo-body of a nation is a man-made territorial definition which creates effects—by classifying, communicating, and enforcement—on people, things, and relationships." Thongchai Winichakul, *Siam Mapped: A History of the Geo-Body of a Nation* (Honolulu: University Press of Hawaii, 1994), 17.
5. Benedict Anderson, *Imagined Communities* (London: Verso, 1993).
6. Anssi Paasi, "Bounded Spaces in the Mobile World: Deconstructing 'Regional Identity,'" *Tijdschrift voor Economische en Sociale Geografie* 93, no. 2 (2002): 139.
7. "Ecevit: Türkiye'de Türk Silahlı Kuvvetleri'nin Özel Bir Konumu Var, Bize Bu Bakımdan Avrupa Ülkeleri Örnek Olabilecek Konumda Değil," *Hürriyet*, January 15, 2001.
8. İlker Başbuğ, "General İlker Başbuğ's Speech during the Handover Ceremony of Turkish General Staff," August 28, 2008. Accessed October 30, 2008. Available from www.tsk.mil.tr/10_ARSIV/10_1_Basin_Yayin_Faaliyetleri/10_1_7_Konusmalar/2008/org_ilkerbasbug_dvrtslkonusmasi_28082008.html.

9. Quoted in Ersel Aydınlı and Dov Waxman, "A Dream Become Nightmare? Turkey's Entry into the European Union," *Current History* 100, no. 649 (2001): 385.
10. *Lise Milli Güvenlik Bilgisi* (Istanbul: Devlet Kitapları, 2004), 7. On this subject, see also Pınar Bilgin, "'Only Strong States Can Survive in Turkey's Geography': The Uses of 'Geopolitical Truths' in Turkey," *Political Geography* 26, no. 7 (2007): 746.
11. Henri Lefebvre, "Reflections on the Politics of Space," *Antipode* 30, no. 2 (May 8, 1976): 31.
12. Jens Bartelson, *A Genealogy of Sovereignty* (Cambridge: Cambridge University Press, 1995), 31.
13. The quote belongs to Suat İlhan, the retired general who has done extensive work on geopolitics since the 1960s and has published various books and articles about Turkey's geopolitics. Suat İlhan, *Avrupa Birliğine Neden Hayır? Jeopolitik Yaklaşım* (Istanbul: Ötüken, 2000), 36. For an exceptional study about the "geopolitical truths," see Bilgin, "'Only Strong States Can Survive in Turkey's Geography,'" 740–756.
14. Bartelson, *A Genealogy of Sovereignty*, 13.
15. Oren Yiftachel, *Ethnocracy: Land and Identity Politics in Israel/Palestine* (Philadelphia: University of Pennsylvania Press, 2006), 43.
16. Akhil Gupta and James Ferguson, "Beyond 'Culture': Space, Identity, and the Politics of Difference," *Cultural Anthropology* 7, no. 1 (February 1992): 9–11.
17. Michel Foucault, *Power/Knowledge* (New York: Pantheon, 1980); Ernesto Laclau, *New Reflections on the Revolution of Our Time* (London: Verso, 1990); Gearóid Ó Tuathail, *Critical Geopolitics* (Minneapolis: University of Minnesota Press, 1996); David Campbell, *Writing Security: United States Foreign Policy and the Politics of Identity* (Minneapolis: University of Minnesota Press, 1992); Anssi Paasi, *Territories, Boundaries, and Consciousness: The Changing Geographies of the Finnish-Russian Boundary* (New York: Wiley, 1996); Pierre Bourdieu, *Reproduction in Education, Society, and Culture* (London: Sage, 1990).

CHAPTER ONE. SEARCHING FOR A NEW LEGITIMACY

1. Ahmet Davutoğlu, *Alternative Paradigms: The Impact of Islamic and Western Weltanschauungs on Political Theory* (New York: University Press of America, 1994), 6–7.
2. Ibid., 118–123.
3. Al-Anbiyaah 21/92.
4. Davutoğlu, *Alternative Paradigms*, 185. *Tawhid* is one of the central concepts in Islam and symbolizes the oneness and absoluteness of God. According to the Koran, "He is Allah, the One, Allah is eternal and absolute. None is borne of him, He is unborn. There is none like unto him."
5. Cyril Glasse and Huston Smith, *The New Encyclopedia of Islam* (Walnut Creek, CA: AltaMira Press, 2003), 111–112.

6. Bernard Lewis, *The Political Language of Islam* (Chicago: Chicago University Press, 1988), 73.
7. Ahmet Özel, *İslam Hukukunda Ülke Kavramı: Darulislam Darulharb* (İstanbul: İz Yayıncılık, 1998), 273.
8. Simon Dalby and Gearóid Ó Tuathail, *Rethinking Geopolitics* (New York: Routledge, 1998), 67–68.
9. For the gaza thesis, see Paul Wittek, *The Rise of the Ottoman Empire* (London: Royal Asiatic Society, 1938). For a detailed analysis about the formation of the frontier zone in Anatolia, see Ralph W. Brauer, *Boundaries and Frontiers in Medieval Muslim Geography* (Philadelphia: American Philosophical Society, 1995), 53–60.
10. Cemal Kafadar, *Between Two Worlds: The Construction of the Ottoman State* (Berkeley: University of California Press, 1995).
11. Colin Imber, *The Ottoman Empire, 1300–1650* (New York: Palgrave Macmillan, 2002), 126.
12. Colin Imber, *Eb'us-su'ud: the Islamic Legal Tradition* (Stanford, CA: Stanford University Press, 1997), 77.
13. Imber, *The Ottoman Empire*, 121.
14. Halil İnalcık, *An Economic and Social History of the Ottoman Empire* (Cambridge: Cambridge University Press, 1997), 1:188.
15. Norman Itzkowitz, *Ottoman Empire and Islamic Tradition* (New York: Alfred A. Knopf, 1972), 69.
16. Imber, *Eb'us-su'ud*, 86.
17. Edward Weisband, *Turkish Foreign Policy, 1943–1945: Small State Diplomacy and Great Power Politics* (Princeton, NJ: Princeton University Press, 1973), 211.
18. Brian Glyn Williams, *The Crimean Tatars: The Diaspora Experience and the Forging of a Nation* (Leiden, The Netherlands: Brill, 2001), 126.
19. Davutoğlu, *Alternative Paradigms*, 48–49.
20. Halil İnalcık, "Turkey," in *Political Modernization in Japan and Turkey*, ed. Robert E. Ward and Dankwart A. Rustow (Princeton, NJ: Princeton University Press, 1968), 43.
21. Gottfried Hagen, "Ottoman Understanding of the World in the Seventeenth Century," in *An Ottoman Mentality: The World of Evliya Celebi*, ed. Robert Dankoff (Leiden, The Netherlands: Brill, 2004), 215–216.
22. Thomas D. Goodrich, *The Ottoman Turks and the New World: A Study of Tarih-i Hind-i Garbi and Sixteenth-Century Ottoman Americana* (Wiesbaden: Harrassowitz, 1990); Svat Soucek, "Piri Res and Ottoman Discovery of the Great Discoveries," *Studia Islamica* 79 (1994): 121–142; Andrew C. Hess, "Piri Reis and the Ottoman Response to the Voyages of Discovery," *Terrae Incognitae* 6 (1974): 19–37.
23. Hagen, "Ottoman Understanding of the World in the Seventeenth Century," 216.
24. According to Ibn Khaldun, the rise and fall of states follow a cycle that resembles that of human life: birth, maturity, and death. Ibn Khaldun, *The*

Muqaddimah: An Introduction to History, trans. Franz Rosenthal (Princeton, NJ: Princeton University Press, 1967).

25. Katip Çelebi, *Tuhfetü'l-Kibar Fi Esfari'l Bihar* (Istanbul: Kervan Kitapçılık ve Basın Sanayii, 1980), 5. Katip Çelebi wrote this book in 1656 as a result of the Ottoman defeat in the beginning of the campaign of Crete. His objective was to warn the Ottoman statesmen about their mistakes and unawareness. The book was translated into English and French; see Haji Khalifeh, *The History of the Maritime Wars of the Turks*, trans. James Mitchell (London: A. J. Valpy, 1831).

26. Because of Katip Çelebi's untimely death, *Cihannüma* remained unfinished. When it was printed in 1732, 325 of 698 pages were added by İbrahim Müteferrika. The printed version also included 27 maps and 13 charts. In the preface of the book, Müteferrika underlined the reasons for printing *Cihannüma:* "the permanence of the state and religion, the protection of the country and nation, the recording of history and events, the conservation of agriculture, education and works of art can only be possible by recording knowledge of books." Bülent Özükan, ed., *Kitab-ı Cihannüma* (Istanbul: Boyut, 2008), 124. For the facsimile edition, see Katib Çelebi, *Kitab-ı Cihannüma* (Ankara: Türk Tarih Kurumu Basımevi, 2009).

27. All seven *iklims* are located in the Northern Hemisphere. The first iklim is located between parallels 0 and 15, the second between parallels 15 and 20, the third between parallels 20 and 28, the fourth between parallels 28 and 34, the fifth between parallels 34 and 39, the sixth between parallels 39 and 44, and the seventh between parallels 44 and 48. It is assumed there are no iklims in the region north of the 48th parallel or in the Southern Hemisphere. See the reprinted version of *Cihannüma* in Turkish and English; Özükan, *Kitab-ı Cihannüma*, 62–63.

28. A. Adnan Adıvar, *Osmanlı Türklerinde İlim* (Istanbul: Remzi Kitabevi, 1970), 130. Bernard Lewis argued that "until the nineteenth century, Muslim writers on history and geography knew nothing of the names which Europeans had given to the continents ... At no time before the nineteenth century was any sovereignty defined in territorial terms." However Lewis's claims are contradictory to the information in *Cihannüma*. Starting with the second half of the seventeenth century, Ottomans were very well aware of the continents and territorial units or, as they called them, *memlekets*. See Bernard Lewis, *Muslim Discovery of Europe* (New York: Norton, 1982), 60.

29. Gottfried Hagen, "Katib Celebi: Cihannuma," in *Exhibition Catalog 400 Jahre Atlas* (Munich: Bayerische Staatsbibliothek, 1995), 48.

30. Hamit Sadi Selen, "Cihannüma," in *Katip Çelebi* (Ankara: Türk Tarih Kurumu, 1985), 132.

31. Katib Çelebi, *Kitab-ı Cihannüma*, 16–17.

32. Katip Çelebi gave a scientific definition of geography in *Cihannüma*. He mentioned that the word "geography" is formed in Greek by joining two words meaning "world" and "writing." Özükan, *Kitab-ı Cihannüma*, 130.

33. Hagen, "Ottoman Understanding of the World in the Seventeenth Century," 227–233.
34. Sonja Brentjes, "Mapmaking in Ottoman Istanbul between 1650 and 1750: A Domain of Painters, Calligraphers or Cartographers," in *Frontiers of Ottoman Studies*, ed. Colin Imber, Keiko Kiyotaki, and Rhoads Murphey (New York: Tauris, 2005), 2:141.
35. İbrahim Müteferrika, *Milletlerin Düzeninde İlmi Usüller* (Istanbul: Milli Eğitim Basımevi, 2000), 23.
36. Müteferrika mentioned the army's leading role as a class compared with three other classes: tradesmen and artisans, civil servants, and peasants. As his book was written in the turbulent years of the Patrona Halil Revolt, Müteferrika emphasized that it was necessary to keep apart the classes from each other for prosperity and order. The principle of four classes (*erkan-ı erbaa*) was an integral part of Ottoman political theory and was elaborated in depth by prominent scholars such as Kınalızade in the sixteenth century. See İbrahim Müteferrika, *Milletlerin Düzeninde İlmi Usüller*, 60; and Kınalızade Ali Efendi, *Devlet ve Aile Ahlakı* (Istanbul: Tercüman, n.d.), 217–218.
37. Müteferrika, *Milletlerin Düzeninde İlmi Usüller*, 64.
38. Ibid., 65–66.
39. Daniel Goffman, "Negotiating with the Renaissance State: The Ottoman Empire and the New Diplomacy," in *The Early Modern Ottomans: Remapping the Empire*, ed. Virginia H. Aksan and Daniel Goffman (New York: Cambridge University Press, 2007), 64.
40. See M. Hakan Yavuz, "Towards an Islamic Liberalism? The Nurcu Movement and Fethullah Gülen," *Middle East Journal* 53, no. 4 (Autumn 1999): 584–605.
41. Goffman, "Negotiating with the Renaissance State," 72–73.
42. Lewis, *Muslim Discovery of Europe*, 297.
43. Gabor Agoston, "Information, Ideology, and Limits of Imperial Policy: Ottoman Grand Strategy in the Context of Ottoman-Habsburg Rivalry," in *The Early Modern Ottomans: Remapping the Empire*, ed. Virginia H. Aksan and Daniel Goffman (New York: Cambridge University Press, 2007), 87.
44. Andrew C. Hess, "The Evolution of the Ottoman Seaborne Empire in the Age of Oceanic Discoveries, 1453–1525," *American Historical Review* 75, no. 7 (Dec. 1970): 1915–1916.
45. Peter Barber, "England II: Monarchs, Ministers, and Maps, 1550–1625," in *Monarchs, Ministers, and Maps: The Emergence of Cartography as a Tool of Government in Early Modern Europe*, ed. David Buisseret (Chicago: University of Chicago Press, 1992), 58–59.
46. Cemal Kafadar, "The Question of Ottoman Decline," *Harvard Middle Eastern and Islamic Review* 4, nos. 1–2 (1997–1998): 51.
47. Tarık Zafer Tunaya, *Türkiye'de Siyasal Partiler* (Istanbul: İletişim Yayınları, 2000), 3:46; Rex A. Wade, *The Russian Revolution, 1917* (New York: Cambridge University Press, 2005), 289; David Styan, *France and Iraq* (New York: Tauris, 2006), 71.

48. Bertrand Badie, "The Impact of the French Revolution on Muslim Societies: Evidence and Ambiguities," *International Social Science Journal* 41 (1989): 6–7.
49. Bernard Lewis, "Watan," *Journal of Contemporary History* 26, no. 3/4 (Sept. 1991): 523; Bernard Lewis, "The Impact of the French Revolution on Turkey," *Journal of World History* 1 (July 1953): 107.
50. Lewis, "Watan," 524–525.
51. While Gellner argued that nations are by-products of industrialization, for Anderson the printing press and capitalism are necessary conditions for the construction of nations. Benedict Anderson, *Imagined Communities* (London: Verso, 1993); and Ernest Gellner, *Nations and Nationalism* (Ithaca, NY: Cornell University Press, 1983).
52. Quoted in Liah Greenfeld, *Nationalism: Five Roads to Modernity* (Cambridge, MA: Harvard University Press, 1992), 162.
53. Ibid.
54. For Bernard Lewis, Ali Esseyid Efendi, the Ottoman ambassador in Paris in 1797 and 1798, was the first Ottoman statesman who used the word *vatan* in a political sense. However, according to Fatih Yeşil, five years before Ali Esseyid Efendi, Ebubekir Ratib Efendi realized that the words "patrie" and "nation" acquired new meanings in the French language. Lewis, "Watan," 526; Fatih Yeşil, "Looking at the French Revolution through Ottoman Eyes: Ebubekir Ratib Efendi's Observations," *Bulletin of SOAS* 70, no. 2 (2007): 283–304.
55. See Yeşil, 291: "bir mezheb ve bir millet ve bir lisan olmalarıyla."
56. Ibid., 302.
57. Fatih Bayram, "Ebubekir Ratib Efendi as Envoy of Knowledge between the East and the West" (Master's thesis, Bilkent University, 2000), 114.
58. Mahmud Raif Efendi, *Osmanlı İmparatorluğu'nda Yeni Nizamların Cedveli*, trans. Arslan Terzioğlu and Hüsrev Hatemi (Istanbul: Türkiye Turing ve Otomobil Kurumu, 1988), 4, 33. This book includes the original French version and also its Turkish translation.
59. Ibid., 3.
60. "Admis, dés ma plus tendre jeunesse, au nombre des secrétaires dans les Bureaux de la SUBLIME PORTE, je me suis senti aussitôt animé du désir de me rendre utile à ma Patrie."
61. Raif Efendi, *Osmanlı İmparatorluğu'nda Yeni Nizamların Cedveli*, 30.
62. This book was republished in French, Ottoman Turkish, and Turkish in 1986. See Seyyid Mustafa, *İstanbul'da Askerlik Sanatı, Yeteneklerin ve Bilimlerin Durumu Üzerine Risale* (Istanbul: Tüyap, 1986).
63. "Selim III, donc, projeta la fondation d'une grande et nouvelle école de mathématiques prés de l'arsenal a Sudlidze: la publication de ce projet ralentit un peu mon ardeur sur le dessein d'un voyage en Europe; l'idée de pouvoir profiter dans le sein de ma patrie, et peut-être encore lui devenir utile, m'enchanta et prévalut; je fis halte." In the Ottoman version he used the word "vatan" in place of "patrie": "Sultan Selim Han Hazretleri, Tersane-i Amire'ye kabil Südlüce nam mahalde bir bab Handesehane müceddeden

bina vu inşasına iradesinin havadisiyle, seyahat maddesinde olan hahisim ta'dil olunup, bir eyyam dahi tevakkufu tasvib eyledim ve kendu vatanım dahilinde tahsil u istifade ve belki fa'ide-dade olmağı tecviz eyledim." See Seyyid Mustafa, *İstanbul'da Askerlik Sanatı, Yeteneklerin ve Bilimlerin Durumu Üzerine Risale*, 70, 89.

64. "Moi-même, ivre de joie de voir ma patrie dans l'état que je desirois si ardemment, éclairée tous les jours davantage du flambeau des sciences et des arts, il ne me fut plus possible de me taire." As the Ottoman version of the book was slightly different, he did not use the word "vatan" in this paragraph. Ibid., 118.

65. Rhigas Pheraios was born in a wealthy Vlach family in 1757. He became familiar with revolutionary ideas when he joined the Greek community in Vienna around 1793 and wrote a new constitution for his envisaged republic. Later Rhigas became a national Greek hero and forefather of the Greek independence movement.

66. Leften Stavros Stavrianos, *The Balkans since 1453* (New York: New York University Press, 2000), 148, 278–279; Michael Angold, *Eastern Christianity* (New York: Cambridge University Press, 2006), 207.

67. Eric J. Hobsbawm, *Nations and Nationalism since 1780* (New York: Cambridge University Press, 1992), 84.

68. Selim Deringil, "The Invention of Tradition as Public Image in the Late Ottoman Empire, 1808 to 1908," *Comparative Studies in Society and History* 35, no.1 (January 1993): 3–29.

69. Anderson, *Imagined Communities*, 86.

70. "... patlayan Kabakçı İsyanı ile bu nisbi aydınlanma ve tereddüt devresi kapandı. Fakat, hayata serpilmiş olan tohumlarını zaruretler beslediği için ölmedi." Ahmet Hamdi Tanpınar, *19. Asır Türk Edebiyatı Tarihi* (Istanbul: Yapı Kredi Yayınları, 2006), 69.

71. Niyazi Berkes, *The Development of Secularism in Turkey* (New York: Routledge, 1998), 90.

72. Cemal Kafadar drew attention to the similarities between Tanzimat reforms in the Ottoman Empire and Mikhail Gorbachev's reforms called *perestroika*, which also means restructuring: "A century and a half earlier than the leaders of the Soviet Union, the ruling class of the Ottoman Empire faced a similar complex of challenges: nationalist stirrings, economic backwardness, and a rapid erosion of both internal and external confidence in the ability of the sociopolitical order to provide state and society with a viable future." Kafadar, "The Question of Ottoman Decline," 65.

73. Deringil, "The Invention of Tradition as Public Image in the Late Ottoman Empire," 5.

74. Kemal H. Karpat, *The Politicization of Islam: Reconstructing Identity, State, Faith, and Community in the Late Ottoman State* (New York: Oxford University Press, 2001), 227–229.

75. Mustafa Sami Efendi, *Bir Osmanlı Bürokratının Avrupa İzlenimleri: Mustafa Sami Efendi ve Avrupa Risalesi*, ed. M. Fatih Andı (Istanbul: Bayram

Matbaacılık, 1996), 70. This book includes Mustafa Sami Efendi's text *Avrupa Risalesi* in Ottoman Turkish and modern Turkish.
76. Ibid., 81.
77. Selçuk Akşin Somel, *The Modernization of Public Education in the Ottoman Empire, 1839–1909: Islamization, Autocracy, and Discipline* (Leiden, The Netherlands: Brill, 2001), 29–30.
78. The memorandum was published in Latin by Faik Reşit Unat: "sayesinde oldukları devletin ve hubb-ı vatan ne olduklarını bilemeyecekleri." Faik Reşit Unat, *Türkiye Eğitim Sisteminin Gelişmesine Tarihi Bir Bakış* (Ankara: Milli Eğitim Bakanlığı, 1984).
79. The Tanzimat text was published in Ottoman Turkish and French. However, there are slight differences between the two texts. In the first sentence of the quoted part of the French version, the words "prince" and "patrie" were used instead of "devlet" (state) and "millet." In the second sentence, in parallel to the Ottoman version, the word "patrie" was used in place of "vatan." The French version is as follows: "S'il y a absence de sécurité à l'égard de la fortune, tout le monde reste froid à la voix du prince et de la patrie; personne ne s'occupe du progrès de la fortune publique, absorbé que l'on est par ses propres inquiétudes. Si, au contraire, le citoyen possède avec confiance ses propriétés de toute nature, alors plein d'ardeur pour ses affaires, dont il cherche à élargir le cercle afin d'étendre celui de ses jouissances, il sent chaque jour redoubler en son cour l'amour du prince et de la patrie, le dévouement à son pays." The Ottoman Turkish version is as follows: "Emniyeti mal kaziyesinin fikdanı halinde ise herkes ne devlet ve ne milletine ısınmayıp ve ne imar-ı mülke bakamayıp daima endişe ve ıztıraptan hâli olamadığı misullû aksi takdirinde yani emval ve emlakinden emniyet-i kâmilesi olduğu halde dahi kendü işi ile ve tevsi-i daire-i taayyüşiyle uğraşıp ve kendisinde günbegün devlet ve millet gayreti ve vatan muhabbeti artıp ona göre hüsnü harekete çalışacağı şüpheden azadedir." For a photograph of the original French version of the Tanzimat Edict, see *Tanzimat: Yüzüncü Yıldönümü Münasebetile* (Istanbul: Maarif Matbaası, 1940), 48–49; for the Ottoman Turkish version in Latin letters, see *Tanzimat Dönemi*. Accessed November 28, 2008. Available from www.tbmm.gov.tr/kultur_sanat/yayinlar/yayin001/001_00_005.pdf.
80. Instead of the word "vatan," the word *pays* was used in the French version: "asker maddesi dahi ber minval-i muharrer mevadd-ı mühimmeden olarak eğerçi muhafaza-i vatan için asker vermek ahalinin farize-i zimmeti ise de"; "Bien que, comme nous l'avons dit, la défense du pays soit une chose importante et que ce soit un devoir pour tous les habitants de fournir des soldats à cette fin . . ."
81. *Ceride-i Havadis*, no. 32, May 31, 1841, p. 3.
82. Hilmi Ziya Ülken, *Türkiye'de Çağdaş Düşünce Tarihi* (Istanbul: Ülken Yayınları, 1966), 51; Tanpınar, 19. *Asır Türk Edebiyatı Tarihi*, 142. Presumably because of a mistake, Ahmet Hamdi Tanpınar argued that this article was published in the twenty-third issue of the *Ceride-i Havadis*.

83. Şerif Mardin, *The Genesis of Young Ottoman Thought* (Syracuse, NY: Syracuse University Press, 2000), 14.
84. Feroz Ahmad, *The Making of Modern Turkey* (New York: Routledge, 1996), 28.
85. Kemal H. Karpat, *Studies on Ottoman Social and Political History* (Leiden, The Netherlands: Brill, 2002), 47.
86. Ahmet Cevdet Paşa, *Tezakir*, ed. Cavit Baysun (Ankara: Türk Tarih Kurumu Basımevi, 1953), 68.
87. Anderson, *Imagined Communities*, 43–45.
88. Karpat, *The Politicization of Islam*, 102.
89. Albert Habib Hourani, *Arabic Thought in the Liberal Age, 1789–1939* (London: Oxford University Press, 1970), 78–79.
90. Quoted in Hourani, *Arabic Thought in the Liberal Age*, 79.
91. Ussama Makdisi, "Debating Religion, Reform, and Nationalism in the Ottoman Empire," *International Journal of the Middle East* 34, no. 4 (November 2002): 604–605.
92. Ibid., 608.
93. Ibid., 606.
94. Fevziye Abdullah Tansel, *Şinasi: Makaleler* (Ankara: Dün-Bugün Yayınevi, 1960), 2.
95. Hikmet Dizdaroğlu, *Şinasi: Hayatı, Sanatı, Eserleri* (Istanbul: Varlık Yayınları, 1954), 55.
96. Hilmi Ziya Ülken, *İnsani Vatanperverlik* (Istanbul: Remzi Kitaphanesi, 1933), 239–241.
97. Ali Sevim, İzzet Öztoprak, and M. Akif Tural, *Atatürk'ün Söylev ve Demeçleri* (Ankara: Divan Yayıncılık, 2006), 186. Mustafa Kemal gave this speech on January 13, 1921.
98. The change in the meaning of *vatan* becomes clearer if Namık Kemal's usage of vatan is compared with Fuzuli's, a well-known poet who lived in the sixteenth century. Fuzuli used the word *vatan* in a lyrical sense to describe one's feeling toward one's native village: "Fuzuli, I cannot leave my lover's village; as it is my homeland [*Edemem terk Fuzuli ser-i kuyin yarin; Vatanımdır vatanımdır vatanımdır, vatanım*]." Namık Kemal established a patriotic relationship between the people and their territory: "Vatan's soil is the essence of the human body; such a body would not hesitate to sacrifice itself and perish to protect the vatan [*Vücudun kim hamir-i mâyesi hâk-i vatandandır; ne gam rah-ı vatanda hak olursa cevr ü mihnetten*]."
99. Karpat, *The Politicization of Islam*, 330–331.
100. Namık Kemal criticized Ottoman statesmen's fear of the Russian armies descending from the north: "If a comet rises in the north of the sky, they [i.e., Ottoman statesmen] will be afraid of it because they believe that it will definitely fall on our heads." According to him, European powers would never allow Russia to control the strategic territories of the Ottoman Empire, because trade routes between Europe and Asia were vital for their economies. Namık

Kemal, "Bir Mülahaza," *İbret*, June 27, 1872, in *Namık Kemal ve İbret Gazetesi*, ed. Mustafa Nihat Özön (Istanbul: Remzi Kitabevi, 1938), 34–37.

101. Namık Kemal, "İttihad-ı İslam," *İbret*, June 27, 1872, in *Namık Kemal ve İbret Gazetesi*, 77.
102. Like Namık Kemal, Renan's famous essay "Qu'est-ce qu'une nation?" (What Is Nation?) identified sacrifices as "the essential condition for being a nation. One loves in proportion to the sacrifices which one has approved and for which one has suffered. One loves the house which he has built and which he has made over. The Spartan chant: 'We are what you make us; we are what you are' is simply the abbreviated hymn of the Fatherland." Ernest Renan, "Qu'est-ce qu'une nation?," in *Nationalism*, ed. John Hutchinson and Anthony D. Smith (London: Oxford University Press, 1994), 17–18. There were also disagreements between Namık Kemal's and Renan's views. Namık Kemal criticized Renan, who regarded Islam as a barrier to scientific development, in his book *Renan Müdafaanamesi* (Defense against Renan). Namık Kemal, *Renan Müdafaanamesi* (Ankara: Kültür ve Turizm Bakanlığı Yayınları, 1988).
103. Namık Kemal, "Vatan," *İbret*, March 22, 1873, in *Namık Kemal ve İbret Gazetesi*, 263–265.
104. Namık Kemal, "İmtizacı Akvam," *İbret*, July 2, 1872, in *Namık Kemal ve İbret Gazetesi*, 82.
105. Ibid., 84. In another article, Namık Kemal emphasized that in the Ottoman Empire, it was impossible to create "Laz, Albanian, Kurdish, Arabic" nationalisms. Namık Kemal, "İstikbal," *İbret*, July 2, 1872, in *Namık Kemal ve İbret Gazetesi*, 33.
106. Namık Kemal, "İmtizacı Akvam," *İbret*, July 2, 1872, in *Namık Kemal ve İbret Gazetesi*, 85.
107. Hilmi Ziya Ülken, *Millet ve Tarih Şuuru* (Istanbul: Dergah Yayınları, 1948), 59.
108. Namık Kemal's two articles, "İttihad-ı İslam" and "Avrupa Şarkı Bilmez" (Europe Doesn't Understand the East), are excellent examples for comparison. See Namık Kemal, "İttihad-ı Islam," *İbret*, June 27, 1872, in *Namık Kemal ve İbret Gazetesi*, 74–78; and Namık Kemal, "Avrupa Şarkı Bilmez," *İbret*, June 22, 1872, in *Namık Kemal ve İbret Gazetesi*, 54–59.
109. Falih Rıfkı Atay, *Başveren İnkilapçı* (Ankara: Türkiye Milli Talebe Federasyonu, 1954).
110. Fuat Köprülü, *Edebiyat Araştırmaları I* (Istanbul: Ötüken, 1989), 212–213.
111. Quoted in Tanpınar, *19. Asır Türk Edebiyatı Tarihi*, 226.
112. Quoted in Ülken, *Türkiye'de Çağdaş Düşünce Tarihi*, 82. Ali Suavi responded to the allegations of the British newspaper the *Saturday Review* that there were not enough Turks in Anatolia because they were assimilated by other nations. See Hüseyin Çelik, *Ali Suavi ve Dönemi* (Istanbul: İletişim, 1994), 620.
113. Ali Suavi, "Osman," *The Mukhbir*, June 12, 1868, 2, quoted in Çelik, *Ali Suavi ve Dönemi*, 623–624.

114. Quoted in İsmail Doğan, *Tanzimat'ın İki Ucu: Münif Paşa ve Ali Suavi* (İstanbul: İz Yayıncılık, 1991), 309.
115. Ali Suavi, "İslam Askerliği Fransız Askerliği," *Muvakkaten* 2, October, 6, 1870, 30, quoted in Seyit Battal Uğurlu, "Ulum Gazetesi'nin Tematik İncelemesi," (Master's thesis, Van Yüzüncü Yıl Üniversitesi, 1997), 43–44.
116. Sultan Abdülhamid, *Siyasi Hatıratım* (Istanbul: Hareket Yayınları, 1974), 107.
117. Ibid., 161–162.
118. Ibid., 166–167.
119. M. Şükrü Hanioğlu, *A Brief History of the Late Ottoman Empire* (Princeton, NJ: Princeton University Press, 2008), 123–129.
120. Mustafa Nihat Özön, "Bazı Küçük Notlar," in *Vatan Yahut Silistre* (Istanbul: Remzi Kitabevi, 1972), 13.
121. Hanioğlu, *A Brief History of the Late Ottoman Empire*, 144.
122. İbrahim Temo was a Muslim Albanian, Mehmed Reşid was a Circassian, and Abdullah Cevdet and İshak Sukuti were Kurds. Stanford J. Shaw and Ezel Kural Shaw, *History of the Ottoman Empire* (New York: Cambridge University Press, 1976), 2:256; M. Şükrü Hanioğlu, *The Young Turks in Opposition* (New York: Oxford University Press, 1995), 168.
123. İbrahim Temo, *İbrahim Temo'nun İttihat ve Terakki Anıları* (Istanbul: Arba Yayınları, 1987), 17.
124. Ahmet Rıza, *Anılar* (Istanbul: Cumhuriyet, 2001), 16–17, 30.
125. The pamphlet was republished in Latin letters in 1988 in the journal *Tarih ve Toplum*. Ali Birinci, "Vatan Tehlikede," *Tarih ve Toplum* 54 (June 1988): 337–342.
126. Ibid., 339.
127. Ibid., 341.
128. *Bedreka-i Salamet* 6, March 12, 1897, 1.
129. Ibid.
130. Temo, *İbrahim Temo'nun İttihat ve Terakki Anıları*, 31–32.
131. Ahmet Niyazi, *Hürriyet Kahramanı Resneli Niyazi Hatıratı* (Istanbul: Örgün Yayınevi, 2003), 134–135.
132. Kazım Nami Duru, *İttihat ve Terakki Hatıralarım* (Istanbul: Sucuoğlu Matbaası, 1957), 6.
133. Yusuf Kemal Tengirşenk, *Vatan Hizmetinde* (Ankara: Kültür Bakanlığı, 1981), 27.
134. Feroz Ahmad, *The Young Turks: The Committee of Union and Progress in Turkish Politics, 1908–1914* (Oxford: Clarendon Press, 1969), 145.
135. There is a saying in today's Turkish culture that is used to describe distant places: "Oh, it is in Fezzan." Although most Turkish people do not know what Fezzan is, presumably this saying was popularized during Abdulhamid's reign to describe those exiled to Fezzan, which was the most remote part of the empire, in the southwest of Libya.
136. Ahmet Mehmetefendioğlu, *İttihat ve Terakki'nin Kurucu Üyelerinden Dr. Reşid Bey'in Hatıraları: Sürgünden İntihara* (Istanbul: Arba Yayınları, 1993), 40.

137. Ibid., 40–41.
138. See Ussama Makdisi, "Ottoman Orientalism," *American Historical Review* 107, no. 3 (June 2002): 768–796; Selim Deringil, "'They Live in a State of Nomadism and Savagery': The Late Ottoman Empire and the Post-Colonial Debate," *Comparative Studies in Society and History* 45 (2003): 311–342.
139. Similarly, the article "Gecelerimden" (From My Nights) written by Müfide Ferit Tek under the pseudonym Suyum Bike and published by the journal *Türk Yurdu* bemoaned the loss of Tripoli. Müfide Ferit Tek spent her childhood in Libya with her father, who was appointed there as an officer. Her father contracted tuberculosis and died in Tripoli. She considered Tripoli as her vatan and felt great pain over its loss: "Tripoli, which was the heaven of my memoirs, was lost . . . Oh my dear father! Can you see from your burial place in a sand hill that does not have even a tombstone, the condition of your country, for which your lungs were lost. Can you hear the footsteps of the enemy, who wander around your burial place?" Suyum Bike, "Gecelerimden," *Türk Yurdu* 64 (April 30, 1914): 253–254. *Türk Yurdu* was republished in Latin script by Tutibay Yayınları in 1999 in Ankara. In this study, all references to *Türk Yurdu* are to the republished version of the journal. See for an informative article about Müfide Ferit Tek's life and her Turanist novel *Aydemir,* published in 1918, Murat Belge, "Müfide Ferit Tek'in Aydemir Romanı," in *Kitap-lık* 63 (July 2003).
140. Selim Deringil argued that colonialism was a "survival tactic" for Istanbul and therefore referred to the intermediary status of the Ottoman Empire as "borrowed colonialism." I think that there are still important problems in using the modified term "borrowed colonialism" to portray the relationship between the center and the periphery of the Ottoman Empire in the nineteenth century. See Seim Deringil, "The Late Ottoman Empire and the Post-Colonial Debate."
141. Khalil Ghanem, who was a Maronite Arab and member of the Young Turk movement, wholeheartedly supported Ottomanism. His words were a clear example of how some Arabs preferred Ottoman rule over European colonial rule: "We Arabs know that if (the Franks) enter our country, in a couple of years our territories will be in their hands; and they will rule it as they wish. As for Turks, they believe in our religion and are acquainted with our customs. In their four centuries of rule, they did not take an inch of our property into their possession. They left to the inhabitants their land, their property, their industry, and their commerce. The Arabs have benefited from trade with the Turks and from our uninterrupted bond. Would it be right for us to replace them with someone else? . . . It is only those who want to curry favor with the ruler who accuse the Muslims of [desiring] to establish an Arab state and the Christians of conspiring with the foreigners . . . The Arab intellectuals and notables have no wish for their umma other than to live within the domain of Ottoman interests." Hasan Kayalı, *Arabs and Young Turks: Ottomanism, Arabism, and Islamism in the Ottoman Empire, 1908–1918* (Berkeley: University of California Press, 1997), 223.

142. Karpat, *The Politicization of Islam*, 66.
143. Makdisi, "Ottoman Orientalism," 787.
144. Ibid., 773.
145. Yusuf Akçura was one of the founders of Turkish nationalism, along with Ziya Gökalp. He was born to a rich merchant Tatar family in Kazan, Russia. At the age of seven, he came to Istanbul and later attended the military college. He was exiled to Fezzan in Libya by the Hamidian regime because of his revolutionary ideas. However, he escaped from Libya to Paris and became a student at the Ecole Libre des Sciences Politiques. In France, Akçura became an ardent supporter of Turkish nationalism, and during the CUP years, he founded institutions and publications that served as an impetus for the development of Turkish nationalism. After the establishment of the Republic of Turkey, he became a member of Parliament and one of the ideologues of nationalism. See François Georgeon, *Türk Milliyetçiliğinin Kökenleri: Yusuf Akçura (1876–1935)*, trans. Alev Er (Istanbul: Tarih Vakfı, 1999).
146. Yusuf Akçura, *Üç Tarz-ı Siyaset* (Ankara: Lotus, 2005).
147. "Osmanlı Devletinin hakiki kuvveti, günümüzdeki coğrafi şeklini korumakta mıdır?" Akçura, *Üç Tarz-ı Siyaset*, 48.
148. Ibid., 54.
149. Ali Kemal, "Cevabımız," in *Üç Tarz-ı Siyaset* (Ankara: Lotus, 2005), 68.
150. Ahmet Ferit was Yusuf Akçura's friend during military college. He was also exiled by the government to Libya and then escaped to Paris. He was a member of Parliament between 1908 and 1912. Later, he became the director of the nationalist Turkish Hearths organization during the CUP rule. After the establishment of the Republic of Turkey, he served as a member of Parliament and ambassador to London, Warsaw, and Tokyo.
151. Ahmet Ferit, "Bir Mektup," in *Üç Tarz-ı Siyaset* (Ankara: Lotus, 2005), 91.
152. "Edirne, Rize, Rodos, Süleymaniye! Bu dört kale Türkün ilk hududunun demir kazıklarıdır." Ahmed Ferid, "Türk Ocakları," in *Nevsal-i Milli* (Istanbul: Artin Asaduryan Matbaası, 1914), 189–191.
153. Ali Fuat Cebesoy, *Sınıf Arkadaşım Atatürk* (Istanbul: İnkılâp ve Aka Kitabevleri, 1967), 108–114.
154. The manifesto was published by Resneli Niyazi in his memoirs. Ahmet Niyazi, *Resneli Niyazi Hatıratı*, 187–188.
155. Ibid., 192, 197–198.
156. M. Şükrü Hanioğlu, *Preparation for a Revolution: The Young Turks, 1902–1908* (New York: Oxford University Press, 2001), 313–317.
157. The ideal of "defending the vatan" has been an important one for the Turkish military. It became a slogan and has been used by the army in military coups against governments and opposition groups such as Kurds, Islamists, and Leftists.
158. Kemal H. Karpat, *Ottoman Population, 1830–1914: Demographic and Social Characteristics* (Madison: University of Wisconsin Press, 1985).
159. Hanioğlu, *Preparation for a Revolution*, 299.

160. Georgeon, *Yusuf Akçura*, 60.
161. In the context of discourse theory, "dislocation" refers to "a destabilization of a discourse that results from the emergence of events which cannot be domesticated, symbolized or integrated within the discourse in question." See Jacob Torfing, *New Theories of Discourse: Laclau, Mouffe, and Zizek* (Malden, MA: Blackwell Publishers, 1999), 301.
162. Kayalı, *Arabs and Young Turks*, 107.

CHAPTER TWO. FROM IMPERIAL TO NATIONAL VATAN

1. Sati Bey, *Vatan İçin Beş Konferans* (Dersaadet: Kader Matbaası, 1913). For a detailed study about Sati Bey and his political views, see William L. Cleveland, *The Making of an Arab Nationalist: Ottomanism and Arabism in the Life and Thought of Sati Al-Husri* (Princeton, NJ: Princeton University Press, 1971).
2. With the end of World War I, Sati Bey left Istanbul and lived in Iraq, Syria, and the Middle East until the end of his life. He institutionalized modern education in Syria, Iraq, and Egypt. In Cairo he became a professor of the Arab nation and, according to Berkes, "taught the Egyptians how to become an Arab." Niyazi Berkes, *Arap Dünyasında İslamiyet, Milliyetçilik, Sosyalizm* (Istanbul: Köprü, 1969), 96.
3. Sati Bey, *Vatan İçin Beş Konferans*, 3.
4. Ibid., 23–25.
5. Ibid., 37, 46–48.
6. The similarities between Josef Alexander Helfert and Sati Bey are striking. Both of them served in the ministry of education and advocated for the construction of a common imperial history to maintain the solidarity between different ethnic groups. Similarly, both Helfert and Sati Bey analyzed the education systems of other European countries to change their imperial and cosmopolitan curriculums to patriotic and practical ones. In his book *Concerning National History and What Is Done in Austria to Promote It*, published in 1853, Helfert envisaged a national history for the Habsburg Empire: "It is true that mankind is divided into a great number of tribes that differ as to language and color. But according to our ideas national history is not the history of any such group defined by its racial origin. We think that national history is the history of the population of a territory that is politically united, subordinate to the same authority and living under the protection of the same law. For us, Austrian national history is the history of the Austrian state and people as a whole. This whole is constituted of a variety of tribes that differ as to education and customs. These live together organically in a very complex system on the vast territory of the Empire either separated in closed groups or intermixed." Josef Alexander Helfert, *Über Nationalgeschichte und den gegenwärtigen Stand ihrer Pflege in Österreich* (Prag: Calve'schen Buchhandlung, 1853). See also Walter Leitsch, "East Europeans Studying History in Vienna," in *Historians as Nation-Builders*, ed. Dennis Deletant and Harry Hanak (London: Macmillan, 1988), 139–143. Sixty years after Helfert, Sati Bey highlighted the

importance of reforming the teaching of history and geography: "Geography is a crucial science to teach the body and the physical characteristics of vatan. History as a science is important to teach the spirit of vatan. These two sciences are the most important tools for the education of patriotism . . . Teaching of these two sciences should be restructured to engender the love of vatan in the hearts of people." Sati Bey, *Vatan İçin Beş Konferans*, 36–37.

7. Josef Alexander Helfert, *Über Nationalgeschichte und den gegenwärtigen Stand ihrer Pflege in Österreich*, 31.
8. Jan Penrose, "Nations, States and Homelands: Territory and Territoriality in Nationalist Thought," *Nations and Nationalism* 8, no. 3 (2002): 283–284.
9. Ernest Gellner, *Nations and Nationalism* (Ithaca, NY: Cornell University Press, 1983), 139–140.
10. Anssi Paasi, "Boundaries as Social Processes: Territoriality in the World Flows," in *Boundaries, Territory and Postmodernity*, ed. David Newman (London: Taylor and Francis, 1999), 81.
11. After the 1908 Revolution, the politics of the empire was dominated by the civil and military officers from the Balkans, who played an important role in the establishment of the Republic of Turkey. According to Zurcher, 48 percent of high-level military and civil officers came from the Balkans after 1908, "with another 26 percent born in the capital. Eleven percent came from the islands and coast of the Aegean, while the vast Asiatic possessions of the empire taken together produced only 13 percent" of the post-1908 leadership. Erik Jan Zurcher, *The Young Turks—Children of the Borderlands?* Accessed December 2, 2008. Available from www.tulp.leidenuniv.nl/content_docs/wap/ejz16.pdf.
12. "Bir taraftan hudutlar kat'i mahiyetini kaybeder, koca imparatorluk harice karşı adeta emniyetsiz yaşar." Ahmet Hamdi Tanpınar used this sentence to define the period between 1776 and 1826. I believe it is more appropriate for the period between 1876 and 1920, when the empire lost almost all of its territories in Europe and the Middle East. Ahmet Hamdi Tanpınar, *19. Asır Türk Edebiyatı Tarihi* (Istanbul: Yapı Kredi Yayınları, 2006), 163.
13. Mustafa Kemal made this speech to the journalist Ruşen Eşref in Amasya on October 24–25, 1919. Ali Sevim, İzzet Öztoprak, and M. Akif Tural, *Atatürk'ün Söylev ve Demeçleri* (Ankara: Divan Yayıncılık, 2006), 22.
14. The use of the terms "Turkism," "pan-Turkism," and "Turanism" is problematic, and their meanings changed according to the circumstances. The difference between pan-Turkism and Turanism is relatively clear compared with Turkism. Pan-Turkism emerged in Russia to unite all Turkic groups against the czarist rule. Compared with pan-Turkism, Turanism was all-encompassing, and in addition to Turkic groups it included Hungarians, Finns, and Mongols. However, most of the Turkish nationalists used these terms interchangeably. For instance, although Ziya Gökalp used the term *Turan* extensively in his articles and poems, a confederation of Turks with Mongols, Hungarians, and Finns was not realistic for him, because he considered

religion an important factor for a political union. The difference between pan-Turkism and Turkism is more ambiguous. Whereas pan-Turkism was used mainly against pan-Slavism by authors in those works that were aimed at Western readers, Turkism as a term was more prominent in publications that were in Turkish and were aimed at Turkish public opinion. Moreover, pan-Turkism had expansionist tones compared with Turkism, which limited its objectives to the Turks in the Ottoman Empire. The main difference between pan-Turkism, Turanism, and Turkish nationalism is that the last one clearly rejected irredentism and restricted its objectives within the "national borders." Ziya Gökalp, "Türkleşmek, İslamlaşmak, Muasırlaşmak," *Türk Yurdu* 35 (March 20, 1913): 186; Niyazi Berkes, *The Development of Secularism in Turkey* (New York: Routledge, 1998), 344.

15. Syria, Jordan, Iraq, and Egypt did not gain their independence as a result of a national liberation war against colonial powers. Algeria was definitely an exception, gaining independence after a long war against France.

16. Although Akçura had a very close relationship with the CUP and from time to time supported its policies, he never became a member. Ziya Gökalp was appointed by the CUP as the inspector of party organizations in the provinces of Diyarbakır, Bitlis, and Van after the 1908 Revolution. In 1910, Gökalp moved to Salonika and became a member of the Central Committee, which was the highest organ of the CUP, and he kept his influential position until 1918. See Taha Parla, *The Social and Political Thought of Ziya Gökalp, 1826–1924* (Leiden, The Netherlands: Brill, 1985), 13.

17. Ali Kazancıgil, "The Ottoman-Turkish State and Kemalism," in *Atatürk: Founder of a Modern State*, ed. Ali Kazancıgil and Ergun Özbudun (London: Hurst, 1981), 51.

18. Yusuf Akçura, *Üç Tarz-ı Siyaset* (Ankara: Lotus, 2005), 59.

19. Muharrem Feyzi Togay, *Yusuf Akçura: Hayatı ve Eserleri* (Istanbul: Hüsnütabiat Basımevi, 1944), 59.

20. Yusuf Akçura, *Yeni Türk Devletinin Öncüleri: 1928 Yılı Yazıları* (Ankara: Aydınlar Matbaacılık, 2001), 229–230.

21. Fuat Köprülü belonged to the well-known Köprülü family, and his great-grandfather was a grand vizier from 1655 to 1661. Fuat Köprülü was a leading historian and known for his contributions to Ottoman history. He later became one of the founders of the Democrat Party and served in the governments of Adnan Menderes as minister of foreign affairs from 1950 to 1955. Mehmet Emin was one of the first ardent Turkish nationalist poets; his poems are still memorized today by Turkish schoolchildren. Mehmet Emin became a member of the CUP in 1907. After the establishment of the republic, he took the surname Yurdakul, which means "slave to the homeland." Ahmet Ağaoğlu (known as Agayev in Azerbaijan) was a prominent Turkist. He was a member of the CUP and became a member of Parliament in 1914. He studied in Paris at the Sorbonne and was influenced by the works of Ernest Renan. Upon the establishment of the Azerbaijan Democratic Republic,

he went to Baku and became a member of the Parliament. After the Soviet invasion, he came to Turkey and continued his political activities as a journalist. Later he became a member of Parliament from the city of Kars, which has a considerable Azeri population.

22. Yusuf Akçura and other Turkist intellectuals established the organization the Türk Ocağı (Turkish Hearths) in 1912. The organization had 3,000 members in 1914 and 30,000 by 1920.
23. Akçura, *Yeni Türk Devletinin Öncüleri*, 235.
24. Yusuf Akçura, "Türk Aleminde," *Türk Yurdu* 1, no. 17 (July 11, 1912): 288.
25. Cemal Pasha wrote his memoirs in 1919 and admitted that the Unionists were unsuccessful in integrating the revolutionary organizations of other ethnic groups into the CUP: "Just as the Ottoman government was formed by the union of all Ottoman nations, we wanted the CUP to be a union of all revolutionary organizations of all the Ottoman nations." Cemal Paşa, *Hatıralar* (Istanbul: Selek Yayınları, 1959), 346.
26. Tarık Zafer Tunaya, *Türkiye'de Siyasal Partiler* (Istanbul: İletişim Yayınları, 2000), 3:47.
27. According to Hasan Kayalı, it is misleading to argue that "the transition from Young Ottoman to Young Turk implies an ungrounded narrowing of interests toward a more ethnically Turkish emphasis." Hasan Kayalı, *Arabs and Young Turks: Ottomanism, Arabism, and Islamism in the Ottoman Empire, 1908–1918* (Berkeley: University of California Press, 1997), 38–39.
28. Tunaya, *Türkiye'de Siyasal Partiler*, 3:373–375. The idea of establishing two types of territorial loyalty was first employed in the Ottoman Empire in 1878 by Albanian intellectual Şemsettin Sami, who argued that he had two different loyalties: one to the Ottoman Empire and the other to Albania. He called the former the "general vatan" and the latter the "special vatan." See Hasan Kaleşi, "Şemsettin Sami Fraşeri'nin Siyasi Görüşleri," in *VII. Türk Tarih Kongresi* (Ankara: Türk Tarih Kurumu Basımevi, 1973), 647.
29. Tunaya, *Türkiye'de Siyasal Partiler*, 3:373–374. For detailed information about Halil Menteşe, see Syed Tanvir Wasti, "Halil Mentese: The Quadrumvir," *Middle Eastern Studies* 32, no. 3 (July 1996): 92–105; İsmail Arar, "Giriş," in *Halil Menteşe'nin Anıları* (Istanbul: Hürriyet Vakfı Yayınları, 1986), 1–106.
30. Erik Jan Zurcher, "Kosovo Revisited: Sultan Resad's Macedonian Journey of June 1911," *Middle Eastern Studies* 35, no. 4 (October 1999): 26–39.
31. Ziya Gökalp, "Yeni Osmanlılar," in *Makaleler I*, ed. Şevket Beysanoğlu (Istanbul: Milli Eğitim Basımevi, 1976), 63. This article was originally published by the newspaper *Peyman* in Diyarbakır on July 12, 1909.
32. Ibid.
33. Ibid., 62–65.
34. Ziya Gökalp, "Eskiliğin Mukavemeti," *Genç Kalemler* 2 (May 9, 1911): 26–29.
35. "İmparatorluk Haricindeki Türkler Ne Diyorlar?" *Türk Yurdu* 20 (Aug. 22, 1912): 336–337.
36. Ibid.

37. Yusuf Akçura, "Türklük Şuunu," *Türk Yurdu* 25 (Oct. 31, 1912): 30.
38. Ibid.
39. Tunaya, *Türkiye'de Siyasal Partiler*, 3:130. Kazım Karabekir (1882–1948), who fought against the Bulgarian army in the Balkan Wars and became one of the most powerful generals during the War of Independence, mentioned in his memoirs the importance of the Balkans for the survival of Turkey: "Macedonia, are you going to remain in our hands? If you leave, will you drag all Turkey with you?" Kazım Karabekir, *Hayatım* (Istanbul: Emre Yayınları, 1995), 365.
40. Şevket Süreyya Aydemir's book *Suyu Arayan Adam* is an excellent account for analyzing the changing discourse of a Turkish intellectual in the first half of the twentieth century. Aydemir was an Ottoman patriot when he was in military school. After the loss of territories in the Balkans, he became a passionate pan-Turkist whose aim was to unite all the "enslaved Turks" in the Russian Empire. He joined the Ottoman army during World War I to fight against Russians on the Caucasus front. After the war, he went to Azerbaijan and Russia and became a socialist. After returning to Turkey, he became a Kemalist intellectual and defended the Kemalist reforms until the end of his life. Aydemir defined the end of his intellectual transformation accordingly: "My life story ended with a turn to the soil of the Central Anatolian steppe." Şevket Süreyya Aydemir, *Suyu Arayan Adam* (Istanbul: Remzi Kitabevi, 1976).
41. Ibid., 48–49.
42. İnci Enginün, *Halide Edib Adıvar'ın Eserlerinde Doğu ve Batı Meselesi* (Istanbul: Dergah Yayınları, 2007), 434. Her speech was published by *Türk Yurdu* on May 29, 1913. Halide Edib, "Felaketlerden Sonra Milletler," *Türk Yurdu* 40 (May 29, 1913): 287–291.
43. Halide Edib, "Felaketlerden Sonra Milletler," 288.
44. Ibid., 289.
45. Ibid., 291.
46. Fuat Köprülü, "Ümit ve Azim," *Türk Yurdu* 32 (February 6, 1913): 139.
47. Tunaya, *Türkiye'de Siyasal Partiler*, 3:562–563.
48. Ömer Seyfettin was a prominent modern Turkish nationalist. He is one of Turkey's well-known short story writers. He graduated from the military academy and served in the army until the Balkan Wars. During the war, he became a prisoner of war and was kept in a prison camp by the Greek army. After returning to Istanbul, he resigned from the military and started writing articles in newspapers and journals. Ömer Seyfettin was an ardent supporter of the nationalist policies of the CUP.
49. Ziya Gökalp, "Türkleşmek, İslamlaşmak, Muasırlaşmak," *Türk Yurdu* 35 (March 20, 1913): 184–186.
50. Ibid., 184.
51. Ibid., 186.
52. Yekta Bahir, "'Milli,' Daha Doğrusu 'Kavmî' Edebiyat Ne Demektir?" *Genç Kalemler* 4, no. 2 (June 8, 1911): 162–167. Ali Canip used the nickname Yekta Bahir for this article.

53. Fuat Köprülü, "Edebiyatı Milliye," *Servet-i Fünun* 1041 (1911): 3–7.
54. Köprülüzade Mehmed Fuad, "Türklük, İslamlık, Osmanlılık," *Türk Yurdu* 44 (July 24, 1913): 373.
55. Ibid., 374.
56. Fevzi Paşa, *Garbi Rumeli'nin Suret-i Ziyaı ve Balkan Harbi'nde Garb Cephesi Harekatı* (Istanbul: Erkan-ı Harbiye Mektebi Matbaası, 1927), 4–5.
57. The word *Turan* is a Persian word for Central Asia that literally means "the land of the Tur."
58. Ziya Gökalp, "Turan," *Genç Kalemler* 14 (1911): 68.
59. Aydemir, *Suyu Arayan Adam*, 54.
60. Ibid., 55. Aydemir pointed out how the journal *Türk Yurdu* and the articles it published changed his worldview from Ottomanism to Turkism.
61. Ibid., 57–58.
62. Ahmet Agayef (Ağaoğlu), "Türk Alemi," *Türk Yurdu* 1, no. 1 (Nov. 30, 1911): 15–16.
63. Hülya Adak, "New Introduction," in Halide Adivar Edib, *Memoirs of Halide Edib* (New York: Gorgias Press, 2004), ix. *Yeni Turan* was translated into German in 1916 and later into Russian and Serbian.
64. Halide Edib Adıvar, *Yeni Turan* (Istanbul: Özgür Yayınları, 2006), 55–56. According to Ahmet Ağoğlu, *Yeni Turan* illustrated that Turkish nationalists were not chauvinists, as was argued by their opponents: "There is not anybody left that does not read the novel *Yeni Turan* written by well-known author Miss Halide. The nationalist author summarized the intention and the ideal of the new movement in her novel. Nobody, not even the hardest opponent of the nationalist movement, can question the sincerity of Miss Halide. Is there such a feeling of revenge among the main characters of the novel? Do they want to harm other [ethnic] groups? Do they want to have more for Turks than others?" "Matbuat," *Türk Yurdu* 65 (May 14, 1914): 295.
65. Yusuf Akçura, "Türklük Şuunu," *Türk Yurdu* 49 (Oct. 2, 1913): 29.
66. Ziya Gökalp, "Türkleşmek, İslamlaşmak, Muasırlaşmak 6," *Türk Yurdu* 47 (Sept. 4, 1913): 426.
67. Yusuf Akçura, "Peyam'a Cevap," *Türk Yurdu* 66 (May 28, 1914): 312–313.
68. Şükrü Hanioğlu coined the phrase "the longest decade" of the empire for the era from 1908 to 1918. The term "the longest century" of the empire was used by İlber Ortaylı to define the previous completed century, namely, the nineteenth century, in the Ottoman Empire. M. Şükrü Hanioğlu, *A Brief History of the Late Ottoman Empire* (Princeton, NJ: Princeton University Press, 2008); İlber Ortaylı, *İmparatorluğun En Uzun Yüzyılı* (Istanbul: Hil Yayın, 1983).
69. Tunaya, *Türkiye'de Siyasal Partiler*, 3:30.
70. Yahya Kemal Beyatlı, *Çocukluğum, Gençliğim, Siyasi ve Edebi Hatıralarım* (Istanbul: İstanbul Fetih Cemiyeti, 1976), 132–133. According to Ali Fuad Erden (1883–1957), who served in the Ottoman army in the Middle East during World War I and later became general secretary of the National Security Council in 1946, the objective of the offensive to the Suez Canal was to block

the linkage between Britain and its colonies in Asia, not to conquer Egypt. He highlighted that the offensive also aimed at blocking the British warships, which transported soldiers from India, Australia, and New Zealand to the Dardanelles. However, both Ali Fuad Erden and Ziya Şakir argued that the Suez offensive was depicted by the ruling elites as a military move to conquer Egypt and was used as a propaganda vehicle for domestic public opinion.

71. Tunaya, *Türkiye'de Siyasal Partiler*, 3:603.
72. Ali Fuad Erden, *Paris'ten Tih Sahrasına* (Ankara: Ulus Basımevi, 1949), 21.
73. During his visit in Medina, Enver Pasha was psychologically in a condition of ecstasy. He constantly cried and prayed in the tomb of the Prophet Muhammad. Ali Fuad Erden, *Birinci Dünya Harbinde Suriye Hatıraları* (Istanbul: İş Bankası Kültür Yayınları, 2003), 220–221.
74. Kayalı, *Arabs and Young Turks*, 139–140.
75. Feroz Ahmad, *The Making of Modern Turkey* (New York: Routledge, 1996), 39.
76. Tunaya, *Türkiye'de Siyasal Partiler*, 3:591–592.
77. Ziya Şakir, *1914–1918 Cihan Harbini Nasıl İdare Ettik* (Istanbul: Ahmet Sait Matbaası, 1944), 112.
78. According to Ziya Şakir, two "first class" Unionists were talking to each other about the signing of the alliance between the Ottoman Empire and Germany on August 3, 1914. One of them argued that after the war the empire would regain the lost territories. Furthermore, he underlined that "a Great Turkistan Empire will be established from the Adriatic Sea to the border of China." It is striking that a similar phrase, "from the Adriatic to the Wall of China," was employed by Turkish statesmen, especially by President Süleyman Demirel, after the collapse of the Soviet Union to define the "emerging Turkic world in Eurasia." Ziya Şakir, *1914 Cihan Harbine Nasıl Girdik* (Istanbul: Muallim Fuat Gücüyener Kitap Deposu, 1943), 68.
79. Bernard Lewis, *The Emergence of Modern Turkey* (New York: Oxford University Press, 2002), 351; Jacob M. Landau, *Exploring Ottoman and Turkish History* (London: Hurst, 2004), 45.
80. *Sultan Osman* and *Reşadiye* were the two battleships constructed by Britain for the Ottoman Empire. Winston Churchill, who was the First Lord of Admiralty in August 1914, requisitioned these warships. Moreover, Britain refused to refund the payments of four million pounds to the Ottoman Empire for these battleships.
81. Ziya Gökalp, "Millet ve Vatan," *Türk Yurdu* 67 (May 28, 1914): 303.
82. Ibid.
83. Although Ömer Seyfeddin gave weight to the unity between Turks and Arabs, he made a clear distinction between the territories inhabited by these two groups. According to him, Arabs were in the majority in the territories south of Kirkuk and Aleppo, which he called the "Arabian homeland." According to Ömer Seyfeddin, "Turkish homeland includes Istanbul, Edirne, Konya, Adana, Sivas, Diyarbakır, Trabzon, Erzurum, Van, Bitlis, Ma'muretül-Aziz [Elazığ], and the north of Mosul and Aleppo. There are few Greeks in the

coastal areas of the Turkish homeland and they are migrating and leaving. In the eastern provinces of Erzurum, Van, and Bitlis, Armenians are in the minority and their population is less than that of the Turks." It is important to note that after World War I, roughly the same territories were claimed by the last Ottoman Parliament and the Kemalists as the "national territories." Ömer Seyfeddin, "Türklük Mefkuresi," in *Türklük Üzerine Yazılar* (Ankara: Bilgi Yayınevi, 2002), 83–85. This article was originally published in 1914.

84. Said Halim Paşa, *Buhranlarımız* (Istanbul: Tercüman, n.d.), 110–111.
85. Mehmed Akif Ersoy, "Hala mı Boğuşmak?" in *Safahat* (Istanbul: İnkilap Kitapevi, 1958).
86. Ahmed Naim, *İslamda Kavmiyetçilik Yoktur* (Istanbul: Bedir Yayınevi, 1991), 40–41. Ahmed Naim wrote a series of articles with the title "There Is No Nationalism in Islam" published in the newspaper *Sebilürreşad* in 1914. These articles were collected in a book published in 1916.
87. The theme of expanding the borders of the empire was dominant even among second-rank army officers. Just after the signing of the Ottoman-German alliance, Ali Fuad Erden participated in a discussion with Colonel von Frankenberg and Ottoman officers in the headquarters of the Second Army in Istanbul. Frankenberg and Ottoman officials were talking about the future borders of the Ottoman Empire on a map. When Ali Fuad Erden appeared distant during this conversation, Frankenberg turned to him and asked him directly about a region in Asia: "Why should not this border be the border of your vatan?" Ali Fuad Erden thought about this question and acknowledged that Frankenberg was right: "There was no reason not to desire [expanding the borders to Asia]." Erden, *Paris'ten Tih Sahrasına*, 17–19.
88. Similarly, the imperial elites of the Habsburg Empire viewed World War I as an opportunity to become a Great Power in Europe. For imperial elites, to be a Great Power was the only justification for the existence of the Habsburg Empire, as accepting the status of a middling power "would be a sign of weakness and convey the wrong signal to all of the domains under Vienna's control." See Solomon Wank, "The Habsburg Empire," in *After Empire*, ed. Karen Barkey and Mark Von Hagen (Oxford: Westview Press, 1997), 52.
89. Tunaya, *Türkiye'de Siyasal Partiler*, 3:295.
90. Ibid., 605.
91. The 11th clause of the Armistice of Mudros follows: "Immediate withdrawal of the Turkish troops from Northwest Persia to behind the pre-war frontier has already been ordered and will be carried out. Part of Trans-Caucasia has already been ordered to be evacuated by Turkish troops; the remainder is to be evacuated if required by the Allies after they have studied the situation there."
92. Tunaya, *Türkiye'de Siyasal Partiler*, 3:560.
93. "Türk Ocağı Kongresi," *Türk Yurdu* 7, no. 160 (July 15, 1918): 250–252.
94. Ibid.
95. Halide Edib, "Evimize Bakalım: Türkçülüğün Faaliyet Sahası," *Vakit*, June 30, 1918.

96. Ziya Gökalp, "Türkçülük ve Türkiyecilik," *Yeni Mecmua* 2, no. 51 (July 4, 1918): 482.
97. Köprülüzade Mehmet Fuat, "Türkçülüğün Gayeleri," *Vakit*, July 16, 1918.
98. The Army of Islam headed by Nuri Pasha captured Baku on September 15, 1918. The Ottoman forces continued to advance toward the north along the Caspian coast and took Petrovsk in Dagestan, 180 miles north of Baku, on October 8, 1918.
99. Köprülüzade Mehmet Fuat, "Türkçülüğün Gayeleri."
100. According to Ali Fuat Türkgeldi, who was the chief secretary of the chancery of the Ottoman Sultan Vahdeddin, there were around 7,000–8,000 Ottoman soldiers in Thrace. According to Stanford Shaw, the number of Ottoman defensive forces in the Thrace region was "no more than 6000 men." Ali Türkgeldi, *Moudros ve Mudanya Mütarekelerinin Tarihi* (Ankara: Güney Matbaacılık, 1948), 25–26; Stanford J. Shaw, *From Empire to Republic* (Ankara: Türk Tarih Kurumu Basımevi, 2000), 1:66.
101. Ahmet İzzet Paşa, *Feryadım* (Istanbul: Nehir Yayınları, 1993), 2:19.
102. Shaw, *From Empire to Republic*, 1:94.
103. Clauses 7 and 24 of the Mudros Armistice were written in a particularly ambiguous way, so that it would give rights to the Allies to occupy any part of the empire without consulting Istanbul. Clause 7: "The Allies to have the right to occupy any strategic points in the event of a situation arising which threatens the security of the Allies." Clause 24: "In case of disorder in the six Armenian vilayets the Allies reserve themselves the right to occupy any part of them." In the Turkish text, "six Armenian vilayets" were called "six vilayets."
104. "British War Aims," *The Times*, January, 6, 1918: 7.
105. The original document can be downloaded from www.ourdocuments.gov/doc.php?flash=true&doc=62.
106. In October 1918, the grand vizier Ahmet İzzet Pasha announced in the Ottoman Parliament that the empire would grant autonomous status to its Arab regions. After the announcement, he was congratulated by the Arab members of the Parliament. Türkgeldi, *Moudros ve Mudanya Mütarekelerinin Tarihi*, 16, 29.
107. Clause 16 of the Armistice of Mudros ordered the surrender of all garrisons in Hejaz, Assir, Yemen, Syria, and Mesopotamia to the nearest Allied commander and the withdrawal of all troops from Cilicia, except those necessary to maintain order, as would be determined under Clause 5.
108. Gotthard Jaeschke, *Kurtuluş Savaşı ile İlgili İngiliz Belgeleri*, trans. Cemal Köprülü (Ankara: Türk Tarih Kurumu Basımevi, 1991), 32–33. Mustafa Kemal became the commander of the Ottoman army in Syria after the armistice, and his communications with the Ottoman government revealed that he was aware of the fact that Allies were aiming to occupy major cities in the south and east of Anatolia by using the geographical and historical terms mentioned in the armistice. On November 3, 1918, only a day after the armistice was publicly announced, Mustafa Kemal asked for clarification of these

terms from the grand vizier Ahmet İzzet Pasha: "Which Cilicia territories were included? Where is the boundary of Syria set? Does the boundary of Syria mean the north boundary of our province of Syria . . . While the area of Cilicia is known to be an important part of the province Adana, its boundaries are not known. Please elaborate on what they are." In another telegram he sent to the grand vizier, he insisted on resisting any further Allied demands: "This article was written by the British to fool us, and no doubt remains that they are giving two meanings to every one of the conditions signed by the Turkish representatives . . . My object in asking about the border of the Cilicia is to find out if the Ottoman government is officially accepting the British definition of the boundaries of the historic term, which includes everything north of Maras. Because to my thinking by substituting the word Cilicia for that of Adana, which we use, the British are trying to extend its boundaries to the north, right up to the borders of Iraq. They want to include Siirt . . . If we bend our neck to everything that the British say, we will not be able to escape their greed . . . If they occupy Anatolia, will we give permission?" Shaw, *From Empire to Republic*, 1:103–104.

109. Mehmet Kalan and İnci Enginün, *Devrin Yazarlarının Kalemiyle Milli Mücadele ve Gazi Mustafa Kemal* (Ankara: Kültür Bakanlığı, 1981), 1:89.
110. Damat Ferit served as the grand vizier of the Ottoman governments between March 4, 1919, and September 30, 1919, and between April 5, 1920, and October 17, 1920. The Sèvres Treaty was signed by his government, and therefore he was identified by Mustafa Kemal as the "traitor to vatan." His political career ascended during Vahdettin's reign due to Damat Ferit's marriage to Vahdettin's sister Mediha Sultan.
111. According to Ali Fuad Türkgeldi, Sultan Vahdettin immediately left the room after his opening speech with Abdülmecid, the heir to the throne. In tears, he told Abdülmecid that "I am crying like a woman." Ali Fuad Türkgeldi, *Görüp İşittiklerim* (Ankara: Türk Tarih Kurumu Basımevi, 1949), 234.
112. Mithat Sertoğlu, "Mütareke Devrinde Saltanat Şurası ve Milli Şura Hazırlıkları," *Belgelerle Türk Tarihi Dergisi* 22 (July 1969): 34–35.
113. Mustafa Budak, *İdealden Gerçeğe* (Istanbul: Küre Yayınları, 2002), 78.
114. Stanford J. Shaw and Ezel Kural Shaw, *History of the Ottoman Empire* (New York: Cambridge University Press, 1976), 2:696.
115. Mustafa Kemal Atatürk, *Nutuk* (Istanbul: Milli Eğitim Basımevi, 1973), 3:1225–1226.
116. Stanford J. Shaw and Ezel Kural Shaw, *History of the Ottoman Empire*, 2:696.
117. Jacob C. Hurewitz, *Diplomacy in the Near and Middle East: A Documentary Record: 1914–1956* (Princeton, NJ: D. Van Nostrand, 1956), 2:74.
118. Ibid., 74–75. For the Turkish version, see Budak, *İdealden Gerçeğe*, 156–157.
119. "Vahdet-i Coğrafiyemiz," *Minber* 8, November 8, 1918.
120. Budak, *İdealden Gerçeğe*, 144.
121. Ibid., 246.

122. Sevim, Öztoprak, and Tural, *Atatürk'ün Söylev ve Demeçleri*, 61. On December 28, 1919, when Mustafa Kemal arrived in Ankara, he gave a speech to city leaders. In his speech, he declared that the southern border included Iskenderun, Mosul, Kirkuk, and Sulaymaniyah. According to Mustafa Kemal, "this border is defended by our army with arms and at the same time it is the border of our vatan, which Turkish and Kurdish elements inhabited." See Sevim, Öztoprak, and Tural, *Atatürk'ün Söylev ve Demeçleri*, 37.

123. The words "Turk," "Turkish," "Turkish people," or "Turkish vatan" were not used in the original texts of the declarations of the congresses and the National Pact. However, the English translations of these texts erroneously used the term "Turkish Empire" instead of "Ottoman Empire." Only the third article of the National Pact used the word "Turkey" as a geographical concept: "The determination of the juridical status of Western Thrace also, which has been made dependent on the peace of Turkey, must be affected in accordance with the votes which shall be given by the inhabitants in complete freedom."

124. This is an excerpt from Mustafa Kemal's speech in the Grand National Assembly in Ankara on May 1, 1920. Sevim, Öztoprak, and Tural, *Atatürk'ün Söylev ve Demeçleri*, 105.

125. Although there were some local guerilla activities against the French army in the southeast of Anatolia, these were local armed campaigns, not major wars fought by regular armies.

126. Cevat Dursunoğlu, "Erzurum Kongresi Sırasında Atatürk'ün Düşünceleri," *Belleten* no. 108 (Oct. 1963): 636.

127. This is an excerpt from Mustafa Kemal's speech in the Grand National Assembly on December 1, 1921. Earlier in the meeting with the American General Harbord in Sivas on September 22, 1919, Mustafa Kemal limited the objectives of the national movement to the national borders: "We consider Turanism as a harmful ideal. We are not interested in illusions like this that are far from our borders." Sevim, Öztoprak, and Tural, *Atatürk'ün Söylev ve Demeçleri*, 267; Jaeschke, *Kurtuluş Savaşı ile İlgili İngiliz Belgeleri*, 170.

128. Shaw, *From Empire to Republic*, 3:1137.

129. Although the article was published without an author's name, it was presumably written by Mustafa Kemal, as some of the themes in the article were very similar to those of his speech in Ankara on December 28, 1919. "Hudut Meselesi," *Hakimiyet-i Milliye* 4, January 24, 1920, in *Devrin Yazarlarının Kalemiyle Milli Mücadele ve Gazi Mustafa Kemal*, 1:208–215.

130. Ibid.

131. "İngilizlerin İslam Siyaseti," *Hakimiyet-i Milliye* 23, April 20, 1920, in *Devrin Yazarlarının Kalemiyle Milli Mücadele ve Gazi Mustafa Kemal*, 1:268–271; "Anadolu," *Hakimiyet-i Milliye* 72, November 7, 1920, in *Devrin Yazarlarının Kalemiyle Milli Mücadele ve Gazi Mustafa Kemal*, 1:346–348.

132. Ibid.

133. Ziya Gökalp, "Çoban ile Bülbül," *Genç Yolcular* 3, January, 1, 1920, in *Devrin Yazarlarının Kalemiyle Milli Mücadele ve Gazi Mustafa Kemal*, 1:137–138.

134. "Milletvekillerinin Heyecanı," *Hakimiyet-i Milliye* 33, May 23, 1920, in *Devrin Yazarlarının Kalemiyle Milli Mücadele ve Gazi Mustafa Kemal*, 1:299–305.
135. Recently, the prevailing Islamic spirit in the national anthem was criticized by the retired army general Doğu Silahçıoğlu in his article "Supporters of Ummah and Nationalists," published by the uncompromising Kemalist newspaper *Cumhuriyet* on February 22, 2008. Doğu Silahçıoğlu argued that whereas the religious Mehmet Akif could not find a place for the word "Turk" in the ten-stanza-long national anthem, he "skillfully installed" in the anthem religious words such as "God," "azan," "paradise," and "faith." Doğu Silahçıoğlu, "Ümmetçiler ve Milliyetçiler," *Cumhuriyet*, February 22, 2008.
136. Sevim, Öztoprak, and Tural, *Atatürk'ün Söylev ve Demeçleri*, 236. The influential and high-circulation daily newspaper *Hürriyet* selected Mustafa Kemal's phrase "Turkey belongs to Turks" as its motto one year after its foundation and has been using it on the front page since 1949.
137. Sevim, Öztoprak, and Tural, *Atatürk'ün Söylev ve Demeçleri*, 194. Six months before Mustafa Kemal's speech, on July 3, 1920, İsmet İnönü argued in his speech in the Parliament that the invasion of Anatolia by Greece was instigated by the "imperialist leaders." *İsmet İnönü'nün TBMM'deki Konuşmaları 1920–1973* (Ankara: TBMM Basımevi, 1992), 1:15.
138. Ruşen Eşref was the first journalist in the Ottoman media to conduct a long interview with Mustafa Kemal, published by the journal *Yeni Mecmua* in 1918. Ruşen Eşref's interview about Mustafa Kemal's military achievements in the Battle of Dardanelles elevated Mustafa Kemal's image in the eyes of the public. Ruşen Eşref became the secretary general of the president of Turkey in 1933. After Mustafa Kemal's death, he served as an ambassador in Rome, London, and Athens. Ruşen Eşref, "Azim ve İman," *Hakimiyet-i Milliye* 257, August 7, 1921, in *Devrin Yazarlarının Kalemiyle Milli Mücadele ve Gazi Mustafa Kemal*, 2:632–636.
139. Falih Rıfkı became a leading journalist after the end of the National Liberation War. He was the chief editor of the newspaper *Hakimiyet-i Milliye* and *Ulus*, both of which were official newspapers of the Republican People's Party. Until Mustafa Kemal's death in 1938, he had been a trusted member of Mustafa Kemal's entourage and regularly attended his dinners in the Çankaya Palace. Falih Rıfkı, "Sakarya'nın Suları Neler Anlatıyor," *Akşam* 1054, August 31, 1921, in *Devrin Yazarlarının Kalemiyle Milli Mücadele ve Gazi Mustafa Kemal*, 2:637–638.
140. Falih Rıfkı, "Allah Senden Razı Olsun," *Akşam* 1076, September 22, 1921, in *Devrin Yazarlarının Kalemiyle Milli Mücadele ve Gazi Mustafa Kemal*, 2:644–646.
141. Yahya Kemal, "İstiklal Hissimiz," *Tevhid-i Efkar* 311, April, 20, 1922, in *Devrin Yazarlarının Kalemiyle Milli Mücadele ve Gazi Mustafa Kemal*, 2:842–845.
142. This sentence comes from the poem "The Song of Vatan" written by Namık Kemal for his well-known play "Vatan or Silistre."

143. Yahya Kemal, "Yeni Türk Ruhu," *Tevhid-i Efkar* 334–337, May 13–16, 1922, in *Devrin Yazarlarının Kalemiyle Milli Mücadele ve Gazi Mustafa Kemal*, 2:852–860.
144. Ziya Gökalp, "Kara Destan," *Küçük Mecmua* 4, June 26, 1922, 13–14, in *Devrin Yazarlarının Kalemiyle Milli Mücadele ve Gazi Mustafa Kemal*, 2:884–885.
145. Ziya Gökalp, "İngiliz'den Sakın," *Küçük Mecmua* 6, July 10, 1922, 11–12, in *Devrin Yazarlarının Kalemiyle Milli Mücadele ve Gazi Mustafa Kemal*, 2:890–891.
146. "Dumlupınar Zaferi Üzerine Türk Milletine Beyanname," in *Atatürk'ün Tamim, Telgraf ve Beyannameleri* 4 (Ankara: Atatürk Araştırma Merkezi, 1991), 474.
147. Sevim, Öztoprak, and Tural, *Atatürk'ün Söylev ve Demeçleri*, 382–383.
148. The original version of the ordinance was published by Tevfik Bıyıklıoğlu, *Trakya'da Milli Mücadele* (Ankara: Türk Tarih Kurumu, 1987), 2:104–105.
149. Budak, *İdealden Gerçeğe*, 362–369.
150. *İsmet İnönü'nün TBMM'deki Konuşmaları 1920–1973*, 1:83.
151. Ibid., 84.
152. Ibid., 137.
153. Ibid., 120.
154. Ibid., 140.
155. Ibid., 114.
156. Sevim, Öztoprak, and Tural, *Atatürk'ün Söylev ve Demeçleri*, 559–569.
157. Tom Nairn, "Scotland and Europe," in *Becoming National*, ed. Geoff Eley and Ronald Grigor Suny (Oxford: Oxford University Press, 1996), 80; Jan Penrose, "Nations, States and Homelands: Territory and Territoriality in Nationalist Thought," *Nations and Nationalism* 8, no. 3 (2002): 285.

CHAPTER THREE. FROM GEOGRAPHY TO VATAN

1. I borrowed the title of this chapter from Remzi Oğuz Arık's book *Coğrafyadan Vatana* (*From Geography to Vatan*). The book includes collected essays written by Arık. It was first published in 1956 in memory of him, two years after his death in a plane crash. This book was later published by the Ministry of National Education. Arık wrote essays on nationalism, and he can be considered one of the earliest founders of right-wing nationalism in Turkey, where it has been an influential political movement since the second half of the 1960s. Arık founded the right-wing Peasant Party of Turkey in 1954, which later became the Republican Peasants' Nation Party in 1958 and eventually the Nationalist Action Party in 1969. See Remzi Oğuz Arık, *Coğrafyadan Vatana* (Istanbul: Milli Eğitim Basımevi, 1969).
2. Ibid., 1.
3. Ibid., 3.
4. Liisa Malkki, "National Geographic: The Rooting of Peoples and the Territorialization of National Identity among Scholars and Refugees," *Cultural Anthropology* 7, no. 1 (1992).
5. Akhil Gupta and James Ferguson, "Beyond 'Culture': Space, Identity, and the Politics of Difference," *Cultural Anthropology* 7, no. 1 (February 1992): 7.

6. There is an extensive literature on the Turkish Thesis of History and the Sun Language Theory. See Büşra Behar Ersanlı, *İktidar ve Tarih: Türkiye'de Resmi Tarih Tezinin Oluşumu, 1929–1937* (Istanbul: Afa Yayınları, 1992); İlker Aytürk, "Turkish Linguists against the West: The Origins of Linguistic Nationalism in Atatürk's Turkey," *Middle Eastern Studies* 40, no. 6 (2004): 1–25. For an interesting article published in the *New York Times*, see "Turks Teach New Theories," *New York Times*, February 9, 1936, E7.
7. See Anssi Paasi, "Territorial Identities as Social Constructs," *Hagar— International Social Science Review* 1, no. 2 (2000): 100–101.
8. İsmet İnönü gave this speech on April 25, 1925. Bilal Şimşir, *İngiliz Belgeleriyle Türkiye'de 'Kürt Sorunu' 1924–1938* (Ankara: Dışişleri Bakanlığı Basımevi, 1975), 58.
9. Arık, *Coğrafyadan Vatana*, 7.
10. Uygur Kocabaşoğlu, *Şirket Telsizinden Devlet Radyosuna* (Ankara: Ankara Üniversitesi, 1980), 116.
11. Uygur Kocabaşoğlu, "Radyo," *Türkiye Cumhuriyeti Ansiklopedisi* (Istanbul: İletişim, 1985), 10:2735.
12. For a detailed report about the history of Turkey's railways prepared by Turkey's Public Workers Union, see *Türkiye'de Demiryolunun Tarihi Gelişimi*. Accessed April 4, 2009. Available from www.kamusen.org.tr/imaj/arge/demiryolu.pdf.
13. Behiç Erkin (1876–1961) was the first director of State Railways of Turkey and a close friend of Mustafa Kemal. The grandson of Behiç Erkin wrote two interesting books based on Erkin's unpublished memoirs. Emir Kıvırcık, *Büyükelçi* (Istanbul: GOA Basım Yayın, 2007); Emir Kıvırcık, *Cepheye Giden Yol* (Istanbul: GOA Basım Yayın, 2007).
14. Ali Sevim, İzzet Öztoprak, and M. Akif Tural, *Atatürk'ün Söylev ve Demeçleri* (Ankara: Divan Yayıncılık, 2006), 494.
15. Susan Schulten, *The Geographical Imagination in America, 1880–1950* (Chicago: Chicago University Press, 2001), 241.
16. Paasi, "Nationalizing Everyday Life: Individual and Collective Identities as Practice and Discourse," *Geography Research Forum* 19, (1999), 13–14.
17. Michel Foucault argued that "the exercise of power perpetually creates knowledge and, conversely, knowledge constantly induces effects of power." Foucault, *Power/Knowledge* (New York: Pantheon, 1980), 52.
18. Donald Quataert, *The Ottoman Empire, 1700–1922* (Cambridge: Cambridge University Press, 2000), 167.
19. Kemal H. Karpat, *The Politicization of Islam: Reconstructing Identity, State, Faith, and Community in the Late Ottoman State* (New York: Oxford University Press, 2001), 100; Ramazan Özey, "Osmanlı Devleti Döneminde Coğrafya ve Öğretimi," in *Osmanlı*, ed. Güler Eren (Ankara: Semih Ofset, 1999), 8:330.
20. Selim Sabit was a leading reformer in education and the first modern pedagogue in the Ottoman Empire. He studied in Paris and returned to the Ottoman Empire after completing his studies in 1861.

21. Osman Nuri Ergin, *İstanbul Mektepleri ve İlim, Terbiye ve San'at Müesseseleri Dolayısıyla Türkiye Maarif Tarihi* (Istanbul: Osmanbey Matbaası, 1939–1943), 460.
22. Ahmet Ali Özer, "Selim Sabit Efendi Hayatı ve Eserleri," *Yağmur Dergisi* 42 (January 2009).
23. Özey, "Osmanlı Devleti Döneminde Coğrafya ve Öğretimi," 330.
24. Benjamin C. Fortna, *Imperial Classroom: Islam, the State, and Education in the Late Ottoman Empire* (Oxford: Oxford University Press, 2002), 177–184.
25. Selim Sabit Efendi, *Muhtasar Coğrafya Risalesi* (Istanbul: Matbaa-i Amire, 1874).
26. See Sabit Efendi, *Muhtasar Coğrafya Risalesi*; Ahmed Cemal, *Coğrafya-i Umumi* (Istanbul: Harbiye-i Şahane Matbaası, 1891); Mehmed Hikmet, *Coğrafya-i Umrani* (Istanbul: Nişan Berberyan, 1895); Ali Tevfik, *Memalik-i Mahruse-i Şahane Coğrafyası* (Istanbul: Kasbar Matbaası, 1900); İbrahim Hilmi, *Memalik-i Osmaniye Cep Atlası: Devlet-i Aliyye-i Osmaniyenin Ahval-i Coğrafya ve İstatikiyesi* (Istanbul: Mahmud Bey Matbaası, 1907).
27. Sabit Efendi, *Muhtasar Coğrafya Risalesi*, 21–25.
28. Ahmed Cemal, *Coğrafya-i Umumi*, 110.
29. Ibid., 112–113.
30. Ibid., 5–6.
31. Mehmed Hikmet, *Coğrafya-i Umrani*, 7.
32. Ibid., 19.
33. Ali Tevfik, *Memalik-i Mahruse-i Şahane Coğrafyası*. Ottoman maps published during Abdulhamid's reign also had an exaggerated view of Ottoman territories: "[A] pocket-sized Ottoman atlas approved by the Ministry of Education in 1906 and published the following year presents a rather fanciful view of the extent of Ottoman dominion. The pink of Ottoman sovereignty is extended to include 'Tunus emareti,' whereas Tunis had been occupied by France since 1881. Likewise, Egypt is presented as Ottoman, even though Ottoman rule was little more than a legal fiction after the British military occupation of 1882. Bulgaria is treated as an Ottoman tributary, and Eastern Rumelia, annexed by Bulgaria in 1885, is presented as a province of the empire like any other. The province of Yemen is drawn without regard for the British presence in Aden or the Hadramawt." Fortna, *Imperial Classroom*, 190.
34. Quoted in Benjamin C. Fortna, "Change in the School Maps of the Late Ottoman Empire," *Imago Mundi* 57, no. 1 (2005): 31.
35. Hasan Kayalı, *Arabs and Young Turks: Ottomanism, Arabism, and Islamism in the Ottoman Empire, 1908–1918* (Berkeley: University of California Press, 1997), 9.
36. Fortna, "Change in the School Maps of the Late Ottoman Empire," 23–24.
37. Ali Tevfik, *Memalik-i Osmaniye Coğrafyası* (Istanbul: Kasbar Matbaası, 1909), 56–57.
38. Behram Münir, *Vatan-ı Mukaddes Yahud Memalik-i Osmaniye Coğrafyası* (Istanbul: Murettibin-i Osmaniye Matbaası, 1912), 2.

39. Ibid., 17.
40. Ibid.
41. After the CUP came to power, Mehmet Ali Tevfik started to work in the Ministry of Public Works. From the beginning of World War I to September 1916, he worked for the *War Magazine (Harp Mecmuası)*, which was sponsored by the Ottoman War Ministry for propaganda purposes. Between September 1916 and July 1919, Mehmet Ali Tevfik worked as geography teacher in various schools in Istanbul. With the establishment of the republic, he was employed by the Ministry of Foreign Affairs. In 1937, he became the consul of Turkey in New York and died in New York in 1941. See Ali Birinci, "Mehmet Ali Tevfik Yükselen," *Türk Yurdu* 27, no. 243 (Nov. 2007): 58–62.
42. Mehmet Ali Tevfik, "Yeni Hayat, Manevi Yurt," *Genç Kalemler* 3, no. 20 (April 27, 1912): 437–444.
43. Mehmet Ali Tevfik, "Yine Manevi Yurt," *Türk Yurdu* 3, no. 25 (Oct. 31, 1912): 18–21.
44. Mehmet Ali Tevfik used the words *vatan* and *yurt* interchangeably in his speeches and writings.
45. Mehmet Ali Tevfik, "Yeni Hayat, Manevi Yurt," 438.
46. Ibid., 443.
47. Mehmet Ali Tevfik, "Yine Manevi Yurt," 19.
48. Mehmet Ali Tevfik's article "First of All Passion and Enthusiasm" analyzed the significance of geography and history education for a patriotic society. It was written on June 27, 1913. Mehmet Ali Tevfik, *Turanlının Defteri* (Istanbul: Milli Hareket Yayınları, 1971), 74–79.
49. Klaus Kreiser, "Geographie und Patriotismus, Zur Lage der Geowissenschaften am Istanbuler Darulfunun unter dem Jungturkischen Regime (1908–1918)," in *Hommes et terres d'Islam*, ed. Xavier de Planhol (Tehran: Bibliothéque Iranienne, 1997), 71–87; Erol Tümertekin, "Development of Human Geography in Turkey," in *Turkey: Geographic and Social Perspectives*, ed. Peter Benedict, Erol Tümertekin, and Fatma Mansur (Leiden, The Netherlands: Brill, 1974), 6–18.
50. Faik Sabri, *Coğrafya-i Tabii Dersleri* (Istanbul: Matbaa-i Orhaniye, 1917), 136.
51. Faik Sabri, *Osmanlı Coğrafya-i Tabii ve İktisadisi* (Istanbul: Kanaat Matbaası, 1917), introduction.
52. Saffet Bey, *Küçüklere Coğrafya Hikayeleri* (Istanbul: Matbaa-i Amire, 1916), 113–114.
53. Faik Sabri, *Çocuklara Coğrafya Kıraatleri* (Istanbul: Matbaa-i Amire, 1916), 85.
54. Saffet Bey, *Coğrafya-i Osmani* (Istanbul: Matbaa-i Amire, 1916), 129–130.
55. Ahmet Cevad, *Musahabat-i Ahlakiye, Sıhhiye, Medeniye, Vataniye ve İnsaniye* (Istanbul: Matbaa-i Orhaniye, 1916), 124–125.
56. Ibid., 128.
57. Saffet Bey, *Coğrafya-i Osmani*, 39.
58. Ibid., 41–42.
59. Behram Münir, *Vatan-ı Mukaddes Yahud Memalik-i Osmaniye Coğrafyası*, 17, 45. Behram Münir considered the missionary activities of the Catholic and

Protestant churches among Ottoman Christians a crucial threat for the social integrity of the Ottoman Empire. He argued that "Christians, who left the Eastern Churches, are dangerous both for their ethnic groups and for the Ottoman vatan." Ibid., 19.

60. Saffet Bey, *Coğrafya-i Osmani*, 91.
61. Ibid., 92.
62. Faik Sabri, *Osmanlı Coğrafya-i Tabii ve İktisadisi*, 47; Mehmet Asım and Ahmed Cevad, *Anadolu Yavrusunun Kitabı* (Istanbul: Orhaniye Matbaası, 1919), 351–352.
63. Mehmet Asım and Ahmed Cevad, *Anadolu Yavrusunun Kitabı* (Istanbul: Matbaa-i Amire, 1917), 188.
64. Ibid., 280.
65. Saffet Bey, *Coğrafya-i Osmani*, 41; Faik Sabri, *Osmanlı Coğrafya-i Tabii ve İktisadisi*, 19. Today, according to the official statistics, the area of Anatolia is 755,688 square kilometers. This number also included the Hatay district, which is 5,403 square kilometers. Hatay became part of Turkey in 1939.
66. Saffet Bey, *Küçüklere Coğrafya Hikayeleri*, 125.
67. Rıza Nur, "Devletimizin Mahiyeti ve Milli Adı," *Türk Yurdu* 15, no. 162 (Nov. 1924): 54.
68. Ibid.
69. Ibid., 56.
70. Sevim, Öztoprak, and Tural, *Atatürk'ün Söylev ve Demeçleri*, 703.
71. *Cumhuriyet Halk Partisi Üçüncü Büyük Kongre Zabıtları* (Istanbul: Devlet Matbaası, 1931), 25.
72. Bernard Lewis, *The Emergence of Modern Turkey* (New York: Oxford University Press, 2002), 358.
73. Ibid., 358–359.
74. Muhiddin Adil, *Malûmatı Vataniye* (Istanbul: Orhaniye Matbaası, 1925).
75. Ibid., 3.
76. Ibid.
77. Ibid., 12–15.
78. Feroz Ahmad, *The Making of Modern Turkey* (New York: Routledge, 1996), 82.
79. Erik J. Zurcher, *Turkey: A Modern History* (London: Tauris, 2005), 189–190.
80. Ibid., 191.
81. Saffet Geylangil, *Umumi Coğrafya Beşinci Sınıf* (Istanbul: İnkılap ve Cumhuriyet Kitapevleri, 1938), 81.
82. Ibid., 120, 136.
83. Mehmet Besim and Cemal Arif, *Yeni Coğrafya Dersleri* (Istanbul: Türk Kitapçılığı Limitet Şirketi, 1934), 180–182.
84. Faik Sabri, *Coğrafya Orta Sınıf 1* (Istanbul: Kanaat Kütüphanesi, 1932), 61–65.
85. Faik Sabri, *Türkiye Coğrafyası* (Istanbul: Devlet Matbaası, 1929).
86. Ibid., 1.
87. Ibid., 10–11.
88. Ibid., 177.

89. Ibid., 177–178.
90. Hamit Sadi, *Coğrafya Dersleri* (Istanbul: Milliyet Matbaası, 1930), 3.
91. Ibid.
92. Besim Darkot, *Türkiye Coğrafyası* (Istanbul: Maarif Matbaası, 1942), 110.
93. Ibid.
94. Thongchai Winichakul, *Siam Mapped: A History of the Geo-Body of a Nation* (Honolulu: University Press of Hawaii, 1994), 130.
95. Mümtaz Soysal, "The Future of Turkish Foreign Policy," in *The Future of Turkish Foreign Policy*, ed. Lenore G. Martin and Dimitris Keridis (Cambridge: MIT Press, 2004), 41.
96. Faik Sabri, *Türkiye Coğrafyası*, 190–191.
97. Ibid.
98. Abdülkadir Sadi, *Yeni Orta Coğrafya* (Istanbul: Remzi Kitabevi, 1935), 6.
99. Ibid., 8.
100. During the National Liberation War, İsmail Habib Sevük ardently supported Mustafa Kemal in the newspaper *Açıksöz* published in Kastamonu. He published two books about his travels in the 1930s. The book *From Danube to the West*, published in 1935, was about his travels in Europe. İsmail Habib Sevük, *Yurddan Yazılar* (Istanbul: Cumhuriyet Matbaası, 1943).
101. Şevket Süreyya Aydemir, *Suyu Arayan Adam* (Istanbul: Remzi Kitabevi, 1976), 69.
102. Sevük, *Yurddan Yazılar*, 5–9.
103. Ibid., 37.
104. Ibid., 158.
105. Alan K. Henrikson, "The Power and Politics of Maps," in *Reordering the World*, ed. George J. Demko and William B. Wood (Boulder, CO: Westview Press, 1994), 102.
106. Kemal Kaya, *İlkokulda Coğrafya Öğretimi* (Istanbul: Maarif Matbaası, 1942), 161–169.
107. The reports and presentations made in the congress were published by the Ministry of Education. In the conclusion of the congress, the minister of education Hasan Ali Yücel praised Faik Sabri Duran and Saffet Geylangil. Yücel emphasized that their books, which were written in the late Ottoman period and included pictures and maps, influenced him deeply. These books, Yücel continued, were totally different than the geography books he had studied during secondary school that were based on memorization. *Birinci Coğrafya Kongresi: Raporlar, Müzakereler, Kararlar* (Ankara: Maarif Vekaleti, 1941), 114.
108. Ibid., 82.
109. Halil I. Tas, "Geographic Education in Turkish High Schools," *Journal of Geography* 104, no. 1 (2005): 35–39.
110. Sırrı Erinç and Sami Öngör, *Türkiye Coğrafyası* (İstanbul: Okul Kitapları, 1950), 6.
111. Ibid., 8.
112. Ibid., 9.

113. Sırrı Erinç and Sami Öngör, *Ülkeler Coğrafyası* (Istanbul: Milli Eğitim Basımevi, 1975); Sırrı Erinç and Sami Öngör, *Türkiye Coğrafyası* (Istanbul: Milli Eğitim Basımevi, 1976).
114. Erinç and Öngör, *Ülkeler Coğrafyası*, 6–11.
115. Erinç and Öngör, *Türkiye Coğrafyası* (1976), 4–6.
116. Erinç and Öngör, *Ülkeler Coğrafyası*, 55.
117. *Milli Coğrafya* (Ankara: Türk Tarih Kurumu Basımevi, 1989), 63.
118. Ibid., 71–95.
119. İbrahim Atalay, *Milli Coğrafya 7* (Istanbul: İnkilap Kitabevi, 1997), 161–166; Fuat Yahşi and Ayşe Başkurt, *Milli Coğrafya* (Istanbul: Düzgün Yayıncılık, 1996), 177–185.
120. Yahşi and Başkurt, *Milli Coğrafya*, 178.
121. Atalay, *Milli Coğrafya 7*, 163.
122. Sam Kaplan, *The Pedagogical State: Education and the Politics of National Culture in Post-1980 Turkey* (Stanford, CA: Stanford University Press, 2006), 197–198.
123. Hayati Doğanay, *Türkiye Beşeri Coğrafyası* (Ankara: Gazi Büro Kitabevi, 1994), 163.
124. Ayşe Kadıoğlu, "Denationalization of Citizenship? The Turkish Experience," *Citizenship Studies* 11, no. 3 (2007): 291.
125. Kenan Çayır and İpek Gürkaynak, "The State of Citizenship Education in Turkey: Past and Present," *Journal of Social Science Education* 6, no. 2 (February 2008): 55.
126. The book was written by a committee of fourteen people headed by Füsun Üstel. Füsun Üstel, *Coğrafya* (Istanbul: TÜSİAD, 2002).
127. Ibid., 4.
128. Ibid., 13.

CHAPTER FOUR. VATAN AND TURKEY'S FOREIGN POLICY

1. David Campbell, *Writing Security: United States Foreign Policy and the Politics of Identity* (Minneapolis: University of Minnesota Press, 1992), 70.
2. Ernesto Laclau, *On Populist Reason* (London: Verso, 2005), 228.
3. According to Torfing, dislocation is "a destabilization of a discourse that results from the emergence of events which cannot be domesticated, symbolized or integrated within the discourse in question. For example, the concurrence of inflation and unemployment in the early 1970s dislocated the Keynesian orthodoxy suggesting 'stagflation' would never occur. Likewise, the process of globalization tends to dislocate the idea of the nation-state as the privileged terrain of economic activity." Jacob Torfing, *New Theories of Discourse: Laclau, Mouffe and Zizek* (Malden, MA: Blackwell Publishers, 1999), 53, 301.
4. The relevant literature is enormous. See especially Meliha Benli Altunışık and Özlem Tür, *Turkey: Challenges of Continuity and Change* (London: Routledge, 2005); Lenore Martin and Dimitris Keridis, eds., *The Future of Turkish Foreign Policy* (Cambridge, MA: MIT Press, 2004); Stephen Larrabee and Ian

Lesser, *Turkish Foreign Policy in an Age of Uncertainty* (Santa Monica, CA: RAND Publications, 2003); Michael Radu, ed., *Dangerous Neighborhood: Contemporary Issues in Turkey's Foreign Relations* (New Brunswick, NJ: Transaction Publishers, 2003); Tareq Ismael and Mustafa Aydın, eds., *Turkey's Foreign Policy in the 21st Century: A Changing Role in World Politics* (Burlington, VT: Ashgate, 2003); Ahmet Davutoğlu, *Stratejik Derinlik* (Istanbul: Küre Yayınları, 2002); Barry Rubin and Kemal Kirişçi, eds., *Turkey in World Politics: An Emerging Multiregional Power* (Istanbul: Boğaziçi University Press, 2002); Alan Makovsky and Sabri Sayarı, eds., *Turkey's New World: Changing Dynamics in Turkish Foreign Policy* (Washington, DC: Washington Institute for Near East Policy, 2000); William Hale, *Turkish Foreign Policy, 1774–2000* (London: Frank Cass, 2000); Mustafa Aydın, ed., *Turkey at the Threshold of the 21st Century: Global Encounters and/vs Regional Alternatives* (Ankara: International Relations Foundation, 1998); Andrew Mango, *Turkey: The Challenge of a New Role* (Westport, CT: Praeger, 1994); Graham Fuller, *From Eastern Europe to Western China: The Growing Role of Turkey in the World and Its Implications for Western Interests* (Santa Monica, CA: RAND Publications, 1993).
5. Gearóid Ó Tuathail and John Agnew, "Geopolitics and Discourse: Practical Reasoning in American Foreign Policy," *Political Geography* 11, no. 2 (March 1992): 192.
6. Nicholas Spykman, "Geography and Foreign Policy II," *American Political Science Review* 32 (April 1938): 236.
7. Hale, *Turkish Foreign Policy*, 322.
8. Ibid., 7–8.
9. Altunışık and Tür, *Turkey: Challenges of Continuity*, 88.
10. Ibid., 88–89.
11. Mümtaz Soysal, "The Future of Turkish Foreign Policy," in *The Future of Turkish Foreign Policy*, ed. Lenore G. Martin and Dimitris Keridis (Cambridge: MIT Press, 2004), 37.
12. Ibid., 37–46.
13. Gearóid Ó Tuathail, "Problematizing Geopolitics: Survey, Statesmanship and Strategy," *Transactions of the Institute of British Geographers* 19, no. 3 (1994): 263.
14. Gearóid Ó Tuathail, *Critical Geopolitics* (Minneapolis: University of Minnesota Press, 1996), 167.
15. Jawaharlal Nehru, *The Discovery of India* (London: Meridian Books, 1960), 352–353.
16. Aptülahat Akşin (1892–1974), who started his career in the Ottoman Ministry of Foreign Affairs in 1913 and was later appointed as Turkey's ambassador to Argentina, Syria, and Poland, heard this argument from the foreign minister of Turkey Tevfik Rüştü Aras. Aptülahat Akşin, *Atatürk'ün Dış Politika İlkeleri ve Diplomasisi* (Ankara: Türk Tarih Kurumu, 1991), 218.
17. George Orwell, *Two Wasted Years: 1943* (London: Secker and Wartburg, 1998), 295.

18. Ali Sevim, İzzet Öztoprak, and M. Akif Tural, *Atatürk'ün Söylev ve Demeçleri* (Ankara: Divan Yayıncılık, 2006), 347.
19. George F. Kennan, *Soviet Foreign Policy, 1917–1941* (New York: D. Van Nostrand, 1960), 51–52.
20. Salahi R. Sonyel, *Türk Kurtuluş Savaşı ve Dış Politika* (Ankara: Türk Tarih Kurumu Basımevi, 1986), 2:50.
21. Ibid.
22. "D'accord sur les principes de la fraternité des nations et sur les droits des peoples à disposer librement de leur sort, constatant leur solidarité dans leur lute contre l'impérialisme, ainsi que le fait que toute difficulté survenue a l'un des deux peuples aggraverait la situation de l'autre, et étant entièrement animes du désir de voir régner toujours entre eux des rapports cordiaux et des relations de sincère amitié continue, bases sur les intérêts réciproques des deux pays, ont décidé de conclure un traite d'amitié et de fraternité et ont a cet effet nomme pour leurs Plénipotentiaires." The full text of the Moscow Treaty in Turkish and French is available at http://ua.mfa.gov.tr/.
23. Harish Kapur, *Soviet Russia and Asia, 1917–1927: A Study of Soviet Policy Towards Turkey, Iran and Afghanistan* (Geneva: Michael Joseph Limited, 1966), 137.
24. Dilek Barlas, "Friends or Foes? Diplomatic Relations between Italy and Turkey, 1923–1936," *International Journal of Middle Eastern Studies* 36 (2004): 232–233; Ahmet Şükrü Esmer, "Türk Diplomasisi: 1920–1955," *Yeni Türkiye* (Istanbul: Nebioğlu Yayınevi, 1959), 76.
25. "The Mosul Agreement," *The Times*, June 7, 1926, 15.
26. John Gooch, *Mussolini and His Generals: The Armed Forces and Fascist Foreign Policy, 1922–1940* (Cambridge: Cambridge University Press, 2007), 64–65.
27. Mehmet Gönlübol and Cem Sar, *Atatürk ve Türkiyenin Dış Politikası* (Istanbul: Milli Eğitim Basımevi, 1973), 73.
28. Barlas, "Friends or Foes?," 237.
29. Gönlübol and Sar, *Atatürk ve Türkiyenin Dış Politikası*, 74–75.
30. Tevfik Rüştü Aras, *Görüşlerim* (Istanbul: Tan Basımevi, 1945), 130.
31. Gönlübol and Sar, *Atatürk ve Türkiyenin Dış Politikası*, 94–95; Dilek Barlas, *Etatism and Diplomacy in Turkey* (New York: Brill, 1998), 127.
32. Sevim, Öztoprak, and Tural, *Atatürk'ün Söylev ve Demeçleri*, 170.
33. Barlas, *Etatism and Diplomacy in Turkey*, 127.
34. Feroz Ahmad, "The Historical Background of Turkey's Foreign Policy," in *The Future of Turkish Foreign Policy*, eds. Lenore G. Martin and Dimitris Keridis (Cambridge, MA: MIT Press, 2004), 16–17. The mutual respect between the two countries was very well depicted in the article published by the *New York Times* during the tenth-anniversary celebrations of the republic on October 29, 1933: "Soviet Russia is undoubtedly republican Turkey's greatest friend. The Russians helped the Turks when the latter were fighting the Greeks, and this has not been forgotten. M. Surritch, the Russian Ambassador at Angora, occupies a privileged position. Several treaties have been concluded between

Angora and Moscow, and the political understanding is so close that no other great power is able to disturb it. On the other hand, the Russians realize that the Kemalists will not tolerate any Communist propaganda among the Turks." Walter Collins, "Kemal's Turkey Is Ten Years Old," *New York Times*, October 29, 1933.
35. "Turkey in the League of Nations," *The Times*, July 19, 1932, 15.
36. Halil Nalçaoğlu, "Turkey: Nation and Celebration: An Iconology of the Republic of Turkey," in *National Days/National Ways*, ed. Linda K. Fuller (Westport, CT: Praeger, 2004), 269.
37. "Ankaraya Gönderilmek Üzere İstanbulun Toprağı Dün Merasimle Alındı," *Vakit*, October 31, 1933.
38. Türkkaya Ataöv, *Turkish Foreign Policy, 1939–1945* (Ankara: Ankara Üniversitesi Basımevi, 1965), 1.
39. Quoted in Henderson B. Braddick, "The Hoare-Laval Plan: A Study in International Politics," in *European Diplomacy between Two Wars, 1919–1939*, ed. Hans Wilhelm Gatzke (Chicago: Quadrangle, 1972), 153.
40. Feridun Cemal Erkin, *Türk-Sovyet İlişkileri ve Boğazlar Meselesi* (Ankara: Başnur Matbaası, 1968), 63–68.
41. The *New York Times* defined the signing of the Montreux Convention accordingly: "In profit and loss of power it brings distinct gain for Turkey, Russia and the League and a loss for Great Britain, Italy, Germany, Japan, France and the United States. The League's gain is most unexpected; Russia's gain is the most complete; Turkey's gain is the most immediately important." Clarence K. Streit, "New Straits Agreement Lifts League Prestige," *New York Times*, July 19, 1936, 5.
42. Avedis K. Sanjian, "The Sanjak of Alexandretta (Hatay): Its Impact on Turkish Syrian Relations (1939–1956)," *Middle East Journal* 10, no. 4 (Autumn 1956): 380–381.
43. Ataöv, *Turkish Foreign Policy*, 3.
44. A record of this conversation was sent by Loraine with a telegram to the British Foreign Office. The full text of the telegram was published by Ludmila Zhivkova, *Anglo-Turkish Relations, 1933–1939* (London: Secker and Warburg, 1976), 119–120.
45. Boris Potskhveriya, "Sovetsko-Turetskie Otnosheniya I Problema Prolivov Nakanuna, V Gody Vtoroi Mirovoi Voiny I V Poslevoennye Desyatiletiya," in *Rossiya I Chernomorskie Prolivy (18–20 Stoletiya)* (Moscow: Mezhdunarodnye Othosheniya, 1999), 438–439.
46. At the closing session of the conference, Litvinov stressed that friendship between Turkey and the Soviet Union since 1923 was "not merely a temporary combination." According to Litvinov, the outcome of the Montreux Conference was the "first crushing blow for those who are seeking the supremacy of brute force." "New Convention of the Straits," *The Times*, July 21, 1936, 15.
47. Hasan Rıza Soyak, *Atatürk'ten Hatıralar 2* (Ankara: Yapı Kredi Bankası, 1973), 525.

48. Cemil Koçak, *Türkiye'de Milli Şef Dönemi: 1938–1945* (Istanbul: İletişim, 1996), 1:127–137.
49. İsmet İnönü, *Hatıralar* (Ankara: Bilgi Yayınevi, 1987), 298–299.
50. Tevfik Rüştü Aras, "Neler Olacaktı," *Milliyet*, March 14, 1971.
51. "İnönü'nün Hatıra Defterinden Sayfalar," *Hürriyet*, January, 19, 1974.
52. Clement Henry Dodd, *Politics and Government in Turkey* (Manchester, UK: Manchester University Press, 1969), 23.
53. Selim Deringil, *Turkish Foreign Policy during the Second World War: An "Active" Neutrality* (Cambridge: Cambridge University Press, 2004), 41.
54. Frederick W. Frey, *The Turkish Political Elite* (Cambridge, MA: MIT Press, 1965), 35.
55. *Ulus*, May 13, 1939.
56. For example, Zekeriya Sertel criticized Turkish broadcasts of Italian radio in March 1939. See Deringil, *Turkish Foreign Policy during the Second World War*, 72.
57. M. Faruk Gürtunca, *Bu Arslana Dokunmayın* (Istanbul: Ülkü Kitap Yurdu, 1939). Faruk Gürtunca was born in Edirne in 1904. He graduated from a teachers' school and worked for the newspaper *Yeni Asır* in Thessaloniki. He published the children's magazines *Çocuk Sesi* and *Afacan*. In 1947, he founded the nationalist newspaper *Hergün*, which later became one of the well-known newspapers of the Nationalist Action Party in the 1970s. Gürtunca was elected to Parliament in 1957 from the Democrat Party and was arrested after the military coup in 1960. He died in 1982.
58. Sixty years after the publication of *Do Not Touch This Lion*, doyen journalist Hasan Pulur wrote in his column that in primary school he had read and could still remember the poem for which it was named, "Do Not Touch This Lion," which was written by Gürtunca in July 1926. Similarly, the leading journalist of the far-right media, Altemur Kılıç, wrote in his column that he could not forget the cover of the booklet itself. See Hasan Pulur, "Türkiye'ye Aşk Mektubu Yazan İtalyan," *Milliyet*, March 25, 2002; Altemur Kılıç, "Dokunmayın Bu Aslana," *Yeniçağ*, February 2, 2008.
59. Bruce R. Kuniholm, *The Origins of the Cold War in the Near East: Great Power Conflict and Diplomacy in Iran, Turkey, and Greece* (Princeton, NJ: Princeton University Press, 1980); Eduard Mark, "The War Square of 1946 and Its Consequences," *Diplomatic History* 21, no. 3 (Summer 1997): 383–416; Mustafa Aydın, "Determinants of Turkish Foreign Policy: Changing Patterns and Conjunctures during the Cold War," *Middle Eastern Studies* 36, no. 1 (Jan. 2000): 103–139; Duygu Bazoğlu Sezer, "Turkey's Grand Strategy Facing a Dilemma," *The International Spectator* 27, no. 1 (Jan.–March 1992): 19; Hale, *Turkish Foreign Policy*, 109–145; Kemal H. Karpat, *Turkey's Foreign Policy in Transition 1950–1974* (Leiden, The Netherlands: Brill, 1975); Kamuran Gürün, *Türk-Sovyet İlişkileri: 1920–1953* (Ankara: Türk Tarih Kurumu, 1991).
60. Hale, *Turkish Foreign Policy*, 109.
61. Ibid., 110.
62. Karpat, *Turkey's Foreign Policy in Transition 1950–1974*, 2.

63. Hıdır Göktaş and Ruşen Çakır, *Vatan Millet Pragmatizm: Türk Sağında İdeoloji ve Politika* (Metis: İstanbul, 1991), 70. This book published at the end of the Cold War has valuable interviews with prominent Turkish right-wing politicians.
64. Ibid., 182.
65. Sonyel, *Türk Kurtuluş Savaşı ve Dış Politika*, 2:9.
66. Ali Fuat Cebesoy, *Moskova Hatıraları (21/11/1920–2/6/1922)* (Istanbul: Vatan Neşriyatı, 1955), 70–71; Stanford J. Shaw, *From Empire to Republic: The Turkish War of National Liberation, 1918–1923* (Ankara: Türk Tarih Kurumu, 2000), 3:1468, 1479.
67. Campbell, *Writing Security*, 1.
68. Djamil Ghasanly, *SSSR-Turtsiya. Ot Neytraliteta K Kholodnoy Voyne 1939–1953* (Moskva: Tsenter Propagandy, 2008), 227.
69. Ibid., 180–181.
70. Campbell, *Writing Security*, 153.
71. Vyacheslav M. Molotov, *Report on the Government's Foreign Policy*. Accessed June 28, 2010. Available from www.hrono.ru/dokum/molotov.html.
72. Nicholas Tamkin, *Britain, Turkey, and the Soviet Union, 1940–45: Strategy, Diplomacy, and Intelligence in the Eastern Mediterranean* (New York: Palgrave, 2009), 22. Since the archives of Turkey's Foreign Ministry is closed for researchers, Tamkin's book based on the archives of the British Signals Intelligence, which intercepted and decrypted Turkish correspondence between Ankara and diplomats overseas during World War II, is an invaluable source to understand the Turkish foreign policy during this period.
73. Ibid.
74. Ibid., 115.
75. Ibid., 133.
76. Ibid., 116.
77. C. L. Sulzberger, "Russia's Ambitions Are Secrets of Kremlin," *New York Times*, February 28, 1943, E3.
78. Ibid.
79. "Choice," *Time*, July 12, 1943.
80. Ibid.
81. Joseph M. Levy, "Turks Sees Russia Reducing Poland," *New York Times*, December 25, 1943, 20.
82. Ibid.
83. Jacob M. Landau, *Pan-Turkism: From Irredentism to Cooperation* (Bloomington: Indiana University Press, 1995), 115.
84. Niyazi Berkes, *Unutulan Yıllar* (Istanbul: İletişim, 1997), 213; Uğur Mumcu, *40'ların Cadı Kazanı* (Istanbul: Tekin Yayınevi, 1990), 41.
85. Faris Erkman, "En Büyük Tehlike," in *Kırklı Yıllar* (Istanbul: TÜSTAV, 2002).
86. Ibid., 21.
87. Orhan Seyfi Orhon, *Maskeler Aşağı: En Büyük Tehlikenin İçyüzü* (Istanbul: Ülkü Basımevi, 1943); Reha Oğuz Türkkan, *Solcular ve Kızıllar* (Istanbul: Stad Matbaası, 1943).

88. Nizam Önen, *İki Turan: Macaristan ve Türkiye'de Turancılık* (Istanbul: İletişim, 2005), 318.
89. Koçak, *Türkiye'de Milli Şef Dönemi: 1938–1945*, 2:216.
90. Ibid., 349.
91. Ibid., 225.
92. Tevfik Rüştü Aras, "Büyük Komşumuz ve Dostumuz," *Vatan*, June 13, 1944.
93. Tevfik Rüştü Aras, "Daha Açık Söyleyeceğim," *Tan*, June 26, 1944.
94. Ibid.
95. Joseph M. Levy, "Turco-Soviet Pact Desired in Ankara," *New York Times*, June 26, 1944.
96. Tevfik Rüştü Aras, "Sovyet Rusya ile İttifak Tabirinden Kastedilen Mana Nedir?" *Vatan*, July 19, 1944.
97. According to the Soviet Information Bureau's announcement, Molotov told Turkey's ambassador Sarper that the Soviet Union, in "recognizing the value" of the treaty, concluded that it would be feasible to maintain friendly relations but, nevertheless, considered that "the great changes taken place, particularly during World War 2," require a new understanding. "Soviet Wants Treaty with Turks Revised," *New York Times*, March 26, 1945, 3.
98. Vladislav Martinovich Zubok and Konstantin Pleshakov, *Inside the Kremlin's Cold War* (Cambridge, MA: Harvard University Press, 1996), 93.
99. Ibid.
100. *İkinci Dünya Savaşı Yılları 1939–1946* (Ankara: Dışişleri Bakanlığı, 1973), 266.
101. Ibid.
102. Zekeriya Sertel, *Hatırladıklarım* (Istanbul: Gözlem Yayınları, 1977), 269.
103. Faik Ahmet Barutçu, *Siyasi Anılar 1939–1954* (Istanbul: Milliyet Yayınları, 1977), 287.
104. "İnkilap Türkiyesi ile S. Rusya, Osmanlı İmparatorluğu ile Çarlık Rusya arasındaki bütün pürüzleri ortadan kaldırmışlardır," *Vatan*, April 29, 1946.
105. "Fuat Köprülü'nün Mühim Beyanatı," *Vatan*, August 2, 1946.
106. İlhan Turan, ed., *İsmet İnönü: Konuşma, Demeç, Makale, Mesaj ve Söyleşiler 1944–1950* (Ankara: TBMM Kültür, Sanat ve Yayın Kurulu Yayınları, 2003), 34–46.
107. Ibid., 36.
108. Ibid., 37.
109. Ibid., 38.
110. Kemal H. Karpat, *Turkey's Politics: The Transition to a Multi-Party System* (Princeton, NJ: Princeton University Press, 1959), 145.
111. Metin Heper, *İsmet İnönü* (Leiden, The Netherlands: Brill, 1998), 190.
112. Karpat, *Turkey's Politics*, 147.
113. Sabiha Sertel, *Roman Gibi: Demokrasi Mücadelesinden Bir Kadın* (Istanbul: Belge Yayınları, 1986), 288–292.
114. *Görüşler*, no. 1 (Dec. 1, 1945).
115. Ibid.
116. Hüseyin Cahit Yalçın, "Kalkın Ey Ehli Vatan," *Tanin*, December 3, 1945.

117. It is striking that toward the end of the 1950s, when the ruling Democrat Party became more authoritarian, it established "the Vatan Front" against opposition parties.
118. One of the best examples of this thinking is Yalçın's article with the title "To Understand the Spirit of Communism" published in 1946. Hüseyin Cahit Yalçın, "Komünistliğin Ruhunu Anlamak İçin," in *Benim Görüşümle Olaylar* (Ankara: Ulus Basımevi, 1946), 28–30.
119. Ibid.
120. In 1967, Kazım Alöç, who was the general attorney of Istanbul at that time, stated that the mob of students were under the leadership of RPP's chief inspector Ali Tiritoğlu. Kazım Alöç, "İfşa Ediyorum," *Yeni Gazete*, April 12, 1967.
121. *Tanin*, December 5, 1945.
122. Soviet Ambassador Vinogradov in Ankara proposed to make an official statement to Britain and the United States that "fascist and anti-Soviet demonstrations in Istanbul may compel the Soviet Union to take adequate measures to ensure its security." He also suggested publishing a Telegraph Agency of the Soviet Union (TASS) report that "owing to the fascist anti-Soviet demonstration in Turkey, the Soviet government decided to reinforce garrisons along the Soviet-Turkish border" and to break off any contacts with Turkey. It was striking that the Politburo of the Central Committee harshly criticized Vinogradov's proposals: "We consider your proposals to be absolutely unacceptable and thoughtless. You must understand that we cannot make any official presentations to the Turkish government regarding the growth of fascism in Turkey, since it is the domestic affairs of Turks. We also consider your proposal about our statement to the British and Americans as inadmissible and not serious, since the sabre-rattling may have provocative consequences. Your proposal on publishing TASS information that the Soviet government, due to the fascist anti-Soviet demonstration in Turkey, decided to reinforce garrisons along the Soviet-Turkish border is too frivolous. We cannot either accept your proposal on discontinuing our contacts with Turks. You should not make thoughtless proposals that may lead to political complications for our government. Think it over once again and be more sober-minded to comply with your post and mission." The reaction of the Politburo against Vinogradov's proposals revealed that the Soviets did not want to provoke their relations with Britain and the United States because of anti-Soviet unrest in Turkey and were careful about not interfering in the internal affairs of Turkey. See Ghasanly, *SSSR-Turtsiya. Ot Neytraliteta K Kholodnoy Voyne 1939–1953*, 310.
123. "Fashistskie Beschinstva V Stambule," *Pravda*, December 6, 1945; "Posle Fashistskoy Demonstratsii V Stambule," *Pravda*, December 12, 1945; "Po Povodu Demonstratsii V Stambule," *Pravda*, December 15, 1945.
124. "Pismo V Redakciyu Gazety 'Kommunisti' O Nashikh Zakonnyh Trebovaniyah K Turtsii," *Pravda*, December 20, 1945. The article was translated into Turkish and published by the journal *Tarih ve Toplum*. S. Canasia and N.

Brerdzenisvili, "Türkiye'den Haklı İstemlerimiz," *Tarih ve Toplum* 8, no. 46 (Oct. 1987): 49–52.
125. Canasia and Brerdzenisvili, "Türkiye'den Haklı İstemlerimiz," 52.
126. *Tanin*, December 27, 1945.
127. Faruk Gürtunca, *Dokunmayın Bu Vatana* (İstanbul: Ülkü Basımevi, 1946).
128. Ibid., 26.
129. John F. VanderLippe, *The Politics of Turkish Democracy* (Albany: State University of New York Press, 2005), 125.
130. *Demokrat Parti Başkanlığı*, no. 60 (Ankara: Arbas Matbaası, 1947), 40.
131. "Fuad Köprülü Cevap Veriyor," *Vatan*, May 17, 1946.
132. "Mecliste Komunistler İçin Dünkü İfşaat," *Cumhuriyet*, January 30, 1947.
133. Ibid.
134. *Demokrat Parti Kurucuları Bu Davanın Adamı Değildirler* (Ankara: Yeni Matbaa, 1949), 34, 66.
135. Gürün, *Türk-Sovyet İlişkileri*, 315.
136. Duygu Bazoğlu Sezer, "Turkey's Security Policies," *Adelphi Papers* 21, no. 164 (1981): 13.
137. Melvyn P. Leffler, "Strategy, Diplomacy, and the Cold War: The United States, Turkey, and NATO, 1945–1952," *Journal of American History* 71, no. 4 (March 1985): 807–825; Thomas G. Paterson, *On Every Front: The Making of the Cold War* (New York: Norton, 1979), 55–56; Haluk Gerger, *Türk Dış Politikasının Ekonomi Politiği* (Istanbul: Belge, 1999), 49–50.
138. Leffler, "Strategy, Diplomacy, and the Cold War," 813.
139. Bruce Kuniholm, "Turkey and the West," *Foreign Affairs* 70, no. 2 (Spring 1991): 34.
140. Nur Bilge Criss, "U.S. Forces in Turkey," in *U.S. Military Forces in Europe: The Early Years, 1945–1970* (Boulder, CO: Westview Press, 1993), 331–349.
141. *Milliyet*, November 23, 1955.
142. Potskhveriya, "Sovetsko-Turetskie Otnosheniya I Problema Prolivov Nakanune, V Gody Vtoroi Mirovoi Voiny I V Poslevoennye Desyatiletiya," 512.
143. Ghasanly, *SSSR-Turtsiya. Ot Neytraliteta K Kholodnoy Voyne 1939–1953*, 575. A similar statement was made by Adnan Menderes on August 27, 1948. See Haluk Kılçık, ed., *Adnan Menderes'in Konuşmaları, Demeçleri, Makaleleri* (Ankara: Demokratlar Kulübü Yayınları, 1991), 1:316.
144. Nikolai V. Kochkin, "SSSR, Angliya, SSHA, I 'Turetskiy Krizis' 1945–1947 GG," *Novaya I Noveyshaya Istoriya*, no. 3 (2002): 70–72.
145. Gavin D. Brockett, "Betwixt and Between: Turkish Print Culture and the Emergence of a National Identity" (Ph.D. diss., University of Chicago, 2003), 121.
146. "Türkiye Kore İşinde Üzerine Düşen Vecibeleri Yapacak," *Hürriyet*, July 1, 1950.
147. Cameron S. Brown, "The One Coalition They Craved to Join: Turkey in the Korean War," *Review of International Studies Association* 34 (2008): 95.
148. *Kore Harbinde Türk Silahlı Kuvvetlerinin Muharebeleri (1950–1953)* (Ankara: Genelkurmay Harp Tarihi Başkanlığı, 1974), 417.

149. Allan Reed Millett, *Their War for Korea: American, Asian, and European Combatants and Civilians, 1945–1953* (Washington, DC: Brassey's, 2002), 266.
150. Füsun Türkmen, "Turkey and the Korean War," *Turkish Studies* 3, no. 2 (Autumn 2002): 170.
151. *Foreign Relations of the United States 1950* (Washington, DC: Government Printing Office, 1978), 5:1282.
152. Brown, "The One Coalition They Craved to Join," 103.
153. Ibid.
154. Türkmen, "Turkey and the Korean War," 170.
155. Pınar Selek, *Barışamadık* (Istanbul: İthaki Yayınları, 2004), 217.
156. *Zafer*, July 29, 1950.
157. Haluk Kılçık, *Adnan Menderes'in Konuşmaları, Demeçleri, Makaleleri*, 2:128.
158. Ibid., 2:129.
159. Ibid., 2:8.
160. *Ayın Tarihi Temmuz 1950* (Ankara: Basın Yayın Genel Müdürlüğü, 1950), 73–74.
161. Ali Naci Karacan, "Bozguncuları Tasfiye Zamanı Gelmiştir," *Milliyet*, August 1, 1950.
162. *Cumhuriyet*, December 31, 1950.
163. John M. VanderLippe, "Forgotten Brigade of the Forgotten War: Turkey's Participation in the Korean War," *Middle Eastern Studies* 36, no. 1 (Jan. 2000): 98.
164. Quoted in Mim Kemal Öke, *Unutulan Savaşın Kronolojisi: Kore, 1950–53* (Istanbul: Boğaziçi Yayınları, 1990), 71.
165. *Kore Savunmasına Katılmamızda Dini ve Siyasi Zaruret* (Istanbul: Acun Basımevi, 1950), 50–51.
166. *Hürriyet*, September 28, 1950.
167. Türkmen, "Turkey and the Korean War," 170.
168. Haluk Kılçık, *Adnan Menderes'in Konuşmaları, Demeçleri, Makaleleri*, 2:203.
169. *T.B.M.M Tutanak Dergisi Dönem 9* (1950), 3:181.
170. Ibid.
171. *Cumhuriyet*, February 8, 1951.
172. Hüseyin Cahit Yalçın, "Mehmetçiklerimiz," *Ulus*, December 3, 1950.
173. Mehmet Tuncer, "Mehmetçik Kore'de Türk Vatanını Müdafaa Ediyor," *Yeni Asır*, December 4, 1950.
174. Ibid.
175. *Demokrat Parti Neşriyatından 7: Türkiye ve Atlantik Paktı* (Ankara: Güneş Matbaası, 1954); *Demokrat Parti Neşriyatından 8: Düşmanı Kore'de Karşıladık* (Ankara: Güneş Matbaası, 1954).
176. *Demokrat Parti Neşriyatından 7: Türkiye ve Atlantik Paktı*, 6.
177. Ibid., 7.
178. Ibid., 14.
179. *Demokrat Parti Neşriyatından 8: Düşmanı Kore'de Karşıladık*, 6, 12.
180. *Foreign Relations of the United States 1950*, 5:1275–1276.
181. Öke, *Unutulan Savaşın Kronolojisi*, 85.

182. Paragraphs 4 and 9a of the conclusions of the Helsinki Summit highlighted the importance of the settlement of the Cyprus problem for Turkey's membership: "4) In this respect the European Council stresses the principle of peaceful settlement of disputes in accordance with the United Nations Charter and urges candidate states to make every effort to resolve any outstanding border disputes and other related issues. Failing this they should within a reasonable time bring the dispute to the International Court of Justice. The European Council will review the situation relating to any outstanding disputes, in particular concerning the repercussions on the accession process and in order to promote their settlement through the International Court of Justice, at the latest by the end of 2004." "9a) The European Council welcomes the launch of the talks aiming at a comprehensive settlement of the Cyprus problem on 3 December in New York and expresses its strong support for the U.N. Secretary-General's efforts to bring the process to a successful conclusion."
183. "Eteğindeki Taşları Döktü," *Radikal*, March 5, 2004.
184. According to Torfing, a hegemonic project is "a political project, including a vision of how state, economy and civil society should be organized, that aspires to become hegemonic." See Torfing, *New Theories of Discourse*, 302.
185. According to Articles 16 and 20 of the Lausanne Treaty, "16) Turkey hereby renounces all rights and title whatsoever over or respecting the territories situated outside the frontiers laid down in the present Treaty and the islands other than those over which her sovereignty is recognized by the said Treaty, the future of these territories and islands being settled or to be settled by the parties concerned." "20) Turkey hereby recognizes the annexation of Cyprus proclaimed by the British Government on the 5th November, 1914." Accessed November 22, 2008. Available from http://ua.mfa.gov.tr/.
186. Fahir Armaoğlu, *Kıbrıs Meselesi: 1954–1959* (Ankara: Sevinç Matbaası, 1963), 20.
187. *Hürriyet*, April 2, 1954; "No 'Cyprus Question' for Turkey," *The Times*, April 3, 1954.
188. Simon C. Smith, *Reassessing Suez 1956: New Perspectives on the Crisis and Its Aftermath* (Burlington, VT: Ashgate, 2008), 124.
189. Berdal Aral, "Fifty Years On: Turkey's Voting Orientation at the UN General Assembly, 1948–97," *Middle Eastern Studies* 40, no. 2 (March 2004): 138–139.
190. Armaoğlu, *Kıbrıs Meselesi*, 46.
191. Ibid., 41.
192. Ibid., 54.
193. Ahmet Emin Yalman, "Neden Bir Kıbrıs Meselesi Var?" *Vatan*, January 18, 1950, quoted in Armaoğlu, *Kıbrıs Meselesi*, 23.
194. For a representative nationalistic book with poems and articles, see F. Cemal Oğuz Öcal, *Kıbrıs'a Seferim Var* (Istanbul: Sinan Matbaası, 1958).
195. *Kıbrıs Türktür* (Ankara: Güzel İstanbul Matbaası, 1958).

196. "Turkish Case on Cyprus," *The Times*, August 25, 1955. For the entire speech, see *Ayın Tarihi*, August 1955. Accessed February 12, 2009. Available from www.byegm.gov.tr/YAYINLARIMIZ/AyinTarihi/1955/agustos1955.htm.
197. *Ayın Tarihi*, August 1955.
198. *Ayın Tarihi*, July 1956. Accessed February 12, 2009. Available from www.byegm.gov.tr/YAYINLARIMIZ/AyinTarihi/1956/temmuz1956.htm.
199. Armaoğlu, *Kıbrıs Meselesi*, 288.
200. Ibid, 287.
201. *Dışişleri Belleteni* (Ankara: Dışişleri Bakanlığı, 1964), 2:63. Emin Dirvana, Turkey's first ambassador to the Republic of Cyprus, revealed that Rauf Denktaş never believed in the newly established state's viability. Dirvana accused Denktaş of "disputing unnecessarily with the Greeks" instead of working for the economic and social development of the Turkish community as the president of the Turkish Cypriot Communal Chamber. "Denktaş Hakikati Tahrif Ediyor," *Milliyet*, May 15, 1964.
202. Niyazi Kızılyürek, *Milliyetçilik Kıskacında Kıbrıs* (Istanbul: İletişim, 2002), 294.
203. Pınar Bilgin, "Turkey's Changing Security Discourses: The Challenge of Globalization," *European Journal of Political Research* 44 (2005): 182.
204. "TÜSİAD: Aman Kıbrıs AB'yle Aramızı Bozmasın," *Hürriyet*, November 17, 2001.
205. *Türkiye İktisat Gazetesi*, August 8, 1974.
206. "İlk Gün Milliyet Aracılığı ile Yarım Milyon Bağış Yapıldı," *Milliyet*, July 25, 1974.
207. "Turkish Leader Says UN's Cyprus 'Negotiable Idea,'" *BBC World Wide Monitoring*, January 5, 2003. Accessed March 11, 2009. Available from LexisNexis.
208. Ahmet Davutoğlu, *Stratejik Derinlik* (Istanbul: Küre Yayınları, 2001), 179.
209. "Tolon: Çakıl Taşı Vermeyiz," *Radikal*, January 18, 2004.
210. Emin Çölaşan, "Kıbrıs Gerçekleri," *Hürriyet*, December 9, 2003.
211. Özgen Acar, "Mazoşistler: 'Haydi Annan, Bastır!'" *Cumhuriyet*, February 10, 2004.
212. İlhan Selçuk, "Yavru Vatan Gitti . . . Anavatan Gidiyor mu?" *Cumhuriyet*, March 5, 2004.
213. Emin Çölaşan, "Kıbrıs Gerçekleri."
214. Özgen Acar, "Mazoşistler: 'Haydi Annan, Bastır!'"
215. *Ayın Tarihi*, February 2004. Accessed March 23, 2009. Available from www.byegm.gov.tr/ayintarihidetay.aspx?Id=71&Yil=2004&Ay=2.
216. "Hükümete Kıbrıs Eleştirisi," *Cumhuriyet*, February 17, 2004.
217. *Ayın Tarihi*, February 2004.
218. "İsimsiz Eleştirdi," *Hürriyet*, January 23, 2004.
219. Hadi Uluengin, "Vatan ve Kıbrıs," *Hürriyet*, November 23, 2001.
220. Cüneyt Ülsever, "'Bensiz Vatan Ne Yapar?' Sendromu," *Hürriyet*, May 19, 2003.

221. Mustafa Balbay, "Recep'le Acep Kuvvet Tanımıyor," *Cumhuriyet*, May 16, 2005.
222. "Yeni Arayış," *Cumhuriyet*, March 8, 2002.
223. "MGK'da Kıbrıs'ta Müzakere Çıktı," *Hürriyet*, January 23, 2004.
224. "Yavrum Vatan," *Star*, December 16, 2003.
225. "On Binler Çözüm Dedi," *Radikal*, January 15, 2003.
226. Sevim, Öztoprak, and Tural, *Atatürk'ün Söylev ve Demeçleri*, 612.
227. Aras, *Görüşlerim*, 3–4.
228. Berkes, *Unutulan Yıllar*, 295.
229. Owen Lattimore, *Inner Asian Frontiers of China* (Boston: Beacon Press, 1951), 434.

CONCLUSION

1. Jean Gottmann, "Geography and International Relations," *World Politics* 3, no. 2 (1951): 153.
2. Jean Gottmann, "The Mutation of the American City: A Review of the Comparative Metropolitan Analysis Project," *Geographical Review* 69, no. 2 (1978): 205. For a detailed analysis of the question and answer, see Jean Gottmann, "Spatial Partitioning and the Politician's Wisdom," *International Political Science Review* 1, no. 4 (1980): 439–440.
3. Ernest Gellner, *Nations and Nationalism* (Ithaca, NY: Cornell University Press, 1983), 140.
4. Benedict Anderson, *Imagined Communities* (London: Verso, 1993). He demonstrated meticulously that nations were not the determinate products of given conditions, such as language or ethnicity or race, but they had been imagined into existence.
5. Ernesto Laclau, *New Reflections on the Revolution of Our Time* (London: Verso, 1990), 169–170, 194.
6. Peter J. Taylor, "The State as Container: Territoriality in the Modern World-System," in *State/Space A Reader*, ed. Neil Brenner, Bob Jessop, Martin Jones, and Gordon Macleod (Malden, MA: Blackwell Publishing, 2003), 102.
7. Süleyman Nazif, "Mukaddime," in *Abdülhak Hamid Tarhan: Bütün Şiirleri 3* (İstanbul: Dergah Yayınları, 1999), 364–368.
8. Carl Mortished, "Turkish Giant Causes Consternation in Brussels," *The Times*, June 18, 2008.
9. "Asker Bankası Yabancıya," *Milliyet*, June 20, 2007.
10. U.S. Senator John McCain's 2008 presidential campaign website was available at www.countryfirstpac.com/. For Hosni Mubarak's speech, see Brooke Baldwin, Michael Holmes, Ben Wedeman, Hala Gorani, Becky Anderson, Ivan Watson, Nic Robertson, and Dan Lothian, "Egyptian President Mubarak Announces He Will Not Run for Reelection," *CNN*, February 1, 2011. Accessed April 4, 2011. Available from LexisNexis. Although CNN used the word "homeland" in the translated version, in the original Mubarak used the word *watan* in Arabic.

ILLUSTRATION CREDITS

Frontispiece Serdar Karaman
- **1.1** Serdar Karaman
- **2.1** Sine-i Millet Exhibition Istanbul
- **2.2** Serdar Karaman
- **2.3** Ministry of National Education
- **3.1** Selim Sabit, *Short Book on Geography*, 1874
- **3.2** Selim Sabit, *Short Book on Geography*, 1874
- **3.3** Saffet Bey, *Geography Stories for Children*, 1916
- **3.4** Mehmet Asım, *The Book of the Anatolian Child*, 1919
- **3.5** Mehmet Asım, *The Book of the Anatolian Child*, 1917
- **3.6** Saffet Geylangil, *General Geography*, 1938
- **3.7** Besim Darkot and Cemal Alagöz, *General Geography*, 1934
- **3.8** Faik Sabri, *Geography*, 1932
- **3.9–3.12** Faik Sabri, *The Geography of Turkey*, 1929
- **3.13** Abdülkadir Sadi, *Geography for Secondary Schools*, 1935
- **3.14** Sırrı Erinç and Sami Öngör, *The Geography of Turkey*, 1950
- **3.15** Sırrı Erinç and Sami Öngör, *The Geography of Turkey*, 1976
- **3.16** Sırrı Erinç and Sami Öngör, *The Geography of Turkey*, 1975
- **3.17** Erdoğan Sağdıç
- **4.1–4.3** Faruk Gürtunca, *Dokunmayın Bu Aslana*, 1939
- **4.4** Faruk Gürtunca, *Dokunmayın Bu Vatana*, 1946
- **4.5** National Library, Ankara

INDEX

Page numbers in italic type refer to illustrations.

Abdulhamid II, 43–45, 51, 61, 65
Abode of Islam: Abode of War vs., 13–14; defined, 13; nation substituted for, 2, 12–13, 18; and Turkish nation-state, 3–4
Abode of War, 13–14
Abyssinia, 156
Acar, Özgen, 204
Aceh, 50
Adil, Muhiddin, *Information about Vatan*, 122
Afghanistan, 159
Ağaoğlu, Ahmet, 61, 64, 68, 70, 230n21
Ahmad, Feroz, 122
Ahmet Cevdet Pasha, 35
Ahmet İzzet Pasha, 79, 80
Akbank, 202
Akçura, Yusuf, 51–52, 60–61, 64–65, 68, 71, 227n145, 230n16; "Three Political Ways," 51–52, 60, 67
Akif, Mehmet, 74, 93–94
Akşin, Aptülahat, 247n16
Akseki, Ahmet Hamdi, 190
Aktay, Haydar, 171
Alagöz, Cemal Arif, *New Geography Lessons*, 123, 125
Albania, 64, 162
Aleppo, 87
Alexandretta district, 155, 157, 159
Algeria, 196
Ali Esseyid Efendi, 220n54
Allies: Istanbul occupied by, 59, 88, 100; national liberation movement and, 90; Ottoman defeat by, 78–80; and Ottoman lands, 76, 80, 82–83, 85, 87, 91, 236n103, 236n108; Turkish opposition to, 95
alphabet, 122, 123
Altunışık, Meliha Benli, 147
Amcazade Hüseyin Pasha, 16
American Military Mission for Aid, 187
Anatolia: Allied partitioning of, 91; borders of, 109, 117, 119; intercommunal conflicts in, 46; occupation of, 59; Ottoman empire and, 15, 64; populations of, 117, *118*; Turkish identity grounded in, 3, 4, 76, 102, 121, 122, 128; Turkish nation-state and, 60, 104, 117; as vatan, 76–100
Anderson, Benedict, 4, 29, 32, 36, 258n4
Anderson, James, 1
Anglo-Turkish Declaration (1939), 162
Ankara, 150

261

Annan Plan, 194, 202, 204, 206–7, 210
anti-colonialism, 149–50
Arabs: conservatism of, 49; in geography textbooks, 117; language and script of, replaced in Turkey, 122; and Ottoman empire, 48–49, 54, 56, 226n141; patriotism of, 37–38; Turkish nation-state in relation to, 87, 90, 92
Aras, Tevfik Rüştü, 152, 153, 155, 158, 159, 168, 172, 174–75, 178, 179, 208
Ardahan, 86, 165, 167–71, 175, 193
Arık, Remzi Oğuz, 102–4; "From Geography to Vatan," 102; *From Geography to Vatan*, 240n1
Arıkan, Saffet, 176
Armed Forces Mutual Assistance Fund (OYAK), 214
Armenia: conflicts involving, 94; rebellions and conflicts involving, 46, 89–90; Soviet, 151, 168, 175; territorial issues involving, 81, 91
Artvin, 169, 182, 193
Asım, Mehmet, *The Book of the Anatolian Child*, 117, 118, 119. See also Us, Asım
Asia: central, 122, 126; map of, 110
Atay, Falih Rıfkı, 42. See also Rıfkı, Falih
Atsız, Nihal, 173, 174
Attila, 162
authoritarianism, 75, 155, 161, 212
Aydemir, Şevet Süreyya, 65, 69–70, 131, 135, 232n40
Aydın, 88

Bahçeli, Devlet, 204–5
Balkan Entente (1934), 155–56, 159
Balkans: in interwar period, 155–56; loss of, 4, 17–18; nationalism in, 36, 37; Ottoman empire and, 41, 65, 232n39; post-1908 influence of, 229n11; sultan's tour of (1911), 62; in World War I, 78–79
Balkan Wars (1913), 51, 52, 54, 56, 65–66, 68, 114–16
Barlas, Dilek, 152
Bartelson, Jens, 9
Başbuğ, İlker, 6
Batum, 85, 86
Bayar, Celal, 160, 174, 176, 179, 182, 185, 187

Baykal, Deniz, 204
Baykurt, Cami, 178, 179
Bedreka-i Salamet (newspaper), 47
Bekir Sami Bey, 150–51
Berdzenishvili, N., 181
Bike, Suyum. See Tek, Müfide Ferit
Blaeu, Joan, *Atlas Maior*, 23
books, publication of, 36
Boran, Behice, 178, 189, 190
Bosnia, 36, 64
Bosporus, 30
Bozkurt (journal), 182
Britain: and Cyprus, 195–96; opposition to, 73–75, 95, 96, 233n70; relations with, 44, 158, 161–62, 185, 187; territorial issues involving, 80, 152, 157
Bulgaria, 65, 66, 70–71, 78, 112, 155
Bustani, Butrus al-, 37–38

Çınaraltı (journal), 182
Çölaşan, Emin, 204
Caferoğlu, Ahmet, 173
Cain, Harry, 188, 189
Campbell, David, 10, 146, 170
Canip, Ali, 67–68
Cartesian perspectivalism, 148
cartography. See maps and cartography
Caucasus, 17–18, 75, 76, 78
Cebesoy, Ali Fuat, 52, 153
Çelebi, Evliya, 23
Çelebi, Katip, 20–23, 107; *Cihannüma*, 21–24, 218n26
Cemal, Ahmet, 111
Cemal Pasha, 62, 231n25
Cemgil, Adnan, 189, 190
censorship: Abdulhamid II and, 45; of Internet, 8
Central Treaty Organization (CENTO), 138, 139
Ceride-i Askeriye (Newspaper of the Military), 38
Ceride-i Havadis (Journal of News), 34
Cevad, Ahmed: *The Book of Anatolian Child*, 117, 118; *Talks on Vatan*, 116
Cevdet, Abdullah, 76, 225n122
Chicherin, Georgy, 150–52
Christianity: expansion of, 24; Islamic solidarity with, 53; national liberation

movement and, 90; role of, in Ottoman empire, 35
Churchill, Winston, 91
Cilicia, 80
Circle of Equity, 19
citizenship, 2
class, 219n36
Clemenceau, Georges, 83
Cluverius, *Introductio geographica tam vetera quam nova*, 22
coat of arms, 33
Coğrafya-i Kebir (Grand Geography), 23–24
Cold War, 14, 104, 137–38, 161–94
colonialism, Ottoman Turkish, 49–50, 226n140
Committee of Union and Progress (CUP), 45–55, 62, 70–75, 113, 230n16
communism, 153–54, 167, 184, 189–90, 209
community. *See* Islamic community (*ummah*)
Comore Islands, 50
constitution, Turkish, 2
Copernicus, 24
cosmography, 19
cosmology, 18
cosmopolitanism, 64, 67
Council for Mutual Assistance, 138
Council of Europe, 138
Crete, 36, 64, 196, 204
Crimea, 16–17
Cumhuriyet (newspaper), 204
CUP. *See* Committee of Union and Progress
Cyprus, 5, 8, 194–207, 209–10, 256n182, 257n201
Cyprus Is Turkish (booklet), 197, *198*
Cyprus Turkish National Party, 197

Danin, Richard, 97
Dardanelles, Battle of (1915–1916), 75, 76
Darkot, Besim, 135; *The Geography of Turkey*, 128, 130; *New Geography Lessons*, 123, *125*
Davutoğlu, Ahmet, 12–13; *Stratejik Derinlik*, 203
Defense of Rights organizations, 80–81

defense of vatan, 2, 5, 7, 34, 39, 43, 46–49, 53–54, 56, 81–82, 88, 91–92, 100–101, 106, 116, 213
democracy: guided, 177–78, 184; increase of, 195; limitations on, 177–79; multi-party, 178
Democrat Party, 136, 179, 182, 184–85, 187, 190–95, 199
Denktaş, Rauf, 200, 201, 204, 206, 207, 257n201
Deringil, Selim, 161, 226n140
Dimaşki, Ebu Bekr ibn Behram el-, 23–24
Dirvana, Emin, 257n201
dislocation, 147, 246n3
Dodecanese Islands, 150, 162, *164*, 203
Doğanay, Hayati, *The Cultural Geography of Turkey*, 143–44
Donizetti, Giuseppe, 33
Duran, Faik Sabri, 114, 117, 135, 245n107; *Geography*, 123, 126; *The Geography of Turkey*, 123, 127–28, *129*, 131, *132*, *133*; *Geography Reading for Children*, 115–16
Duru, Kazım Nami, 48

Eastern Rumelia, 64. *See also* Rumelia
Eastern Thrace, 71, 86
Ebubekir Ratib Efendi, 29–30, 220n54
Ebu's-su'ud Efendi, 14
Ecevit, Bülent, 6–7, 200, 205
economy: Ottoman, 27, 35; Turkish, 195
Edib, Halide, 65–66, 76–78, 82; "Let's Take Care of Our Own Home," 77; *Yeni Turan* (The New Turan), 70, 233n64
Edirne, 54, 56, 66, 70–71
education: Sati Bey and Helfert on, 228n6; expansion of, in nineteenth century, 107; geography curriculum in, 106–44; national identity inculcated through, 105–6; promotion of vatan in, 7, 33–34, 56–57, 112–16, 122
Egypt, 37, 44, 64
Emin Yurdakul, Mehmet, 61, 82, 230n21
Enosis, 195, 197, 209–10
Enver Pasha, 62, 71–73, 173
Erden, Ali Fuad, 173, 233n70
Erdoğan, Tayyip, 202–5
Erinç, Sırrı: *Geography of States*, 137–38, 140; *The Geography of Turkey*, 137–38, *138*, *139*

Erkilet, Hüseyin Hüsnü, 173
Erkman, Faris, *The Greatest Danger*, 173
Ertegün, Münir, 171
Erzurum, 171
Erzurum Congress, 85, 86, 88
Eşref, Ruşen, 95, 239n138
Esperanto, 68
Esprey, Franchet d', 78
ethnicity: in geography textbooks, 117; political unity and, 39–48, 53–54, 57, 60, 62, 64. *See also* majorities, ethnic
Europe and Europeans: advances of, 21, 24, 26–27, 33; comparisons to, 116; relations with, 104–5, 140
European Economic Community, 138
European Union (EU) membership, 6–7, 104–5, 145, 194–95, 201–7, 256n182
Eurosceptics, 203–7

fatherland, 57
Fazil Ahmet Pasha, 23
Felicity Party, 204
Ferguson, James, 103
Ferit, Damat, 82–83, 85, 89, 91, 237n110
Ferit Tek, Ahmet, 52, 76, 227n150
Fevzi Çakmak Pasha, 68, 155, 160, 173, 176, 184
First Geography Congress (1941), 135–36
foreign policy, 146–210; Cold War (1945–1991), 161–94, 208–9; geography and, 147–48; Korean War, 187–94; nonaligned (1923–1939), 149–61, 207–8; Ottoman, 64–65; periods of, 146–47; post–Cold War, 194–207, 209–10; scholarship on, 147–48, 185–86; significance of, 146; and Soviet threat, 165–86; and vatan, 5
Foucault, Michel, 10
Four Power Pact (1933), 155
France, 80, 150, 157, 159, 162, 196
French Revolution, 27–29, 38, 46, 61
Frey, Frederick, 155
Friendship and Non-Aggression Treaty (1925), 152, 168, 175
Fuad Pasha, 37–38
Furetière, Abbé, *Dictionnaire Universel*, 29
Fuzuli (poet), 223n98

Gasprinski, İsmail, 64
Gellner, Ernest, 29, 58
Genç Kalemler (Young Pens) [journal], 67–69, 113
geo-body, 3–4, 108, 130, 215n4
geographical determinism, 7, 114, 147–48
geographical unity, 87–88
geography: economics and, 26–27; in educational curriculum, 106–44; as fixed and unchanging factor, 147–48; foreign policy and, 147–48; historico-political factors in, 7–8; and the nation-state, 1, 3–4, 106–44; in Ottoman empire, 19; political value of, 20–25; revision of Ottoman, 20–26; as science, 20–26, 107, 114; and security, 6–7; Turkification of, 120–31; vatan and, 83, 102; Western advances in, 26–27. *See also* maps and cartography
geography curriculum and textbooks: alternative, 145; post-republic, 122–31; post–World War II, 136–41; pre-republic, 108–20
The Geography of Turkey (textbook), 137
geopolitics, 141, 143, 147–48, 211
Georgeon, François, 54
Georgia, 168, 175, 181
Gerger, Haluk, 185
Germany, 157, 165, 172–75
Ghanem, Khalil, 226n141
globalization, 213
God, 18, 19
Gökalp, Ziya, 60–62, 64, 67–69, 71, 73–74, 77–78, 92–93, 96, 227n145, 229n14, 230n16; "Beware of Britain," 96; "Kızıl Destan" (Red Epic), 73; "The Resistance of the Old," 64; "Shepherd and Nightingale," 93; "Turan," 69; "Turkification, Islamization, Modernization," 67
Gökbörü (journal), 182
Gorbachev, Mikhail, 221n72
Görüşler (Views) [journal], 178–80
Gottmann, Jean, 211
Great Depression, 153
Great Powers: detachment from, 146, 159; Ottoman empire among, 75; threat of, 147–48, 150, 155

Greece: conflicts involving, 65, 67, 89–90, 94, 96–97, 143; and Cyprus, 195–97, 199–200; independence of, 32; population exchange with, 98; self-determination movements supported by, 196; territorial issues involving, 59, 81–83, 91; treaty with, 155
Greek minority, in Istanbul, 196
Gupta, Akhil, 103
Gürtunca, Faruk, 250n57; *Do Not Touch This Lion*, 162, *163*, *164*, *166*, 250n58; *Do Not Touch This Vatan*, *182*, *183*
Gürün, Kamuran, 185

Habsburg Empire, 15, 57
hadiths, 13
Hakimiyet-i Milliye (National Sovereignty) [newspaper], 91–92
Hale, William, 147, 165, 169
Halil Menteşe Bey, 62, 66
Hanioğlu, Şükrü, 54
Hashemite Revolt (1916), 72, 75
heimatlos, 2
Hejaz, 83
Hejaz railway, 44–45, 51
Helfert, Josef Alexander, 57, 228n6
Helsinki Summit (1999), 194–95, 256n182
Henrikson, Alan K., 135
Hess, Andrew, 26–27
hijra (emigration to Medina), 16, 18
Hikmet, Mehmed, 111
Hikmet, Nazım, "Traitor to Vatan," 207
history. *See* Turkish Historical Thesis
Hitler, Adolf, 173
Holy War, 14–15
homeland, 1, 103. *See also* vatan
Hugessen, Hughe Knatchbull-, 171
Hugo, Victor, 38–39
Huns, 162
Hürriyet (newspaper), 190, 196, 204, 205, 239n136

İnönü, İsmet Pasha, 97, 98, 100, 104, 120, 135, 152, 153, 155, 159–61, 168, 170, 173, 174, 176–81, 186, 189, 191–92, 200, 208–9
identity: national, 58, 105–6; in Ottoman empire, 3, 41, 51, 53; territoriality and, 211; Turkish, 3, 4, 103–5, 211

iklims (climates), 21, 218n27
"Independence March" (Akif), 93–94
ING Bank, 214
intellectuals: on Ottoman empire, 20, 36–37, 54; and Ottomanism, 35, 41–42; and Turkish nationalism, 51–52, 61, 69
International Straits Commission, 91, 98, 156–57
Internet, censorship of, 8
Iran, 159
Iraq, 83, 92, 152, 159
irredentism, 173
Iskenderun, 59, 85, 88, 97–98
Islahat Edict (1856), 35
Islam: Abdulhamid II and, 44–45; Christian solidarity with, 53; cosmology of, 18; modern dissociation from, 4–5, 35–36; in national anthem, 93–94; pan-Islamism, 25; political philosophy of, 18–19; vatan and, 35, 43, 57, 75, 89
Islamic community (*ummah*), 2, 13, 37
Islamic symbolism, 51
Islamism, 51–54, 67, 72, 74–75
Istanbul, 59, 88, 100, 200
Italy, 54, 64, 150, 152, 155–59, 162, *166*
Izmir, 81–82, 88
Izvestiya (newspaper), 181

Janashia, S., 181
Janissary corps, 32
Janissary Revolt (1807), 32
JDP. *See* Justice and Development Party
Juan Manuel, Prince, 14
Justice and Development Party (JDP), 201, 202, 204
Justice Party, 185

Kadızadeli movement, 20
Kafadar, Cemal, 14, 221n72
Kaplan, Sam, 143
Kara Mustafa Pasha, 24
Karabekir, Kazım, 87, 153, 232n39
Karacan, Ali Naci, 190
Karakol Association, 81
Karaosmanoğlu, Fevzi Lütfi, 192
Karlowitz, Treaty of (1699), 15–16
Karpat, Kemal, 33, 165, 167, 169, 178

Kars, 86, 165, 167–71, 175, 182, 193
Kashgar, 50
Kaya, Şükrü, 160, 208
Kayalı, Hasan, 231n27
Kazancıgil, Ali, 60
Keçeciler, Mehmet, 167
Kemal, Ali, 52
Kemal, Mustafa, 39, 52, 58, 59, 80–81, 83, 85–92, 94–95, 100–101, 103–6, 120–22, 130–31, 149–51, 153–55, 157–61, 168, *198*, 206, 211–12, 236n108, 239n136, 239n138
Kemal, Namık, 39–41, 47–48, 51, 95, 96, 180, 223n98, 223n100, 223n102; "Uproar," 41; *Vatan, or Silistre*, 39, 41, 45
Kemal, Yahya, 75, 96
Kemalists, 5, 60, 91–92, 94, 102–4, 120–21, 131, 135, 150–56, 159–61, 207–8, 211–12
Kennan, George F., 150
Kerim, Cevdet, 154–55
Khaldun, Ibn, 20, 217n24
Kılınç, Tuncer, 206
Kirkuk, 87, 99
Kochkin, Nikolai, 187
Kommunisti (newspaper), 181
Köprülü, Fuat, 61, 66–68, 177–79, 182, 187, 189–90, 193, 196, 230n21; "The Aims of Turkism," 78; "Turkism, Islamism, Ottomanism," 68
Koraltan, Refik, 178, 182
Koran, 13
Korean War, 5
Küçük, Fazıl, 197
Küçük Kaynarca, Treaty of (1774), 16
Kuniholm, Bruce, 186
Kunu-ri, Battle of (1950), 192
Kurds: conflicts involving, 104, 143, 152; denigration of, 143–44; disregard of, 104, 130; in geography textbooks, 117, 130; and National Liberation War, 94; territorial issues involving, 88; vatan and, 7, 8

Laclau, Ernesto, 10, 212
Landau, Jacob, 73
language: alphabet reform, 122; national, 67–68; nationalism and, 78, 122; Turkish origins of, 103

Lattimore, Owen, 209
Lausanne Conference (1922), 85, 97–98, 120, 151
Lausanne Treaty (1923), 59, 100, 130, *133*, *134*, 156–57
Lazistan, 99
League of Nations, 85, 98, 151–56
Lebanon, 36, 37, 49
Lefebvre, Henri, 7–8
Leffler, Melvyn, 185–86
Lenin, Vladimir, 150–51
Lewis, Bernard, 13, 28–29, 73, 121, 218n28, 220n54
Libya, 48–49, 54
literacy, 107
Litvinov, Maxim (Soviet diplomat), 152, 158, 168, 249n46
Lloyd George, David, 79, 82, 96
Loraine, Percy, 157–58

Macid, Ali, 114
Mahmud Raif Efendi, 32; *Tableau des Nouveaux Règlements de l'Empire Ottoman*, 30
Mahmud the Second, 32–33
majorities, ethnic: Arab, 87; Kurdish, 88, 104; Muslim, 87; Turkish, 79–81, 83, 86, 88. *See also* ethnicity
Makarios, Archbishop of Cyprus, 195, 197
Makdisi, Ussama, 50
Mansur, Selim, 114
maps and cartography: of Cyprus, 197, *198*; in geography curriculum and textbooks, 107–10, 123, *124*, *125*, 130–31, *132*, *133*, *134*, *137*, *138*, *140*, *141*; of Italy, *166*; of Lausanne Treaty borders, *133*, *134*; Ottoman, 21–22, 242n33; of races, *124*; of Sèvres Treaty borders, *132*, *134*; of Turkey, *ii*, *163*, *164*, *183*; of Turks' locations, *125*; of world, *138*
Marseillaise (song), 28
Marshall Plan, 187
McBride, Horace, 193
McCain, John, 214
McCarthyism, 184
Mehmed Reşid Bey, 48–50, 225n122
Mehmet the Conqueror, 200

memleket (country), 22
memorandum to Allies (1919), 82–83, 85
Menderes, Adnan, 178, 179, 182, 186, 187, 189, 191, 196–98, 207
Menemencioğlu, Numan, 173, 174
Mercator, Gerardus, *Atlas Minor*, 22
Mesopotamia, 80
Middle East, 4
military: and Cyprus, 200, 202, 206; defense of vatan by, 34, 53–54, 213–14, 227n157; EU limitations on, 6–7; European advances in, 24; geography education influenced by, 136–37; and Korean War, 187–88, 191–92; Ottoman campaigns, 14–15; on Ottoman defeat, 68
Millet (journal), 102
millet (politics), 3, 12, 29–30, 32–33
Milli Gazete (newspaper), 204
Milliyet (newspaper), 160, 214
Minber (newspaper), 87–88
Ministry of National Education, 136, 141
USS *Missouri*, 187
Moldavia, 36
Molotov, Vyacheslav (Soviet foreign minister), 167, 169–71, 175–76, 186
Monroe Doctrine, 92
Montenegro, 36, 65
Montreux Convention (1936), 155–58, 168, 170, 172, 175, 249n41, 249n46
Morocco, 196
Moscow, Treaty of (1921), 94, 151
Mosul, 59, 97–99, 151–52
Mubarak, Hosni, 214
Mudros Armistice (1918), 76, 79–80, 92, 236n103
muhajirs (Muslim migrants), 18
Muhammad, Prophet, 14, 20, 37
Muhbir (newspaper), 42
Münir, Behram, *Sacred Vatan or the Geography of Ottoman Domains*, 112–13, 117, 243n59
Mussolini, Benito, 150, 152, 155–57, 162
Mustafa Reşid Pasha, 33, 35
Mustafa Sami Efendi, 33
Müteferrika, İbrahim, 218n26, 219n36; *Usul el-Hikem fi Nizam el-Ümem*, 24–25, 30

Naim, Ahmed, 74
Naima (historian), 16
NAP. *See* Nationalist Action Party
Napoleon Bonaparte, 6
Nasser, Gamal Abdel, 196
national anthems, 33, 74, 93–94
National Geography (textbook), 140
nationalism: criticisms of, 56; defense of rights organizations and, 81; defined, 103; Kemalist, 60; and Korean War, 191–92; language and, 78, 122; Ottoman empire and, 27–28, 32, 61–62; political uses of, 1–3; print capitalism and, 36; rise of, 57–58, 68; territorial, 60, 77, 90, 121. *See also* Turkish nationalism
Nationalist Action Party (NAP), 167, 203, 204, 240n1
national language, 67–68
national liberation movement, 80–81, 90
National Liberation War, 4, 5, 59, 65, 80–81, 83, 87–93, 96, 120, 122, 130–31, 149, 208, 245n100
National Organization of Cypriot Fighters, 197
National Pact, 5, 59, 85, 87, 91, 97–98, 151, 195, 238n123
National Rights Societies, 82
National Security Council, 194, 206
National Students Federation of Turkey, 196–97
Nation Party, 191
nation-states: emergence of, 12; foundations of, 57–58; territoriality of, 1, 12, 57–58, 211; as Western concept, 13
NATO. *See* North Atlantic Treaty Organization
Nazif, Süleyman, 213
Nehru, Jawaharlal, 149, 189
newspapers, 36
New World, 19
New York Times (newspaper), 171, 172, 248n34, 249n41
Nicosia, 206
Niyazi, Resneli Ahmet, 47–48
Nonaligned Movement, 149
nonalignment, 149–61

non-Turkish groups: disregard of, 104, 137; in geography textbooks, 128, 130, 137; Islamism and, 72–73, 92; role of, 50, 52, 53; Turkification of, 54, 104, 128
North Atlantic Treaty Organization (NATO), 136–39, 147, 167, 186, 187, 193–94
Nur, Rıza, 120, 153
Nuri Pasha, 78, 173
Nyon Conference (1937), 159
Nyon Treaty (1937), 159

Oğuz Khan, 68
Okyar, Fethi, 87
Öngör, Sami: *Geography of States*, 137–38, 140; *The Geography of Turkey*, 137–38, 138, 139
opposition. *See* political opposition
Orhon, Orhan Seyfi, 173
Orhun (journal), 182
Ortellius, Abraham, *Theatrum orbis terrarum*, 22, 26
Orwell, George, 150
Others, Turkish nationalism vs., 104
Ottoman empire: borders of, 129; British relations with, 44; centralization of, 27; cultures within, 25–26, 48, 54; defining, 41; deterioration of, 16–18, 36, 39, 54, 64–65, 69, 72, 75, 111, 114–16; economy in, 27, 35; expansion of, 14–15; foreign policy of, 64–65; French Revolution and changes in, 27–34; and geography, 20–26, 108, 111–13; identity in, 41, 51, 53; legitimacy of, 14, 31–32, 37, 50; liquidation of, 52–53; maps of, 17, 242n33; military campaigns of, 14–15; nationalism and, 27–28, 32, 61–62; and patriotism, 34–45; political philosophy of, 19; population of, 54; rule of peripheral regions by, 49–50, 226n140; sovereign power in, 14; Turkish identity in, 3; unity of, 42, 45; and vatan, 34–45; worldview of, 19–20; in World War I, 75–76, 78–79. *See also* Sublime Porte
Ottomanism, 38, 51–54, 59–62, 62, 64, 67, 70, 112–13
Ottoman Turkish language, 67–68

Ottoman Unity Society, 45
Ó Tuathail, Gearóid, 10, 148
Özkök, Hilmi, 206

Paasi, Anssi, 10, 106
Palestine, 83
pan-Islamism, 25, 90
pan-Turkism, 51–55, 60–61, 68–69, 73–75, 90, 172–74, 197, 229n14
Paris Peace Conference (1919), 81
Parliament: democratic reforms proposed by, 178; dissolution of, by Abdulhamid II, 43; and National Pact, 59, 87; post-1908, 48; territorial issues in, 85, 87, 97–98; and war powers, 188, 189, 191
Paterson, Thomas, 185
patriotism: competing conceptions of, 37–38; European concept of, 28–29, 31; Ottoman, 34–45, 56–57; territorial, 37; as threat, 43–44; and vatan, 2. *See also* vatan
Patrona Halil Revolt (1730), 24
Peasant Party, 240n1
pedagogy of space, 106
perestroika (restructuring), 221n72
Peter the Great, 24
Pheraios, Rhigas, 31–32, 221n65
Piri Reis, Hadji Ahmed Muhiddin, 19, 107
Pleshakov, Konstantin, 175
pogroms, 196
Poland, 96
political opposition: Abdulhamid's suppression of, 45; anti-RPP, 178–81, 184; CUP's suppression of, 71; on Cyprus, 204–5; in Democrat Party, 184–85; İnönü and, 161; Kemal's suppression of, 155; and Korean War, 191–94; left-wing, 104, 143; multiparty democracy and, 178; in RPP, 178; Soviet threat wielded against, 170, 179–80, 184–85, 190
population exchange, 52, 83, 98
Porte. *See* Sublime Porte
Potsdam Conference (1945), 169–70
Potskhveriya, Boris, 158
Pravda (newspaper), 181

Preveza, Battle of (1538), 162
print capitalism, 36
Progressive Party of Working People (Cyprus), 195
Ptolemy, 20, 21
Pulur, Hasan, 250n58

Qasim, Abd al-Karim (general), 28

races, map of, 124
radio, 105
Radio Baghdad, 28
railways, 105
Rauf Orbay Bey, 79
regional pacts, 159, 208
The Religious and Political Necessity of Our Participation in the Defense of Korea (Religious Affairs Directorate), 190
Renan, Ernest, 40, 223n102
Republican Peasants' Nation Party, 240n1
Republican People's Party (RPP), 105, 136, 170, 178–79, 181, 184–85, 191–92, 203, 204
Reşad, Mehmed, 62, 72
Resulzade, Mehmet Emin, 173
revenge, 66, 114–15, 115
Revolution of 1908, 48, 54, 63, 112
Rıfkı, Falih, 95–96, 239n139. *See also* Atay, Falih Rıfkı,
Rıza, Ahmet, 45
Rize, 99
Romania, 36, 155
RPP. *See* Republican People's Party
Rumelia, 56, 58, 66, 69, 109, 114–16. *See also* Eastern Rumelia
Russia: and Muslim migration, 16, 42; Ottoman conflict with, 24, 27, 31, 65, 73, 75, 78, 223n100

Sati Bey, 56–57, 228n2, 228n6; *Vatan İçin Beş Konferans*, 56
Şeyh Said Revolt, 104
Şinasi, İbrahim, 38–39
Sabancı Holding, 202
Sabetai movement, 20
Sabit, Nüzhet, 76–77
sacrifice. *See* self-sacrifice
Sadabad Pact, 159

Sadak, Necmettin, 195
Sadi, Abdülkadir, *Geography for Secondary Schools*, 131, 134
Sadi, Hamit, *Geography Courses*, 128. *See also* Selen, Hamit Sadi
Safavids, 15
Saffet Geylangil Bey, 116–17, 135; *General Geography*, 122–23, 124; *Geography Stories for Children*, 114–15, 115, 119; *Ottoman Geography*, 116
Said Halim Pasha, 72–73, 74, 75
Sait Pasha, 65
Sakarya Battle (1921), 95
Sami, Şemsettin, 231n28
San Francisco Conference (1945), 175, 177, 178
Saraçoğlu, Şükrü, 168, 171–73
Sarper, Selim, 167, 169–70, 176
Saydam, Refik, 160–62
science: geography as, 20–26, 107, 114; and national progress, 33–34
Second İnönü Battle (1921), 92
security, geography as factor in, 6–7
Selçuk, İlhan, 204
Selen, Hamit Sadi, 135. *See also* Sadi, Hamit, *Geography Courses*
self-sacrifice, 7, 46
Selim Sabit Efendi, 107–11, 241n20; *Short Book on Geography*, 108, 109, 110
Selim the Third, 16, 17, 30, 31, 32
Serbia, 32, 36, 65
Sertel, Sabiha, 178, 179
Sertel, Zekeriya, 178
Servet-i Fünun (Wealth of Sciences) [journal], 67
Sèvres Treaty (1920), 59, 91, 130–31, 132, 134
Sevük, İsmail Habib, 245n100; *Writings from the Homeland*, 131, 135
Seyfettin, Ömer, 67, 74, 232n48, 234n83
Seyyid Mustafa Efendi, *Diatribe Sur L'état Actuel de L'art Militaire*, 31
Sezer, Duygu Bazoğlu, 185
shariah (Islamic law), 16
Sheikh ul-Islam, 15
Shiism, 15
Simavi, Sedat, 196
Sivas Congress (1919), 86

Slavic alliance, 65
Sökmensüer, Şükrü, 184
Southeast Asia Treaty Organization, 138
Soviet Union: foreign policy of, 253n122; and Korean War, 190–93; *perestroika* in, 221n72; positive relations with, 150–54, 157–59, 165, 175–76, 208, 248n34, 249n46; as threat, 5, 165–86
Soyak, Hasan Rıza, 159
Soysal, Mümtaz, 130–31, 148
space, 19
Spykman, Nicholas, 147
Stalin, Joseph, 154, 167, 175, 176
Star (newspaper), 207
Straits, 91, 98, 131, 141, 151, 155–58, 167, 168, 170, 171, 175, 176, 186, 187, 193
Strange, Susan, 106
Suavi, Ali, 39, 42–43, 47, 51; "Türk," 42
Sublime Porte, 30, 33, 35. See also Ottoman empire
Suez Canal, 75, 196, 233n70
Sukuti, İshak, 225n122
Sulaymaniyah, 87, 99
Suleiman the Magnificent, Sultan (Süleyman the Lawgiver), 14, 20
sultans, modern dissociation from, 4–5
Sun Language Theory, 103
Suphi, Hamdullah, 76–77, 92–93. See also Tanrıöver, Hamdullah Suphi
Syria, 80, 83, 88, 92, 143, 150, 157

Tahtawi, Rifa'a al-, 37, 38
Talat Pasha, 62, 71
Tamkin, Nicholas, *Britain, Turkey, and the Soviet Union, 1940–45*, 251n72
Tan (newspaper), 174, 178, 180, 181
Tanin (newspaper), 73, 180, 182
Tanpinar, Ahmet Hamdi, 32, 34
Tanrıöver, Hamdullah Suphi, 191. See also Suphi, Hamdullah
Tanzimat Edict (1839), 31, 33–35, 38, 71, 222n79
Tanzimat reforms, 25, 44, 67, 221n72
Tarih-i Hind-i Garbi (A History of the West India), 19
Tasvir (newspaper), 181
Tatars, 16–17

tawhid (God as one), 18
Tek, Müfide Ferit (pseudonym: Suyum Bike), 226n139
Temo, İbrahim, 45, 46, 47, 225n122
Tengirşenk, Yusuf Kemal, 48
Tenth Year Anthem, 105
Tercüman (newspaper), 204
Tercüman-ı Ahval (Interpreter of Conditions) [newspaper], 38
territoriality: construction of, 211; globalization and, 213; identity and, 211; nationalism and, 60, 77, 90, 121; nation-states and, 1, 12, 57–58; patriotism and, 37; Turkey and, 104, 211; *vatan* and, 40, 212
Tevfik, Mehmet Ali, 113–14, 243n41; *Geography of Ottoman Domains*, 112
theology, 20, 23
Thrace. See Eastern Thrace; Western Thrace
Three Districts, 86, 87
time, 20
Time (magazine), 171
The Times (London), 152, 154
Togan, Zeki Velidi, 173, 174
Tolon, Hurşit, 203
Torfing, Jacob, 246n3, 256n184
Toydemir, Cemil, 173
Trabzon, 99, 182
traitors, 2
transportation, 105
treason, 2
Tripartite Treaty (1939), 162
Trotsky, Leon, 154
Truman Doctrine, 187
Tulip Era, 24
Tunaya, Tarık Zafer, 61–62
Tuncer, Mehmet, 192
Tunis, 64
Tunisia, 40, 196
Tür, Özlem, 147
Turan and Turanism, 69–70, 73–75, 77, 117, 119, 119–20, 174, 229n14
Türk (journal), 52
Türkeş, Alparslan, 174
Turkey: Anatolian *vatan* and, 76–77; borders of, 3–4, 60, 83, 84, 85–89, 97, 99, 129, 130–31, 132, 133, 134, 136, 137, 151; changing conceptions of, 1–5; construc-

tion of, 33, 58–101, 130; democracy in, 177–79, 184, 195; economy in, 195; establishment of, 59, 100, 128, 238n123; and identity, 103–5; maps of, *ii, 84, 99, 130–31, 132, 133, 134,* 137, *138,* 140, 141, *142, 163, 164*; population of, 127, *127*; roots of, 3; state presence in, 105; tenth anniversary of, 154–55; territory of, 60
Turkey and the Atlantic Pact (Democrat Party), 193
Turkish Association, 61
Turkish Association of Peace-Lovers, 189–90
Turkish Hearths, 76, 81, 231n22
Turkish Historical Thesis, 103, 122
Turkish Industrialists and Businessmen's Association (TÜSİAD), 136–37, 145, 201–2, 204
Turkish nationalism: and Cyprus, 197; in educational curriculum, 117; emergence of, 50–55, 60–62, 227n145; and geography curriculum, 120–31; and national state, 76–78, 92, 94–98, 100–101, 121, 239n136; Others of, 104; Ottomanism vs., 64–68, 70; terminology concerning, 229n14
Turkish Republic of Northern Cyprus (TRNC), 200, 207
Turkism, 229n14. *See also* pan-Turkism; Turkish nationalism
Türkkan, Reha Oğuz, 173, 174
Turks and Turkishness: Anatolia as homeland of, 3, 4, 76, 102, 121, 122, 128; origins of, 42, 103, 122–23; Ottomanism vs., 89; outside Turkey, 123, *125,* 137, 141; political emphasis on, 61, 79–83, 95; promotion of, 64–68; unification of, 52, 60, 69. *See also* pan-Turkism; Turkish nationalism; Turkism
Türk Yurdu (journal), 61, 64, 67, 68, 70, 71, 120, 226n139
TÜSİAD. *See* Turkish Industrialists and Businessmen's Association

Ülken, Hilmi Ziya, 34, 41–42
Ülsever, Cüneyt, 205
Uluengin, Hadi, 205
Ulus (newspaper), 182

Ulusoy, Coşkun, 214
ummah. See Islamic community (*ummah*)
Unionists, 61–62, 71, 75, 79
United Nations: and Cyprus, 197, 200, 206; and Korean War, 187–88, 191–92; San Francisco Conference (1945), 175. *See also* San Francisco Conference (1945)
United States, 184–87
Unity of Islam, 42
Unity of the Elements, 42, 62
universalism, 38–39
Us, Asım, 181. *See also* Asım, Mehmet, *The Book of the Anatolian Child*

Vahdettin, 79, 82, 89
Vakit (newspaper), 77, 78, 181, 204
vatan: Abdulhamid II and, 44–45; Anatolia as, 76–100, 121; concepts related to, 2; conferences on, 56–57; Cyprus and, 194–97, 199, 203–4; defense of, 2, 5, 7, 34, 39, 43, 46–49, 53–54, 56, 81–82, 88, 91–92, 100–101, 106, 116, 213–14; education and propaganda promoting, 7, 33–34, 56–57, 105–6, 112–16, 122; French Revolution ideals and, 28–29, 46; geography and, 102; historical construction of, 2–5, 8–9, 212; Islamic, 35, 43, 57, 75, 89; and Korean War, 190–94; meanings of, 2, 29, 31, 39, 69, 100, 121, 220n54, 223n98; military defense of, 34, 53–54, 227n157; Namik Kemal and, 39–41; non-territorial conception of, 40, 69–70; Ottoman empire and, 34–45; Ottoman vs. Turkish, 89; patriotism and, 34–45; political uses of, 9–10; pre-modern meaning of, 3; and security concerns, 7; study and analysis of, 9; territoriality and, 40, 212; territory-specific, 62, 231n28; Turkish nation and, 155; types of, 73–75, 113, 122; Young Turks and, 45–55
Vatan (newspaper), 174
Vatan Tehlikede (Vatan Is in Danger) [CUP], 46–47
Vienna, siege of (1683), 23–24
Vinogradov, Sergei (Soviet ambassador), 253n122

Wallachia, 36
Warsaw Pact, 138
Weber, Max, 1
We Countered the Enemy in Korea (Democrat Party), 193
Weisband, Edward, 16
Western Thrace, 59, 80, 85, 86, 87
Williams, Brian Glyn, 16–17
Wilson, Woodrow, 79–80, 82, 89, 91
Winichakul, Thongchai, 130, 215n4
World War I, 54, 72, 73, 75–76, 78–79
World War II, 172–75

Yalçın, Hüseyin Cahit, 112, 178, 180–81, 192
Yalman, Ahmet Emin, 175, 197
Tutibay Yayınları, 226n139
Yazıcı, Tahsin, 190
Yemen, 40, 49, 83
Yeni Asir (newspaper), 192
Yeşil, Fatih, 220n54
Young France, 36
Young Germany, 36
Young Italy, 36
Young Ottomans, 36–39, 42–43, 47, 62
Young Turks, 45–55, 62, 112
Yücel, Hasan Ali, 135, 245n107
Yugoslavia, 155

Zeybek, Namık Kemal, 167
Zubok, Vladislav Martinovich, 175

www.ingramcontent.com/pod-product-compliance
Lightning Source LLC
LaVergne TN
LVHW020554211224
799415LV00003B/93